PAUL DEBACH

Professor of Biological Control
University of California, Riverside

Biological control by natural enemies

W9-BWJ-593

CAMBRIDGE
UNIVERSITY PRESS

Published by the Syndics of the Cambridge University Press
Bentley House, 200 Euston Road, London NW1 2DB
American Branch: 32 East 57th Street, New York, N.Y.10022

Library of Congress Catalogue Card Number: 73-90812

ISBNS:
0 521 20380 5 hard covers
0 521 09835 1 paperback

First published 1974

Set in Great Britain
at the University Printing House, Cambridge
(Brooke Crutchley, University Printer)
Printed in the United States of America

Contents

Preface

Years ago, when I was a 19-year-old sophomore student at the University of California at Los Angeles taking a course in Economic Entomology from Professor A. M. Boyce, Professor Harry S. Smith, the late world authority on biological control, was invited over from the then University of California's Citrus Experiment Station at Riverside to give a series of lectures on biological control. This was the turning point in my professional career. Biological control was so intellectually satisfying, so biologically intriguing and so ecologically rational a means of pest control that I immediately opted to become a specialist in this field and to do my PhD research when the time came under Professor Smith at Riverside. This I did and I have always been happy with my choice. It is also why I am writing this book.

The main purpose of this book is to outline the workings and potentialities of biological control of pests for the general reader and student interested in environmental phenomena. It is not primarily to discuss the drawbacks and dangers of pesticide usage. The only reason for bringing in any discussion of pesticides is that these two approaches to pest control have been virtually incompatible since the widespread unilateral use of pesticides became so greatly emphasized in recent years. Biological control cannot operate effectively, if at all, in the face of modern chemical pest control as it is generally practiced.

The insecticide crisis is a multifaceted one affecting society and the environment in diverse ways. The adverse effects have furnished the source for numerous scientific papers, reports and books. Some pertinent ones are cited in this book but I shall not go into more detail here.

It is ironic that the adverse effects of pesticide chemicals on biological control have received relatively little public attention as compared to, say, the widely publicized effects on fish or birds, yet these effects on biological control hold the main key to the whole chain of events leading to the massive proliferation of insecticide usage. This will be illustrated in Chapter 1. If we can maintain, improve and, when necessary, increase biological control, pesticide chemical usage can be very greatly reduced overall and at times, places and on certain crops dispensed with entirely. It is as simple as that, and technologically much more readily achievable than is generally realized.

The term biological control has come to be used in a variety of ways. Professor H. S. Smith coined the term in 1919 to apply to the control or regulation of pest populations by natural enemies, i.e. by predators, parasites or pathogens and this is briefly what biological control means in this book.

Other biological methods of pest control exist and are discussed in Chapter 9. All differ basically in philosophical, biological and ecological principles from biological control and this is why I maintain the distinction in terms.

This book advocates that the first and most important step in pest control (particularly in agriculture where most pest control is required) should be aimed at the achievement of classical biological control by the discovery, importation and colonization of new natural enemies from abroad. But at the same time it stresses as always being indispensable, the conservation or protection from adverse factors of established natural enemies and further shows that at times, and as necessary, natural enemy activity can be purposefully aided by man as, for instance, by insectary mass production and periodic field colonization.

I fully recognize that all pests are not equally susceptible to classical biological control – although we have to learn this by trying – and that the method may not be of any practical consequence at all for a few pests, so that other non-chemical or *selective* chemical methods will continue to be required and should be developed or utilized as dictated by sound bio-ecological research in each major habitat of every agro-ecosystem. Such research on biological and integrated control is still in its infancy and until it grows up massive use of chemical pesticides is not likely to become much reduced.

PAUL DEBACH

International Center for
Biological Control and
Division of Biological Control,
Department of Entomology,
University of California,
Riverside

Acknowledgments

My greatest thanks for help toward the successful completion of this book go to my wife, Margaret L. DeBach, who typed and edited and retyped and re-edited, ad infinitum. Especial thanks for substantial assistance also go to Stanley Warner and Marilyn Huftile. I am also most appreciative of the help of numerous others who include W. D. Bedard, G. Bhaskaran, Shirley A. Briggs, T. O. Browning, D. E. Bryan, James R. Cate, Jr, Harold Compere, Clifton J. Davis, E. J. Dietrick, R. L. Doutt, K. G. Eveleens, T. W. Fisher, Donald L. Flaherty, John E. Foster, Richard D. Goeden, Gordon Gordh, D. D. Hardee, William G. Hart, David J. Horn, Carl B. Huffaker, R. M. Ireland, F. R. Lawson, Diego E. Navas, Earl K. Oatman, Asher K. Ota, Harold T. Reynolds, Michael J. Rose, David Rosen, Yoram Rössler, Allen G. Selhime, J. B. Siddall, F. J. Simmonds, Robert L. Stoltz, George Tamaki, Mary Ann Walsh, George W. Ware and Douglas F. Waterhouse.

Photographs have been graciously taken by, furnished by, or their permission to use granted by the following individuals and organizations: Max Badgley, Harold Compere, Donald L. Flaherty, T. W. Fisher, Gordon Gordh, Kenneth Hagen, Robert Hendrickson, Carl B. Huffaker, Charles Kennett, Kenneth Middleham, Michael J. Rose, Frank Skinner and Robert van den Bosch, all of the University of California; R. H. Foote, Frank D. Parker and R. L. Ridgeway, all of the United States Department of Agriculture; David P. Annecke, Department of Agriculture Technical Services, Division of Entomology, Pretoria, South Africa; Roland Chatham, Bryan, Texas; W. H. Haseler, The Alan Fletcher Research Station, Queensland, Australia; Petr Stary, Czechoslovakian Academy, Entomology Laboratory, Vinicna 7, Prague 11, Czechoslovakia; Asher K. Ota, Hawaiian Sugar Planters Experiment Station, Honolulu, Hawaii; Douglas F. Waterhouse, CSIRO, Canberra, Australia; Commonwealth Agricultural Bureaux, Slough, England; and the Plenum Publishing Corporation, New York. Plates of Eucalyptus snout-beetle, *Gonipterus scutellatus* Gyll. by F. G. C. Tooke as originally published in *Entomology Memoir 3*, reproduced under Copyright Authority 4672 of 6.3.1972 of the Government Printer of the Republic of South Africa.

TO
HAROLD COMPERE
*Emeritus Specialist, University of
California, Riverside*

My first inspiration and subsequent
colleague of many years

Foreign explorer *par excellence*, internationally known taxonomist in the
parasitic Chalcidoidea, expert biologist
and biological control historian. His
personal experience, tying back through
his father George Compere's career, spans
in just two lifetimes all of the developments in biological control since the first
great success occurred in Los Angeles
nearly 85 years ago.

(For photographs see Fig. 20, pp. 90–1.)

I
Fostering pests through misuse of chemicals

The vast majority of objections to the application of chemical pesticides does not come from the people who use them most – the farmers. By and large, the man who depends for his livelihood on crop production is convinced that he must use pesticides regularly or perish. Such conviction has been actively and effectively fostered by the pesticide industry. All sorts of data and discussions in scientific and lay journals have emphasized the apparent need for, and the great good derived by the farmer from, the faithful use of pesticides.

Although these claims are certainly justified in particular cases, they cannot be accepted as general broad truths, as many entomologists and farmers have learned to their sorrow. The pros and cons of this controversy will be left for somewhat later. What I wish to emphasize in this chapter has been largely ignored or overlooked by the sellers and users of chemical pesticides. It is that pesticides often cause actual pest increases rather than controlling them, and more and more frequently are creating new pests of species that formerly were innocuous rarities. Sometimes it is claimed that chemicals are harmless to natural enemies because the latter may be common following pest outbreaks where chemicals were used previously. This does not indicate harmlessness of chemicals, merely that enemies have finally built-up again following a chemical-induced pest outbreak; but usually too late.

Some general references broadly covering nearly all aspects of the subject of adverse environmental effects of pesticides include Briejér (1967), Carson (1962), Doutt (1964a), Graham (1970), Harmer (1971), Mellanby (1967), Newsom (1967), Pimentel (1971), Rudd (1964), Rudd (1971), Report of the Secretary's Commission on Pesticides (1969) and the Report of the Environmental Pollution Panel (1965).

Some recipes for fostering pests

My main area of field research has been with citrus pests and I can provide recipes for the use of several insecticides that are perfect for raising citrus pest insects in tremendous numbers in the field. So perfect in fact that anytime I wished I could use DDT (previous to its banning*) to cause such great increases in certain scale insects and mites on citrus trees that complete tree defoliation, even death, would result. Some of my colleagues have done the same thing with various insecticides on other crops. We did not do this in an endeavour to find out how much good chemicals do; rather the opposite, to find out how much good natural enemies do. Thus we used chemicals purposely to decimate natural enemies on certain trees and by comparing pest trends on these with trees in the same grove on which biological control was undisturbed the extent of biological control was revealed. The major requirement is that the chemical must kill a greater proportion of natural enemies than it does pests and it also helps greatly if it has a persistent residue, which incidentally has also been the goal of insecticide manufacturers. Additionally, it appears as if some insecticides actually stimulate the reproductive rate of certain pests. Of course, if one can apply insecticides purposely to cause explosions of pest insects, it is obvious that such explosions can occur accidentally when the purpose of application is the opposite, i.e. to control pests.

There follow several recipes for use of insecticides which in our experience, and that of others, generally have produced exceptional pest increases. Of course, such demonstrations must be done in plots where natural enemies have not already been recently killed by insecticides.

California red scale on citrus

Take 4 lb of 50 percent wettable DDT* and mix into 100 gallons of water. Using a three-gallon garden sprayer, spray one or two quarts of this mixture lightly over the tree, repeating at monthly intervals until the tree is defoliated or dying as a result of the increase in red scale. This may require from about six to twelve applications depending upon the degree of initial infestation; the higher the numbers initially the faster the explosion occurs. Most growers do not like this sort of test and have usually insisted that we stop before the trees were killed

* The use of DDT is no longer legal in many countries.

Table 1. *Adverse effects of DDT, southern California*
Relative California red scale population densities in various biological control plots (untreated) and in plots in which natural enemy activity had been suppressed by prior applications of a light DDT spray

| Property and location | No. of DDT applications | Final scale population density‡ | | Fold increase, DDT/ untreated |
		Untreated	DDT-sprayed	
Bothin, Santa Barbara	11*	3	425	142
Sullivan, Santa Barbara	11*	16	575	36
Beemer, Pauma Valley	9†	1	580	580
Irvine Company, Irvine	29*	6	1336	223
Rancho Sespe, Fillmore	54*	1	1250	1250
Ehrler, Riverside	10†	4	390	98
Sinaloa Ranch, Simi	55*	3	1015	299
Stow Ranch, Goleta	37*	8	850	112
Hugh Walker Grove, Orange County	47*	1	463	463

* Monthly applications.
† Quarterly applications.
‡ Initial scale population densities were similar in all plots.

but it is a wonderful way to raise red scale. Table 1 shows results from such tests obtained in a variety of citrus groves in southern California over a period of years.

From these figures it is readily seen that, as used, DDT caused pest increases of anywhere from 36-fold to over twelve-hundred-fold in from one to several years. A typical effect of such DDT-caused outbreaks is seen in Fig. 1, which shows a lemon tree nearing complete defoliation. Fig. 2 shows graphically month by month the progress of a DDT-induced outbreak. DDT caused the economic injury level to be significantly exceeded within a matter of months.

3

Fig. 1. A lemon tree (right) nearing complete defoliation from massive increases of the California red scale caused by previous DDT sprays. A nearby unsprayed tree (left) showing dense foliage is under complete biological control.

Fig. 2. Increases in California red scale infestation caused by light monthly applications of DDT spray as compared to nearby untreated trees under biological control in the same grove.

Yellow scale on oranges

The identical formulation and application of DDT used for the California red scale caused similar outbreaks of the yellow scale on orange trees. A typical result after only five months of DDT usage shows a scale population density index of less than one on the untreated check trees as compared to 105 on the DDT-sprayed trees. This represents over a one-hundred-fold increase and is an easier way to raise yellow scale than it is in the insectary.

Purple scale on oranges

Both endrin and dieldrin have been used to produce massive infestations of the purple scale. The formulations and dosage used for both are as follows: take 50 percent wettable powder and mix with water at the rate of two pounds per 100 gallons. Apply two-thirds of a gallon per tree monthly with a Hudson sprayer. This results in a light, scattered coverage. These materials did not cause quite such rapid outbreaks as DDT does with California red scale but persistence was rewarded, so that after about thirty-six months the purple scale population density index remained a low 158 on the untreated trees as compared to massive increases to 7402 on the dieldrin-sprayed trees (about a 47-fold increase) and to 20615 on the endrin-sprayed trees (a 130-fold increase). The latter infestation index represents a tree virtually encrusted with purple scales and suffering from dead and dying leaves, twigs and small limbs.

Citrus red mite on citrus

This species and probably mites in general are about the easiest pests to increase by the application of a variety of pesticidal chemicals. The formulation of DDT used for the California red scale also works wonders in causing enormous citrus red mite infestations to develop. In some of the first tests we used $12\frac{1}{2}$ percent DDT in talc applied both as a dust and spray at the rate of two pounds per tree ($\frac{1}{4}$ lb actual DDT). Only one application was made. After some two and one-half months the citrus red mite population index on the DDT-treated trees was 2303 as compared to only 377 on untreated trees in the same grove. We also found that cryolite and zinc sulfate (a nutritional spray) caused significant increases in mite populations. The use of DDT on

5

Fig. 3. Population increase of Pacific mite in carbaryl-sprayed plots in a previously unsprayed vineyard. Redrawn after Flaherty and Huffaker (1970).

citrus in southern California was abandoned early in the game by citrus growers because of its obvious effect in causing such mite increases.

Pacific mite on grapes

Carbaryl has been shown experimentally to cause marked increases of the Pacific mite on grapes in the San Joaquin Valley of California when used in a mixture of two pounds of 50 percent wettable powder per 150 gallons of water per acre (Flaherty and Huffaker, 1970). Fig. 3 shows graphically a typical population trend resulting from carbaryl treatment in a vineyard with no previous pesticide history and Fig. 4 shows the actual mite damage to the vines as a consequence of carbaryl treatment.

Cyclamen mite on strawberries

Following field observations that commercial use of parathion was associated with subsequent increases in cyclamen mite populations on strawberries, Huffaker and Spitzer (1951) and Huffaker and Kennett (1956) deliberately used parathion dust in paired-plot comparisons to

Fig. 4. Severe Pacific mite damage of upper foliage on Thompson Seedless grape vines as a result of treatment with carbaryl. From Flaherty and Huffaker (1970).

evaluate this phenomenon. In the first work cited they dusted certain strawberry plots with parathion in the second half of July and left other plots untreated. Cyclamen mite population indices obtained at about the peak of infestation, 4–6 weeks following the parathion application, are shown in Table 2. It is clear that the use of parathion dust caused increases in cyclamen mite populations of from about 120

Table 2. *Relative population indices of the cyclamen mite on strawberry plots treated with parathion dust and on untreated plots. Counts made 4–6 weeks after the treatment.* (Adapted from Huffaker and Spitzer, 1951.)

Plot no.	Untreated	Treated	Approximate % increase, treated over untreated
1	7	23	230
2	17	37	120
3	13.5	40	195
4	13.5	34	150

to 230 percent within a month to six weeks, thus showing that parathion is another chemical one can use to create marked increases in pest populations in the field.

Cottony-cushion scale on citrus

DDT again was an excellent material to use to produce massive increases in cottony-cushion scale in the field. In fact this was one of the first cases in which it was found that DDT could produce such remarkable results. A reliable formulation consisted of $1\frac{1}{2}$ pounds of 50 percent wettable DDT powder, two gallons of kerosene and two ounces of blood albumen spreader mixed in 100 gallons of water and applied as a complete coverage spray with a commercial spray rig. For best results applications were made in early May and repeated again in July or early August. When light to moderate cottony-cushion scale populations were present initially, tree defoliation, even death, would be attained by the massive scale increase occurring within about one year. With lighter infestations to start with, four applications over two years would be required for the same spectacular results. The greater the acreage treated the more effective will be the population explosion.

Olive scale on olives

My colleagues Carl Huffaker, Charles Kennett and Glen Finney (1962) deliberately used light dosages of DDT on olive trees in the field to provoke massive 'upsets' of the olive scale. They repeated the procedure over a period of several years in many olive groves, so its reliability is undisputed. Their real purpose of course, as in most of the instances already discussed, was to evaluate the effectiveness of parasites by eliminating them with a chemical which did not control the host population, thence following the resulting increase in the host. A resume of some of their typical results is shown in Table 3. The relative population increase due to DDT over unsprayed trees is truly amazing, ranging from 75-fold to nearly 1000-fold within the period of two years. The results were so visually striking as to be used for the cover jacket on one recent book.

Table 3. *Relative population density increases of the olive scale on unsprayed trees and on DDT-sprayed trees.* (Adapted from Huffaker, Kennett and Finney, 1962.)

Location	1958 Fall		1959 Spring		1959 Fall		1960 Spring		1960 Fall		Relative fold increase, DDT-sprayed to unsprayed
	DDT-sprayed*	Un-sprayed	DDT-sprayed	Un-sprayed	DDT-sprayed	Un-sprayed	DDT-sprayed	Un-sprayed	DDT-sprayed	Un-sprayed	
Lindsay	0.0	0.0	0.3	0.3	5.5	1.2	25.5	1.9	67.6	0.9	75:1
Seville	2.0	1.6	4.2	9.0	2.7	0.0	12.6	0.0	29.8	0.03	993:1
Hills Valley	0.8	1.3	10.6	0.1	12.1	0.4	25.6	0.2	90.7	0.1	907:1
Clovis	1.2	3.0	12.4	0.2	43.9	0.5	55.6	1.9	287.8	2.5	140:1
Herndon	2.0	3.8	38.1	3.2	134.0	0.7	60.4	0.0	169.8	1.5	113:1
Madera	16.9	11.6	23.9	3.4	43.5	0.4	120.3	0.6	204.2	0.5	408:1

* Pretreatment counts.

9

Fig. 5. Increase in bollworms induced by spraying cotton plants with TEPP. Redrawn after van den Bosch *et al.* (1971).

Bollworm on cotton

The insecticide TEPP has been used experimentally to promote substantial increases of the bollworm as shown in Fig. 5. Most evidence indicates that other commercially used insecticides produce similar results. These insecticides are used primarily against lygus bugs but the bollworm usually increases following their application.

Bagworms on oil palms

In Malaysia, Wood (1971*a*) was able to deliberately increase bagworm populations by applying low-volume dieldrin sprays to two two-acre plots of oil palms within larger blocks of trees. Population trends in these plots were compared to untreated trees extending some 500 yards away from the centrally treated plot. There was approximately a 5- to 10-fold increase in bagworm larvae in the treated plots as compared to populations unaffected by the spray. This was the result of just one spraying.

The foregoing are but a few of the striking instances where chemicals can be used, either purposefully or accidentally, to cause great increases in pest insect or mite populations. Such population explosions are generally referred to as 'upsets' or 'upsets in natural balance' when non-target organisms are affected and as 'resurgences' when target pests increase very rapidly following chemical treatments and often become more serious than they were originally.

Upsets of natural balance by chemicals

There was a period following the widespread adoption of the post-World War II chlorinated hydrocarbon and organophosphorus pesticides when the first documented reports of striking upsets in crops generally met with disbelief or disavowal on the part of pesticide-oriented entomologists and the industry. Today few, if any, knowledgeable professionals deny such effects to be rather commonplace. They are in fact extremely commonplace, as can readily be ascertained from the entomological literature. Hence it is truly amazing that so little general attention, publicity and recognition has been directed toward this very broad and basic problem as compared to the effects of pesticides on some other groups of organisms such as fish or birds. The differential in emphasis alluded to is evident in the *Report of the Secretary's Commission on Pesticides and their Relationship to Environmental Health* (1969) and in Pimentel's (1971) major review of the ecological effects of pesticides on non-target species. In the former, Chapter 3 on 'Effect of pesticides on nontarget organisms other than man' includes less than one page dealing with adverse effects on natural enemies. In the latter, the treatment of mammals, birds and fishes is much more comprehensive than that of non-target insects and mites, concerning which only about ten instances of upsets are listed. This is a mere handful of those that have been recorded in the literature. Nonetheless these works are otherwise extremely valuable to the ecologist interested in this general problem of pesticides and environmental quality. However, when and if pesticide usage is significantly reduced by greater use and conservation of natural enemies and other non-chemical methods the problems with non-target organisms and of rapid rebound of target pests will be automatically alleviated. Not that the side problems are unimportant, but as will soon be discussed, the production of upsets by chemicals in agro-ecosystems, where more than 50 percent of the pesticides are used, leads to

11

ever increasing chemical usage. It follows that a major solution to reduction in the use of chemical pesticides lies in minimizing upsets and resurgences.

It would take a large book to adequately cover the recorded literature concerning upsets and resurgences. I can only refer to a few, better studied major cases here and indicate as well some general references. In my experience, in that of various of my colleagues and from numerous literature reports, it seems clearly evident that in almost all intensively treated crops today, chemical applications are being made against upset pests (i.e. ones that formerly were innocuous) nearly as frequently as against the few key pests actually lacking established effective natural enemies. It is probably safe to generalize that in intensively treated crops it is no longer possible to distinguish between real pests (i.e. ones actually lacking established effective natural enemies) and man-made upset pests unless long-term basic ecological studies are conducted.

I have seen the citrus red mite increase over the years since the chlorinated hydrocarbons and organophosphorus chemicals were introduced, from a minor or non-pest status to the number one pest of citrus in California. In fact similar events seem to have commonly occurred worldwide with mites of many crops, as has been reviewed by Huffaker, van de Vrie and McMurtry (1969, 1970) and McMurtry, Huffaker and van de Vrie (1970).

A major review of the adverse effects of pesticides on insect and mite pests and their natural enemies was made by Ripper (1956). He covered upsets and resurgences involving some fifty pest species occurring in a wide variety of taxonomic groups. Diverse chemicals were responsible, such as the chlorinated hydrocarbons, the organophosphorus compounds, sulfur, lime-sulfur, copper carbonate, calcium arsenate, derris, zinc sulfate and thiuram, and even carrier materials and diluents such as talc, used to mix with the toxicants. DDT was the worst offender. Another comprehensive review of upsets and resurgences among pest insects has appeared more recently (Newsom, 1967). Some other important references which furnish a picture of the magnitude of the problem, which deal with the basic biological and ecological phenomena involved, and which in themselves cite many other cases include: Conway (1969), Doutt (1964a), Huffaker (1971), Massee (1954), Pickett and Patterson (1953, plus a long continuing series of papers from the same laboratory), Reynolds (1971), Smith (1971b), Smith and Reynolds (1972), van den Bosch (1971a, b), van den Bosch *et al.* (1971) and Wood (1971*a*). Only a few of the more impressive cases covered by these authors and others can be mentioned.

Upsets are not new phenomena; some were recognized and reported in the 1920s and 1930s, but it was the widespread use of DDT and its relatives beginning about 1945 and of parathion and related compounds a little later that opened Pandora's box. I studied one of the first great DDT-induced upsets, that of the cottony-cushion scale in California in 1946 and 1947. As will be related in Chapter 5 this scale was the first pest to be subjugated by importation of a natural enemy and the result literally was the saving of the citrus industry in California. The scale remained a rare insect on citrus from 1890 until DDT was widely used on citrus and other crops in the Central Valley. This caused the virtual extinction of the controlling predatory vedalia beetle and an unbelievable population explosion of the scale extending from Bakersfield in the south to Hamilton City in the north. Many groves actually looked as if they were covered with snow because of the density of the cottony egg masses. Some trees were killed and many groves defoliated with subsequent loss of crop in the short two to three years before the use of DDT was voluntarily dropped or drastically modified. In order to reattain control as rapidly as possible, growers paid $1.00 each for vedalia beetles which still were locally present in southern California. This recolonization along with modification of the DDT program rapidly resulted in a return to the normal biological control.

Another scale insect, the brown soft scale, has been a major pest of citrus in the Rio Grande Valley of Texas for some years now, as a result of being upset by pesticide chemicals primarily applied to adjacent cotton. This scale is under excellent biological control by parasites worldwide unless they are decimated by pesticides. Parathion-caused outbreaks have been recorded in California and South Africa.

Perhaps the most amazing chronicle involving pesticide-induced upsets and resurgences has occurred with cotton, which has been the recipient of nearly half of the agricultural insecticides used in the United States and is similarly heavily treated in many countries. Reports have come from virtually all areas of the world where insecticide usage has been intensive. The effects, along with the development of pest resistance to insecticides, have been so severe as to result in the curtailment of cotton production in some major areas and the increasingly real threat of this happening in others such as the Rio Grande Valley of Texas, the Imperial and Central Valleys of California and various

13

Central American countries, particularly Nicaragua and Guatemala, where the situation is becoming truly disastrous.

In the Matamoros–Reynosa area of northeast Mexico, cotton acreage declined from more than 710 000 acres in 1960 to some 1200 acres in 1970. As this was happening, production was moved to the new Tampico–Mante area about 200 miles south where about 500 000 acres were planted to cotton in 1966. A similar but more rapid decline occurred there. By 1970 only 1200 acres of cotton were left. This is attributed to the increase in intensity of pests, particularly the tobacco budworm, which is an upset species, and the inability to cope with them any longer by the unilateral use of chemical pesticides in spite of attempts to increase dosages and frequency of application. Economic ruin and loss of employment have been widespread. As Adkisson (1971) has said, 'The seeds for the destruction of the Mexican cotton industry were planted when the producers decided that their insect pest problems could be best solved by the unilateral use of regularly scheduled applications of broad-spectrum insecticides.'

In the Rio Grande Valley, cotton pests, mainly the boll weevil, were adequately controlled with chlorinated hydrocarbon insecticides for nearly 15 years until the boll weevil became resistant to them in the late 1950s. The organophosphorus compounds, especially methyl parathion, were then used for boll weevil control and as a result DDT became necessary to control the upset pests, the bollworm and tobacco budworm. By 1962, the latter two became resistant to DDT, other chlorinated hydrocarbons and to carbamate insecticides, but could still be killed by heavy dosages of methyl parathion. This control began to become unsatisfactory by 1968 when some growers treated 15–18 times and failed to obtain satisfactory results. Now the pest control situation was suddenly reversed as the bollworm and tobacco budworm, two pests formerly of minor importance, became more serious than the boll weevil which faded to insignificance. Currently the growers and entomologists are faced with a real dilemma in pest control and ironically the worst pest species, the tobacco budworm, which no available insecticide will now adequately control, has been brought to its present status by the use of insecticides.

Similar insecticide-induced problems have occurred in California. In the Imperial Valley, the organic insecticides such as DDT, toxaphene and endrin gave outstanding results during the early 1950s. Then they became less effective; resurgences and upsets began to occur and other pesticides were substituted. The same pattern was repeated with formerly minor pests or innocuous insects such as the cotton leaf perforator, cabbage looper, beet armyworm, salt marsh caterpillar, omnivorous leaf roller and spider mites becoming more serious. Finally it became urgently obvious that changes in pest control were necessary. Ecological research by University personnel stressing selective insecticides and treatment based on actual need as determined by field surveys, greatly reduced the use of pesticides and alleviated the problem until 1965 when the serious pink bollworm invaded the Valley from Arizona and literally exploded in this new area. Applications of broad-spectrum insecticides were made at six-day intervals in an ill-advised eradication attempt and soon the other potential pest species already named again became so serious that today continued cotton production is threatened as cotton yields have dropped to the lowest level since World War II. Area-wide side effects on other crops have been noticed; for instance vegetable crops and sugar-beets have had the most severe pest infestations ever seen on these crops.

In the Central Valley serious target-pest resurgence and upsets on cotton were experimentally induced and studied in large-scale field experiments by University personnel. In 1964 it was found that azodrin used to control the bollworm actually did not reduce the bollworm as compared to the untreated checks; in fact the azodrin-treated plots suffered significantly more damaged bolls than the untreated checks. Again in 1965, after three applications of azodrin, more bollworms and more damage were recorded from the azodrin plots than in the untreated checks. In 1966, it was demonstrated that bidrin-treated plots sustained a cabbage looper infestation about three times as great as the checks with considerably greater leaf damage. Three toxaphene–DDT treatment programs for lygus bug control were compared with untreated check plots in 1969. The tests covered one square mile. Beet armyworm populations were increased in all of the treated plots and in two of them were 16- and 18-times higher than in the checks. Cygon for lygus bug control was used in similar tests in 1970. Where July treatments were used, outbreaks of both beet armyworm and cabbage looper occurred. The overall conclusions have been that the serious lepidopterous pest problems in the Central Valley involving bollworm, beet armyworm and cabbage looper are largely pesticide-induced upsets, that the cotton industry is actually losing more money with the current insecticide programs than if *no* insecticides were used and that, while some growers would suffer severe damage if they were to abandon all use of insecticides,

15

most would realize little or no loss and others would even obtain greater yields.

The sad tale of pesticide-induced problems on cotton in the Cañete Valley of Peru is best told in the words of Smith and van den Bosch (1967).*

The Cañete Valley is one of the most technologically advanced of these Peruvian agro-ecosystems. The growers in it are organized into an association (La Asociación de Hacendados de Cañete) and they have their own experimental station (La Estación Experimental Agrícola de Cañete) to serve their 22000 hectares of cultivated land. Originally the valley was largely planted to sugar-cane, but in the 1920s a shift was made to the cultivation of cotton. Currently about two thirds of the valley (approximately 15000 hectares) is planted to that crop. The Cañete agricultural operations are the most highly mechanized in Peru. Other advanced agricultural, agronomic, horticultural, and plant-protection techniques have also been adapted to crop production in the valley.

It was the adoption of modern synthetic organic insecticides for cotton pest control which led the valley to the brink of economic disaster and ultimately to its salvation in integrated control.

The Cañete story stands as a classic example of the problems that can beset pest control which ignores ecology and relies on unilateral use of broad-spectrum insecticides. Once this approach to pest control was initiated, the Cañete was doomed to disaster because of certain factors peculiar to it. The most important of these was its status as an oasis in an otherwise arid and biologically impoverished land. Thus when synthetic organic insecticides were brought into use they were essentially applied as a blanket over the entire ecosystem. As a result, literally the entire biota of the valley was repeatedly exposed to these materials. This had two critical effects: (1) decimation of the parasite and predator fauna, which in turn relieved the key pest species as well as potential pests from biotic repression, and (2) rapid selection for insecticide resistance in the pest species.

Both developments occurred with great rapidity and with devastating effect. For example, though use of synthetic organic insecticides, principally DDT, BHC, and toxaphene, was not initiated until 1949, resistance to these materials had already developed by 1955. Where 5% DDT, 3% BHC, and a 3:5:40% BHC–DDT–sulfur mixture had proved effective in 1949, 15% DDT, 10% BHC, and a 5:10:40% BHC–DDT–sulfur mixture often applied at elevated dosages, were necessary for control by 1955. Furthermore, the interval between treatments was progressively shortened from a range of 8–15 days down to 3 days. Meanwhile, a whole complex of previously innocuous insects had risen to serious pest status. Included were *Argyrotaenia*

* Copyright ©1967, Academic Press, New York. Reprinted by permission.

sphaleropa, Platynota sp., *Pseudoplusia rogationis, Pococera atramenalis, Planococcus citri,* and *Bucculatrix thurberiella.*

Substitution of new insecticides, including organophosphorus compounds, for the older chlorinated hydrocarbons finally became necessary and then even these failed. Finally, as a result of pest resistance to the insecticides and the burgeoning complex of injurious species, the cotton yield plummeted alarmingly; the average yield per hectare in 1956 was the lowest in more than a decade.

The solution to this crisis will be detailed in Chapter 10.

Striking upsets or resurgences have been carefully documented on oil palms and cocoa in Malaysia. In general, these developed during the late 1950s and early 1960s following the use of insecticides, particularly DDT, endrin and dieldrin, having long-term residues. On oil palms several generally innocuous species of bagworms and nettle caterpillars occasionally reached damaging levels, or other species appeared to threaten, so the use of DDT, endrin or dieldrin was initiated. Initial results were good but populations sooner or later resurged to very high densities necessitating more treatments. This led eventually to the insects becoming serious continuous pests rather than occasional ones. The successful solution to this particular paradox and certain other chemically induced pest problems also will be discussed in Chapter 10.

Cocoa was a new crop in Sabah in 1956, planted in cleared forest areas. The acreage increased rapidly and soon some indigenous insects were observed attacking cocoa trees. The first serious pests were three species of lepidopterous borers, which led to spraying with high concentrations of DDT or dieldrin in 1959. That year several other potential pests including leaf-eating caterpillars, aphids and mealybugs were noticed and considered to be dangerous, so in 1960 general spraying was carried out as a prophylactic measure, using endrin, dieldrin, DDT, BHC, lead arsenate and a white oil, alone or in combination. This was repeated in 1961. Meanwhile the pest situation was becoming worse. Branch borers became abundant by early 1961. Within months, outbreaks of four other pests occurred, two leaf-eating caterpillars, one nettle caterpillar and one homopterous plant hopper. All became extremely abundant, the latter to the extent that when disturbed they rose in large clouds from the branches. Then in July 1961 the most serious outbreak of all occurred involving several species of bagworms, which produced large numbers of defoliated and dying trees. Continued spraying had no effect on the bagworms. Eventually

17

field studies and experiments showed that virtually all of these out-breaks were insecticide-induced with the main exception of one species of ring bark borer.

The situation on tea in Ceylon will be used as our last example of induced upsets. For years a shot hole borer has been a serious pest there. Cultural control was largely used until dieldrin was tried in the fifties with good results. This subsequently resulted in upsets of the tea tortrix, which earlier had been brought under complete biological control by importation of a parasitic wasp. These tortrix outbreaks, however, could be dealt with by DDT applications, so because of the importance of shot hole borer damage, dieldrin was recommended for shot hole borer control with follow-up DDT sprays to be made when-ever tortrix upsets were noted. This policy was commonly followed with good results for several years, although DDT appeared to induce mite attacks. Then upsets of the tea tortrix became more severe and persistent and major outbreaks of two other leaf-eating caterpillars occurred. One of these had never been previously recorded and the other had been reported as only an occasional minor pest of tea in Ceylon. Both of the latter caused greater damage than the shot hole borer or the tea tortrix ever had. Subsequent studies and observations showed all of these outbreaks to be the result of insecticide usage.

Most of the upsets and resurgences described have been correlated with, or proven by experimental tests to be due to, adverse effects of pesticides on natural enemies. In some cases, particularly with mites, it appears that the pesticide also may act to cause increases in the reproductive or survival capacity of the organism. This may result from an indirect physiological effect on the host plant or from making the physical substrate more suitable. Such an effect, of course, can only add to the adverse effect of pesticides on natural enemies to cause more rapid and severe resurgences or upsets.

The foregoing rather harsh indictment of pesticides still does not present the whole problem within agro-ecosystems or of other environ-mental, social and economic problems derived from the use of chemicals in crops. However, as I mentioned earlier, we are here stressing adverse effects as they relate to biological control. In this regard there is one additional major drawback within the agro-ecosystem to pesticide usage, the development of resistance to them by the pests. This is not only an extremely serious disadvantage to the use of pesticides *per se* but, as they begin to fail, dosages and number of applications are increased which magnifies the adverse effects on natural enemies.

More than 220, possibly 240, pest species are now resistant to pesticides, many to several pesticides and some to virtually all that are available for use. Resistance has been increasing in a geometric ratio since about 1950 when less than 20 species were resistant. For anyone advocating strong reliance on chemicals the resistance picture is truly frightening. A very good review of the resistance problem has been made by Georghiou (1971).

Insecticides: the ecological narcotics

A very realistic comparison can be drawn between the pattern of effects from use of hard narcotics by humans and the pattern resulting from the unilateral use of 'hard' pesticides in crops. First the method of use is simple and feasible and at an early stage of usage the effects appear to be salubrious and desirable. The results that are sought are generally obtained. However, sooner or later, dosages and frequency of use have to be increased as tolerance or resistance to the chemicals develops. Applications become more frequent and often different materials are resorted to in attempts to reproduce the original results. Ultimately usage becomes habit-forming in that reliance on the materials becomes essentially absolute. Meanwhile severe physiological and psychological problems (in humans) or ecological problems (in crops) develop which may disrupt the whole system. Recognition of this state does not immediately solve the problem because withdrawal is slow, difficult and painful, and reattainment of normality a lengthy process both in humans and generally in agro-ecosystems. How pesticide addiction can be alleviated will be discussed in Chapter 10.

In spite of all the foregoing discussion of the adverse effects of pesticides, for practical reasons one cannot advocate their immediate general deletion from agro-ecosystems. The problem is not that simple. To do so would result in heavy pest damage and financial loss in the short term in many cases, although in some other cases elimination of pesticides could be achieved immediately. I do strongly urge that our ultimate *goal* be the complete elimination of pesticides and that the strongest research efforts possible be directed toward this end. This means concentration on biological control and other ecologically non-disruptive, non-pollutive methods of control.

Why the great pesticide boom?

The question naturally arises as to why, if there are such severe adverse effects, pesticide usage came to be so great and, in fact, is still increasing markedly. Nearly one billion pounds of registered pesticides were used in the United States alone in 1970 and over half of this was for agricultural purposes, whereas in 1964 only 143 000 000 pounds of insecticides were used in agriculture.

Part of the reason was just explained. There is a reaction akin to narcotic effects in humans that tends to make pesticides increasingly self-perpetuating and this phenomenon has generally been recognized too late. However there is more to the story.

Until the past few centuries most potential pests were natives and generally had effective natural enemies that evolved with them. As commerce and trade increased pests were translocated without their enemies and created new, more serious problems. The reasons for these outbreaks were often not understood and led to the use of chemical poisons as attempted solutions. Insecticides began to be fairly commonly used in the 1800s as chemistry improved, as large-scale commercial farming developed, as monoculture increased and, especially as mentioned, new invading pests from abroad increased to damaging proportions and immediate remedies were sought. What could seem more logical than poisons to kill them? Only the glimmerings of other methods of control were then being perceived. There is also a certain satisfaction, perhaps the psychology of achievement, in applying a poison and seeing the pests die rapidly as a result.

Such ready acceptance by the farmer rapidly led to development of commercial pesticides and eventually to the huge pesticide industry of today. As in any business the profit motive is king and advertising is the key to profits. I think it safe to say that over the past years very much more information on pest control has reached farmers around the world from salesmen's contacts, magazines, pamphlets, newsletters, calendars, and highway signs telling only the pesticide story than from all governmental, university, or other sources combined which present a more balanced approach. Promotion of pesticide sales is big business and has tended toward the motto used by one company for a time on TV that 'the only good bug is a dead bug'. I have no doubt that most pesticide companies and individuals associated with them have acted ethically, honestly and in good faith in promoting their products. I think they generally believe what they say and advertise. However, they have overstressed the need for pesticides to eliminate the last thrips scar or mite russeting on fruit when no actual damage either in quality or quantity is involved; their treatment recommendations are often based on unreal or undetermined economic injury levels (state and federal entomologists share the blame here) and crop losses from failure to spray are commonly magnified – unintentionally I am sure – by the inadequate method generally used by those testing insecticides to determine losses by pest insects and mites. That is, a crop area of variable size is selected and divided into subplots, generally all of which are replicated and treated with different materials, dosages, and intervals of application except one subplot which is 'untreated'. Such a plot often is surrounded by treated plots and receives drift chemicals, plus it is part of a larger field or orchard which has been treated previously, hence has natural enemies decimated. In no sense is it an adequate check of the potential natural or biological control that might be attained in the complete absence of treatment (see Chapter 3 on the evaluation of natural enemies). Naturally the pests tend to explode in such a plot and by comparison with such a check plot the pesticide plots generally look much better and the amount of damage prevented by treatment appears correspondingly greater. Rudd (1964, Chapter 4) covers the pros and cons of loss from pests and the costs as compared to the gains resulting from pesticide use. In referring to some figures provided by the National Agricultural Chemicals Association in 1957 documenting gains derived from the use of pesticides he states that:

Caution must be observed with such sets of figures. The means of arriving at such values are not very refined and are often unreliable. Moreover, they tell only part of a story. Too frequently, they reflect an unrealistic 'optimism' not in keeping with their source.

'Insurance' or 'by the clock' treatments are commonly pushed by pesticide salesmen and are readily practiced by farmers who expect to avoid risk of loss thereby. They are especially bad from an ecological standpoint. Such treatments ignore real need or scientific determination of economic treatment thresholds. The farmer is told something like, treat for thrips at petal-fall or spray for aphids on May 15, when it may not even be known that such insects are in fact present at that time or, if present, constitute any real hazard. A good illustration is related by Rudd:

One may wonder about the accuracy of specific loss figures. In 1953 the rice leaf miner outbreak was credited with ruining 10 to 20 percent of the

California rice crop. Judged by my personal damage appraisal at the time of the outbreak, this range was certainly correct for many of the rice fields. Even at that time, however, by far the greater part of the rice acreage was not hit at all. To the presumed loss of yield must be added a cost of some $1.25 million for pesticides (and a very large wildlife loss). Curiously, however, rice yields that year were among the highest on record to that date. Equally inexplicable was the reduced yield per acre and consequently reduced total production that occurred with much greater acreages in 1954, the year following the outbreak and treatment. The price of rice was also substantially lower in the year following the outbreak. I conclude, therefore, that growers extrapolated single-field losses to the total acreage, and the 'insurance' spraying was the rule. Economically, insect damage seems relatively much less important than other factors. One may perhaps be permitted to wonder if perspective as well as accuracy were not somehow awry in reporting of the 'threat' to the rice crop.

It will be recalled from various instances of upsets related earlier, that in the early phases of pesticide use in crops, perhaps for quite a few years, the results may be quite satisfactory, even spectacular. At the same time the adverse effect of pesticides on biological control makes the need for chemicals seem greater and greater and the effectiveness of natural enemies increasingly poorer. However, we must also keep sight of the fact that in most crops there are one or more pests for which other methods of control have not as yet been discovered or perfected, hence some pesticide use is to be expected.

The philosophy of pest control by chemicals has been to achieve the highest kill possible, and percent mortality has been the main yardstick in the early screening of new chemicals in the laboratory. Such an objective, the highest kill possible, combined with ignorance of, or disregard for, non-target insects and mites, is guaranteed to be the quickest road to upsets, resurgences and the development of resistance by the pests. The pesticide industry has something of a parallel in the cigarette industry in that it took many years to recognize and prove the magnitude of the adverse effects but there are still many users and advocates and the industries still push their products vigorously. Fortunately there is a change in scientific understanding and in public attitude which portends the development of more biologically and ecologically sound practices in the future.

2
Pests and their natural enemies

It is a rare organism that has no natural enemies, if indeed there are any such. Natural enemy populations have the unique ability of being able to interact with their prey or host populations and to regulate them at lower levels than would occur otherwise. Some are effective at extremely low prey levels, others only at higher levels. Biological control operates within and often below the levels permitted by the physical factors of the environment such as temperature, moisture, light and others. This is briefly the biological control mentioned here and there in Chapter 1 and which will be discussed in more detail in the next chapter.

In order to appreciate the biological workings and ecological basis of biological control it is first desirable to have an idea of different pest groups and their major characteristic natural enemies. Although this book will stress natural enemies of insect pests and weeds because it is with these groups that nearly all applied biological control has been practiced, there are pests in nearly all groups of organisms and each is attacked by some other kind of organism ranging from parasitic microbes to predatory mammals.

Pest mammals have their predators, parasites and pathogens as do birds, fish, reptiles, nematodes, molluscs, plants (weeds) and so on through the lists of plant and animal groups. A pest, of course, is often made by definition and one man's pest may be another's food. Some well known cases of impact of natural enemies among mammals include applied biological control of pest rabbits in Australia by the imported myxoma virus and natural biological control of deer in Arizona by mountain lions.

Many natural enemies operate unsuspected and it is amazing how complex the bio-ecological interactions may be when detailed studies of any given organism are made. Recent evidence of a deer explosion in Texas is linked to the control of the screw-worm fly of cattle by the mass release of sterile male flies. This fly not only attacks cattle but also deer and evidently was having an unrealized but decided impact on the deer population previous to fly control. At a lower level of the phylogenetic scale, the crown of thorns starfish is currently being indicted as a pest of living coral reefs and considerable alarm has been created by its reported damage in some areas. In this case the starfish is a predator apparently tending to produce biological control but it is also a pest because it is attacking a wanted organism – the coral. Similarly coyotes are considered pests by some in the West but they might be considered quite useful elsewhere in rabbit control. Space prevents any attempt to even briefly cover all major phyla; suffice to say that biological control projects have included species as beneficial agents, i.e. natural enemies, in such diverse groups as mammals, birds, amphibians, fish, snails and nematodes, in addition to the predaceous and parasitic insects, the predatory mites and the pathogenic micro-organisms that are emphasized in this book and have been used predominantly in biological control.

The reasons for such emphasis lie in the fact that around 80 percent of all animals are insects and they include the vast majority of pests of man. They seriously affect his crops, his domestic stock and his forests and structures, as well as man himself. Efforts to control them with chemicals are responsible for a vast amount of environmental pollution and degradation. By far the greatest amount of poisonous chemicals are used against insects and mites and over 50 percent is used for agricultural pests. Weeds are also great pests and in recent years the use of herbicidal poisons has increased tremendously. Biological control was conceived and developed by entomologists against agricultural insect pests as well as against weeds, and most biological control projects have been directed against these groups. Hence it is only logical that we largely restrict coverage to natural enemies of insect pests (including also mites) and weeds. This is not meant to de-emphasize possibilities for biological control in other groups. There is much potential but relatively little research emphasis has been expended in this regard.

Natural enemies of insects

There is no accurate estimate available of the total number of insect natural enemies of other insects but there are probably as many, perhaps more, entomophagous insects as there are prey or hosts. It is commonly estimated that there are over 1 000 000 species of insects and this figure would include insect natural enemies. It has also been estimated that only about 15 percent of the insect natural enemies in existence have been discovered and named. Based on the many detailed studies of natural enemies of major insect pests in their native homes it would seem that most plant-feeding insects have more than one and generally several to many natural enemies. Some pest species have well over 100 recorded enemies. Many natural enemies attack several different host or prey species but others are rather specific. Considering everything, I would hazard an estimate that there are probably as many insects that are entomophagous as there are prey or host insect species, i.e. about one million natural enemy species. Obviously even of the ones known we can only treat broad groups. Among the best general references to these groups and their biologies are the books *Parasitic Insects*, Askew, (1971, Part 2), *Entomophagous Insects*, Clausen (1962), *Biological Control of Insect Pests and Weeds*, DeBach, ed. (1964a, Chapters 6 and 7) and *Beneficial Insects* by Swan (1964). The latter book will be found especially helpful to the non-specialist.

In biological control parlance, natural enemies are referred to as parasites, predators or pathogens. The first two are termed entomophagous, the latter entomogenous. Parasitic insects, sometimes referred to as parasitoids, develop as larvae on or in a single host individual from eggs generally laid on, in or near the host. They usually consume all or most of the host body, killing the host, and then pupate, either within or external to the host. The free-living adult parasite emerges from the pupa and starts the next generation anew by actively searching for hosts in which to oviposit. Most adult parasites require food such as honeydew, nectar or pollen and many feed on exudations from the host caused by the puncture made while depositing eggs. Some require free water.

Parasites may have one generation to one of the host (univoltine) or two or more generations to one of the host (multivoltine), and they tend to attack only one host stage, i.e. eggs, larvae, or pupae, although there is also some overlapping in certain cases – adult insects do not serve as hosts very often. Life cycles are commonly short, ranging from 10 days to 2 weeks or so in midsummer but correspondingly longer in cold weather. However some require a year or more if they have hosts with but a single generation per year. In general, they all have great *potential* rates of increase.

According to the species one or more parasitic larvae may characteristically develop per host individual; thus we have either solitary or gregarious parasitism. Sometimes two different species of larvae develop from eggs laid in the same host. This is multiple parasitism. There is also ectoparasitism and endoparasitism, depending upon whether the larva develops externally or internally. A parasite developing on a non-parasitic host insect is a primary parasite, whereas a parasite larva developing on another parasite species is a secondary or hyper-parasite. The latter are carefully screened out in quarantine rooms in all biological control importation projects. Superparasitism refers to the case where more eggs of a given species are deposited per host than can develop in one host because of nutritional limitations. This is generally not a cause for concern in the field because it tends to be a mechanism regulating balance between host and parasite.

Predatory insects differ from parasitic ones in that the larvae or nymphs, as the case may be, require several to many prey individuals to attain maturity. The adults generally deposit their eggs near the prey population and after hatching the active mobile immatures search out and consume prey individuals. This need of the larvae or nymphs to search is an important distinction from parasitic forms whose larvae develop on a single host individual and thus have the advantage of not having to discover additional hosts. Metamorphosis among predators may be complete or incomplete according to the insect order. Adults of many if not most species are also predatory. There may be one or several generations to one of the prey.

Pathogenic micro-organisms attack insects and have life cycles more or less characteristic of similar micro-organisms developing in other groups of animals. Insects are probably subject to as wide a variety of diseases as are the vertebrates. Except for the fungi, disease organisms gain entry and infect the host via the mouth and the digestive tract. That is, the insect host must eat plant or other food contaminated with the pathogen. In the case of fungi, entrance is gained through the insect's integument and free water or very high humidity is generally required. Thus fungi tend to be restricted to moist environments. However, fungi do have the advantage of attacking sucking insects, which because of the nature of their feeding on sap, tend to be fairly free of diseases caused by other micro-organisms because they rarely ingest them. Virtually no insect disease organisms also occur in mammals and none have been recorded from man. Thus they are safe to use in applied biological control, even in large-scale microbial spraying operations.

The major groups occur in two orders of insects, Hymenoptera (bees, wasps, ants, etc.) and Diptera (flies).

HYMENOPTERA. This is the dominant order among all entomophagous insects both numerically and as regards their successful use in biological control. Over two-thirds of the cases of successful biological control of pest species have been achieved by hymenopterous parasites.

There are many extremely interesting biological adaptations among the Hymenoptera that are discussed in some detail in the publications previously cited. One is the ovipositor which is a specialized egg-laying organ composed of long interlocking chitinous plates through which the egg passes. The ovipositor acts as a drill to pierce the host or the material surrounding the host and in many cases it also serves as a hypodermic to inject paralyzing venom into the host. It is the same organ as the stinger in bees and large wasps. In some species it is used to secrete and form a feeding tube through which the adult parasite sucks the host body fluid, much as through a straw, in order to obtain protein for continued egg production. Being chitin, the ovipositor lacks muscles except at the base but it is supplied with nerves extending its length to the tip which bears highly sensitive sense organs that can discern by chemical stimuli whether a host is suitable or not and in fact whether it already contains a parasite egg. In spite of the fact that the ovipositor itself is non-muscular it can be manipulated by the muscles attached to the base to rotate back and forth like a drill and to curve and bend in any given direction as it is used to explore either the surface or the interior of a host.

The well known reproductive method of female production from fertilized eggs and male production from unfertilized eggs (arrhenotoky) is supplanted in some species by obligatory parthenogenesis or uni-parental reproduction (thelytoky) wherein females give rise to females and males have become lost or only occur quite rarely. Polyembryonic reproduction in insects occurs only in Hymenoptera. This unusual phenomenon involves the production of two or more, sometimes hundreds, of individuals from a single egg. It is known to occur in at least four parasitic superfamilies. Phoresy is another interesting habit of certain parasites, especially of species that lay their eggs in the eggs of the host, i.e. egg parasites, and of species whose first instar larvae attach themselves to an adult host in order to reach the host

27

larvae in the nest or colony. Phoretic adult parasites are small and attach themselves to the females of the host insect, then, when that female lays eggs, the parasite female leaves her and proceeds to oviposit in the newly deposited host eggs. The most important and numerous hymenopterous parasites occur in the major groups commonly known as chalcids, braconids, ichneumonids and proctotrupids.

The chalcids. This term refers to a large superfamily, the Chalcidoidea that includes some twenty-odd families and thousands of species. The chalcids attack species in nearly all orders of insects, the preferred ones being Coleoptera, Diptera, Homoptera, and Lepidoptera which also happen to include the bulk of our chief crop pests. The immature stages of chalcids predominantly develop in host eggs or larvae but they also commonly attack pupae, and some develop in adults of Homoptera. The adults are free-living winged 'wasps' ranging in size from the smallest of insects to ones $\frac{1}{2}$ inch or more in length. They generally require honeydew or nectar as food and some construct the feeding-tube, already mentioned, in order to feed on host body fluids. They have been responsible for more successful cases of applied biological control than all other groups combined. I do not consider this to be especially due to intrinsic superiority as much as to the fact that they include the families that specialize in attacking scale insects, mealybugs, aphids and whiteflies and that these pest groups have received a great deal of research emphasis in biological control.

Among the chalcids, two families, the mymarids and the trichogrammatids, consist entirely of species that are egg parasites and consequently are usually very minute, some being less than 0.25 mm in length. It is difficult to collect many insect eggs in the field and hold them in a rearing container without obtaining numerous individuals of one egg parasite species or another. The encyrtids and aphelinids include many that specialize in attacking scale insects, mealybugs, whiteflies and related forms and have been so outstandingly successful in applied biological control.

Fig. 6a shows a tiny adult chalcid parasite of the family Encyrtidae in the act of oviposition in its scale insect host. This is *Metaphycus helvolus*, which is responsible for complete biological control of the black scale of citrus in many places. The other photograph (Fig. 6b) shows an adult chalcid parasite of the family Eupelmidae.

The braconids. This is a major large family of parasitic wasps in the superfamily Ichneumonoidea. They have been commonly used in applied biological control and include many species effective in natural

28

(a)

(b)

Fig. 6. (a) A small (1.5 mm) chalcid parasite (family Encyrtidae) in the act of ovipositing in a young black scale. This is *Metaphycus helvolus*, which is responsible for complete biological control of the black scale on citrus in many areas. (b) A chalcid parasite of the family Eupelmidae.

control. Only an occasional rare species is hyperparasitic, hence the family is nearly entirely beneficial. Their general biology and life cycle is similar to the chalcids. Parasitism may be external or internal, solitary or gregarious. The type of parasitism is usually correlated with the habits of the host, external parasitism tending to occur in hosts living in protected places like tunnels and internal parasitism in free-living hosts. Their host preferences are principally lepidopterous larvae and coleopterous larvae but also commonly Diptera, including the damaging fruit flies, and Homoptera, particularly aphids. When females that have larvae which develop externally on the host oviposit, they nearly always permanently paralyze the host with a venom. This prevents the mobile host larva from dislodging the parasite eggs. The internal parasitic species seldom paralyze the host. The free-living adults require food and some make feeding tubes, as do the chalcids. They tend to average somewhat larger in size than the chalcids. Fig. 7 shows examples of two adult braconids.

Various braconid subfamilies and genera specialize in distinctly particular host groups; some (Vipioninae) are primarily gregarious external parasites on lepidopterous larvae of which nearly all have the common habit of occurring in a burrow, cell, cocoon or within a web. Thus the adult parasites tend to search for and choose particular sites for oviposition as much as, or more so than, the individuals of the host species attacked. This is true of many other braconids. Others (Cheloninae) are principally solitary internal parasites of lepidopterous hosts. The Microgasterinae also specialize predominantly in lepidopterous larvae, many of which are free-living. The Opiinae includes the important genus *Opius*, species of which mainly attack dipterous fruit fly larvae. The Aphidiinae are exclusively solitary internal parasites of aphids and include species used successfully in biological control.

The ichneumonids. This is a very large family numbering thousands of species also of the superfamily Ichneumonoidea, and has great potential in biological control to judge from many studies showing their important natural regulatory effects in crop pest populations. According to Townes (1971), 'There are more species of Ichneumonidae than all the vertebrate animals combined.' In other words, more than all the mammals, birds, reptiles, amphibians and fish. The Ichneumonidae comprise about 20 percent of all parasitic insects. Surprisingly, thus far only a few have produced appreciable results when imported in applied biological control projects. Most are primary parasites, hence

(a)

(b)

Fig. 7. An example (a) of an adult braconid parasite, *Aphidius ervi*, ovipositing in an aphid (left). Courtesy of Petr Stary. (b) An adult braconid, *Meteorus vulgaris*, ovipositing in a larva hidden in a cotton boll. From van den Bosch and Hagen (1966).

31

Fig. 8. A large ichneumonid parasite with an especially long ovipositor.
Photo by Kenneth Middleham.

the family is predominantly beneficial. Some of the largest and most conspicuous parasite species occur in this family. The ovipositor especially is often noticeable and may be extremely long in relation to the size of the body (see Fig. 8).

The host preferences of the family are quite varied but many sub-families or genera tend to be fairly uniform with respect to parasitism of particular host groups. For example, the Joppinae occur only as internal parasites of larvae and pupae of Lepidoptera. Most of the Ichneumonidae probably parasitize wood- and stem-boring larvae in the Lepidoptera, Coleoptera or Hymenoptera but many attack lepidopterous pupae and the remainder have quite varied habits. Some species have a very wide host range, tending, as in many braconids, to choose situations, such as borings, rather than particular host species for oviposition. Most of the Tryphoninae are solitary parasites of sawflies. The Ophioninae are predominantly internal parasites of lepidopterous larvae although a few develop in the grubs of root-feeding scarabs in the soil.

This is such a large family that the biological phenomena cover a tremendously wide range of interesting and curious occurrences. Only some generalized or interesting patterns can be mentioned. Both external and internal parasitism are common and most species oviposit on or in the host stage upon which the parasite larvae is to complete development. The external parasites commonly oviposit on hosts enclosed in cocoons, pupal cases or burrows and may permanently paralyze the host. This causes the host to remain in a fresh condition, yet not develop past the preferred stage, for weeks or even months. Some drill deep into bark or wood with the ovipositor and the very long stalked eggs pass down the narrow channel and into the hidden host. The adults live for appreciable periods, often 6–8 weeks, which is advantageous when hosts are scarce. Many require free water and depend for food on nectar or pollen from particular plant species. This may affect their occurrence or efficiency in certain localities. Oviposition is keyed to the habits of the host. Free-living host larvae provide a direct stimulus via the antennae and the ovipositor for egg deposition but host larvae enclosed in cocoons, burrows, etc. cannot be reached except by the ovipositor. Initial attraction in the latter case is probably by odor or tactile responses and final selection of the host by sense organs on the ovipositor. The adult females of many species feed upon the body fluid of the stage they parasitize as it exudes from the ovipositor puncture, others go so far as to consume an entire host with the mandibles, hence become true predators but none construct tubes for host feeding as many chalcids and braconids do.

The serphoids. This superfamily, the Serphoidae, contains several families, the most important of which are the Platygasteridae and the Scelionidae. All are parasitic on the immature stages of other insects and they are predominantly primary internal parasites.

The species of platygasterids differ relatively little in appearance, habits and host preferences. They are internal parasites of cecidomyiid fly larvae and of homopterous nymphs, some of which are serious crop pests. The adults are necessarily small in size because their hosts are all small insects ranging from about 1 mm to several mm in length, and most of them are black. The polyembryonic reproduction which occurs in the genus *Platygaster* has occasioned much biological interest. Only a few species have been utilized in biological control; one is reported to have had a substantial controlling effect on the pear midge in New Zealand and two imported species of *Amitus* have been important in biological control of pest whiteflies. Species of *Alloptropa* are important parasites of mealybugs. Fig. 9 shows an adult

33

(a)

(b)

Fig. 9. (a) A small scelionid parasite, *Amitus spiniferus*, that is an effective enemy of the woolly whitefly. (b) Mummified woolly whitefly pupal cases showing exit holes through which *Amitus* adults have emerged after developing as an internal parasite.

34

Fig. 10. An adult of the scelionid *Trissolcus basalis*, in the act of chemically marking an egg of the green vegetable bug to inform other females that the host egg has already been parasitized. Courtesy Division of Entomology, CSIRO, Canberra, Australia.

of *Amitus spiniferus*, an important parasite of the woolly whitefly of citrus. It is only about 1.5 mm in length.

The scelionids comprise a fairly large family numerically; all are small, again because they all develop in small hosts – insect eggs exclusively in this case. For the most part they parasitize eggs of Lepidoptera, Hemiptera and Orthoptera, as well as of certain flies and spiders. They generally develop as solitary individuals. Several species have been successfully utilized in biological control importation projects. In addition to interesting cases of phoresy in this group, the females of certain species exhibit the remarkable adaptation of marking the host egg with the ovipositor, much as with a pencil, following oviposition. The marking substance evidently is a chemical secreted at the tip of the ovipositor. This informs subsequent females that the host egg already contains a parasite egg, and consequently they refrain from oviposition in it. An adult of *Trissolcus basalis* in the act of marking an egg of the green vegetable bug is shown in Fig. 10.

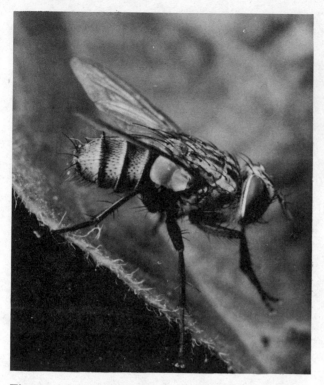

Fig. 11. Adult of a parasitic tachinid fly. From van den Bosch and Hagen (1966).

DIPTERA. In addition to the tachinids which comprise the most important dipterous family in biological control, this order contains several parasitic families including the Cyrtidae, Nemestrinidae, Pipunculidae, Conopidae and Pyrgotidae. Most Bombyliidae are parasitic, and parasitic species occur in many of the families that principally have other habits. However the tachinids constitute the major parasitic family both in numbers of species and in economic importance and have been the only group utilized extensively in biological control importation projects.

The tachinids. This is a very large family containing a number of subfamilies having species important in natural and applied biological control. There are no hyperparasitic species. As would be expected in a large group, host preferences cover a wide range. An appreciable number of species are highly specific in their host preferences whereas others are very polyphagous. Some have the greatest host range known

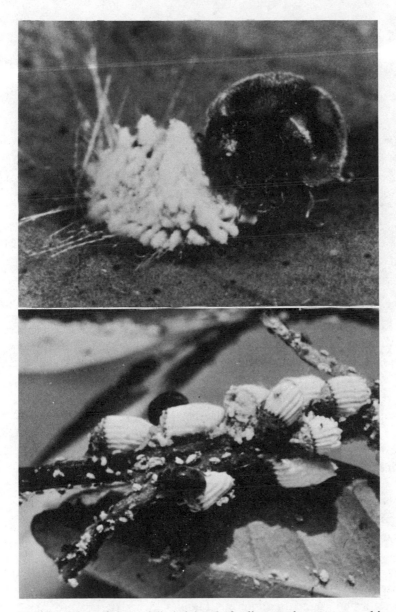

Fig. 12. Adult of the vedalia ladybeetle feeding on the cottony-cushion scale. This beetle produced the first outstanding case of biological control.

37

Fig. 13. A common ladybeetle *Hippodamia* feeding on an aphid. From van den Bosch and Hagen (1966).

in any parasitic group. For instance, *Compsilura concinnata*, a parasite imported against the gypsy moth, has been recorded from some 100 species of hosts just in the United States. All in all it appears that tachinids are less host-specific than are the hymenopterous parasites. A tachinid is shown in Fig. 11.

The subfamily Exoristinae is the most important, both numerically and economically. It includes many well-known genera that attack important crop pests. The hosts are predominantly lepidopterous larvae, and adult beetles in the scarab, chrysomelid and carabid families. The Tachininae principally include species that parasitize boring or otherwise concealed lepidopterous larvae. The Gymnosomatinae largely parasitize adult hosts, but sometimes nymphs, of the pentatomid, pyrrhocorid, and coreid hemipterous families. Scarab grubs are commonly attacked by species of Dexiinae which also include in their host preferences adult scarabs and boring larvae of beetles and moths.

Such a wide variety of taxonomic groups of diverse habits and host preferences occur among predators that only a few of the larger and more ecologically important ones can be touched upon. In general, predators lack the highly specialized adaptations which are correlated with the parasitic mode of life. Both larvae or nymphs as well as the corresponding adults may be predaceous or only one stage may exhibit the habit.

COLEOPTERA. The beetles contain many families with a large number of predaceous species and all told probably more than half of all predators are in this order. The principal predaceous families are the Coccinellidae (the well-known ladybeetles), Silphidae, Staphylinidae, Histeridae, Lampyridae, Cleridae, Cantharidae, Meloidae, Cicindelidae, Carabidae, Dytiscidae and Gyrinidae.

The coccinellids and the carabids are of most importance in biological control of agricultural pests. The ladybeetles especially have produced outstanding results in biological control importation projects in a number of cases and the vedalia ladybeetle was responsible for the first outstanding success in biological control. Fig. 12 shows adults of the vedalia beetle feeding on the cottony cushion-scale. This common worldwide family specializes mainly in feeding upon scale insects, mealybugs, aphids and whiteflies. Fig. 13 shows the common ladybeetle, *Hippodamia*, feeding on an aphid.

Other families having rather specialized feeding habits include the lampyrids which commonly feed both as larvae and adults on snails and earthworms; the meloids that prey upon the eggs of locusts in the soil or develop in the cells of bees; the generally nocturnal carabid ground beetles that commonly feed on lepidopterous larvae and pupae, and the checkered clerid beetles which predominantly feed both as adults and larvae on scolytid and other wood-boring beetles and are an important factor in the control of these forest pests. Other families tend to be restricted to particular habitats but may be rather generalized feeders. Thus the dytiscid diving beetles are aquatic and feed on nearly everything of the right size including various aquatic insects, snails, tadpoles and earthworms, although most feed on the immature stages of dragonflies, mayflies or aquatic bugs. The agile cicindelid tiger beetles are predominantly terrestrial and favor a wide variety of prey in exposed habitats such as open sandy areas, roadways or paths. A large number of the staphylinid rove beetles prey upon dipterous larvae in manure and other refuse, in decomposing animal carcasses and in the soil.

NEUROPTERA. Most of the species of this order are predatory. It contains such familiar forms as the common green lacewings and the ant lions whose pits are seen so often in sandy or dusty areas. The larvae of nearly all neuropterans possess long curved mandibles which act like forceps to grasp and pierce the prey and suck out the body fluids.

The most important families in biological control have been the Chrysopidae (green lacewings) and Hemerobiidae (brown lacewings) which attack many agricultural pests including scale insects, mealybugs, aphids, whiteflies, mites and a variety of others. The eggs of the green lacewings are characteristically borne on long slender stalks and commonly in groups. The larvae when magnified appear ferocious, which indeed they are, and nearly dragon-like because of their large scimitar-shaped mandibles. They feed mainly on aphids and mealybugs but on a variety of other insects and mites as well. The beautifully bright green adults frequently have golden eyes. They are often abundant in orchards, fields and gardens. The adults tend to feed on the same kinds of prey as the larvae. Fig. 14 shows the stalked eggs, larva and adult of a green lacewing.

The brown lacewings eat aphids, mealybugs, whiteflies, chermids, scale insects and a variety of others. The adults appear similar to the green lacewings in form, perhaps smaller, but are brown and drab in appearance as compared to the former. Population studies have shown them to be quite effective in natural biological control of mealybugs.

HYMENOPTERA. About one-quarter of the families of this order are strictly predaceous. Most of the predatory forms tend to be social and live in colonies. The ants (Formicidae) probably comprise the most important predatory group and are important in natural control even though many are classed as pests. They are fostered in Europe in the biological control of forest insects and in the Orient for biological control of certain citrus pests. Ants are particularly effective against soil-inhabiting larvae, pupae or adults of a diverse variety of forms.

The colonial vespid wasps provision their paper nests with the bodies of caterpillars and other soft-bodied insects. The family is important in natural control, especially of exposed foliage feeding

Fig. 14. (a) The stalked eggs, (b) a larva feeding on an aphid and (c) an adult of a green lacewing. From van den Bosch and Hagen (1966).

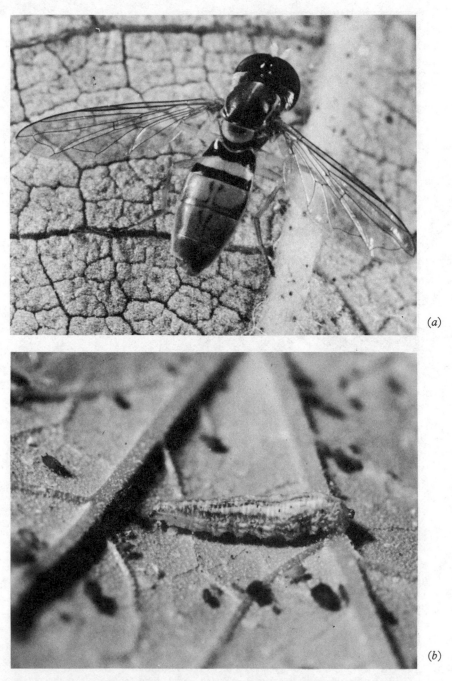

(a)

(b)

Fig. 15. (a) A syrphid fly adult and (b) larva. From van den Bosch and Hagen (1966).

larvae. Species of *Polistes* have been used in several biological control projects.

The specoid wasps likewise provision their nests with other insects but tend to be much less social than the vespids. The nests range from one cell to a group. They are commonly built in the soil or else in stems of plants. Some construct nests of mud or sand. Host preferences are very diverse and include prey in all the common insect orders, especially the Orthoptera, Hemiptera, Homoptera, Hymenoptera, Lepidoptera and Diptera. When large hosts are used only a single egg may be placed in a cell, hence the developing larva is parasitic in this case; usually however more than one prey individual is used to provision a cell, so they qualify as predators. They generally paralyze the prey for a greater or lesser duration of time.

DIPTERA. Quite a few families are entirely predaceous and many others contain predatory species. Either or both larvae and adults may be predators, generally on noxious insects. They are of decided importance in natural control and some have been utilized in applied biological control. The more common or important economic families include the Syrphidae, Asilidae, Cecidomyiidae, Bombyliidae, Anthomyiidae, Calliphoridae, and Sarcophagidae. Of the latter four, many are predaceous in the egg masses of grasshoppers. The syrphid larvae are common and valuable predators of aphids especially, although some attack scales and related forms; the asilid robber flies prey as adults on many flying insects, often including beneficial ones, but the larvae feed in the soil or in decaying wood largely on pest insects. Fig. 15 shows a syrphid fly larva and adult. The tiny cecidomyiid gnats or midges include a substantial number of species whose larvae prey upon aphids, scale insects, whiteflies, thrips and mites, especially the eggs or younger stages.

HEMIPTERA. Although this order is predominantly plant-feeding, a substantial number of species in various families have evolved to become predaceous. Many attack important economic crop insects and are considered to be of great importance in natural control. A predatory hemipteran, *Geocoris*, is shown sucking the body fluids from a leafhopper through its proboscis in Fig. 16. Some have been used in biological control importation projects of which *Cyrtorhinus mundulus*, which controlled the sugar-cane leafhopper in Hawaii (see Chapter 5), is the outstanding example. It feeds exclusively on the leafhoppers'

43

Fig. 16. A big-eyed bug *Geocoris* sucking the body fluids from a leafhopper through its proboscis. From van den Bosch and Hagen (1966)

eggs. A considerable number, if not most, of the species of this same family, the Miridae, are predaceous. Among the anthocorids the best known predator is *Orius insidiosus* which sucks the body fluid of a variety of prey including thrips, Homoptera, Hemiptera, Lepidoptera and mites. It is a fairly effective predator of corn earworm eggs and young larvae as well as of various thrips and mites. The reduviid assassin bugs prey on a wide range of plant-feeding insects including caterpillars, leafhoppers and aphids. There are several families primarily aquatic in habit which prey upon aquatic insects and other organisms. These are included in the superfamily Gerroidea.

ODONATA. The well-known large dragonflies and damselflies number several thousand species, all of which are predaceous both as nymphs and as adults. The nymphs are virtually all aquatic and feed on a wide range of aquatic insects and other organisms. The adults capture their prey on the wing and tend to prefer mosquitoes and other flies, Lepidoptera and Hymenoptera. Active predation on swarming termites has been recorded.

Pathogenic micro-organisms

The most common diseases of insects are caused by bacteria, fungi, viruses, protozoa and nematodes. Because of their small size usually only the symptoms will be seen by the non-specialist. In terms of numbers of species, relatively few pathogens are known as compared to the numbers of described entomophagous insects. However, many of them, such as *Bacillus thuringiensis* and the fungi, *Entomophthora sphaerosperma, Beauveria bassiana* (white muscardine), and *Metarrhizum anisopliae* (green muscardine), attack a large range of host species. Their effects are sometimes spectacular in natural control, especially when epizootics occur to devastate great outbreaks of pest insects. However, pathogens have the handicap that they are not active searchers for the host or prey as are entomophagous insects, hence generally do not limit host population densities at low levels.

In classical biological control importation projects, very little has been done regarding introduction of new exotic insect pathogens. Of those purposely imported, I know of no case where a pathogen alone has produced outstanding biological control at low levels but certain viruses have played a prominent role.

The greatest emphasis with pathogens in recent years has been with their mass production and application in the field as microbial insecticides. This offers much promise in integrated control programs because microbial insecticides appear to have none of the toxic residue drawbacks of chemical pesticides. However, the possibility exists that resistance may develop. For some reason federal agencies have been reluctant to approve the registration for commercial use of insect viruses. This has been unfortunate because viruses offer much hope as microbial insecticides. It currently appears that this problem is being solved. Bacterial preparations of *Bacillus thuringiensis* are available from several commercial firms and have given good results against various pests, especially Lepidoptera. The milky disease, *Bacillus popillae*, of the Japanese beetle is also produced commercially and used successfully in the eastern United States.

Insect pathology is a whole field in itself and probably has nearly as many research specialists as are engaged in any other major area of biological control. Important references include: DeBach, ed. (1964*a*) [Chapter 18 by E. A. Steinhaus, Chapter 19 by Y. Tanada, Chapter 20 by M. E. Martignoni and Chapter 21 by I. M. Hall]; Steinhaus (1946, 1949, 1963); and Swan (1964).

45

Natural enemies of weeds

The insect natural enemies of weeds do not fall into specialized taxonomic groups as is true of the entomophagous insects. Instead they are just as diverse as the entire range of phytophagous insects and any weed-feeding insect of whatever feeding habit in any order, family, or genus can be considered potentially important in biological control of weeds. Thus we cannot categorize any particular order or family as being of outstanding importance. The critical aspect in biological weed control is the choice, by careful screening, of weed-feeders which are so highly adapted to the weed species that they are unable to develop on any other plants – at least any economic ones. This often means the choice of an insect with specialized habits but it can just as well mean one with very high host (weed) specificity. Thus insects in such diverse groups as the moths, thrips, mealybugs, scale insects, chrysomelid and other beetles, sucking bugs as well as dipterous leaf miners, gall midges and others have been more or less successfully used in biological control of weeds; some outstandingly so, such as the *Cactoblastis* moth which killed prickly pear cactus over millions of acres in Australia and reclaimed the land for agricultural use.

Diseases of weeds offer great potential but thus far there has been reluctance to try them in fear that they might also attack desirable plants. However, there should be no more hazard here than in the case of weed-feeding insects, provide l proper screening tests are carried out to determine near absolute specificity of the pathogen for the weed in question. This remains an important field for research and application. The effects of accidently imported plant pathogens, albeit on certain desirable plants, demonstrate not only that the method is feasible but that native species of weeds may be controlled. This is illustrated by the 'control' of chestnut trees in the eastern United States forests by the accidentally introduced fungus, *Endothia parasitica*, from Asia. Not only was a native plant controlled but the pathogen was highly specific to it.

Other organisms have been little utilized but may offer considerable potential in some cases. Carp have been used for control of aquatic weeds and snails may offer promise in this regard. Mites have shown possibilities and parasitic plants such as dodders and mistletoes have been considered.

3
Biological
control ecology

Biological control is a part of the broader overall phenomenon of natural control. Natural control may be defined as the regulation of populations within certain more or less regular upper and lower limits over a period of time by any one or any combination of natural factors. Such factors have sometimes been classed into two groups, biotic (living) and abiotic (non-living). However, rarely if ever do they act alone, although any one may be the key regulatory factor largely responsible for a particular density in a given situation.

Natural control

The most important factors in natural control are (1) natural enemies (parasites, predators and pathogens), (2) weather and other physical factors, (3) food (quantity and quality), (4) interspecific competition (other than natural enemies), (5) intraspecific competition, and (6) spatial or territorial requirements. Population movement is a complicating factor applying to some organisms which we shall not deal with. In this discussion natural control and biological control of insects is stressed but the principles involved apply broadly to all organisms.

Over the years there has been considerable disagreement and misunderstanding between two so-called schools of thought wherein certain ecologists have stressed population regulation by weather and others have stressed regulation by natural enemies. Perhaps a third group that stresses competition should be distinguished. Actually, in the broad sense, competition between individuals of the same or different species for some common requisite or other is generally involved in all regulatory processes, whether they entail weather, natural enemies, food or spatial needs. All of the factors mentioned are important and all are capable of regulating the population density

47

of an organism. However, their mode of action and interaction is not the same and the degree of natural control of a given species attributable to any one may differ markedly between different habitats or even microhabitats. Additionally, some workers emphasize genetic feedback in the determination of population densities, i.e. that selection for better adaptation may change the density at which the populations are regulated. We see this possibility as an evolutionary process but not as a regulatory process (Huffaker, Messenger and DeBach, 1971, pp. 56–61).

Weather produces natural control in the sense defined. I have been able to demonstrate this experimentally with several insects, including both pests and natural enemies (DeBach, 1958). Proof can be obtained by making paired plot comparisons in which other factors, such as natural enemies, are excluded or can be shown to have absolutely no effect in population regulation. For example, starting with a low population density so that competition is not a factor, natural enemies can be eliminated in one plot by an insecticide which is non-toxic to the pest but not decimated in an adjacent plot. If no appreciable population increase of the pest occurs in either plot, one can conclude that natural enemies were inconsequential and that weather therefore was responsible for the observed low population density. Of course weather or other physical factors always act ultimately to determine the limits of distribution of an organism. There are certain tolerable limits for each species. Within an organism's range of distribution weather determines within any given habitat the ultimate basic limits within which certain 'average' but fluctuating population densities may be obtained, theoretically even in the absence of other possible regulatory factors. Such natural control may occur at very high or at very low densities because natural control does not involve any characteristic density that is inherent for a species.

Weather acts to regulate insect population densities by interacting with the other physical and biotic aspects of a habitat. It must be severe on occasion at least, to have any effect. Otherwise it will be continuously permissive, i.e. more or less ideal or optimum, and the organism will increase until checked by other factors. Severe weather (in the relative sense) operates to restrict the number, size and quality of inhabitable spots in a given habitat and may produce its results by direct effects on food or shelter or by increasing competition for such requisites. For instance, the higher the temperature and the lower the humidity, the fewer are the places on a plant that a phytophagous insect may be able to survive. Thus weather acts in a density-dependent manner but it is not density-dependent in the sense that natural enemies are (see later discussion of density-dependence). Like a density-dependent factor, given weather conditions will kill a higher proportion of a dense population than of a sparse one because in the dense population a greater percentage of the population will be unable to find suitably sheltered microhabitats because the number of sheltered sites tends to be fixed.

If weather is permissive or optimal and natural enemies absent or ineffective, then ultimately an insect population will be regulated by the quantity of food or other requisites interacting with interspecific and/or intraspecific competition. However, the last three factors usually do not control insect pest populations at sufficiently low levels to be economically satisfactory, hence are not generally important factors in applied insect ecology. In other words, if a plant-feeding insect becomes sufficiently abundant to reduce or destroy its food supply thus limiting its further increase, this would be a case of natural control of interest to the basic ecologist but not to the farmer or applied entomologist, except that they would seek additional more effective means of regulation.

Thus it seems obvious that in agricultural crops, in forests and other habitats of economic significance to man, if weather is generally favorable for a pest, natural control of an economically satisfactory nature must generally derive from the actions of natural enemies. Of course there are other non-chemical means of achieving control, but this is not the natural control under discussion here. Chapter 9 will cover other approaches.

Biological control

Biological control in an ecological sense can be defined as the regulation by *natural enemies* of another organism's population density at a lower average than would otherwise occur. Fluctuations about the mean are expected and may either be marked or essentially unnoticeable. This falls within the definition of natural control and, as in that case, does not attempt to prescribe the population densities involved – only that they be lower than would be true if the responsible factors were withdrawn or made ineffective. Thus, this definition does not cover the degree of biological control in the economic sense, which must be stated separately in relation to any particular pest organism. Nor does the definition necessarily imply any activity by man, although man may import and establish new natural enemies and thereby achieve biological control. However, a vast amount of biological control is natural, as will be shown in the next section. I sometimes use applied biological control for the cases involving manipulation by man and natural control for the others. To go a step further, applied biological control can be achieved in differing degrees of economic importance, which have been distinguished as partial, substantial or complete. These qualifications can also be applied to natural biological control of potential pests. For instance, if the natural enemies of a potential pest under complete biological control are killed off by insecticides a great upset will occur; if the potential pest is under partial biological control only a mild upset may occur. Additionally the term biological control also is used in a broad sense to refer to the professional field of biological control and to cover all the activities man may engage in to foster the effectiveness of natural enemies.

Biological control and population phenomena

Thus far we have talked only about the fact of biological control and what it is but not how the remarkable interactions which bring it about occur. Scientists engaged in research on biological control have contributed a great amount to an understanding of how it occurs as well as to other theories and principles of population ecology.

The mechanisms of regulation by insect natural enemies, and of climate by comparison, were visualized partially by Howard and Fiske (1911) in connection with the gypsy moth parasite work, by Muir working with parasites and predators in Hawaii within the next decade or so, then, and most importantly, by A. J. Nicholson in Australia and H. S. Smith in California mainly in the early 1930s. Professor Smith developed the important concept of density-dependence to explain how predator–prey or host–parasite systems interact to produce biological control. C. B. Huffaker in recent years has done much to clarify this concept and bring together opposing views. Huffaker and Messenger (1964) and Huffaker, Messenger and DeBach (1971) cover this subject in some detail.

Density-dependence is the term covering the special attributes of a natural enemy which enables it to regulate the prey or host population.*

* In this discussion predator, parasite and natural enemy are often used interchangeably, as are prey and host.

It operates by means of an intensification of the mortality-causing actions of enemies as the host or prey population increases and a relaxation of these actions as the host population density falls, so that host population increase beyond a characteristic high is prevented and decrease to extinction is prevented (except perhaps locally on occasion). A negative feedback process between population density and rate of increase is involved. This reciprocal interaction also results in regulation of the enemy's own population because as it reduces the host population during one phase of the cycle it necessarily reduces its own population. Then as its repressive pressure reaches a minimum and the host population again increases, the enemy population correspondingly is enabled to increase until it again overtakes the host and the cycle is repeated.

Such reciprocal interaction results in the achievement of a typical average population density or 'balance' in a given habitat or area. The concept of density-dependence explains how natural enemies can regulate host populations but it does not explain at what density they will do so. The balance may occur at high, low or intermediate population densities. The determination of this rests primarily with the inherent characteristics of the natural enemy and secondarily with how these innate capabilities may be restricted or reduced by adverse environmental conditions. Characteristics of the host may also be modifying.

All natural enemies having an appreciable degree of prey specificity will exhibit density-dependence with respect to that prey. A natural enemy that is highly density-dependent can regulate the prey (host) population density at very low levels, whereas one that is weakly density-dependent will only do so at high levels. Very closely related species may have quite different capabilities in this regard. This is another way of describing an effective enemy as compared to an ineffective one. The difference is that the effective enemy responds very rapidly to any tendency of the prey (host) population to increase so that its relative reproductive rate quickly increases with respect to the prey and it overtakes and reverses the trend before any important increase has occurred. An ineffective enemy responds slowly and shows much greater lag effects, thus permitting the prey to achieve much higher maxima and mean population densities.

The degree of density-dependence or efficiency of an enemy is linked to its searching ability more so than anything else. Only an enemy that has a high searching ability can find prey when they are scarce and this is absolutely necessary if it is to be able to regulate the prey population at low levels. It also is able to respond rapidly by finding proportionately more prey as the prey population tends to increase. Poor searchers can never do so.

In addition to searching ability, the qualities most important to the effectiveness of a natural enemy in prey population regulation are: (1) a high degree of prey (host) specificity, (2) a high reproductive capacity with respect to the prey, and (3) good adaptation to, and tolerance of, as broad a range of environmental conditions as the prey. Item (1), high prey specificity, is strongly correlated with nearly all natural enemies that have produced outstanding results in biological control. Items (2) and (3) must be favorable to the natural enemy in order for it to be highly effective but they can also be possessed by a poor searcher and they alone will not make an efficient enemy of it.

Thus far we do not know how to measure with any accuracy the searching ability of a natural enemy or its potential effectiveness except by the effect it has in prey population regulation. In other words it must be tested or evaluated in the field. Laboratory studies have done no more than give an idea of some of the processes involved in searching, but none have yet explained why, of two closely related or even sibling species of natural enemies, one is efficient in prey population regulation and the other poor. More often than not, detailed laboratory studies of the bio-ecological characteristics of newly imported natural enemies have led to predictions of future field results that were the opposite of those obtained. We can get a good idea of the degree of prey specificity from field and laboratory studies and of potential reproductive capacity in the laboratory, as well as a fair idea – but often misleading – of adaptability to environmental conditions. How to put everything together to choose a potentially effective enemy *beforehand* with certainty is still beyond our grasp.

Additionally, even if a natural enemy possesses all the inherent qualities to be effective in prey population regulation, adverse environmental conditions can so reduce its potential as to transform it into an ineffective enemy. Weather extremes can do this and, as we have seen in Chapter 1, so can insecticides. Also shortage of requisites such as food (honeydew, pollen, nectar, etc.) or free water for adult parasites or predators or of alternate prey or host plants can produce the same effects. What happens is that the enemy's density-dependent response is weakened so that it has a lessened ability to cause an increasing rate of mortality of the prey population as prey population density tends to increase. This results in the prey population achieving 'equilibrium' or 'balance' at a higher average density than otherwise would be the case.

We can perhaps envision this better from a simple numerical example. Assume that a given prey species in a particular climatically ideal habitat requires 90 percent mortality of the immature stages on the average in each generation to remain in equilibrium. This would apply if the species possesses a 50:50 sex ratio and the females consistently produced 20 eggs each. Thus starting at any point in time at an equilibrium density of 200 prey adults (100 females), 2000 eggs would be laid (100 females × 20 eggs each) which, subjected to a total of 90 percent mortality from parasites through the egg, larval and pupal stages would result in the survival of 200 prey adults (100 females and 100 males) in the next generation. The same would be repeated in such subsequent generation to maintain equilibrium.

However, if instead we arbitrarily started with an equilibrium density of 2000 adults and assume no other changes, the same 90 percent mortality would maintain equilibrium. This makes it clear that a certain total percent mortality is necessary on the average to maintain the equilibrium position of a given species in a particular habitat and that the characteristics of that species as finally expressed by its actual birth rate determine the level of mortality needed to maintain balance, i.e. mortality must equal natality. It is also evident from the example that percent mortality does not determine the *equilibrium position* or average density but only that equilibrium will occur at *some* density if an average mortality that equals natality occurs generation after generation.

What then does determine the average population density? Broadly, and as already pointed out, it is the degree of density response of the environmental mortality factors. If, for example, the mortality factors involved in the preceding example are exclusively parasites, and the parasites were adversely affected by a spray beginning in a given host generation so that they then caused only 80 percent host mortality instead of 90, the adult host population would double in the next generation to 4000. If, then, as the spray dissipated the parasites recovered quickly and increased their progeny production in the next generation in response to the greater host density so that they caused 95 percent parasitization, the adult host population would again return to 2000 at the beginning of the next generation. Thereafter the parasites would produce 90 percent mortality and the system would remain in balance, given no more sprays. The numbers would be as follows, original generation → 2000 host adults → 20000 progeny which are 80 percent parasitized giving in generation 1, 4000 host adults → 40000 progeny which are 95 percent parasitized giving in generation 2, 2000 host adults. The fluctuation in host adults would be 2000 → 4000 → 2000. This would be an example of high density-dependence of a parasite as expressed by a high relative rate of increase of host mortality with respect to increasing host density. In another case consider that the parasite was affected by the spray longer so that its response to increasing host density was slowed after its parasitization was first reduced to 80 percent and the next host generation became doubled, so that parasitization increased in the next generation only to 90 percent. The adult host population therefore would remain at 4000. Only an increase to 95 percent in the third generation would reduce the adult host population again to 2000 but meanwhile a higher average host density would have been achieved for the period in question. The numbers would be as follows: original generation, 2000 host adults → 20000 progeny which are 80 percent parasitized, giving in generation 1, 4000 host adults → 40000 progeny which are 90 percent parasitized, giving in generation 2, 4000 host adults → 40000 progeny which are 95 percent parasitized, giving in generation 3, 2000 host adults. The fluctuation in host adults would be 2000 → 4000 → 4000 → 2000 for a total of 12000 adults during the four generations, or a mean density of 3000. In the first case only 10000 adults would be produced during the same four generations for a mean density of 2500. Thus we see how insecticides or other adverse factors can make a poor natural enemy out of an efficient one merely by reducing their ability to respond rapidly to increases in host density. If we visualize the two preceding cases as representing different parasite species attacking the same host in different habitats, it is clear that the relative ability of the two species to cause increasing rates of host mortality with respect to increasing host density would determine the average host population density.

Many population phenomena have been illustrated by biological control research, some coming as challenges to popular ideas. Thus, a numerically rare enemy species is not necessarily an ineffective one. The best natural enemies are often the rarest because they regulate prey populations at low levels and thereby regulate their own at even lower levels. By doing so they tend to eliminate competitors which can only exist at high prey densities. By the same token some of the commonest, most numerous, parasites or predators are the least effective in prey population regulation. With abundant prey they are enabled to remain abundant. Weather interactions may modify otherwise expected effects. If the weather is suboptimum for the prey but even more so for a potentially effective enemy, the prey may escape regulation and become abundant, while the enemy remains less common. Thus, both would be more common than they would be in a climatic zone optimal for both, where the enemy could regulate at low densities. In the latter instance we have the anomaly of scarcity being correlated with ideal weather conditions.

Some few ecologists have propounded the hypothesis that species have so evolved to fit their environment that this results in a certain characteristic population density. There is, of course, usually a characteristic average population density in a given habitat – this is natural control. But there is no inherent characteristic density for a species. All of the outstanding examples of applied biological control refute this because by modifying the habitat, i.e. by introducing and establishing a new mortality factor, natural enemies, the equilibrium population density of numerous pest species has been greatly reduced. It is easy, in fact, by appropriate experimental techniques to maintain different population densities of a phytophagous species on adjacent plants or, with small more or less sessile species, on different portions of the same plant, or even on different parts of the same leaf. This is done by modifying the microhabitat either to favor the prey as for instance by excluding or inhibiting enemies, or perhaps by favoring enemies by provision of necessary adult food which otherwise might be lacking. Of course all the cases of 'upsets' of equilibrium of non-target species by insecticidal interference in crops further demonstrate that it is the properties of the environment both biotic and abiotic that determine the population density of a species. Thus there are no organisms that are inherent pests.

The important ecological principle of competitive displacement between ecological homologs (i.e. species having identical requisites such as different parasite species requiring the same stage of the same host species) has probably been more thoroughly demonstrated or proven with cases of natural enemies seeking to utilize the same identical host, than with any other group of organisms. Our studies (DeBach and Sundby, 1963) with scale insect parasites showed that ecological homologs cannot coexist, rather that one species will eliminate the other but the food (host or prey) must be *identical*, even to the point of its being the same larval stage, or the egg or pupal stage. It was further shown that species whose food differs slightly can coexist, thus egg or larval or pupal parasites of the same host species do coexist and in effect do not compete as ecological homologs. This has an important bearing on biological control importation policy.

When individual larvae of two species of parasites occur simultaneously in the same individual host insect, this is known as multiple parasitism in the biological control literature, and such parasites are ecological homologs and cannot coexist in the same habitat unless they possess different alternative hosts or there is some other modifying factor. Multiple parasitism and the associated displacement of one parasite species by another caused concern among biological control researchers beginning in the 1920s. They thought that an efficient parasite might be displaced by the introduction of one less effective in host population regulation. This idea has been repeated by some until recently, but with rare theoretical exceptions all data show that if one parasite species displaces another, the winner is the more efficient in host population regulation and better control will result. Even during the highly competitive process of displacement no ill effects on host population regulation will occur. If a second parasite species is imported that attacks a different host stage and becomes established, it will add to the effectiveness of control, as was independently shown deductively in the late 1920s and early 1930s by H. S. Smith and A. J. Nicholson and has been demonstrated conclusively in various biological control projects.

Many, probably most, ecologists subscribe to the idea that species diversity is highly correlated with community population stability, that is with natural control, and this includes biological control. As a consequence it is commonly held that this principle applies to biological control of single species populations. In fact, L. O. Howard and W. E. Fiske propounded the sequence theory more than sixty years ago which suggested that a sequence of parasite species including egg, larval and pupal parasites was probably most likely to achieve satisfactory biological control. Actually this has proven to be true in only a few cases of outstanding applied biological control where the prey has been reduced to consistently low population densities. The opposite is true in the great majority of highly successful cases in which one highly specific natural enemy species acting alone or two acting in combination have been responsible rather than several or many. As has been previously pointed out, a diversity of several established enemy species has often been replaced by a single newly imported highly effective one with the result that better prey population regulation is obtained. Thus the theory of biological control must include the precept that, in general, increasing species diversity of natural enemies per given prey species is inversely correlated with regulation of a prey population at low levels In other words, we should seek to *reduce* the number of natural enemy species established against a given prey species by introducing a highly specific, more effective enemy which is capable of replacing them and as a result producing better biological control. If we pursue this thought a little further one might begin to wonder whether species diversity in a community, especially with insects, might be the *result* of many separate, more or less independent, cases of natural biological control, rather than being the *cause* of community stability. When many species are held under biological control in a community, this would conserve the plant food sources thereby enabling more species to utilize it.

Plant diversity also is generally held by ecologists to contribute to stability of phytophagous insect populations by providing better environmental conditions, including alternate prey as well as better chronological continuity of prey for entomophagous forms. A good many examples have been cited in the literature where diversification of crops, as opposed to monoculture, has resulted in achievement of better biological control or better integrated control. However, it seems that one should not generalize regarding the advantages of crop diversification in enhancement of biological control. Recently it was shown (Robinson, Young and Morrison, 1972) that, where cotton had other crops planted on either side of it as compared to a check having no other crop planted on either side, the planting of corn, alfalfa, or peanuts adjacent to cotton resulted in greater damage by the bollworm in the cotton. Only when sorghum was planted adjacent to cotton was there any indication that bollworm damage in the cotton might be reduced over the monoculture check. It is interesting that the adjacent planting of corn resulted in the greatest bollworm damage and the least seed cotton because corn is commonly used as a 'trap crop' for the bollworm. The cotton with sorghum and the check produced the most seed cotton and the cotton with sorghum had the most predators. Various other examples could be cited showing increases in certain pest problems to be correlated with diversification of crops. Thus each habitat must be viewed separately and the best procedures for each case determined by appropriate experimental and observational studies.

One very important aspect of biological control ecology concerns means of evaluating the relative and absolute importance of factors responsible for prey population regulation. Indeed this is a critical problem in all population ecology. We shall cover the subject of means of evaluation of effectiveness of natural enemies in some detail in Chapter 7, so will only comment briefly here.

There has been much controversy, and doubtless it will continue for some time, as to how best to measure the impact of environmental factors on populations and to determine which factors, or groups, are regulatory and which are mainly, or entirely, responsible for an observed degree of natural control or biological control. A substantial number of ecologists have attempted to do this quantitatively by correlation analysis utilizing periodic censuses and life table data and thereby determine the 'key factor'. We and others (DeBach and Huffaker, 1971; Huffaker and Kennett, 1969) have tried these approaches but have concluded that used alone they are quite inadequate for the job described above. In practice it appears impossible to obtain the highly accurate and detailed mortality data necessary to be statistically meaningful and in any case, a positive correlation between, say, prey and predator population trends will not show which is cause and which is effect. Modeling methods and regression analysis, however, can be of considerable value in understanding other aspects of the problem.

Experimental 'check methods' appear to be the only satisfactory means of rating the efficiency of natural enemies or of weather and other factors for that matter. These involve paired-plot comparisons of a suitable size and number of replicates to fit the occasion. One series of unmodified plots serve as the check, the other series have one parameter, such as natural enemies, excluded or inhibited *without* disturbing anything else or otherwise modifying the microhabitat. If no subsequent change in prey population density occurs in the two series, it can be concluded that natural enemies were inconsequential and non-regulatory. If, on the other hand, the prey population rises to a new average density, this is proof that the natural enemies were responsible for the original observed density. This method isolates particular parameters and shows what their total effect is, but not how they produce this effect. The method can just as well measure the effect of climate by isolating or removing other regulatory factors which are nearly always natural enemies, if we select insects occurring at reasonably low densities so that food shortage is not a factor. If we then exclude natural enemies from the system and no change in density occurs it is climate that is responsible for maintenance of the original observed density.

The differences in the philosophy and ecological basis of biological control and chemical control have been touched on before in Chapter 1. Classical biological control, as far as man is concerned, has no ecological drawbacks that we recognize, whereas chemical control has many. A comparison is shown in Table 4.

Table 4. *A comparison of biological and chemical control: the disadvantages*

Category	Biological control	Chemical control
Environmental pollution; danger to man, wildlife, other non-target organisms, soil, etc.	None	Considerable
Upsets in natural balance and other ecological disruptions	None	Common
Permanency of control	Permanent	Temporary – must repeat one to many times annually
Development of resistance to the mortality factor	Extremely rare, if ever	Common
General applicability to broad-spectrum pest control	Theoretically unlimited but not expected to apply to all pests. Still underdeveloped. Initial control may take 1–2 years but then pest remains reduced	Applies empirically to nearly all insects but not satisfactory with some. Can rapidly reduce outbreaks but they rebound. Psychologically satisfying to the user at first

The extent of natural biological control

This aspect of biological control cannot be overemphasized. Upon it rests our entire ability to successfully grow crops because without it, the *potential* pests would overwhelm us. It is variously estimated that

59

from less than 1 percent to perhaps 2 percent of phytophagous insects that are potential pests ever achieve the status of even minor pests. By and large this is due to natural enemies. However, only field ecologists or naturalists who have made detailed studies can fully appreciate the fact. Most of the work of natural enemies goes unnoticed but especially so where a non-economic insect is concerned. Enough cases of highly effective natural biological control have been studied however to indicate that the figure of 99 percent or more of potential pests being under natural biological control is close to the truth. At a Conference of Experts in Biological Control in Canada as early as 1936 it was stated that only about 1 percent of insects became pests and the 1968 *Bulletin of the Entomological Society of America* carried figures showing that only 1425 out of 85 000, or 1.7 percent, of known United States and Canadian insects were important enough to have common names, i.e. in general to have achieved some sort of pest status, although some beneficial insects also are included in the list. Dr J. D. Tothill, famous for his achievements in biological control in Fiji, considered it to be a well-established fact that virtually all insects in their native homes are controlled by natural enemies and L. O. Howard and W. F. Fiske, the former, the Chief of the United States Department of Agriculture, Bureau of Entomology, published in 1911 that 99 percent of phytophagous insects were under natural biological control. The famous French entomologist, Professor Paul Marchal, wrote that if phytophagous insects could multiply without hindrance in proportion to their natural reproductive powers, in a short time they would eliminate all species of terrestrial vegetation. However, he stated that the increase of the destructive insects is fortunately kept within limits by parasitic and predatory insects.

I concur that these estimates are substantially accurate. I have been amazed during more than twenty-five years of field research at the vast amount of natural biological control that occurs. However, one virtually has to live with the insects to see or to measure it, unless it is brought into brilliant focus by chemically induced upsets which are so common now as to further emphasize the extent of natural biological control. Yet another form of proof of the natural occurrence of biological control comes from the mounting number of successful cases of applied biological control resulting from importation of enemies because these represent cases of natural control in the original home.

I like to compare the ratio of actual pests to potential pests under natural biological control, to an iceberg. The tip of the iceberg (like our pests) may appear very large but it represents only a small fraction of the great bulk (represented by natural control) which is hidden from view and hardly believable even to the more than casual observer. Viewed ecologically this is a tremendous asset which obviously must be preserved. In our efforts to control the approximate 1 percent of insects that are pests we must make every effort to conserve the natural enemies of the estimated 99 percent that are under natural biological control.

Even a cross-section list of some selected, documented cases of natural control would be unwieldy. A fairly detailed coverage of some cases in North America will be found in articles by Hagen, van den Bosch and Dahlsten (1971), Rabb (1971) and MacPhee and MacLellan (1971 a). A worldwide list wherein over twenty-five species of predatory mites are considered to be important predators of many phytophagous mites on a variety of crops is given by McMurtry, Huffaker and van den Vrie (1970); also a worldwide record of natural biological control of phytophagous mites is given by Huffaker, van den Vrie and McMurtry (1970). A multitude of other cases is scattered throughout the literature which I shall not attempt to review. Although most of the cases documenting natural control by enemies are based on careful quantitative studies generally backed by expert experience, relatively few have been subjected to proof by the use of experimental check methods. It may come as a surprise that the majority of natural control cases studied and demonstrated have been with 'so-called' pests. This is because there has been more motivation and research money available. However, either they were not actual pests when studied under undisturbed conditions of no chemical applications, or they were only occasional pests normally under biological control for lengthy periods of time, or else they were pests in one area but under biological control in others.

Some idea of the generality of natural biological control can be had by mentally extrapolating from the number of cases of naturally occurring biological control documented by one observer – the author. This is based on field studies mainly involving homopterous insects on citrus in California and abroad. In California most of these cases have been proven by use of experimental check methods (often replicated in different localities and by use of different check methods). Abroad, I have relied on experience, observations of chemical upsets of non-target organisms, the observed quantitative actions of natural enemies with respect to host density in the field and the use of naturally occurring experimental check comparisons such as one tree with honey-dew-seeking ants (which interfere with enemies) compared to another without ants, or to natural microexclusion 'cages' or other protected situations as spider webbing on certain leaves which will exclude parasites from scales or mealybugs. Table 5 does not include cases which might have been judged to represent natural biological control based upon experience but the observation or information was insufficiently thorough.

One might ask the question; if natural biological control is so commonplace why don't we hear more about it? Why is it so overlooked, even by many professional entomologists and ecologists? Perhaps the main reason is that in applied research most scientists are paid to work on pests and they rarely have had the opportunity or motivation to study natural control. Happily this is changing, but the great population studies conducted on forest insects in Canada, Europe and elsewhere in recent years furnishes a case in point. The stress has been on the study of periodic major outbreaks or epizootics and the factors involved in their diminution, but little emphasis has been placed on their population dynamics during the long non-outbreak periods of endemicity, or on other related non-outbreak species. In crops the stress has naturally been on the major pests, i.e. ones that often lack effective established enemies. As a result such studies have emphasized the population dynamics of the few insects and mites that lack effective natural enemies or whose enemies are periodically depressed by unusual conditions, but these very studies have been most used to furnish generalizations regarding population theory and the presumed paucity of effective biological control. Attention was called earlier to some of the weaknesses in evaluating the role of natural enemies especially in crops, but this applies to a considerable extent to forests and other natural habitats. The general lack of adequate experimental evaluation techniques and the reliance upon quantitative methods of correlation analysis do not permit an accurate interpretation of the role of enemies.

Professor Alvah Peterson, late of Ohio State University, covered these points very succinctly as long ago as 1936 as follows:

I sometimes wonder if most entomologists, including myself, have not approached the question of biological control from a too narrow and restricted point of view. For the most part all of our biological control studies today have been directed toward and with insects of economic importance. All of us know the reasons for this situation. Has this approach

Table 5. *Cases of natural biological control documented by author**

Species	Common name	Host plant	Country or area	Type of natural enemy
Aleurocanthus woglumi	Citrus blackfly	Citrus	India and Orient	Parasites
Aleurothrixus flocossus	Woolly whitefly	Citrus	Mexico Brazil	Parasites
Aonidiella aurantii	California red scale	Citrus	Japan to India	Parasites
Aonidiella citrina	Yellow scale	Citrus	Japan to Pakistan	Parasites
Toxoptera aurantii	Black citrus aphid	Citrus	California	Parasites and predators
Aspidiotus nerii	Oleander scale	Olive, lemons, ornamentals	Cosmopolitan	Parasites
Chrysomphalus aonidum	Florida red scale	Citrus	Hong Kong and Orient	Parasites
Coccus hesperidum	Brown soft scale	Citrus, ornamentals	Cosmopolitan	Parasites
Coccus viridis	Green scale	Citrus	Orient	Parasites
Dialeurodes citri	Citrus whitefly	Citrus	Japan to Pakistan	Parasites
Diaspis echinocacti	Cactus scale	Cacti	California and Mexico	Parasites
Ferrisia virgata	Striped mealybug	Citrus, avocado, ornamentals	Mexico	Parasites
Hemiberlesia lataniae	Latania scale	Avocado, ornamentals	California and Greece	Parasites
Hemiberlesia rapax	Greedy scale	Citrus, ornamentals	California and Greece	Parasites
Lepidosaphes beckii	Purple scale	Citrus	Hong Kong to India	Parasites
Panonychus citri	Citrus red mite	Citrus	California	Predators
Parlatoria oleae	Olive scale	Olive	Pakistan and Mid-East	Parasites
Planococcus citri	Citrus mealybug	Citrus	Cosmopolitan	Parasites and predators
Pseudococcus adonidum	Long-tailed mealybug	Citrus, avocado, ornamentals	Cosmopolitan	Predators
Unaspis citri	Snow scale	Citrus	Hong Kong	Parasites

* Certain of these have also been documented or confirmed by others.

distorted our view or concept of the entire biological control picture? Are we not restricting ourselves too closely when we work with so-called economic species only. By so doing are we not attempting to develop biological control principles and theories from insect hosts that are more successful in their environment than many closely related species which are held in check by natural enemies or environmental factors?

Briefly stated it may be said that many economic insects are misfits so far as the average balance of nature is concerned. Economic pests frequently develop in numbers and extent far beyond what usually takes place in nature. In other words as investigators we are studying for the most part unsuccessful cases of biological control.

If we consider the numerical relationship of economic species to all other insects in almost any geographical area, a very conservative estimate will show less than one insect pest to one hundred non-destructive species. As economic entomologists we devote all our time to one percent or less of all insects.

Supposing in our biological control studies we reversed the picture and devoted some or all of our time to some of the 99 percent of insects that are apparently unimportant. There is very little doubt in my mind that if we did this we would find many outstanding examples of biological control in nature, and from such studies of naturally successful cases we would learn fundamental principles, and probably learn them more rapidly than from economic pests that are out of control. In simple language would it not be a wise policy to devote some time studying successful examples of biological control in nature? In other lines of study and in the business field investigators frequently devote much time analyzing successful ventures in order to learn principles and gain ideas that will improve less profitable lines.

Unfortunately times have not changed to a great extent since Professor Peterson spoke these words.

Fortuitous biological control

Strictly speaking, natural biological control may be limited by definition to cases where an indigenous natural enemy controls an indigenous insect. There is another category, however, which I have termed fortuitous biological control, that does not involve any manipulation by man, hence in this sense is also natural biological control. This includes all cases where biological control has occurred as a result of the accidental immigration and establishment (ecesis) of an exotic natural enemy or conversely of ecesis of an exotic pest which is then attacked and controlled by indigenous natural enemies. Fortuitous biological control is probably more overlooked than natural biological control *per se*. The results of classical biological control from purposeful importation of enemies are often self-evident. However, equally successful results can occur accidentally and go unheralded, even though their importance in pest control is just as great. I know of no general review of such cases, so again perhaps we can extrapolate and generalize from data on fortuitous biological control acquired during my studies on biological control of scale insects by species of the parasite genus *Aphytis*.

The purple scale has been a notorious citrus pest in many countries in past years. Its dominantly important parasite, *Aphytis lepidosaphes*, was discovered and imported in 1948–9 into California from Hong Kong and Taiwan where it is native (DeBach, 1971 *a*). It was not then known to occur elsewhere outside its range in the Orient but it may possibly have already spread undetected to one or more other countries.

Subsequent to the parasite's successful establishment in California we have sent it to thirteen other countries with establishment being recorded from nine thus far. However, I have found or recorded the parasite to be accidentally established in thirteen other countries to which it was not sent or purposely imported, and in nearly all of which it is producing excellent fortuitous biological control. These include such diverse and distant places as Hawaii, Florida, Turkey, Israel, Puerto Rico, Guadaloupe, Jamaica, Australia, New Caledonia, El Salvador and Argentina. In nearly all of these places the presence of the parasite and its good work was unknown until specifically sought out. These fortuitous cases are just as valuable as if they had been accomplished purposely and are currently saving millions of dollars a year just with the purple scale alone.

There is so much movement of plant products internationally today that it is reasonable that sometimes natural enemies accompany their prey or subsequently reach it accidentally. If they move with their prey originally, fortuitous biological control may occur from the beginning and the presence of the *potential* pest may remain undetected. Regarding the accidental movement of parasites, we regularly find live parasitized scale in California food markets on citrus fruit from Texas and Florida. We have even started parasite cultures from such. Obviously establishment of these parasites in the field could easily occur accidentally.

Another parasite studied by me, *Aphytis chrysomphali*, has become nearly cosmopolitan by accidental spread. Its presumed native home area is the Mediterranean area but it is now definitely known to occur in Taiwan, the Philippines, Australia, South Africa, Argentina, Chile, Brazil, Peru, Panama, Costa Rica, Mexico, the Caribbean, Florida, Texas and California. It attacks the California red scale and others which have been moved worldwide with their host plants. It has been responsible for appreciable fortuitous biological control in various places. Yet another parasite of the California red scale, *Aphytis lingnanensis*, was dispersed accidentally from its home in the Orient to Mexico and then to south Texas; originally perhaps to Mexico many years ago via the Manila galleons. It was unknown when we imported it to California from south China in 1948 and it turned out to be much more effective in biological control of the California red scale than *Aphytis chrysomphali*, yet for unknown years it had occurred at Hermosillo, Sonora, Mexico only about 300 airline miles from the citrus areas of San Diego County in California. A survey throughout all Mexico and the citrus area of Texas made shortly after the importation into California from China showed the parasite to be thoroughly established everywhere in those areas and made it clear that the parasite had been in Mexico for many years. It was responsible for fortuitous biological control in most Mexican citrus areas but its presence was unknown there or in Texas.

Aphytis chilensis primarily attacks the oleander scale, usually a minor or non-economic insect, and is considered to be native to the Mediterranean area. It has spread accidentally and is thoroughly established in North America, South America, Australia, New Zealand and South Africa.

Aphytis mytilaspidis, an important parasite of the oyster-shell scale and the San Jose scale of fruit trees over much of North America, is an accidental import from Europe, even though it was first described from Illinois by William Le Baron in 1870. This parasite probably involves the first written record of a case of fortuitous biological control, although LeBaron (1870) doubtless thought it to be a native parasite at the time. He stated:

The oyster-shell bark louse of the apple tree has, for a number of years past, been gradually disappearing, so that it no longer occupies the rank which it has heretofore so preeminently held, of a first-class noxious insect...Already the smoother bark, the greener foliage, and the fairer fruit proclaim to the orchardist that this deadly insect is loosening its hold upon the apple tree; and many, no doubt, have prided themselves upon the successful application of some infallible wash, or patent nostrum; but underneath all this goodly show, busily intent upon the accomplishment of her own curious economy, and heedless of the momentous results she is effecting in human interests, works unseen our infinitesimal friend, the apple-tree bark louse parasite (*Chalcis* [*Aphelinus*] *mytilaspidis*).

These only represent part of the records I have for ecesis and fortuitous biological control by species of only one genus. Were the same information available for all parasite and predator genera it is obvious that a fantastic amount of fortuitous biological control has occurred and is going on unnoticed. These results suggest some interesting conclusions: (1) since fortuitous biological control has occurred accidentally time and again, man could have brought about the results much sooner in each case, thereby providing substantial financial savings in reduced chemical pest control costs in addition to the reduction in environmental pollution; (2) sometimes exotic natural enemies may be more easily and cheaply found and imported from a country where they have become accidentally established than from their native home. For example, the purple scale parasite was in Hawaii and the California red scale parasite was in nearby Mexico, yet California went to much more trouble and expense to seek them out and obtain them from their native home in the Orient.

The ecological basis of classical biological control

Classical biological control seems to be an apt term to cover the applied phase involving the discovery, importation and establishment of exotic natural enemies. Most applied biological control successes have resulted from this approach; in fact it is probably thought of by many as constituting essentially all there is to biological control. This supposition and other aspects will be dealt with in Chapters 5, 6 and 7.

The broad ecological aspects of the process are relatively simple. The basic theory is that the average population density of an organism may be lowered by the introduction of additional density-dependent mortality factors into its environment. In most cases the target organisms are exotic insects that have invaded a new habitat (or country) and become pests. When such is the case the assumption is usually correct that essential natural enemies have been left behind. Their discovery abroad, importation and establishment by man constitutes an attempt to reduce the pest to a non-economic status and achievement of success constitutes a case of classical biological control.

The ecology involved applies as well to indigenous (native) pests.

67

Natural enemies obtained from related pests abroad can be imported and established to constitute a new regulatory factor. This was the case with the famous coconut moth in Fiji which is discussed in Chapter 5. There are a number of other well-documented cases in the literature. Obviously one should not assume as some do that native pests are not amenable to classical biological control.

Management of natural enemy populations

The discussion thus far in this chapter of the ecology of natural enemies has related principally to their operation in a more or less optimum undisturbed environment. Often this does not occur in nature or in agro-ecosystems. Also the only manipulation of enemies by man was that discussed in the last section – importation and establishment of new exotic enemies.

However, the ecology of *established* enemies also can be manipulated to man's advantage in pest control. This can be likened to wildlife management in many respects and is assuming an important role in biological control. As discussed earlier in this chapter and as shown by numerous examples of pesticide interference in Chapter 1, inherently effective enemies can be rendered ineffective in prey population regulation by a variety of adverse environmental phenomena. In addition to the effect of insecticides, which is by far the most adverse factor in agro-ecosystems, these include, among others: weather extremes, lack of food or other requisites for adults, lack of alternative prey which are necessary to provide year around propagation because of periodic shortages of the primary prey, asynchronization of natural enemy and prey life cycles, disturbing effects of ants on natural enemies and killing effect of airborne dust. Precise determination of which factors are adverse or which requisites are insufficient coupled with the formulation of methods of alleviating them constitute natural enemy management. A most important premise to bear in mind is that the enemy we choose to manipulate should be an *inherently* effective one. Management requires considerable research and expenditure of money and in general should not be wasted on an enemy which is intrinsically incapable of satisfactory biological control under favorable conditions.

The determination of the impact of adverse environmental conditions on natural enemy efficiency depends on basic bio-ecological studies involving periodic field censuses, life-table construction and analysis, and experimental check methods conducted in an adequate-sized plot that has not, or will not, receive chemical pesticidal treatment (if at all possible), preferably for several years. Sufficient time is essential to determine basic undisturbed predatory–prey population interactions, as well as the long-term effect of other parameters. Biological, behavioral and even physiological, studies in the laboratory will be desirable and necessary to supplement the field information. Only after the adverse factors are pinpointed can the environment be knowledgeably manipulated to favor natural enemies. It is to be expected however that in some instances the information obtained will indicate (1) that the natural enemy(ies) is inherently ineffective and manipulation should not be tried, or (2) that the type of manipulation needed is impossible or impracticable to attain. In these cases major emphasis should be placed on the discovery and importation of new exotic enemies.

The latter recourse turned out to be the case with our project on biological control of the California red scale on citrus. A tiny parasite (1 mm in length), *Aphytis lingnanensis*, had been imported from south China and was found to be highly effective in scale population regulation in the mild coastal areas of southern California but it proved to be much less effective in intermediate areas and generally ineffective in the more climatically extreme interior areas of Riverside and San Bernardino. Basic bio-ecological studies showed that weather extremes, especially low winter temperatures, but also to an extent, high summer temperatures combined with low humidities, caused such great periodic mortalities of the parasite that it was rendered ineffective in control of the host which was much less affected by the same conditions.

We found many interesting and unsuspected facets of the effect of weather. Prolonged periods of cool winter weather (days below 18 °C (65 °F) maximum for 1 or 2 weeks) proved to be as severe in causing heavy mortality to all stages as several nights of rather heavy frost. It was found that the sperm stored in the spermatheca of the female would be killed by subjection to −1 °C (30 °F) for eight hours (not uncommon during the winter in Riverside) hence they were sterilized to become 'factitious virgins' and would produce only male progeny. Furthermore they would not mate again. The effect on males was as bad or worse; all sperms were killed and no regeneration occurred, so that they were permanently sterilized. It should be noted that to all intents and purposes these adults appeared to be normal insects after they were sterilized. Even more surprisingly it was found that short exposures (twenty-four hours) to temperatures in the 15 °C (60 °F) range altered sex ratios unfavorably by increasing the proportion of males produced and also severely reduced total progeny production. The *effective* progeny production (number of female progeny per female parent) was cut from a normal of 21.4 to only 4.5 by such an exposure – a drastic reduction of about 78 percent. The ability or inability to control the host population because of differences in local weather were found to occur within distances of just a few miles in some instances.

As a result of the knowledge obtained that *Aphytis lingnanensis* was prevented from controlling its host in certain areas by adverse effects of weather, it was reasoned that insectary mass production and periodic colonization of the parasite in the field following unfavorable periods might solve the problem. This was tried and found to be satisfactory and economically feasible in intermediate climatic areas, but results were not consistently reliable in interior areas. Hence additional natural enemies were sought and discovered in the Orient and one, *Aphytis melinus*, has very nearly solved the problem because it is inherently better adapted to interior area conditions than was *A. lingnanensis*.

Management of enemies can be divided into two major headings: Augmentation and Conservation. Research and application toward these ends will be covered more fully in Chapters 7 and 10. The periodic colonization technique just mentioned is a type of augmentation in that the natural enemy itself is manipulated. Another type of augmentation would involve selective breeding for genetic improvement. Conservation involves manipulation of the environment to favor the natural enemy. This includes elimination or mitigation of adverse factors or provision of necessary requisites that are lacking. Aside from the importation of new natural enemies in classical biological control, conservation is by far the biggest, most important, aspect of biological control. Successful conservation permits natural enemies to operate to their full effectiveness; its lack more often than not denies the possibility of obtaining satisfactory natural or applied biological control.

4
Early naturalists and experiments

The concept and development of biological control necessarily occurred within the framework of the gradual accumulation of biological and ecological knowledge as man's civilization progressed. The history of biological control is the history of early naturalists, biologists and experimental scientists. The information in this chapter has been derived from various sources but the following especially have been drawn upon: Doutt (1964*b*), Essig (1931), Howard and Fiske (1911), Riley (1893), Silvestri (1909) and Steinhaus (1956).

The first use of predators

There were some apparently empirical developments that preceded even the earliest intellectuals and skilled professionals. Probably primitive agriculturalists, who usually were surprisingly good naturalists, observed the more obvious insect predators feeding on phytophagous insects. This would be straightforward and understandable, as it would were they to observe a lion preying on a gazelle. It took much more biological sophistication to perceive and understand insect parasitism, as we shall see.

The first record of the use of predatory insects by man is lost in history but it is known that the ancient Chinese fostered the ant *Oecophylla smaragdina* in their citrus trees to control caterpillars and large boring beetles. This ant builds great paper nests in trees containing thousands of individuals. These colonies not only could be purchased or else moved from wild trees but the movement of ants between cultivated trees was engendered by placing bamboo runways from one tree to another. I observed this practice still being continued in the Shan States of north Burma not long ago and it reportedly continues in China. A similar development was recorded among the Yemenese date growers of Arabia by P. Forskål in 1775. Each year they brought

71

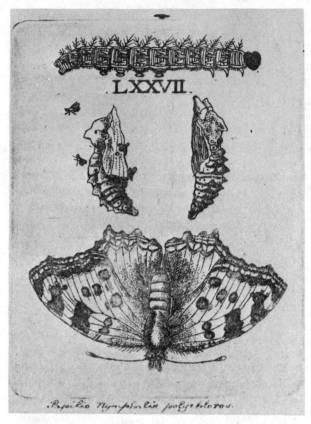

Fig 17. Parasites emerging from a butterfly pupa (center left). Published by Johannes Goedaert, 1662.

colonies of a predatory ant down from the mountains and put them among their date palms to control pest insects.

The first known successful introduction of a natural enemy from one country to another occurred about this same time and indicates that the idea of using predators may have been more than a rarity even by then. The red locust, *Nomadacris septemfasciata*, was the most serious pest of agriculture in Mauritius in those days. In order to possibly solve the problem the mynah bird was introduced from India by the Count de Maudave in 1762. By 1770 it was credited with the successful control of the locust. The predaceous pentatomid bug *Picromerus bidens* of Europe not only is an important predator of various Lepidoptera and other foliage feeders but has a preference for bedbugs. Its use for biological control of bedbugs was apparently tried as early as 1776. A few specimens placed in an infested room reportedly cleaned out the bedbugs in a matter of weeks.

Observations during the Late Renaissance

Meanwhile, the necessary biological basis for the scientific development of modern biological control was accumulating in Europe. It took the entire seventeenth century for learned men to pass from the first vague observations of insect parasitism to an understanding of the process. Silvestri (1909) pointed out that U. Aldrovandi, who published in 1602, was the first person to observe insect parasitism. He recorded the exit from the common cabbage butterfly larva of parasitic larvae of *Apanteles glomeratus* in order to spin their external cocoons, but he mistakenly supposed these to be eggs of the butterfly. Later F. Redi published the same observation in 1668, as well as another involving insects of different species being born from the same pupa – again a misunderstood observation of parasitic insects. Another parasite of butterflies was noted in print in 1662 by Johannes Goedaert in Volume 1 (Plate 77, p. 175) of *Metamorphosis et Historia Naturalis Insectorum*. It is not clear that Goedaert fully understood what he observed but his figure (see Fig. 17) clearly shows small gregarious adult parasites emerging from a butterfly pupa. He reared butterfly adults from several pupae but from each of two others he obtained eighty-two small 'flies'. Inasmuch as there is no known parasitic tachinid or other parasitic fly of this size having such gregarious habits, these 'flies' are undoubtedly parasitic hymenopterans, probably pteromalids. This is probably the first published illustration of a hymenopterous parasite.

Credit has been given by Silvestri to Antonio Vallisnieri of Padua who in 1706 finally correctly interpreted the phenomenon of insect parasitism and who wrote about the form and biology of many he discovered. It appears, however, that this honor may actually be due to Van Leeuwenhoek, who in 1701 wrote of and pictured a parasite of a sawfly that feeds on willow. A colleague of Vallisnieri's, one Cestoni, also corresponded with Vallisnieri, discussing parasites of the cabbage aphid, the cabbage butterfly and the cabbage whitefly.

Knowledge of parasites rapidly increased thereafter. Among the leaders R. A. F. de Réaumur (who also invented the Réaumur thermometer) published principally from 1734 to 1742 (*Mémoires pour*

Fig. 18. Details of an ichneumonid parasite ovipositing (top), details of the ovipositor (center), and other parasites (bottom). From de Réaumur's *Mém. 9 de l'Hist. des Insectes*, vol. 6, 1742.

Servir à l'Historie des Insectes in six volumes) and Baron Carl DeGeer, a pupil of Linnaeus, from 1752 to 1778. Both carefully worked out the biologies of a number of parasitic as well as predatory insects. Réaumur's beautifully detailed and accurate illustrations of 1742 (see Figs. 18 and 19) show how significantly the knowledge of entomophagous insects increased between 1700 and 1750.

The recognition and understanding of insect diseases was developing during this same general period of the Late Renaissance (see Steinhaus, 1956). This came about largely from man's study of the diseases of the silkworm, mainly in Europe, but also in Japan and China. However,

Fig. 19. Details of the morphology and behavior of a predatory ant-lion showing capture of prey (lower left) and a laboratory observation unit (lower right). From de Réaumur's *Mém. 10 de l'Hist. des Insectes*, vol. 6, 1742.

diseases of bees were known to the Greeks and were commented on by Aristotle. Pliny also wrote about bee maladies in A.D. 77.

The Italian poet Vida published a poem in 1527 on the silkworm which contained descriptions and remedies for diseases. During the sixteenth, seventeenth and eighteenth centuries literally hundreds of works were written on silkworm diseases in Europe. Silkworm culture of course was a major industry. Vallisnieri, who correctly observed insect parasitism in 1706, also was the first to mention the disease now known as muscardine. However, the first actual publication depicting an observed disease *organism* was by de Réaumur, who in

1726 included drawings of insect larvae killed by a fungus which we now know to belong to the genus *Cordyceps*. DeGeer also comes into the picture again with the publication in 1776 of the first description of what is now known to be an *Empusa* infection in flies. The microbial nature of these diseases was not actually realized, however.

Biological knowledge matures during the 1800s

In the nineteenth century biology, including biological control, came of age. The philosophical and biological foundations of modern insect pathology were laid, beginning principally with William Kirby's chapter on 'Diseases of Insects' in Volume 4 (1826) of Kirby and Spence, *An Introduction to Entomology*. This was the first at all comprehensive account of diseases of insects in general, and by this time Kirby and others recognized that true fungi actually grew in the bodies of some insects, some clearly as saprophytes but others, they believed, possibly as parasites.

Agostino Bassi of Lodi, Italy, is considered the father of insect pathology and by some the founder of the doctrine of pathenogenic microbes. In this respect his studies helped overthrow the theory of spontaneous generation. He was the first to demonstrate experimentally the *parasitic* nature of white muscardine diseases of the silkworm, an account of which was published in 1835. Thus Bassi was the first to show experimentally that a micro-organism (*Beauveria bassiana*) was the cause of an infectious disease of an animal.

This brief account of basic contributions must be terminated with the great work of Louis Pasteur, who began his career by saving the silk industry of France. Like Bassi, his later contributions to higher animal diseases and pathology began with research on silkworm diseases which were ravaging the great French industry. He spent about five years (1865–70) on these studies and published among others the famous two-volume treatise *Etudes sur la Maladie des Vers à Soie*. His was apparently the first laboratory to use a microscope for the diagnosis of infectious diseases. He finally differentiated two main diseases, pebrine and flacherie. With pebrine he observed that the pathogen could be transmitted through the silkworm egg, as well as by contact and ingestion of contaminated food. By microscopic examination of the moth that laid a given batch of eggs, he could determine if disease corpuscles were present. If so, the eggs and the moth were burned; if not, he could obtain eggs yielding pebrine-free silkworms.

Distribution of such eggs to producers, along with sanitary precautions, gradually enabled the industry to control the disease. With Pasteur's work, following Bassi's, the real scientific development of insect pathology was initiated.

Meanwhile beginning about the mid-1800s the idea of using microorganisms to control insects began to appear. This concept grew out of the increasing knowledge that insect diseases were infectious and contagious and could be transmitted from diseased to normal individuals. Again Bassi appears first on the scene. In 1836 he published a suggestion to utilize putrified liquids to spray the leaves of plants to kill pest larvae. Not until 1873, apparently, was such a suggestion again made. In August of that year at the Annual Meeting of the American Association for the Advancement of Science, the American entomologist J. L. LeConte read a paper in which he proposed the production of diseases, especially the muscardine fungus of the silkworm, and its artificial transmission in the field to other lepidopterous larvae. Then in 1874, Pasteur suggested the possible use of pebrine against the notorious grape phylloxera in France and again in 1882 he noted that the grape phylloxera must have its own diseases which should be sought out and utilized artificially by man. About the same time, suggestions and some laboratory experiments were made in America with commercial yeast as a possible insect pathogen, but, as would be expected today, they were fruitless.

In the meantime, probably unbeknownst to the Americans and others, Elic Metchnikoff began conducting experiments in 1878–9 with three diseases of the wheat cockchafer *Anisoplia austriaca*, a serious pest of cereal crops in his area of Odessa, Russia. In 1879 he published an important paper on the green muscardine fungus *Metarrhizium anisopliae*. He envisioned and recommended the practical application by man of disease organisms in insect control and successfully tested this possibility experimentally in the laboratory. His observations on natural epizootics led him to believe that pathogens could not be depended upon alone but that with man's application, effective control might be obtained. Toward this end he discovered a method of producing spores artificially on sterilized beer mash. Thus the main ingredients were at hand for the application of insect pathology as it is mainly practiced today.

Metchnikoff's suggestions and experiments led Isaak Krassilstschik to develop a small *Metarrhizium* spore production plant in Smela, Russia in 1884. Over 120 pounds of spores were produced and subsequent field tests caused mortality of *Cleonus* larvae of from 55 to 80 percent from green muscardine. From this time on interest quickened in the use of fungi to control insects and ultimately to today's actual or potential use of a wide variety of pathogens.

Ideas and efforts directed toward the biological control of weeds apparently did not arise until after 1850. The American entomologist Asa Fitch was probably the first to suggest the biological control of weeds about 1855 when he observed that the toad-flax, a European weed very destructive in New York pastures, had no American insects feeding on it and speculated that the importation of insects feeding on it in Europe might solve the problem.

The first practical attempt at biological control of weeds according to my co-worker, Dr R. D. Goeden, dates from 1863, when stem segments of the prickly pear cactus *Opuntia vulgaris*, infested with an imported cochineal insect *Dactylopius ceylonicus*, were distributed for cactus control in southern India after they unexpectedly had been observed to decimate cultivated plantings of this same cactus in northern India. In 1856, the first international importation for biological weed control took place when this same insect was transferred from India to Ceylon, where in a few years time, widespread feral populations of this same cactus were effectively controlled. It has been commonly supposed that the first use of insects to control a weed was that undertaken in Hawaii in 1902 against *Lantana camara*, an introduced ornamental plant that escaped and ran wild (see Holloway, 1964).

Developments with insect parasites and predators moved considerably more rapidly than with pathogens during the 1800s, as might be expected if only because of the technical difficulties of studying minute pathogenic micro-organisms in those days. Work with weeds was probably restricted because of the fear that the introduced insects might transfer to cultivated plants. In view of the limited knowledge of that period it is well that more wasn't attempted. Today's sophisticated studies of weed-feeding insects excludes the importation of any that might be able to feed on economically valuable plants.

Basic studies of the taxonomy and biology of insect parasites and predators and later of their ecology were a necessary prelude to the scientifically sound, practical applications of biological control. Among an increasing number of workers who published good taxonomic studies of parasites should be mentioned M. M. Spinola who published his *Insectorum Liguriae* in Genoa in 1806, J. W. Dalman of Sweden who published on *Encytrus* in 1820, J. L. C. Gravenhorst who described

1300 European Ichneumonidae about the same period, J. O. Westwood the great English entomologist who published voluminously from 1827 on through most of the 1800s, Francis Walker, who specialized in the Chalcidoidea from 1833 to 1861 and erected the family Encyrtidae in 1837, the Italian C. Rondani (publ. 1840–60) who also tabulated host–parasite relations, the German A. Förster (publ. 1841 to the 1800s) and J. T. C. Ratzeburg, another German who published between 1837 and 1852. His *Die Ichneumonen der Forstinsekten* (1844) was the best European contribution devoted to the biology of hymenopterous parasites and remained a standard for many years. Other leaders in the taxonomy of parasites, some of whom continued well into the 1900s, can only be mentioned. They include Holmgren and Thompson (Sweden), Mayr (Austria), Motschulsky (Russia), Hartig and Schmiedeknecht (Germany), Wesmael (Belgium), Haliday, Marshall and Cameron (England), Brulle, Giraud and Decaux (France), Provancher (Canada), Cresson (the pioneer American hymenopterist who described many parasites and published a serial list of the Ichneumonidae of North America), Riley, Howard and Ashmead (USA).

Practical ideas and tests gradually accelerated as the nineteenth century advanced. Dr Erasmus Darwin, the grandfather of Charles Darwin, started the century off by stressing the controlling effect of certain parasites and suggesting in his book on agriculture and gardening, *Phytologia*, published in London in 1800, that aphids in hothouses might be controlled by the artificial use of predaceous syrphid fly larvae. Kirby and Spence devoted considerable space in their *Introduction to Entomology* (London, 1815) to strongly stressing the good work of parasites and predators, as well as to a discussion of the major groups and their habits. They state:

I observed in a former letter, that the devastations of insects are not the same in every season, their power of mischief being evident only at certain times, when...an unusual increase of their numbers, [may occur]...The great agents in preventing this increase, and keeping the noxious species within proper limits, are other insects; and to these I shall now call your attention.

Numerous are the tribes upon which this important task devolves, and incalculable are the benefits which they are the means of bestowing upon us; for to them we are indebted,...that our crops and grain, our cattle, our fruit and forest-trees, our pulse and flowers, and even the verdant covering of the earth, are not totally destroyed.

Noting the value of the common English ladybeetle in destroying the hop aphis they suggested the desirability of discovering means of artificially increasing the ladybeetles for use in aphid control on hops and in glasshouses and also suggested that certain hemipterous predators of bedbugs ought to be encouraged because six or eight of the predators shut up in a room swarming with bedbugs would completely 'extirpate' the latter in several weeks. Obviously, this referred to the small test of 1776 with *Picromerus bidens*, mentioned earlier in this chapter. They noted that gardeners and florists in England had used ladybeetles for *very many* years by transferring them from one place to another and that the authors also had done this to good effect. Thus this empirical use of predators possibly may antedate that of the date growers in Yemen or of the mynah bird in Mauritius.

Kirby and Spence used the term parasite as we use it today, but insect predators they referred to curiously as imparasites. In their discussion of the types, habits, and effectiveness of parasites they covered the ground surprisingly well, including, it appears, all the major families or higher groups we know today (i.e. their Ichneumonidae equals today's Ichneumonoidea). Apropos of habits and effectiveness they say:

The habits of the whole of this tribe, which properly includes several families (*Ichneumonidae, Chalcididae*, &c.) and a great number of distinct genera, are similar. They all oviposit in living insects, chiefly while in the larva state, sometimes while pupae...; at others while in the egg state...The eggs thus deposited soon hatch into grubs, which immediately attack their victim, and in the end insure its destruction. The number of eggs committed to each individual varies according to its size, and that of the grubs which are to spring from them; being in most cases one only, but in others amounting to some hundreds.

From the observations hitherto made by entomologists, the great body of the Ichneumon tribe is principally employed in keeping within their proper limits the infinite host of *lepidopterous* larvae, destroying, however, many insects of other orders; and, perhaps, if the larvae of these last fell equally under our observation with those of the former, we might discover that few exist uninfested by their appropriate parasite. Such is the activity and address of the Ichneumonidans, and their *minute* allies..., that scarcely any concealment, except, perhaps, the waters, can secure their prey from them; and neither bulk, nor ferocity avail to terrify them from effecting their purpose. They attack the ruthless spider in his toils; they discover the retreat of the little bee, that for safety bores deep into timber; and though its enemy Ichneumon cannot enter its cell, by means of her long ovipositor she reaches the helpless grub, which its parent vainly thought secured from every foe, and deposits in it an egg, which produces a larva that destroys it. In vain does the destructive *Cecidomyia* of the wheat conceal its larvae within the glumes that so closely cover the grain; three species of these minute benefactors of our race, sent in mercy by Heaven, know how to introduce their eggs into them, thus preventing the mischief they would otherwise occasion, and saving mankind from the horrors of famine...Even the clover-weevil is not secure within the legumen of that plant; nor the wire-worm in the earth, from their ichneumonidan foes...The ichneumonidan parasites are either external or internal...But the great majority of these animals oviposit within the body of the insect to which they are assigned, from whence, after having consumed the interior and become pupae, they emerge in their perfect state. An idea of the services rendered to us by those Ichneumons which prey upon noxious larvae may be formed from the fact, that out of thirty individuals of the common cabbage caterpillar...which Reaumur put into a glass to feed, twenty-five were fatally pierced by an Ichneumon...The parasites are not wholly confined to the order Hymenoptera: a considerable number are also found amongst the tribe of flies, many of the species of the Dipterous genera *Tachina* Meig.;...depositing their eggs in caterpillars and other larvae, often in such great numbers, that from a larva of *Sphinx atropos*...which had sufficient strength to assume the pupa state, not fewer than eighty flies of *Senometopia atropivora* came out of it...Generally speaking, parasitic larvae do not attack insects in their perfect state, but to this rule there are several exceptions.

Theodor Hartig of Germany, when only 22 years of age in 1827, perhaps was the first to suggest the construction of rearing cages for parasitized caterpillars in order to recover the parasites in large numbers for release where needed. Vincent Kollär, also of Germany, clearly understood the value of entomophagous organisms, especially insect parasites and predators, in natural control. He stated that we often owe the preservation of our agricultural products to natural enemies. The Austrian Emperor Francis I, sponsored the publication of his work in 1837. Kollär described in rather accurate detail the biology and habits of various predators and parasites, including egg parasites, and stressed the need for ample knowledge of natural enemies in order to protect man from injurious insects. For example he states:

The manner in which the Ichneumonidae accomplish their work of destruction is highly curious and interesting. All the species are furnished at the end of the body with an ovipositor, composed of several bristles attached together, with which they pierce the larvae of other insects, and introduce their eggs into the flesh of the wounded animals. In some this sting is longer than the whole body, sometimes more than an inch long, namely, in those species which seek the object of their persecution in the interior of trees or wood that has been much and deeply perforated by the insects which reside therein. They perceive, either by their sense of smelling or by their antennae, that their prey is at hand, and introduce their eggs, not without difficulty, into the bodies of the larvae living in the wood. Some attack caterpillars feeding openly on plants, others perforate the various excrescences or, gall-nuts, which also contain larvae; there are even many species, scarcely visible to the naked eye, which lay their eggs in the eggs of other insects, such as butterflies, and thus anticipate their destruction.

The eggs are hatched within the body of the living insect, and the young parasites, in the most literal sense, fatten on the entrails of their prey. At last the wounded caterpillar sinks, the enemies escape through the skin, and become pupae; or the caterpillar, notwithstanding its internal parasites, enters the pupa state, but instead of a butterfly, one or more Ichneumonidae appear. To these wonderful animals we often owe the preservation of our orchards, woods and grain.

Kollär concluded that:

We can only protect ourselves from the injurious influence of insects by an ample knowledge of the reciprocal relation in which one stands to another, and in order to obtain this, it is essentially necessary to acquire a knowledge of those kinds which are directly or indirectly injurious to man, their different stages of life, their nourishment, propagation, duration, and finally their natural enemies.

Another student of natural enemies, the Italian Rondani, proposed the use of parasitic insects for the control of pests in the 1850s.

Actual tests using insect predators collected and translocated in the field were reported in Europe in the 1840s. Professor Boisgiraud of Poitiers, France, used the predatory carabid *Calosoma sycophanta* in 1840 in an attempt to control gypsy moth larvae on willows. He also tried predatory staphylinids against earwigs in his garden and claimed success in both cases. This led an Italian Society for the Promotion of Arts and Crafts in 1843 to offer a gold medal for presentation in 1845 to anyone who meanwhile had conducted successful tests with artificial breeding of predatory insects for control of agricultural pests. Antonio Villa, just preceding the deadline, presented a written account of such tests to the Society on December 26, 1844. He used climbing carabid predators for phytophagous larvae, staphylinids for flower insects and ground carabids for soil-inhabiting insects. He claimed that most of the predators used increased and gave good control. As a result he was awarded the gold medal.

The second *international* transfer of a predatory bird, or apparently of any natural enemy for that matter, took place about 1850. The Spanish governor of the Philippines, Juan Martinez, introduced the Chinese starling or crested mynah from China or India for the control of migratory locusts. It became established in Luzon with unreported results (Baltazar, 1966).

The scene now switches largely to America, where by the 1850s the ravages of accidentally imported Insect pests were beginning to bestir ideas of *importing new* natural enemies from their homeland. Some American entomologists were quite cognizant of the fact that many pests of European origin were considered to be held under control by natural enemies in Europe.

Vigorous suggestions and actual attempts to import the European parasites of the disastrous pest, the wheat midge *Sitodiplosis mosellana*, were made by Asa Fitch, famous State Entomologist of New York, in 1855. He had documented the spread of the midge, studied it carefully in the field, correctly identified it as the European species, observed a lack of effective parasites in New York and knew that it was held under natural control in Europe. In his own words:

There must be a cause for this remarkable difference. What can that cause be? I can impute it to only one thing; we here are destitute of nature's appointed means for repressing and subduing this insect. Those other insects which have been created for the purpose of quelling this species and keeping it restrained within its appropriate sphere have never yet reached our shores. We have received the evil without the remedy. And thus the midge is able to multiply and flourish, to revel and riot, year after year, without let or hindrance. This certainly would seem to be the principal if not the sole cause why the career of this insect here is so very different from what it is in the Old World.

As a consequence in May 1855, he wrote to Mr John Curtis, President of the London Entomological Society, informing him of the damage in the United States and the lack of effective enemies and asking co-operation in obtaining shipments of parasites. He even suggested how to collect and ship the parasitized larvae. The request was received with favor by the London society but no shipments ever resulted. Although the Rev. C. J. S. Bethune, a Canadian entomologist, was credited by C. V. Riley as probably being the first to suggest the importation of the European parasites of the wheat midge, his suggestion apparently was not made until 1864. Again nothing came of the idea.

Benjamin D. Walsh, as State Entomologist of Illinois, subsequently actively continued the written campaign started by Fitch to obtain

83

wheat midge parasites and apparently tried to obtain them through some English friends. In several publications he strongly criticized the inactivity of the government and State Entomological Societies for failing to import parasites. He pointed out the damage in New York State alone amounted to fifteen million dollars in one year and that the midge frequently took half of the crop, whereas in England the largest amount ever destroyed was five percent. He stressed that there were no parasites in this country but at least three species in England and this was the reason for the difference in damage. His efforts are summed up in a nutshell by the statements published in the September 29, 1866 issue of the *Practical Entomologist*:

The plain common sense remedy...is, by artificial means to import the European parasites, that in their own country prey upon the Wheat Midge, the Hessian Fly and the other imported insects that afflict the North American farmer. Accident has furnished us with the bane; science must furnish us with the remedy. [He went on to say:] Vaccination, Gas, the Steam-engine, the Steam-boat, the Rail-road, the Electric Telegraph, have all been successively the laughing-stock of the vulgar, and have all by slow degrees fought their way into general adoption. So will it be with the artificial importation of parasitic insects. Our grandchildren will perhaps be the first to reap the benefit of a plan, which we ourselves might, just as well as not, adopt at the present day. The simplicity and comparative cheapness of the remedy, but more than anything else the ridicule which attaches, in the popular mind, to the very names of 'Bugs' and 'Bug-hunters', are the principal obstacles to its adoption. Let a man profess to have discovered some new Patent powder pimperlimpimp, a single pinch of which being thrown into each corner of a field will kill every bug throughout its whole extent, and people will listen to him with attention and respect. But tell them of any simple commonsense plan, based upon correct scientific principles, to check and keep within reasonable bounds the insect foes of the Farmer, and they will laugh you to scorn. [and finally:] But we should not stop here. [with introduction of parasites of the wheat midge.] The principle is of general application; and wherever a Noxious European Insect becomes accidentally domiciled among us, we should at once import the parasites and Cannibals that prey upon it at home.

Obviously Walsh was vigorously proposing classical biological control but unfortunately again nothing practical came of his efforts.

The well-established and older Walsh appears to have transmitted his enthusiasm for biological control to young C. V. Riley who in 1868, when only twenty-five years of age, was appointed State Entomologist of Missouri during the height of Walsh's campaign in nearby

Illinois to import parasites. Riley began his career reporting on economic entomology for the *Prairie Farmer* in Chicago in 1864 and probably got to know Walsh at once. In fact, they published 478 papers together and jointly started the *American Entomologist* in 1868.

Riley appears to have been the first to *transport insect parasites* from one locality to another. In studying the parasites of the plum curculio in 1869–70 he determined that they could be easily collected and distributed from Kirkwood, Missouri, and sent two species of parasites to several correspondents in other parts of the State. Then in 1871, he proposed *conservation* of parasites of the rascal leaf-crumpler of apple and other fruit trees by collecting larvae in their cases in mid-winter and then removing them a short distance from the trees so that the larvae could not return but the adult parasites emerging from the parasitized ones the next spring easily could.

In writing of this procedure toward the close of his career in 1893, he considered that conservation of natural enemies was one of

but two methods by which these insect friends of the farmer can be effectually utilized or encouraged, as, for the most part, they perform their work unseen and unheeded by him, and are practically beyond his control. These methods consist in the intelligent protection of those species which already exist in a given locality, and in the introduction of desirable species which do not already exist there.

In this same 1893 paper Riley was certainly among, if not *the* first, to recognize the adverse ecological effects deriving from the use of insecticides and to visualize the interactions of natural enemy–prey populations to produce natural biological control. He states:

Year in and year out, with the conditions of life unchanged by man's actions, the relations between the plant-feeder and the predaceous and parasitic species of its own class remain substantially the same, whatever the fluctuations between them for any given year. This is a necessary result in the economy of nature; for the ascendancy of one or the other of the opposing forces involves a corresponding fluctuation on the decreasing side, and there is a necessary relation between the plant-feeder and its enemies, which, normally, must be to the slight advantage of the former and only exceptionally to the great advantage of the latter.

This law is recognized by all close students of nature, and has often been illustrated and insisted upon by entomologists in particular, as the most graphic exemplifications of it occur in insect life, in which fecundity is such that the balance is regained with marvelous rapidity, even after approximate annihilation of any particular species. But it is doubtful whether another equally logical deduction from the prevalence of this law has been sufficiently recognized by us, and this is, that our artificial insecticide methods have little or no effect upon the multiplication of an injurious species, except for the particular occasion which calls them forth, and that occasions often arise when it were wiser to refrain from the use of such insecticides and to leave the field to the parasitic and predaceous forms.

It is generally when a particular injurious insect has reached the zenith of its increase and has accomplished its greatest harm that the farmer is led to bestir himself to suppress it, and yet it is equally true that it is just at this time that nature is about to relieve him in striking the balance by checks which are violent and effective in proportion to the exceptional increase of and consequent exceptional injury done by the injurious species. Now the insecticide method of routing this last, under such circumstances, too often involves, also, the destruction of the parasitic and predaceous species, and does more harm than good. This is particularly true of those of our Coccidae and Aphididae and those of our Lepidopterous larvae which have numerous natural enemies of their own class; and it not only emphasizes the importance of preventive measures [cultural control], which we are all agreed to urge for other cogent reasons, and which do not to the same extent destroy the parasites, but it affords another explanation of the reason why the fight with insecticides must be kept up year after year, and has little cumulative value.

Riley's remarks concerning insecticides are even more true today.

One cannot help but reflect that during this early period the great American economic entomologists and national leaders in the profession were primarily strong advocates of biological control and in several cases were accomplished expert taxonomists in the parasitic Hymenoptera as well. Both Riley and his successor as Chief of the US Bureau of Entomology, L. O. Howard, outstandingly filled both categories. Then recall also the great early State Entomologists, Asa Fitch of New York and Benjamin Walsh of Illinois (as well as Riley in Missouri) plus University advocates such as J. H. Comstock of Cornell. Relatively speaking I am afraid that the very deep appreciation and actual study of natural biological control by many of the top men of those early days was gradually replaced by entomologists having more and more one-sided interest in insecticidal control. Hopefully today this trend is being reversed toward a state of broader ecological understanding and appreciation of the need to rebalance the overuse of chemicals with adequate stress on non-chemical approaches to pest control.

Just after Riley's 1871 proposal for conservation of natural enemies, F. Decaux, a French entomologist, made essentially the same suggestion

86

in 1872. He was impressed by the large number of parasites that emerged from apple buds attacked by the *Anthonomus* weevil and advised, instead of collecting and burning these buds, as was generally done, placing them in boxes covered with gauze and then opening the boxes from time to time to permit the parasites to escape. He later tested the idea personally in 1880 by collecting more than one million *Anthonomus*-infested buds from which he obtained and liberated about 250000 parasites which during the following year aided in the control of the weevil. He repeated the experiment again that year and reportedly this stopped all serious damage in the treated orchards for ten years. Decaux also made some tests in 1872 in transporting parasites from one locality to another.

During the same period of the early 1870s, Dr William Le Baron, State Entomologist of Illinois, was conducting intensive studies on the oyster-shell scale of apple and its parasite, *Aphytis mytilaspidis*. In the winter of 1871–2 he moved twigs bearing parasitized scales from one locality, Galena, to another, Geneva, where the parasite did not exist. At the end of 1872, the parasite was established in the new location.

Although these tests by Riley, LeBaron and Decaux were progressive for their time and a sign of things to come, they were not well-designed experiments in the modern sense. In the transfer tests the possibility existed that the parasites actually were already present in low numbers in the new locality and in the conservation of parasites by collecting parasitized material and permitting the parasites but not the host to escape, there were no adequate checks.

Riley comes back into the picture in 1873 by making the first successful international transfer of an *arthropod predator* by sending the predaceous mite *Tyroglyphus phylloxerae* of the grape phylloxera to Planchon in France. The mite, although established, did not prove to be of importance in control however.

International shipments of aphid predators, and possibly also parasites, were made from England to New Zealand in 1874 but without any startling results although the ladybeetle, *Coccinella undecimpunctata*, was reported to have become established. This would represent the first overseas establishment of a predaceous *insect*.

Another international movement of a vertebrate predator of insects was made in 1875. The Surinam toad *Bufo marinus* was introduced into Bermuda from British Guiana by Captain Nathaniel Vesey especially for control of roaches. It became established and is now abundant.

It is a very general predator which has been distributed into various Caribbean islands.

The first authentic *inter-country* transfer of a *parasitic* insect appears to have been the importation of *Trichogramma* from the United States to Canada by W. Saunders, President of the Entomological Society of Ontario, in 1882 for the control of the gooseberry sawfly. Results, if any, are unknown.

It will be recalled that the first parasite species recorded by man was by Aldrovandi in 1602, although he did not recognize it as such. However, it is evident from his description that the parasite was *Apanteles glomeratus*, a common and fairly effective parasite of the cabbage butterfly. Two hundred and eighty-one years later in 1883 this became the first *parasite species* to be *shipped intercontinentally* and successfully *established*. Riley, with the co-operation of G. C. Bignell of Plymouth, England, was responsible for this importation to the United States. The species was colonized in the District of Columbia, Iowa, Nebraska and Missouri and rapidly spread throughout the country. It remains today one of the more effective enemies of the cabbage butterfly.

The stage is now set for the first great success in classical biological control – that of the cottony-cushion scale in California which firmly established biological control as a major pest control method. The story is related in the next chapter. Riley again was the mastermind; in fact he had begun gathering data on the cottony-cushion scale and its enemies in California as early as 1872 and over the years into the mid-1880s continued to seek information on the native home of the scale in order to obtain effective natural enemies. In his writings one can almost feel the surge of his great drive, enthusiasm and confidence in the yet unproven biological control method. As will be related, he was more successful than he could ever have dreamed.

5
The first foreign explorers

Foreign exploration for new exotic natural enemies is the classical approach to biological control and still remains the major one. It furnishes the big pay-off. Its evolution was sketched in the preceding chapter. Its beginnings often were fraught with adventure, danger and hardships for the explorers, as will be related in some of the individual stories that follow.

These early projects cover the period from the first great success beginning in 1888–9 to about the beginning of World War II, i.e. 1938 or 1939. During this period nearly all foreign exploration and importation of natural enemies entailed lengthy trips primarily involving steamship and railway travel supplemented by local and even long distance travel by foot, ox-cart, camel, horse and, if lucky, sometimes by auto. In those days the explorer often had to accompany his shipments home on lengthy sea voyages in order to maintain the live cultures en route. Some illustrative views from various trips made by Harold Compere for the University of California at Riverside during the 1920s and 30s are shown in Fig. 20. The commercial development of international and overseas air transport marked the end of this era. The first long distance intercontinental air shipment of natural enemies I have documented was from Japan to Israel in 1939, although some shorter air shipments occurred in the mid-1930s.

I have chosen the following fifteen projects from among many. Most, but not all, represent great successes and between them illustrate the main principles and practices of classical biological control. Projects involving classical biological control, it will be recalled, should be triggered when a new exotic insect invades and becomes a pest. In order to establish a new natural balance below the pest-status level, the origin of the pest is sought out and a search made for its natural enemies. When found these are imported and colonized and, if they prove to be efficient, successful biological control occurs, permanently solving the problem.

Fig. 20. Aspects of foreign exploration for natural enemies by Harold Compere *circa* 1930. (*a*) Field collecting in Eritrea, (*b*) cages containing parasitized black scale on host plants being transported to ship on camels, Eritrea, (*c*) cages being loaded on board S.S. *President Polk*, Red Sea, (*d*) cages en route on deck, (*e*) protection of cages on deck from salt spray and hot sun, Red Sea, (*f*) cage repair in India, (*g*) transport in India.

(e)

(f)

(g)

91

Some foreign explorers and famous projects

Cottony-cushion scale in California, 1888–9

This project established the biological control method like a shot heard around the world. About 1868, the cottony-cushion scale *Icerya purchasi* Maskell was discovered on *Acacia* in Menlo Park in northern California and spread rapidly. By 1886 its effect on the new and growing citrus industry in southern California was devastating to the point of destruction. Growers tried washes and HCN fumigation but these were not sufficiently effective. Damage was so extensive that many growers pulled out or burned their trees and real estate values plummeted.

The alarmed California horticultural officials started inquiries and early in the game enlisted the aid of Charles Valentine Riley, Chief of the United States Department of Agriculture Division of Entomology. Riley emerged as the dominant and guiding figure in this odyssey but others made more important active contributions. Riley's earlier interest and experiments in biological control have already been mentioned in Chapter 4.

Albert Koebele was the foreign explorer involved. He became famous and followed the same career for many years. D. W. Coquillett, the third man of the team so to speak, played the important role of receiving and colonizing the imported natural enemies.

Setting the stage began in 1885 when Riley sent his assistant, Koebele, to Alameda, California, at a salary of $100.00 per month to conduct an 'investigation of the history and habits of insects of California'. About the same time he appointed Coquillett, a skilled amateur entomologist residing in Anaheim, California, as field agent to work on the control of the cottony-cushion scale *Icerya purchasi* Maskell, around Los Angeles. In February 1886, both men were assigned to work together at Los Angeles on this latter problem.

Meanwhile, Riley apparently had been endeavoring by correspondence to determine the native home of the *Icerya* in order to discover and import its natural enemies and probably – at least by 1887 – California officials were doing likewise. Possibly stimulated by such correspondence (here the story is cloudy) Frazer Crawford, an entomologist of Adelaide, Australia, discovered in 1886 the parasitic fly *Cryptochaetum iceryae* Will., an effective natural enemy of the cottony-cushion scale. Early in 1887 Crawford wrote to Riley that *Icerya* in Adelaide was destroyed by a dipterous parasite and sent drawings of the fly and also specimens which the USDA received in February 1887. At first Riley was dubious of its parasitic status, because no true dipterous fly parasites of scale insects were then known. Later he became so convinced of its importance that this assumed the main objective in Koebele's future trip.

In his Annual Report of 1886 Riley recommended that the natural enemies of the cottony-cushion scale be investigated in Australia and introduced into California. The same year the California Fruit Growers' Convention petitioned Congress to appropriate funds for the USDA to do this work. Politics and pressures then were much like now. However, Congress not only refused but maintained the regulation that USDA funds could not be spent in foreign travel.

In April 1887, as invited speaker at the California Fruit Growers' Convention, Riley was asked to provide a remedy for the cottony-cushion scale scourge. He stated his belief that the scale came from Australia, where it was harmless, and probably not from New Zealand where it was recorded as a serious pest. He assumed that parasites kept the scale in check in Australia and again recommended that those be sought out and imported into California. He offered to send an entomologist to do this but said that the US Congress would laugh at the idea and asked California, or even Los Angeles County, to appropriate a couple of thousand dollars to import the parasites. Although the Convention again adopted a resolution in favor of sending someone to Australia for natural enemies, no money was forthcoming from California.

About this same time, W. G. Klee, the California State Inspector of Fruit Pests corresponded with W. M. Maskell in Auckland, New Zealand (Maskell described the cottony-cushion scale as a new species from Auckland in 1878) and with Frazer Crawford in Adelaide, Australia. Maskell told Klee positively that Australia was the native home (letter published in *Pacific Rural Press*, May 7, 1887). Subsequently Riley, who meanwhile had had second thoughts as to the country of origin and was suggesting Mauritius (letter in *Pacific Rural Press*, June 4, 1887), agreed that Australia was probably the native home (letter in *Pacific Rural Press*, March 4, 1888).

Late in 1887, as a result of Klee's correspondence, Frazer Crawford with considerable effort, collected and sent some live *Cryptochaetum* to Klee who liberated the flies on cottony-cushion scale in San Mateo County near San Francisco in early 1888 *before* Koebele sailed for Australia – ostensibly to get the same flies. There is good reason to believe that this resulted in establishment, because it eventually became common in California and there is doubt that Koebele's later shipments to Los Angeles did survive after release.

The financing for Koebele's trip to Australia came about through some adroit political maneuvering. In 1888 an International Exposition was to be held in Melbourne, Australia, and a US exhibit was planned through the US State Department. Through the efforts of Riley, N. J. Coleman, the California Commissioner of Agriculture and others, the US Secretary of State was persuaded to set aside $2000.00 to pay the travel expenses of an entomologist who, ostensibly, was to represent the US State Department at the Exposition. Riley selected Albert Koebele who sailed from San Francisco, August 25, 1888.

In Australia, Koebele had none of the problems that beset some of the later foreign explorers. As an official representative of the US State Department and the USDA he received utmost co-operation and was nearly everywhere accompanied by knowledgeable local entomologists or growers, who often led him to known pockets of the otherwise rare cottony-cushion scale. Additionally the State railways throughout Australia furnished him with free passes.

Arriving in Sydney, September 20, 1888, Koebele searched for four days and found only a few *Icerya* and no natural enemies. The local orange growers had no knowledge of the scale. Proceeding to Melbourne by train, he searched for some six days but found no *Icerya*. Next he went to Adelaide with a letter of introduction to Frazer Crawford (the discoverer of *Cryptochaetum* in 1886). The next day in gardens in Adelaide they found *Icerya* and the very first scale examined contained nine pupae of the parasitic fly. In fact nearly all the scales examined were parasitized. We can well imagine Koebele's excitement, especially when the scale was so rare that most local entomologists hardly knew of its existence.

On October 15, while collecting scales for shipment to California with Crawford in a North Adelaide garden, Koebele relates 'I discovered there, for the first time, feeding upon a large female Icerya, the Ladybird, which will become famed in the United States – *Vedalia cardinalis*.' (Note that this report was written in July 1889, after his return and after vedalia was showing its potential in California.) Koebele wrote Riley about this discovery and Riley replied that *Cryptochaetum* was probably the most promising but to try others as well. As we shall see, he was both right and wrong regarding *Cryptochaetum*.

Searching further afield for more scales, Koebele went to Mannum in the Murray River valley, where so much of today's oranges are grown. There he found the scale along with *Cryptochaetum*, the lady-bird vedalia, and a predatory green lacewing. He returned within a week to Adelaide with considerable material which was placed in a cool cellar to await shipment to California. On October 24–25 he collected more scales in North Adelaide, along with many parasitic flies and green lacewings. The first shipment was described by Koebele thus:

I finished collecting for my first shipment on the 25th and estimated that I had about 6000 Icerya, which in return would produce at an average about four parasites [Lestophonus = *Cryptochaetum*] each. They were packed partly in wooden and partly in tin boxes. Small branches generally full of scales were cut so as to fit exactly lengthwise into the box. With these the boxes were filled and all loose scales placed in between, plenty of space remaining for any of the insects within to move about freely without danger of being crushed by loose sticks. Salicylic acid was used in small quantities in the tin boxes to prevent mold, yet these, as I have been informed by Mr Coquillett, arrived in a more or less moldy condition, while those in wooden boxes always arrived safe. In addition, Dr Schomburgh, director of the botanical gardens at Adelaide, kindly fitted up for me a Wardian case which was filled with living plants of orange and *Pittosporum* in pots. Large numbers of Icerya were placed in this, and such larvae as were found feeding upon them... The object of this was to have the *Lestophonus* go on breeding within the case during the voyage. No doubt many infested scales arrived in Los Angeles.

I found [later] on examining the tree [in Los Angeles], on April 12, 1889, under which this case had been placed with a tent over it, that from several of the Iceryas the *Lestophonus* had issued. This case, as Mr Coquillett informed me in a letter of November 30, arrived in good condition, except that the putty had been knocked off in several places, leaving holes large enough for the parasites to escape. Before opening the case he found two coccinellid larvae crawling on the outside, and these when placed with the Icerya attacked it at once. He further said that there were only about half a dozen living *Chrysopa* adults. This would show that the Lestophonus was still issuing on arrival in California and all turned out more favorably than I had anticipated on seeing the box handled in such a rough manner by the steamer hands at Sydney, to which point I accompanied this as well as all the subsequent shipments. I expected little good would come out of this method of sending and therefore concluded to send only small parcels on ice thereafter, as had been partly done at first. If once the insects could be placed in good condition in the ice-house on the steamer just before leaving, where a temperature of 38° Fah. at first and about 46° Fah. on arrival in San Francisco existed, they must arrive safely. To accomplish this, the parasites with their hosts were all collected the last three days before leaving

95

Adelaide, and on arriving home were immediately placed in a cool cellar. On the trip from Adelaide to Sydney, which takes two days by train, my insects came generally in an ice-box on the sleeping-car.

Following this he surveyed other areas of Victoria and New South Wales but concluded that the Adelaide area was best, so returned on November 8, 1888. After collecting about 6000 scales in five days and making a trip to Melbourne for additional material, he left Adelaide for Sydney with the second shipment.

On the 26th I left Adelaide on my way to Sydney, with what I considered even a better shipment than the first. Unfortunately this lot arrived in a bad condition at San Francisco, owing to a gale on the route when the parcels fell off the shelving in the ice-house, in which they had been placed, and most of them were crushed by cakes of ice falling on them.

A third shipment was made about the end of December. Meanwhile Koebele travelled to Brisbane, where he found only a few specimens of *Icerya* and slowly returned to Melbourne with similar very poor collecting along the way. At Melbourne he collected *Cryptochaetum* on a related scale insect, *Monophloebus* sp. Nearing the end of his stay in Australia, he collected *Icerya* with parasites and about 200 vedalia, mostly in the Sydney Town Hall garden. Either he now knew how to search better or was luckier than during his first trip to Sydney when he drew a blank. Then under instructions from Riley to study *Icerya* in New Zealand on his way home, he boarded ship on January 23, 1889 with his insects in the cold room, and arrived in Auckland, New Zealand, January 28. The scales with parasites and ladybirds were found to be in excellent condition at Auckland and were repacked in wooden boxes with fresh *Icerya* found in Auckland, and apparently sent on to California. He found no natural enemies in Auckland; however at Napier he found large numbers of vedalia beetles feeding on *Icerya*. This was unknown before; according to Koebele the vedalia arrived in Auckland by chance, where *Icerya* was destroying everything five years previously, and there cleaned nearly the whole district around Auckland within about two years. At the time of Koebele's visit the vedalia was dispersing into new areas, hence his big collection of about 6000 specimens of vedalia at Napier. Returning to Auckland, these were placed in the ship's cool-room at 4 °C (38 °F). He left Auckland on February 25 and arrived in San Francisco, Saturday evening March 16, 1889. The material could not be sent to Coquillett at Los Angeles until the following Monday and he received it on

March 20 – 34 days since collection and 29 days on ice – yet they arrived in better condition than any shipment previously received. The specimens were liberated under the same caged tree that had received the earlier specimens. This was on the F. W. Wolfskill property in Los Angeles.

According to Coquillett's records live vedalia arrived in Los Angeles as follows:

November 30, 1888	28	(Shipment 1)
December 29, 1888	44	(Shipment 2)
January 24, 1889	57	(Shipment 3)
Total	129	

These were placed under the caged tree at Wolfskill's.

On February 21, thirty-five vedalia (shipment 4) arrived and were colonized at the J. R. Dobbins property at San Gabriel. The final shipment of 350 live vedalia that was brought personally by Koebele on shipboard, arrived and was colonized on March 20, 1889. About one-third went to the Dobbins' grove, and the remainder to the large A. Scott Chapman grove in San Gabriel valley.

All told about 12 000 *Cryptochaetum* arrived in Los Angeles from Koebele. These were all put under one caged tree and when he examined this tree on April 12, 1889 he noted that very few *Cryptochaetum* remained of the vast numbers of flies received. I have found no record as to whether this resulted in establishment, because at this time vedalia was beginning to explode and clean up the scale. Apparently everyone forgot the fly in the excitement. If this release didn't cause establishment then the 1888 release by Klee at San Mateo surely did, because the fly is common in all coastal areas today.

By early April 1889, nearly all the *Icerya* in the caged tree at Wolfskill's were destroyed by vedalia, so one side of the cage was removed and the beetles allowed to move to adjoining trees. On April 12, Coquillett began sending colonies to other parts of the State. By June 12 – two months after the cage was opened – 10 555 vedalia had been distributed to 208 different growers and successful colonization occurred in nearly every case. At this time, i.e. within six months of the first release of twenty-eight beetles and with a total release of only 129, the original trees in Wolfskill's were virtually clean of *Icerya* and the beetles had spread to a distance of three-quarters of a mile away. In his Annual Report for 1889 Riley states that in the original orchard (Wolfskill's) practically all the scales were killed before August 1889 and further that by the end of 1889, *Icerya* was no longer a factor to be considered

97

in citrus growing in California. The following season saw this statement completely justified.

According to Coquillett in mid-1889, regarding the San Gabriel colonization of February and March:

All of these colonies have thrived exceedingly well. During a recent visit to each of these groves I found the lady-birds on trees fully one-eighth of a mile from those on which the original colonies were placed, having thus distributed themselves of their own accord. The trees I colonized them on in the grove of Dobbins were quite large and were thickly infested with the *Iceryas*, but at the time of my recent visit scarcely a living *Icerya* could be found on these and on several adjacent trees, while the dead and dry bodies of the *Iceryas* still clinging to the trees by their beaks, indicated how thickly the trees had been infested with these pests, and how thoroughly the industrious lady-birds had done their work.

The citrus grower, J. R. Dobbins, stated in July 1889 only some four months after the first beetles were released:

The vedalia has multiplied in numbers and spread so rapidly that every one of my 3200 orchard trees is literally swarming with them. All of my ornamental trees, shrubs, and vines which were infested with white scale, are practically cleansed by this wonderful parasite. About one month since I made a public statement that my orchard would be free from *Icerya* by November 1 [1889], but the work has gone on with such amazing speed and thoroughness that I am today confident that the pest will have been exterminated from my trees by the middle of August. People are coming here daily, and by placing infested branches upon the ground beneath my trees for two hours, can secure colonies of thousands of the vedalia, which are there in countless numbers seeking food. Over 50000 have been taken away to other orchards during the past week, and there are millions still remaining, and I have distributed a total of 63000 since June 1.

Dobbins' orchard was so completely free of *Icerya* that on July 31 he posted a notice that he had no more beetles for distribution. The other colonized grove in San Gabriel was similarly cleaned of scale. In 1888 the owner, Mr A. Scott Chapman, had stated that he was being forced to abandon citrus growing by the scales; in October 1889 he stated that the vedalia had cleaned up the scale on 150 acres. In just one year shipments of oranges from Los Angeles County increased dramatically from 700 to 2000 carload lots.

Yet another testimonial was published by Riley in 1893 as follows:

Mr William F. Channing, of Pasadena, son of the eminent Unitarian divine, wrote two years later [in 1891]: We owe to the Agricultural Department the rescue of our orange culture by the importation of the Australian lady-bird, *Vedalia cardinalis*.

The white scales were incrusting our orange trees with a hideous leprosy. They spread with wonderful rapidity and would have made citrus growth on the whole North American continent impossible within a few years. It took the Vedalia, where introduced, only a few weeks absolutely to clean out the white scale. The deliverance was more like a miracle than anything I have ever seen. In the spring of 1889 I had abandoned my young Washington navel orange trees as irrecoverable. Those same trees bore from two to three boxes of oranges apiece at the end of the season (or winter and spring of 1890). The consequence of the deliverance is that many hundreds of thousands of orange trees (navels almost exclusively) have been set out in southern California this last spring.

From a total original stock of 514 beetles colonized from the end of November 1888 to late March 1889 the rapidity and extent of this control was nearly unbelievable. Coquillett in a letter to Riley, October 21, 1889, summarized it as follows:

The first half of the year I devoted nearly the whole of my time to propagating and distributing the Australia Lady-bird (*Vedalia cardinalis*) recently introduced by this Division. At the present time it is very difficult to find a living Fluted Scale (*Icerya purchasi* Maskell) in the vicinity of this city [Los Angeles], so thoroughly has the Lady-bird done its work; and, indeed, the same is true of nearly the entire southern part of the state, as well as of many localities in the northern part.

By 1890 all infestations in the State had been completely decimated. The cost, aside from Koebele's and Coquillett's salaries, was about $1500.00; and all told less than $5000.00. Benefits to the citrus industry of California have amounted to millions of dollars annually ever since and as an aftermath similar successes have been attained over the years in more than fifty countries around the world by transfer of vedalia, and to a lesser extent of *Cryptochaetum*.

As mentioned earlier, Koebele immediately became famous and continued as a foreign explorer for the USDA and later for Hawaii, although he never again achieved such a spectacular success. As a fitting finale to his great achievement the Californians raised a fund and presented Koebele with a gold watch and Mrs Koebele with a pair of diamond ear-rings.

The sequel to this story is that, meanwhile, *Cryptochaetum* had been increasing in California and eventually it became strongly dominant in all coastal areas, including Los Angeles, where vedalia attained its first notoriety. This part of the account rarely is heard. From the evidence we have today it is certain that had *Cryptochaetum* alone been introduced it would have done just as spectacular a job in control of the scale in the citrus areas of 1890 as did the vedalia beetle. Today, however, the vedalia beetle remains dominant in all interior and desert citrus areas. (See Doutt, 1964*b*; Koebele, 1890.)

Gypsy moth and brown-tail moth in New England, 1905–11

These two moth species, *Porthetria dispar* (Linnaeus) and *Nygmia phaeorrhoea* (Donovan), are invaders from Europe and can, if unchecked, defoliate large tracts of forest and shade trees. The gypsy moth actually was purposefully imported by an astronomer about 1869 into Medford, Massachusetts, but only to be studied in the laboratory in connection with its silk production. Unfortunately to the everlasting embarrassment of Professor Leopold Trouvelot it escaped and was soon wreaking havoc over the New England countryside. Today, of course, importation of potentially dangerous organisms is strictly prohibited. This dual biological control project, like quite a few that have followed, was undertaken only after attempts at chemical eradication had failed.

This was the first of only a few 'super-projects' conducted thus far in biological control and was broadly directed by Riley's successor, Dr L. O. Howard, Chief of the Bureau of Entomology of the USDA. I say super-project because, for the period, considerable money and a very large number of co-operating entomologists were involved. Howard had great faith in the parasite method, as it was called in those days, and was a leading taxonomist in parasitic Hymenoptera. A large number of young American entomologists who later on became famous in their own right were employed on this dual project and some are still quite active although retired, such as my colleague, the uncle of President Richard Nixon, P. H. Timberlake. Others were Professor Harry S. Smith, Dr W. R. Thompson and Dr J. D. Tothill, all famous names in biological control.

They worked principally at two converted laboratory–insectaries: the first at North Saugus, Massachusetts, beginning in the fall of 1905. This proved insufficient and by the end of the 1907 summer they moved to the famous Melrose-Highlands laboratory–insectary remodeled from a large house. Numerous innovations, rearing techniques, use of cold storage for synchronization of host and parasites, as well as exciting biological discoveries were worked out at Melrose-Highlands and served as guides for years to come. Mr E. S. G. Titus was in charge of the laboratory work, with strict emphasis on identification, quarantine and biology until his health broke down and he was forced to resign in May 1907 due to the irritating and poisonous effects of the barbed hairs of the brown-tail moth larvae. His physician ordered this in order to save his life because of intense lung irritation. Some assistants also resigned in spite of efforts to solve the problem by the use of goggles, masks, and protective clothing. W. F. Fiske, who succeeded Titus, pretty well solved the difficulty by confining the larvae to closed cages having two sleeved openings with attached gloves so that the material inside could be safely handled. A large number of foreign entomologists were employed to collect material following survey trips by L. O. Howard in Europe and Professor Kincaid, of the University of Washington, in Japan and Russia.

In general, the two moth projects were conducted simultaneously. Some of the natural enemies were common to both but most were not. As is well known today, the gypsy moth still remains a problem even though quite a few parasites and predators were established against it. According to Clausen (1956):

It is believed, however, that the combined effect of the parasites and predators has given appreciable control. Instead of occurring frequently in epidemic form and for extended periods, the gypsy moth outbreaks are now reduced so that they are comparable in range and severity to those occurring in Europe.

On the other hand the brown-tail moth is now considered to be at best a minor problem in New England and is reported to be under complete biological control in Canada from some of the same natural enemies originally imported into New England.

The conclusions have been drawn by some, including certain entomologists and others in decision-making positions, that biological control of the gypsy moth has been completely tried and is hopeless. True, it was given a mighty effort but largely in the early days when a lot remained to be learned. Even L. O. Howard concluded:

It has been found impossible to secure certain of the parasites in adequate numbers for colonization under satisfactory conditions. The proportion of such is very small, it is true, but at the same time it may easily be that ultimate success or failure may depend upon the establishment, not of the most important among the parasites and other natural enemies, but of a group or sequence of species which will work together harmoniously toward

101

the common end. Viewed in this light, the importance of parasites which otherwise might be considered as of minor interest is greatly enhanced.

It is impracticable to determine certain facts in the life and habits of those parasites which have been colonized under conditions believed but not known to be satisfactory. Further detailed knowledge is necessary before we can judge whether the circumstances surrounding colonization were in truth the best that could be devised. Furthermore, so long as original research is confined to the study of material collected by foreign agents, some of whom are technically untrained, it is practically impossible to secure the evidence necessary to refute published statements concerning the importance of certain parasites abroad which the results of first-hand investigations have not served to confirm. It is believed that these statements are largely based upon false premises, but should this belief prove ungrounded it would mean that there are important parasites abroad of which little or nothing is known first-hand.

In view of this and of what we know of the successful conclusions of other programs taking place by the discovery of new effective natural enemies many years after the projects were considered impractical of solution, and especially in view of the enormous millions of dollars spent in repetitive chemical campaigns over the years, it seems necessary that strong additional biological control research on importation of exotic natural enemies of the gypsy moth be conducted.* It is known that in many countries of Europe, Asia, and especially Japan, the gypsy moth rarely, if ever, becomes a pest due to the action of parasites. This is not universally true, for as Howard noted in parts of Russia parasitic control was obviously inefficient and that although disease became prevalent it was not sufficient to keep the gypsy moth from increasing until defoliation of large areas resulted.

However, the general degree of biological control accomplished abroad and therefore potentially possible in the US is evident from Howard's statements:

The study of the tussock moth has resulted in demonstrating another fact which is of peculiar interest in this connection, which is, that the parasites which assist in effecting its control in country districts where this control is perfect are sometimes entirely absent in the city. Something of the same sort may be true of the parasites which assist in effecting the control of the gypsy moth in many localities in Europe where it is so uncommon as to make collection of material for exportation in any quantity impossible. Some

* After this was written the Plant Protection Division, United States Department of Agriculture reported in 1973 the importation of four new exotic parasites of the gypsy moth.

of the most interesting lots of caterpillars or pupae which have been received were from such localities, and it may well be that there are parasites abroad which have not been received at the laboratory in Massachusetts in sufficient quantity for colonization, and which can never be received there until new methods for collecting and importing them are devised, but which at the same time are actually among the important species. This fact can only be determined definitely by careful study of the gypsy moth in localities where it was not sufficiently abundant to permit of its collection in large quantities. [To my knowledge no adequate follow-through on this has ever been made – author.] Professor Kincaid's reports upon the effectiveness of the parasites, even when taken with more than the prescribed grain of conservatism, have been so consistently optimistic as to leave no room to doubt that the parasitism to which the moth is subjected in Japan, even in localities where it is more than normally prevalent, is sufficient to meet and overcome the rate of increase of the gypsy moth in America...How these parasites work together in bringing about the control of the moth in Japan is indicated in Table I, which, with its explanation was published in a somewhat abbreviated form in the popular bulletin by the junior author which was issued through the office of the State forester of Massachusetts a year ago...The addition of the names of the species marked with an asterisk (ones not considered important) makes the list complete, so far as it may be completed through the information now available. The species so designated are those which have never been received in sufficient abundance to make their colonization possible, and among them are some which are doubtless of wholly insignificant importance from an economic standpoint, while others may, upon investigation, prove to be of more than sufficient importance to justify an attempt to secure their introduction into America... It will be noted that the parasites not designated by the asterisks, and which are therefore to be considered as of some importance in effecting the control of the moth, form, when taken together, a perfect sequence, and that every stage of the moth from the newly deposited egg to the pupa is subjected to attack...From a technical standpoint it was exceedingly interesting and valuable, since there were found to be present [in Russia] in the boxes of young gypsy-moth caterpillars the cocoons of several species of hymenopterous parasites which had either not been received from other sources or which were not known to be sufficiently abundant in any other part of Europe to make possible their collection in large quantities.

In Russia the reports were quite variable. According to Professor Trevor Kincaid in Bessarabia:

Bendery, Bessarabia, Russia, June 11, 1909. The season here is in full swing, but the situation causes me considerable anxiety, as the whole business is so utterly different from my experience in Japan. The damage wrought by *dispar* in the forests and orchards of Bessarabia this season is enormous and parasite control seems to be most inefficient in checking the depredations of the caterpillars. When I think of the masterly and well-ordered attack of the Japanese sites and the splendid fashion in which they wiped out the caterpillars in large areas before depredation took place I am surprised by what I see here. [But in Kiev,] Kief, June 26, 1909. From what I can see in the field and from what I can gather from Prof. Pospielow, *dispar* was almost exterminated in this district last year through the activity of the parasites. Only a few isolated colonies seem to have survived, the most important of these being at Mishighari, a small place on the river about two hours by steamer from Kief. In this place, which is perhaps 100 acres in extent, the trees are plastered with cocoons of *Apanteles fulvipes*. The attack of the parasite was so thorough that the first generation seems to have been sufficient to wipe out the caterpillars, as I can find no large caterpillars about the place, and a few days will doubtless witness the complete wiping out of *dispar*.

The Russian observations seemed on the whole to indicate that in that country the gypsy moth is not controlled by its parasites to an extent which serves to remove it from the ranks of a destructive pest. Again according to Howard:

Conditions similar to those prevailing in Russia emphatically do not prevail in western Europe, nor, according to all accounts, in Japan. Natural conditions in western Europe and in Japan are in many respects more like those of our own Eastern States than are those of Kharkof Province. Conditions in Kief Province, even, are much more like those of Massachusetts than are those of Kharkof, and in Kief parasite control seemed to be an accomplished fact, although of course there is no assurance that it is continuous and perfect.

All told, Dr Howard made five foreign exploration trips to Europe, including Russia, in 1905, 1906, 1907, 1909, and 1910. During these trips he met virtually all the important and concerned entomologists of the day and through them, or agents they suggested, he arranged for the collection and shipment of the great masses of natural enemies that ultimately were received and colonized in Massachusetts. Prominent and especially helpful entomologists he consulted included Prof. F. Silvestri and Dr Leonardi, Portici (Naples), Italy; Prof. A. Berlese, Florence; Miss Marie Ruhl, Zurich; Dr G. Horvath, Prof. A. Mocsary and Prof. Josef Jablonowski, Budapest; Dr Paul Marchal, Paris; Dr Gustav Mayr, Vienna; and Prof. Sigismond Mokshetsky, Simferopol, Russia, to name but a few. He surveyed throughout the most important part of the European range of the moths from Transylvania and Russia on the southeast, to Brittany on the northeast and from Spain and Portugal on the southwest to the Baltic shores on the northeast. He rode the famous Oriental Express from Paris to Budapest, waded through newly fallen volcanic ash from Vesuvius to get to Silvestri's laboratory at Portici, and even rented an orchard in Kief, Russia, for the State of Massachusetts. Ultimately he perfected arrangements so that shipments from any part of Europe to Boston only spent at most 48 hours subjected to summer temperatures, 24 in Europe and 24 in America. The remainder of the time was spent in a special low-temperature holding room in Cherbourg, France, where all European collections were consigned or in the ship's cold-room. In the US, official arrangements were made for passage of shipments through customs without delay or opening. Professor Trevor Kincaid, a skilful collector and investigator on leave from the University of Washington, made two foreign trips, the first to Japan in 1908 and the second to Russia in 1909. The Japanese trip was quite successful. Kincaid knew various Japanese entomologists and received great co-operation from many of them, especially from Professor S. I. Kuwana, who was officially assigned to this work by the Japanese government. A large amount of material was sent home and many parasites colonized in New England. The Japanese devised excellent shipping boxes and material often arrived in better condition than that from Europe. The Japanese continued to ship material over subsequent years under Dr Kuwana's supervision. Later, under a new project during the period 1922–33, much additional material was sent in from Japan.

Kincaid surveyed the provinces bordering the Black Sea in the spring and summer of 1909. As noted earlier, the work of the natural enemies was not as impressive here as elsewhere in Europe but he made various shipments, especially from Kiev. However, owing principally to deficient transportation facilities the material received proved to be generally unsatisfactory.

The total numbers of parasites of both moth species imported and colonized from 1905 to 1911 is as follows:

	Number	
	Species	Individuals
Hymenopterous parasites	11	1 794 640
Tachinid parasites	16+	68 343
Predatory beetles	7	18 835
Total	34+	1 881 818

All told and including later shipments from Japan, as during the period 1922–33, more than forty species of natural enemies of the gypsy moth were imported and colonized. Eleven species – nine parasites and two predators – became established and between them they cause quite appreciable mortality of the gypsy moth, but generally this affords only partial control. Many parasites were reared or collected from established colonies and redistributed, so that by 1927 about ninety-two million parasites had been spread throughout the infested areas. Additionally, a wilt disease, or polyhedral virus, appeared in New England in 1907, doubtless introduced unknowingly with the European material. It becomes important only when infestations are damagingly heavy. The question persists if among the remaining twenty-nine natural enemy species not established, or others not yet discovered, the ultimate successful solution lies hidden. (See Clausen, 1956; Howard and Fiske, 1911.)

Sugar-cane leafhopper in Hawaii, 1904–20

In the early days sugar was king in Hawaii and any threat to it caused consternation. The sugar-cane leafhopper *Perkinsiella saccharicida* Kirkaldy was discovered in the islands by Dr R. C. L. Perkins in 1900 and by 1902 it was doing serious damage on Oahu. By mid-1903 it had been found on all of the Hawaiian islands and the next year a sharp drop in the total yield of sugar occurred. Large areas of sugar-cane actually were killed out. This emergency led the Hawaiian Sugar Planters Association to create a Division of Entomology and to employ a staff of entomologists on a full-time basis in 1904. Dr Perkins was appointed superintendent and his staff consisted of O. H. Swezey, G. W. Kirkaldy, F. W. Terry, Alexander Craw and Albert Koebele. These men and their successors proved to be pre-eminent in the field of biological control.

Kirkaldy, a specialist in leafhoppers, determined that closely allied species occurred in Java. Then Dr Perkins found leafhoppers on cane cuttings newly arrived from Queensland, Australia, and determined by correspondence and exchange of preserved specimens that the same species as in Hawaii occurred at Cairns, Queensland, but did no noticeable damage there. Thus the most important clue as to where to obtain effective natural enemies occurred from this simple detective work.

Dr Perkins and Koebele left for Queensland to search for natural enemies on May 11, 1904. Upon arrival in Brisbane and at Bundaberg in South Queensland they at once found the same leafhopper as in Hawaii, and observed a number of parasites. Koebele soon discovered the minute and previously unknown egg parasite, *Paranagrus optabilis* Perkins, that played a dominant role in the early reduction of the leafhopper in Hawaii. It was found to be generally distributed in Queensland and several shipments were made to Honolulu but the slow and difficult transport by ship resulted in nearly everything arriving greatly weakened or dead. However, a few direct colonizations of parasites were made by Terry on Oahu in August, October and November 1904. Then Dr Perkins stocked a breeding cage in Australia, arriving by ship in Honolulu December 14, 1904 with a few parasites surviving. In late January 1905, half of the parasites were liberated and half kept for breeding purposes. Dr Perkins' insectary culture prospered and more field liberations made. By the end of 1905 this parasite, *Paranagrus optabilis*, was recovered in the field. It became abundant and widespread in 1906 and during 1907 the leafhopper was greatly reduced by it. Meanwhile, a closely related species, *Anagrus frequens* Perkins, was found to be established, presumably from the late 1904 releases made by Terry, but it was of lesser importance. Another parasite species, *Ootetrastichus beatus* Perkins, was discovered in Fiji by Koebele during his return voyage from Australia. He returned with stocks of this in April 1905 and it rapidly became established and spread throughout the territory, but it also was of minor importance. At this time, after more than ten years of arduous foreign collecting for Hawaii, Koebele's health was failing, so he was put on a consulting basis and Dr Frederick Muir was engaged for the foreign work.

Dr Muir left nearly immediately and soon (March 1906) sent in another new parasite species from Fiji, *Haplogonatopus vitiensis* Perkins, but which again added little to the effect of the others. Then in China he discovered at Mei Chow another new parasite species, *Pseudogonatopus hospes* Perkins, which after much difficulty he succeeded in shipping alive to Honolulu in December 1906 and early in 1907. This became established and was additionally helpful to the other parasites. From 1907 to 1916 Muir explored extensively throughout the Malay archipelago, the Philippines, New Guinea, Formosa and Japan in connection with a variety of projects, but always searching for sugarcane leafhopper enemies. In Formosa during February 1916, he discovered another new species of egg parasite, *Ootetrastichus formosanus* Timb., and brought it alive to Honolulu. This was cultured and colonized in the field and proved to be an additional help to the already established species. Thus from 1904 to 1916, five species of parasites were successfully established, which produced excellent biological control on most of the Hawaiian sugar plantations. However, outbreaks continued to occur from time to time in certain areas and it seemed to be particularly where heavy rainfall normally occurred during much of the year.

By 1919 it was evident that in the wet areas such as the Hilo, Hawaii district, the leafhopper remained an especial problem. Thorough trials with chemical and other control measures proved futile and additional evidence confirmed the opinion that heavy and frequent rains seriously interfered with the egg parasites introduced by Koebele, Perkins and Muir. It was concluded that additional natural enemies that could operate efficiently under such conditions were needed.

Thus in May 1919 Muir went to Queensland, Australia, to carry out extended and detailed field studies. Nearly a year later he discovered *Cyrtorhinus mundulus* (Bredd) to be a highly effective predator of sugar-cane leafhopper eggs whereas previously it had been thought to be a sugar-cane-feeding insect and in fact had been recorded as a minor pest in Java. Both Koebele and Perkins, as well as Muir and others, had previously overlooked this predator principally because it belongs to the family Miridae in which most of the species suck plant sap.

Muir's discovery of its habits combined careful basic science and good luck – often the main ingredients in important discoveries. The story is best told in Muir's own words.

In 1919 I went to Australia to make further investigations of the habits of a small carabid beetle which I had noted previously preying upon Perkinsiella, but owing to the very exceptionally dry season these beetles were so scarce I could make no progress with this work, so turned my attention to other phases of the question. It soon came to my notice that a very large percentage of Perkinsiella eggs were dead and attacked by a fungus, a fact that Perkins noticed in 1903–4. I found the fungus in the form of yeast-like spores present in old egg shells from which the young had hatched, which could be recognized by the egg cap being off, and also in unhatched eggs, which in itself was intriguing. In moist cells these spores gave rise to mycelia and then to fruiting bodies and yeast-like spores similar to the original ones. Further investigation showed that these spores were present in all young and adult leafhoppers in the body cavity, where they multiplied by division; that they passed through the walls of the ovarian tubes and entered the young eggs, congregating in a small round ball at one end of the egg, and eventually becoming mostly incorporated into the embryo. As these were universal, it then became evident that the fungus could not be the cause of the dead eggs, as otherwise all could be destroyed. Upon killing the egg by pricking, the spores developed. This led to observations in the field to discover what led to the death of the egg. The fact was then revealed that *Cyrtorhinus mundulus* pierced the egg and sucked it. In some cases the egg was sucked nearly dry, in others the egg was only pierced and very little sucked, but it led to the death of the egg and to the development of the fungus. Thus the fungus is symbiotic and passes from adult to embryo and is always present. Whether the leafhopper can be reinfected by spores developed outside is not known. It is highly probable that the spores play some part in the metabolism of the insect, as similar bodies are found in all species of Delphacidae and many other Homoptera.

Thus we see that the least obvious of the death factors was the keystone of the complex and one that was overlooked by observers in different parts of the world.

How often this statement has proven to be true in succeeding projects over the years!

Muir returned with a cage of live *Cyrtorhinus* in June 1920, and after thorough testing to be absolutely certain that it would not live on sugar-cane leaves but required leafhopper eggs for food, releases were made in July 1920. In fact, according to Dr J. G. Myers, the West Indian entomologist, Dr Muir once told him that he had spent several sleepless nights considering the risks of the introduction should the bug not remain faithful to its egg-eating habit. C. E. Pemberton then went immediately to Fiji where *Cyrtorhinus* was known to occur and sent six well-stocked cages by ship to Honolulu from September through November. Abundant material was released in the field and some was cultured for future releases. It became established at once and by 1923 the leafhopper everywhere subsided to an insignificant level where it has remained ever since.

H. P. Agee wrote:

The value of this work in economic entomology cannot be measured in millions of dollars, regardless of how high we carry the count. It saved an industry that has been the mainstay of modern Hawaii...

(See Muir, 1931; Pemberton, 1948.)

This insect, *Rhabdoscelus obscurus* (Boisd.), was the second major pest in Hawaii to become the object of a biological control project. It was of south Pacific origin, quite possibly native to New Guinea and neighboring islands where it probably fed on sago and other palms as well as banana. It presumably adopted sugar-cane upon the intro- duction of that plant and was spread from island to island by natives carrying sections of sugar-cane along in their travels. It was a pest on cane in Hawaii as early as 1865. Albert Koebele regarded this beetle as the most injurious enemy of the sugar-cane in Hawaii in 1896 because of the damage its boring did to the cane and its difficulty of control.

It was conservatively estimated by Hawaiian entomologists that before parasites were introduced the annual loss from this insect amounted to from $750000 to $1000000, i.e. up to 1910. It did not threaten to wipe out the industry but was a continuing source of appreciable loss and complaint.

Dr F. A. G. Muir of the Hawaiian Sugar Planters Experiment Station commenced the foreign exploration for natural enemies of the borer from south China in January 1907. The successful completion of his mission occurred over three long years later and entailed a nearly unique odyssey in foreign exploration for natural enemies. The story has been well told by Pemberton (1948):*

At the time Muir began this adventure there was some published information concerning the borer. It received its name from specimens collected on New Ireland in 1835. In 1885 it was recorded from the Island of Larat and by 1895 literature referred to its presence in New Guinea. It was also known in Tahiti and was supposed to have reached Fiji from Hawaii. It had also reached North Queensland presumably in cane brought in from New Guinea. Muir thus had some grounds for suspecting that the native home of this borer was somewhere in New Guinea or the Malay Archipelago to the west. He began by spending about two months in the Federated Malay States searching for the borer but found none. He then spent 10 weeks in West Java studying borers allied to the cane borer. Here he found no true parasites; but a number of predatory insects (Histeridae and Hydrophilidae) were observed feeding on the grubs of these related borers that he found in palms and banana stumps. He failed to find the sought after cane borer in Java.

* Copyright ©1948, *Hawaiian Planters Record*, Honolulu. Reprinted by permission.

Muir then went to Borneo in July 1907 to undertake similar borer studies. He failed to find the cane borer; but again found predatory insects similar to those found in Java which fed on other borer grubs occurring in palms and banana stumps. He remained in Borneo until October 1, 1907 and then returned to Java to ship more of these predatory insects to Honolulu. These failed. Having found no promising natural enemy of various borers which he studied in Java and Borneo, Muir decided to move into regions where the cane borer was known to occur and on October 1, 1907, he left Batavia, Java and journeyed some 1500 miles eastward to the Island of Amboina, where he had reason to believe the borer could be found. Arriving at Amboina on October 9, he spent 6 weeks searching for the borer in sugar cane, but failed to find it. He then departed for Larat, a six-day steamer trip to the southeast, where the cane borer had been found by a wandering naturalist in 1885. Arriving at Larat on November 29, 1907, he soon found the cane borer in sugar cane and in sago-palm stalks and betel-nut palm stems. A month's study of these revealed no parasites and he returned to Amboina about January 9, 1908. Having learned at Larat that the borer occurred commonly in sago-palm leaf stalks, he renewed his search for borer parasites on Amboina and was rewarded with success as soon as he visited a sago-palm swamp. Here he immediately found the borer in the palm-leaf stalks and also discovered that from 25 to 90 percent of the borer grubs were parasitized by a tachinid fly, which was later described and named *Ceromasia sphenophori* by Dr J. Villeneuve. This is the parasite which ultimately checked the borer ravages in Hawaii. It is now known as *Microceromasia sphenophori* Vill. [The current name is *Lixophaga sphenophori* – author.]

To import this fly from Amboina to Honolulu alive in those days was a disheartening problem. Transportation was very slow and irregular and all material had to be sent to Macassar, Celebes, thence to Hong Kong and from there transshipped to Honolulu. Muir remained in Amboina eight months striving in various ways to surmount these difficulties. Several shipments of the fly were attempted but all failed. Mr Terry had been sent out to Hong Kong to receive and send on the consignments from that point to Honolulu. Muir sent 18 consignments of beneficial insects in all, many of which were histerid beetles which he found preying on borer grubs. With Terry's aid in handling this material at Hong Kong many of these beetles or their larvae reached Honolulu alive and were liberated in Hawaiian cane fields, but were never seen again. None of the flies survived the trip. Finally in September 1908, Muir personally conducted a consignment of the flies from Amboina to Hong Kong, but all died en route.

Muir then decided to return east to the Island of Ceram to devise other means, if possible, by which the parasite could be introduced into Hawaii. He had as a companion J. C. Kershaw, who had the year before published an excellent book on the butterflies of Hong Kong. They worked together in Ceram for a month without success. Knowing that the cane borer occurred in New Guinea, Muir laid plans to investigate its parasites there, if such could be found. He returned again to Macassar and obtained transportation to Port Moresby, New Guinea, on April 9, 1909. Soon after reaching Port Moresby he found the borer in sugar cane some 15 miles inland and immediately discovered the same parasite, which he first found in Amboina. This he soon attempted to bring to Honolulu alive via Thursday Island and Brisbane, Queensland, but he was forced into a hospital with typhoid fever at Brisbane and his consignment of flies, which was transshipped to Honolulu by a friend, arrived dead. After 5 weeks hospitalization in Brisbane, Muir returned to Honolulu to recuperate.

On January 8, 1910, Muir left Honolulu for Queensland to resume his labors on this problem. During the same month Mr Kershaw was engaged on the entomology staff. A relay station for breeding the parasite was established at Mossman, North Queensland, with Kershaw in charge. Muir then proceeded to Port Moresby again to obtain the parasite. A mail shipment to Kershaw failed and on April 22, 1910, Muir left Port Moresby for Mossman with a large consignment of parasite material in a living condition. After unexpected delays and other difficulties he finally reached Mossman with a good lot of living parasites. The borer being common in cane at Mossman, Kershaw had experienced no difficulty in having three large cages well stocked with borers awaiting Muir's arrival. This was on May 5. Some of these parasites were used to stock the cages for the production of a new generation. Though suffering from an attack of malaria at the time, Muir took the remainder of the parasites and departed for Fiji on the first available steamer. At Fiji, where the borer was numerous in cane, a cage containing borer-infested cane had been previously prepared by the Colonial Sugar Refining Company to await Muir's arrival. Upon reaching Fiji, Muir immediately placed the parasites in the cage and then was forced to enter a hospital for treatment and rest because of his malarial condition. Kershaw reached Fiji from Mossman, Queensland, on August 9 with the remainder of the parasites and by then Muir had sufficiently recovered to depart for Honolulu with Kershaw's cages and the one he had already prepared in Fiji. Muir arrived at Honolulu August 16 with a good stock of living parasitic material and a month later Kershaw arrived from Fiji with more which he had reared in Fiji from a portion he kept out of the original lot brought by Muir.

These flies were multiplied at the Station in large cages and distributed to the plantations for more than two years, resulting in the establishment of this beneficial insect on all parts of Hawaii where sugar cane was grown, and, during the ensuing years, in the savings of millions of dollars.

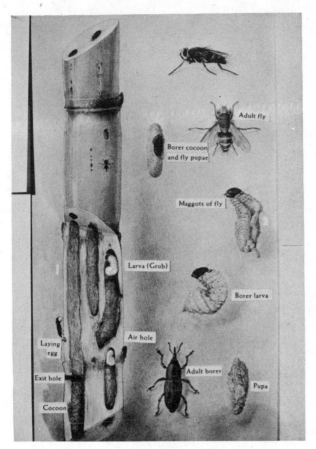

Fig. 21. Various developmental stages of the sugar-cane beetle borer and its parasite. Courtesy of Asher K. Ota, Hawaiian Sugar Planters Experiment Station.

Fig. 21 shows various developmental stages of the beetle and the parasite.

To make the story more complete, a subsequent change in variety from soft- to hard-rind canes which are not as susceptible to the borer, along with the constant operation of the parasites from New Guinea further reduced the borer so that damage became even more negligible (see Pemberton, 1948). However, in the 1960s an inadvertent change to susceptible varieties on the island of Kauai again led to an increase in the borer problem. This is being ameliorated by replanting with partially resistant varieties. It is expected that this change, combined with the biological control being exerted by *Lixophaga*, will keep the borer below economic levels.

This work was undertaken at the time the gypsy moth and brown-tail moth parasite work was at its peak and was generating considerable enthusiasm. The citrus whitefly *Dialeurodes citri* Ashmead then was by far the most serious pest of citrus in the gulf states from Florida to Texas. Overall, considering the injury it caused and the difficulty in control, it could be considered the most serious pest of citrus in the entire country. In Florida it was estimated that the loss in an average infested grove was 45–50 percent of the normal value of the crop and statewide the annual loss was over half a million dollars. This led to demands from Florida for foreign exploration to discover natural enemies of the whitefly.

Dr L. O. Howard assigned Russell S. Woglum to travel abroad and import any natural enemies he might discover. Just previously Woglum had been perfecting the HCN fumigation method for scale insect control in California. The US Congress, contrary to its stand when money was sought for the cottony-cushion scale project, readily made a special appropriation in 1910 for the purpose of searching the world to discover the native home of the citrus whitefly and to learn if it was held in check by natural enemies. Woglum soon decided that special emphasis should be placed on a search of tropical and sub-tropical oriental areas based upon the presumption that citrus was native to the Orient and because specimens of the citrus whitefly from Japan, southern China and India were present in the collection of the Bureau of Entomology in Washington. He set sail on July 31, 1910 via the Mediterranean where he failed to locate any citrus whitefly in the citrus groves of Spain, Italy or Sicily. Proceeding to Ceylon, again no citrus whitefly was found.

His first objective in India was the great Indian Museum in Calcutta where he soon found specimens of the citrus whitefly collected in the northwestern Himalayas about 1893 and also some from a remote locality named Kulu in northwest India. Kulu was virtually impossible to reach with the primitive transportation available, so Woglum decided to concentrate on government botanical gardens in north India which generally had a large variety of fruit trees. The oldest botanical garden in a known citrus area was learned to be at Saharanpur. Soon after arriving he found the citrus whitefly to be generally distributed but rather scarce and not a pest. Nearly at once he found a tiny ladybeetle, *Cryptognatha flavescens* Motsch., feeding on eggs and larvae of the whitefly. After several days' collecting, he carefully prepared a shipment which was forwarded to the American Consul-General at Calcutta, who placed it in charge of the captain of a cargo steamer sailing directly to the United States. Unfortunately all specimens arrived in Florida dead. A second sending also failed.

Moving on to Lahore in the Punjab in November, Woglum found a fine botanical garden and abundant citrus. Again the citrus whitefly was found to be generally distributed but scarce. He soon found emergence holes made in the mummified whitefly pupae by the exit of a minute parasitic wasp but due to the cold weather no adult parasites could be found. From infested leaves sent to Dr Howard, the parasite was determined to be new to science and was named *Prospaltella lahorensis* Howard.

Because it was then winter and live specimens were scarce, Woglum decided to survey as much new territory as possible. Throughout India he found the whitefly wherever citrus was grown and nearly always found evidence of the parasite as well. He proceeded on through Burma, Java, south China, and the Philippines but saw a few citrus whiteflies only at Macau near Hong Kong. Howard had cabled Woglum to return to Lahore and prepare shipments of the natural enemies for Florida but Woglum fell ill, probably with malaria, and had to spend a month in the hospital in Manila. He finally returned to Lahore in April 1911 and after a painstaking search found a fairly good source of whiteflies on an ornamental citrus hedge which became his main material.

Elaborate special preparations had to be made to get the natural enemies alive from north interior India to Florida in the year of 1911. The trip from India to Florida took five to six weeks and the entire life cycle of the parasite was only about three weeks, so that the adult parasites would emerge and die en route unless living whitefly material was available in which they could lay eggs and start a new generation. This meant considerable innovation in artificially infesting nursery trees with citrus whitefly in different stages and in cages in order to exclude and eliminate other pests. These infested trees, inoculated with the natural enemies, would then be shipped in Wardian cages – a sort of portable miniature greenhouse.

With the coming of the monsoon rains in August the fall brood of adult whiteflies emerged and laid eggs on the potted nursery trees. Good infestations developed and by mid-October all was ready. Three Wardian cages were filled with material parasitized by *Prospaltella*

Fig. 22. Wardian cages on oxen used to transport infested plants bearing natural enemies of the citrus whitefly at the beginning of their long journey from Lahore, India, to Florida in 1911. From Woglum (1913).

lahorensis and two with the predator, *Cryptognatha*. A sixth cage contained uninfested trees. Woglum's cages being started on their trip by ox cart are shown in Fig. 22. Leaving Lahore on October 20, Woglum proceeded by train to Bombay and thence by steamer for Europe as there was no through vessel to New York. Careful planning enabled good connections and trans-shipments to be made at Port Said and Naples, so little delay occurred. En route he cared for the cages like a mother hen, finally arriving in New York exactly one month out of Bombay and five weeks from Lahore.

The cages were immediately sent by express to Orlando, Florida, arriving December 2 at the government laboratory. Examination showed twenty-eight live healthy beetles and eight adult parasites, as well as a large number of developing immature parasites. Sufficient material was on hand for successful culture and all seemed promising.

Unfortunately at this time the whiteflies in Florida were in the winter-dormant pupal stage which is not suitable for either the predator or parasite which only attack younger stages; the result being that both species were lost before spring. For reasons unknown such importations to Florida were never tried again, although Woglum outlined what he considered to be a feasible procedure.

Only today is the finale being written. The citrus whitefly was found at several places in California in 1967, and in 1968 the author began importations of *Prospaltella lahorensis* from India and West Pakistan, only this time much more simply and rapidly by airmail. We now have this parasite established in California and are sending it to Florida as well. The predator is next in line and should be easy to import today.

The sad part of the story is that these natural enemies could have been reimported to Florida and doubtless established many years ago, thus, probably preventing considerable economic loss and reducing or eliminating the necessity for chemical sprays for the whitefly. (See Woglum, 1913.)

Spiny blackfly in Japan, 1925

This is an example of how simply some pest problems can be solved by biological control. The project was casually arranged on a co-operative basis and as far as I can learn, cost nothing. Nonetheless, it is a great economic success ranking among the best in the world.

The so-called spiny blackfly *Aleurocanthus spiniferus* Quaint., which technically is a member of the whitefly family Aleurodidae, was discovered near Nagasaki in Japan by Professor I. Kuwana and Dr T. Ishii about 1922, although it probably already had been present and spreading for some time. Within a few years it became one of the serious pests of citrus trees in the southern island of Kyushu. Spraying and fumigation failed to bring relief.

No effective natural enemies occurred in Japan and it was surmised that the pest came from south China which is in the native home range of citrus and where the spiny blackfly was known to occur. Entomologists and horticulturalists were considering an attempt to discover natural enemies on the mainland when Professor F. Silvestri of Portici (Naples), Italy, who was on a temporary foreign exploration mission for the University of California to find parasites of the California red scale, visited Japan. At that time he was requested by the Japanese to be on the look-out for enemies of the spiny blackfly upon his return to the Asiatic mainland.

Professor Silvestri obliged and on his second trip to Nagasaki, Japan, May 23, 1925, brought with him a parasite, *Prospaltella smithi* Silv., and a ladybeetle, *Cryptognatha* sp. Professor Kuwana met him there and on May 25 Silvestri and Ishii colonized them on heavily infested trees in the village of Ikiriki, near Nagasaki. In all there were twenty parasites and ten beetles. The beetles apparently were never seen again, but the parasites were a different story. By the end of November, adult parasites were easily found on the leaves of the original release tree. However, because Nagasaki has a colder winter than Canton it was feared that the parasites might not overwinter successfully.

These fears were allayed when parasite activity was noted on the release tree in June 1926 and it was found that 74 percent of the whitefly pupae had exit holes from which adult parasites had emerged. Spread occurred rapidly and was aided by distribution of leaves bearing parasitized pupae, so that within a short time the pest was almost completely eliminated. All this came about from an initial stock of only twenty parasites hand carried in a small vial. Control remains perfect to the present day, as I can attest from personal observations made throughout the citrus areas of Japan in recent years. (See Kuwana, 1934.)

Prickly pear cactus in Australia, 1920–5

This was a massive, long-term project comparable in this respect to the gypsy and brown-tail moth project and represents the first striking success in biological control of a weed. Numerous entomologists and assistants were employed and a great deal of foreign exploration carried out in the Americas ranging from the United States to Argentina.

Ironically, but for an unfortunate fluke, the natural enemy *Cactoblastis cactorum* Berg, which caused the ultimate destruction of the prickly pear, could have done the job at least ten years earlier than it did and with a minimum of cost. It would have been another simple, nearly miraculous success like the cottony-cushion scale–vedalia project. It seems that Mr Henry Tyron, one of a pair of members of a Queensland Prickly Pear Travelling Commission, was impressed by the potentialities of the *Cactoblastis* work he saw in Argentina and actually brought a small number of larvae back to Australia in 1914; unfortunately he was not able to rear these through to maturity or we might have had quite a different story. No project activity followed this until 1920 and *Cactoblastis* was not imported until 1925.

The enormity of the prickly pear problem in Australia is difficult to conceive. Evidently various species were brought by the early settlers as ornamentals and escaped. Two species, *Opuntia inermis* and

O. stricta, assumed major catastrophic pest proportions but several others were pests in more localized districts. These two obtained their footing in the 1800s when the country was being opened for grazing and population was sparse. From 1900 on, the cacti spread rapidly, reaching a peak about 1925 when 60000000 acres were heavily infested, 30000000 of which were so dense that the land was completely useless. Actually hundreds of miles were impenetrable to man or beast. Otherwise it was good grazing land with potential for dairying and general farming. Eighty percent of the infested land was in Queensland and 20 percent in New South Wales. The cost of chemical or mechanical control was more than the land was worth, hence was out of the question. During the peak years the rate of spread of the cactus was alarming; year by year more land became unoccupied and more holdings and homesteads deserted.

The project which led to ultimate and complete success began with the appointment of the Commonwealth Prickly Pear Board in 1920. Their first steps were to send entomologists to America and to establish insectaries and quarantine facilities in Australia. They early decided to concentrate on cactus-feeding insects rather than disease organisms because disease didn't appear to be important in the field, several diseases occurred accidentally in Australia already, and there was the question of the disease perhaps transferring to other plants. The entomological work in America centered in the United States, Mexico, and Argentina where experimental centers were maintained; however, virtually all other American countries were surveyed.

Altogether 150 species of insects restricted to feeding on cactus of one sort or another were discovered. About fifty species were sent to Australia, totaling more than 500000 individuals. All imported material was screened through a central quarantine and culture laboratory at Brisbane and subjected to starvation tests on a wide variety of other plants before being sent out to local breeding or colonization stations. Final tabulation showed that twelve species of prickly pear insects had become established and were exerting some measure of control when the establishment and final success by *Cactoblastis* put an end to further trials.

Larvae of *Cactoblastis cactorum* were collected, apparently by Alan P. Dodd, at Concordia, Argentina, in late January 1925, and taken to Buenos Aires. It is interesting to note that they came from two different species of *Opuntia* than those they were destined to subjugate in Australia. Moths emerged in February and readily laid many eggs.

119

Six Wardian cages were filled with *Opuntia* for food and 3000 *Cactoblastis* eggs were placed on the prickly pear in the cages. In March the shipment went by steamer via Cape Town to Australia. Some 250 larvae were removed for examination at Cape Town so the original shipment then included 2750, and this gave rise to all Australian stocks. The unsupervised cages arrived in Brisbane ten weeks and 14000 miles later in May 1925 in excellent condition, containing about half-grown larvae. This was readily possible as cactus pads may last several months. These larvae were given food and they successfully pupated in August–September 1925, producing 1137 cocoons. One thousand and seventy moths emerged and produced 100605 eggs, a return of nearly 36-fold. From then on success was assured.

Had this shipment not succeeded, it is problematical whether, or at least when, another would have been made. Dodd returned to North America following the shipment because Argentina had a limited fauna of *Opuntia* insects and he had no particular reason to believe that *Cactoblastis* might be more successful than other *Opuntia* feeding insects. According to Dodd, 'certainly, its remarkable achievements could not have been foretold'. Thus, if the one shipment had not resulted in establishment, further investigations in the Argentine may not have been undertaken for several years. Again we see the common combination for successful scientific discovery – good basic research along with a measure of serendipity.

The first colonizations of *Cactoblastis* consisting of 2263150 eggs were made in various localities in Queensland and New South Wales during February–March 1926. By March 1927, 10196150 eggs had been released in the field. Redistribution of eggs obtained from field material finally amounted to 389225520 by November 1929.

Establishment and increase occurred so rapidly that by 1930–2 the general collapse and destruction of the original stands of prickly pear had occurred. Mile after mile of dense growth collapsed in a few months under the concentrated attack of enormous numbers of larvae. Some spectacular examples showing prickly pear infestations before and after clean-up by *Cactoblastis* are shown in Figs. 23 and 24. According to Dodds the most optimistic scientific opinion could not have foreseen the extent and completeness of the destruction. The spectacle of mile after mile of heavy prickly pear growth collapsing *en masse* and disappearing in the short space of a few years did not appear to fall within the bounds of possibility. The other cactus natural enemies were generally eliminated at the same time but this

(a)

(b)

Fig. 23. Biological control of prickly pear cactus by *Cactoblastis* in Queensland, Australia. (*a*) Cactus-infested range before the establishment of *Cactoblastis*, (*b*) virtual elimination of cactus following release of *Cactoblastis*. From Dodd (1925).

121

Fig. 24. Biological control of prickly pear cactus by *Cactoblastis* in Queensland, Australia. (*a*) Homestead abandoned because of prickly pear infestation, (*b*) homestead reoccupied following clean-up of cactus by *Cactoblastis*. From Dodd (1925).

Fig. 25. Various stages of the coconut moth, *Levuana irridescens*; (1) adult male, (2) adult female, (3) egg cluster on coconut leaf, (4) fifth instar larva, (5) pupa. From Tothill, Taylor and Paine (1930).

made no difference. Following the kill-off of the cactus plants, the *Cactoblastis* population naturally collapsed and during 1932–3 a heavy regrowth of cactus occurred from the roots. However, *Cactoblastis* responded to this and destroyed the regrowth during 1933–5. From then on until today the prickly pears have remained under virtual complete control and the former densely infested country reclaimed and brought into production. (See Dodd, 1940.)

Fig. 26. Destruction of coconut palms in Fiji by the coconut moth *Levuana irridescens* before the importation of natural enemies. From Tothill, Taylor and Paine (1930).

Coconut moth in Fiji, 1925

This pretty little purple moth, *Levuana irridescens* B-B. (see Fig. 25), had become such a pest by 1924 that the entire copra industry was threatened with disaster and the Government of Fiji offered a prize of £5000 (quite a sum then) to anyone who could devise a remedy. Before any solution was forthcoming, and having become convinced that the best approach lay in biological control research by professional entomologists, the offer was withdrawn, and J. D. Tothill, R. W. Paine and T. H. C. Taylor were hired and brought in to attack the problem. They were to co-operate closely with H. W. Simmonds, Government Entomologist.

The coconut was the chief source of wealth of the native Fijians and it enabled islands to be inhabited and prosperous that otherwise would be barren. Historically the coconut moth had been restricted to the large island of Viti Levu and was considered native there. As a consequence of the damage, coconuts were never considered a commercial crop. The threat developed as the moth spread to other islands causing defoliation and crop failure. The coconuts on islands attacked

124

by *Levuana* turned from the normal fringe of shining green fronds to a band of lifeless grey. At the close of an outbreak not a single green palm was to be seen. An example of the destruction is seen in Fig. 26.

Because *Levuana* was originally known only from Viti Levu and there it had no parasites of any consequence, it was suspected that it might be an exotic invader. However, after painstaking search throughout the south Pacific islands and southeast Asia the species was never found other than in Fiji. H. W. Simmonds searched in this regard during 1923 in the New Hebrides, Bismarcks, Solomon Islands and New Guinea but found neither *Levuana* nor any allied species. However, a related moth, *Artona catoxantha*, had been known for some time to occur in Java and Malaya and to be well parasitized. In 1924 attempts were made through co-operating entomologists to obtain the *Artona* parasites. Several parasite species were collected in abundance in Java and twice sent by ships' cold storage to Fiji but necessarily via Sydney because there was no direct route. The long unattended sea voyages of 4000 miles and one month duration resulted in failure of the insects to survive.

Tothill, the new project director, arrived early in 1925, and along with the Levuana Committee procceded to draw up a plan of action. So little was known of realistic possibilities at that time that such miscellaneous approaches were decided upon as the importation of a series of general parasites of non-related hosts from Hawaii in the hope that one or two might attack *Levuana*, trials with the predatory ant, *Oecophylla smaragdina*, which is used in the Orient to control certain citrus pests, and possible importation of coconut-inhabiting insectivorous birds from Ceylon, India, etc. These approaches either failed or were finally rejected as impractical, undesirable, or unfeasible. The part of the plan that paid off was the decision to continue the search for *Levuana* or closely related forms and their parasites, and to reattempt the introduction of the parasites of *Artona catoxantha*. Even the latter was a long-shot because it meant that the parasites would have to transfer from *Artona* to *Levuana*, which not only is a different genus but, in fact, a different subfamily. Often host specificity prevents such transfers but from previous studies he had made of forest moths in Canada, Tothill had learned that in certain cases the same parasites could attack distinctly different host species, hence he concluded that a similar result might be feasible with *Levuana*.

Beginning in 1925 foreign exploration was conducted throughout Melanesia and Indonesia by Taylor, Tothill and Paine. Nine species related to *Levuana* ultimately were found, mostly quite rare and heavily parasitized, and Taylor even returned to Fiji once with a shipment of *Artona* parasites but none survived. Because of the rarity of most species, coupled with the fact that *Artona catoxantha* was more readily available in Java and other parts of Indonesia and was known to have at least two promising parasites, *Ptyochomyia* and *Apanteles*, it was decided to concentrate on importing these two. This would be the third attempt.

H. W. Simmonds was sent to Kuala Lumpur early in 1925 to seek out a possible *Artona* outbreak and meanwhile Taylor was travelling in the then Federated Malay States when he located a small outbreak of *Artona* about 300 miles from Singapore at Batu Gajah. Both species of parasites were present. Simmonds joined him there to prepare as large a shipment as possible for Fiji. This was to be effected in seventeen large Wardian-type ventilated cages, each of which would hold four or five small coconut seedlings infested with both parasitized and unparasitized larvae of *Artona*. The latter were to serve as hosts for egg-laying by parasites emerging en route. Finally about 20000 larvae were placed on the 85 young palms and sent the 300 miles to Singapore by rail.

The difficulties facing them in getting a shipment through alive to Fiji were stupendous. It had been decided for a variety of reasons that direct shipment from Singapore to Fiji was required but principally because of Australian quarantines. However, there were virtually no direct sailings, so most went by Australia. Also the collections and shipments had to be made when the insects were available, but this had to coincide with the availability of a ship which often was months apart. About the only hope was the Clan Line of cargo boats which ran between London and Fiji, sometimes via Singapore. In June it was learned by cable that the *Clan Mackay* would sail from Singapore on July 10 for Fiji but not direct. Meanwhile it was learned, again by cable, that *Clan Matheson* was sailing from Java direct to Suva, Fiji, on July 10, so for an extra £250 sterling the *Clan Mackay* was instructed to call at Surabaya, Java, to transfer the parasites to the *Clan Matheson* which would be ready to sail. Thus several days were saved although it still took twenty-five days following collection to reach Suva. Taylor accompanied this shipment to supervise and care for it en route, arriving in Suva on August 3, 1925, and immediately conveyed the cages to the quarantine insectary built for this purpose (see Fig. 27).

Fig. 27. (a) Landing on Ra island of the first colony of the coconut moth parasite *Ptychomyia remota* to be released from the Suva insectary. (b) The *Ptychomyia* insectary at Suva. (c) *Ptychomyia* breeding cages outside the insectary after release from quarantine. From Tothill, Taylor and Paine (1930).

Examination showed about 315 live adult parasitic flies of *Ptychomyia* (Fig. 28) but no *Apanteles* which had all perished on the way. The tachinid flies were transferred to cages stocked with *Levuana* larvae and to everyone's joy proceeded to attack them at once. By August 21 the first generation of new adult flies began to emerge and insectary culture was assured. Within six months, i.e. by January 20, 1926, over 15000 flies had been bred and colonized over the *Levuana*-infested districts. The potential of the fly was first realized when just two months after importation, the parasites were found to be accidentally

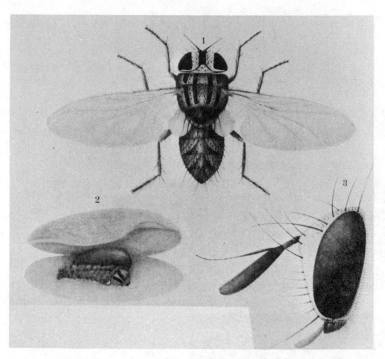

Fig. 28. *Ptychomyia remota*, the parasitic tachinid fly that controlled the coconut moth in Fiji. (1) Adult, (2) cocoon of the coconut moth opened to show the skin of the larva (below) that has previously been killed by the larval tachinid parasite which has pupated (above), (B) side view of head of adult *Ptychomyia*. From Tothill, Taylor and Paine (1930).

established around the insectary. From this time in October onward, the dispersal of the fly was remarkably rapid and it was found to be established throughout all *Levuana* zones within six months of the first liberation.

The control results were just as remarkable. Within three months of liberation of the Suva colony, *Levuana* was exterminated on the original release trees. Six months after the initial introduction of *Ptychomyia*, many of the outbreaks of *Levuana* had subsided completely. When the final report was written in 1929, there had been no new outbreak of *Levuana* for three years and the insect had become so rare that reputedly a visiting entomologist searching specially for it would almost certainly fail. It seems especially significant that this single natural enemy, *Ptychomyia remota*, apparently has given better control of its adopted host *Levuana* than it did of its native host

Artona, although such control was perfectly satisfactory. This should serve as a good indication of some of the unexplored possibilities remaining in biological control research. (See Tothill, Taylor and Paine, 1930.)

Eucalyptus snout-beetle in South Africa, 1926

In the early 1920s, species of *Eucalyptus* were highly important timber and ornamental trees in South Africa. Mining companies alone had had about 10000 acres of plantations and many times more thousands of acres were held by municipalities and private individuals. These trees had been remarkably free of insect problems but in 1916 the eucalyptus snout-beetle *Gonipterus scutellatus* Gyll. was discovered at Cape Town. The beetle spread rapidly and by 1924 was found at Pietermaritzburg, Natal, a great distance from Cape Town, as well as in the highveld of the Transvaal. By now the beetle was threatening the entire eucalyptus-growing industry of the country, and continued to rapidly invade new areas. Continued feeding damage actually killed trees but most damage resulted from greatly reduced growth and the formation of knots and malformations in the wood. Many blocks of trees were felled as no longer worth keeping owing to the depredations of the beetle.

C. P. Lounsbury, Chief of the Division of Entomology, believed that the solution of the problem lay in the introduction of natural enemies from the native home, Australia. Additionally, all other control measures had failed. After fruitless negotiations with Australian and New Zealand authorities to have a study made and parasites shipped, he finally got the financial backing he needed from his own government and in January 1925 appointed Dr F. G. C. Tooke to head up the project and to go to Australia in search of natural enemies in 1926.

Before leaving for Australia in June 1926, Tooke corresponded with Australian entomologists regarding the snout-beetle and its parasites, but about all he learned was that the beetle was extremely scarce, probably ranged from Queensland, through New South Wales and Victoria to South Australia and Tasmania, and that nothing was known of its natural enemies. It appeared to Tooke as if he would be looking for the proverbial needle in a haystack. He arrived at Adelaide, South Australia, on July 19, 1926 and at once contacted Mr A. M. Lea, a taxonomic specialist in the genus *Gonipterus,* who had specimens of *G. scutellatus* from Tasmania, New South Wales, Victoria and South

Fig. 29. The mymarid egg parasite *Anaphoidea   tens* that controlled the eucalyptus snout-beetle in South Africa. (*a*) Adult, (*b*) adult ovipositing in an egg mass of the snout-beetle on a eucalyptus leaf. From Tooke (1953).

Australia. Inasmuch as *Eucalyptus viminalis* was known to be a preferred host, he searched out this species in the countryside near Penola and eleven days after arrival, on August 1, he found some egg masses of the beetle in question. Returning to Adelaide, dissection of the eggs showed many eggs to contain a small hymenopterous mymarid parasite. This proved to be new to science and was described by Girault as *Anaphoidea nitens* (see Fig. 29). Subsequent searching around Melbourne and elsewhere failed to yield any beetles, so he returned to Penola on August 20 to collect parasitized egg masses. Enough material was collected to send off the first shipment from Adelaide to Durban, South

Fig. 30. F. G. C. Tooke's living quarters and laboratory in the bush in South Australia where he spent nearly a year during 1926–7 in his quest for parasites of the eucalyptus snout-beetle. From Tooke (1953).

Africa, on August 24, 1926. At this time he also found the snout-beetle larvae to be parasitized by a tachinid fly but in low numbers.

Although Tooke scouted considerably on several occasions in Victoria and New South Wales he never found collecting to be as good as in the *Eucalyptus* stand some ten miles from the small town of Penola, so he set up field headquarters there, where he was compelled by necessity to live and work in a small wooden shack (see Fig. 30). He put in the best part of a year here, which must have been a lonely, but most surely, a dedicated existence. He soon learned from field and laboratory counts that the egg parasite was highly effective and lacked any hyperparasites. The latter point meant that there was no danger in making direct shipments to South Africa.

An idea of the extent of natural control of the beetle was gained from the fact that he had to search several square miles of country to collect 200 egg capsules and this was in the Penola district, the best collecting area he discovered. In South Africa at that time, many egg capsules could be collected from one small tree in a few minutes.

Once he had found the parasites, Tooke's big problem, like so many other foreign explorers, was how to get them home alive. The long journey by sea from Adelaide to Durban took three weeks and at least

131

a week was needed to collect material prior to shipment. This meant that the parasite which had a life cycle of 17–24 days at normal temperatures would emerge en route, and the adults would in all likelihood die. The scarcity of material precluded such a risk being taken. Tooke chose the alternative of using the ship's cool-room (about 35–40 °F) to slow down the development of the egg parasite and this proved successful using specially constructed, well-insulated teakwood boxes.

The second shipment of parasitized eggs was made on September 23, 1926 from Adelaide and a third shipment on October 12. On February 27, 1927, Lounsbury cabled instructions to concentrate on the tachinid larval parasite as the egg parasite *Anaphoidea* was then definitely established in South Africa. This was just six months after the first shipment was made.

Although three shipments of the tachinid were sent to South Africa, most flies were dead on arrival and those that emerged subsequently failed to reproduce. Tooke arrived back in Cape Town, December 31, 1927 after more than a year and a half away from home.

Mass production and widespread field colonization of *Anaphoidea* was then rapidly increased. From 1926 to 1933, 736 395 parasites were released in hundreds of plantations throughout the Union. Its ability to spread long distances was demonstrated; in one case it dispersed more than 100 miles from the nearest site of liberation within one year.

According to Tooke, the control exercised by the parasite far exceeded expectations. Results in South Africa were spectacular in some districts but much slower in others. This is the only known case of complete biological control where rates of control varied so greatly in different districts. This was due to differential effects of climate on the parasite's rate of increase. The period varied from three years, which is the more usual, to as much as twenty-three years in the most extreme climates. Perhaps a strain of the parasite slowly developed to operate successfully in the extreme climates. Complete control was achieved by 1933 in all of the southwestern and southern Cape province, which has a climate similar to that of South Australia. By 1936 complete control had occurred everywhere on all *Eucalyptus* species at elevations below 1200 m (4000 ft), as well as on 62 of the 65 species of *Eucalyptus* occurring above this altitude.

It is significant that this is the only case of complete biological control attributed to an egg parasite acting alone. How much better and more rapid the control might have been had the tachinid parasite been successfully established remains an intriguing question. (See Tooke, 1953.)

As the biological control of the coconut moth was drawing to a successful conclusion, another serious menace to coconuts and the copra industry was rapidly increasing. The coconut scale *Aspidiotus destructor* Sign., first recorded as a pest of bananas in 1912, then of coconuts in 1916, was spreading at an alarming rate on coconuts by 1920. Damage was great enough to cause H. W. Simmonds, the Government Entomologist of Fiji, to seek natural enemies in Tahiti in 1920 where the scale was known to be present but much less severe. He imported and established two parasite species, *Aphytis chrysomphali* Mercet and *Aspidiotiphagus citrinus* Craw, and by 1925 had distributed them to many islands of the group. The spread of these parasites was rapid and they were considered to be doing some good, but the scale continued to spread to new islands and to cause severe outbreaks.

This insect, like all other scales, as well as whiteflies, mealybugs and aphids, sucks the plant juices. It prefers the undersides of the leaves and in severe infestations forms a continuous overlapping crust of countless thousands per coconut leaf. This results in the leaf turning yellow, withering, and even dying in severe cases.

By 1927, in spite of rigid quarantines, the scale had spread to nearly all of the Fiji island group and was the most serious pest of coconut in Fiji, since *Levuana*, the coconut moth, had been decimated by the imported parasite *Ptychomyia*. The coconut scale was not quite so generally severe as the *Levuana* moth had been but it was not unusual for trees to become completely defoliated and many trees were killed after two or more outbreaks. Neither chemical nor mechanical control methods proved feasible for a variety of reasons.

In 1926, an attempt was made to secure additional natural enemies, this time from Java. T. H. C. Taylor was given this assignment which was fraught with transportation difficulties because of the lengthy sea voyage and the paucity of ships sailing from Java to Fiji. However, as luck would have it, Taylor was able to make arrangements to ship his parasites and predators on a vessel carrying a cargo of other organisms to Fiji: Indian coolies. Little did these indentured laborers dream that some day they and their descendents would be the numerical and political majority in Fiji.

The coolie steamer *Ganges* out of India, stopped in Java on January 1, 1927 and sailed on to Fiji on January 2 with Taylor bringing his infested coconut palms in Wardian cages. Three weeks later they arrived in Fiji, but a severe outbreak of smallpox on board prevented the shipment being landed at Suva but rather on the quarantine island of Nukulau, where the insects had to be tended for another five weeks with poor rearing facilities and limited stocks of scales. As a result, although some parasites and predators were colonized on Nukulau and later around Suva and some recoveries made, no permanent establishment occurred.

After mid-year 1927, it was evident that the enemies from Java either were ineffective or were not established at all. Consequently, J. D. Tothill, then Director of Agriculture for Fiji, assigned Taylor to go to Trinidad to investigate several species of ladybeetles which Urich had recorded as being important factors in the control of the coconut scale there.

Taylor started work in Trinidad in September 1927 with a survey of the natural enemies present. He found five species of ladybeetles to be more or less common and effective, even though at times they were heavily attacked by parasites of their own. These latter he subsequently took care to exclude from the shipments. By January 28, 1928, his collections of live ladybeetles and his stocks of scale-infested palms were ready and were loaded on board ship. Nine large cages were used, holding from six to eight or more infested young palms. Three newly designed extra large cages required four men to lift and move them. Additional food for the predators in the form of eighty heavily scale-infested young palms were carried along in five-gallon tins. All had to be carefully arranged to protect them from rough handling and damage from salt water during the voyage.

Although Taylor limited his initial predator stocks to 200 adult beetles, plus some larvae and pupae, per cage, the predators increased so rapidly during the voyage that many had to be removed to keep them from completely eliminating the food supply and thus starving to death before arrival in Fiji. Trans-shipment of the stock was made at Panama, February 1, 1928 to a steamer going via Tahiti to Suva, Fiji. The entire trip took just over five weeks.

All five species of ladybeetles arrived in Fiji in sufficient numbers to enable culture to be started, but more than twice as many *Cryptognatha nodiceps* Mshl. (1517) as compared to all of the other four species (746) came through, which may have been an indication of the ultimate exclusively dominant role played by *Cryptognatha*.

Problems developed with insectary culture in Fiji, so with a little ingenuity Taylor devised a method of breeding in the field within cloth-sleeve-covered, heavily infested banana leaves. In each sleeve, starting with twenty beetles, he would recover about 300 in one month's time, a return of fifteen to one with very little expense or labor. By September 1928, it was evident that *C. nodiceps* had by far the greatest potential, so breeding of the others was stopped and the small stocks of those remaining were liberated. Some of these became temporarily established but evidently eventually disappeared after *Cryptognatha nodiceps* became completely dominant.

Cryptognatha nodiceps was a remarkable and spectacular success. Only nine months after the introduction of this beetle into Fiji, the coconut scale was reduced to non-economic levels in all important islands of the group. After eighteen months (i.e. in September 1929) the scale was controlled completely on every single island and was so rare in many localities, where formerly it had been heavy, that it was difficult to find individual specimens. During the peak of the clean-up, adult beetles and larvae swarmed on every tree and the adults could be readily seen flying around in the air. The trees soon changed from yellow to bright green. Such rapid and thorough results exceeded all expectations.

When Taylor published his report of this success in 1935, not a single new outbreak had occurred. The ladybeetle constituted a permanent and effective check. The same results occurred on all host plants, many of which had been as badly infested as coconuts. The writer visited Fiji in 1969 and carefully surveyed for coconut scale. The scales – even single individuals – were virtually impossible to find on coconut, even though an occasional *Cryptognatha* adult was seen rapidly searching the clean leaves. It evidently is an excellent searcher that can survive at very low host densities like the vedalia beetle. Additionally, it probably feeds on alternative host scales on other host plants. It is interesting to note, however, that the *Aphytis* mentioned earlier is still rather common on coconut scale in Fiji. I found only one light infestation of the scale in 1969, and that only on avocado, but parasitization by *Aphytis* was considerable. Perhaps, after all, *Cryptognatha* should not be given all the credit, just as the vedalia beetle likewise should not in California. (See Taylor, 1935.)

Citrophilus mealybug in California, 1928

The highly successful biological control of the citrophilus mealybug *Pseudococcus fragilis* Brain (= gahani) ranks second only to that of the

135

cottony-cushion scale in California. Today this insect is so extremely rare that few field entomologists or citrus growers have ever seen it. Yet in the 1920s it was a spreading scourge on citrus and many other plants. The discovery of its place of origin and of its parasites constitutes one of the best deductive pieces of scientific detective work in the annals of biological control.

The citrophilus mealybug was first found on citrus in southern California in 1913. How it arrived no one knew. It spread rapidly and in a few years became a major, highly destructive, pest of citrus, other fruit trees and ornamentals in the State. Fumigation and spraying were ineffective in controlling it, so mass production of a mealybug ladybird predator, *Cryptolaemus montrouzieri* Mulsant, introduced by Koebele years before, was tried. *Cryptolaemus* did not overwinter well in California and was ineffective when unaided. The mass-release program developed under Professor Harry S. Smith's guidance provided a fair degree of control but the mealybug continued to spread and each year more heavy infestations developed. In desperation some growers even turned to high-pressure water washing in 1927, but this method was very expensive, necessitating the installation of water-pipe systems.

As the mealybug situation became more alarming in 1927, Professor Harry Smith of the University of California at Riverside (then UC Citrus Experiment Station) decided to send a collector abroad to attempt to secure effective natural enemies. Harold Compere was chosen to make the trip.

The citrophilus mealybug was obviously an invader from abroad in California but its country of origin was unknown to entomologists. It was recorded from England and South Africa but all evidence indicated that these also represented accidental importations. Dr C. P. Clausen, then of the US Department of Agriculture, Bureau of Entomology, had searched unsuccessfully for it in China, Japan, the Philippines and Taiwan. Professor Filipo Silvestri, on temporary assignment for the University of California in 1924–5, had covered the same general area as Clausen plus Indo-China and failed to locate this species. Also Professor I. Kuwana, the Chief Entomologist of the Japanese Empire, and specialist on Coccidae (including the mealybugs) of the Orient, had not seen this mealybug.

The Mediterranean citrus areas were excluded deductively because it was reasoned that the mealybug would have been discovered if it occurred there because of the presence of numerous competent citrus entomologists in that part of the world.

This narrowed the range down considerably. Then the assumption was adopted that it was likely the citrophilus mealybug came from a climate similar to southern California and from a locality closely linked by steamer to England, South Africa and California – the three places the mealybug was known to occur. The most likely common denominator appeared to be Sydney, Australia; thus this port became Compere's target.

He arrived in Sydney in September and on the 27th, the first day spent searching, he found seven specimens of the citrophilus mealybug in the Sydney Botanical Garden. Several more weeks elapsed before a few more were found, so generally rare was the species. Drawing on past experience, Compere recalled that isolated plants sometimes become heavily infested because the pests may find and build-up on a plant before their enemies discover it. Therefore he deliberately made a search of the Sydney industrial district where plants were widely scattered – only an occasional one being seen there in a yard. On the second day's search, January 18, 1928, an old mulberry tree was found completely infested in the front yard of a small dwelling. At that time the mealybugs appeared to be healthy and devoid of parasitism.

Meanwhile beginning in September 1927, Compere was endeavoring to develop a small insectary using sprouted potatoes to grow the mealybugs but over a period of several weeks of searching around Sydney he found only sixty-nine citrophilus mealybugs. Cultures were started from these, but some of them contained undetected, small, immature parasite larvae or eggs and parasites got started in all the cultures. By January 1928, these parasites, mostly *Coccophagus gurneyi* Compere, later destined for fame in California, had increased to the point of overwhelming the cultures. They could not be held down sufficiently even with constant removal of individuals. Moreover, the potato stock had deteriorated badly, so that the short-term culture situation was very precarious.

Because of these problems Compere decided that the best plan was to personally transport the material on the first steamer leaving for California using the many parasites and reduced numbers of mealybugs on hand supplemented by fresh mealybug material to be collected from the heavily infested mulberry tree found on January 18. Professor Harry Smith approved this plan by cable and arrangements were at once made to depart on the steamship *Tahiti* on February 23, 1928.

On February 19, Compere visited the infested mulberry tree for the second time in order to obtain the mealybug stocks to be used as hosts for the insectary-reared parasites during the voyage to California. To his surprise close inspection showed that virtually all the mealybugs had been parasitized and contained parasite pupae. Countless thousands of parasites were present, principally *Tetracnemus pretiosus* Timberlake, which also was to become famous in California. Fortuitously, the timing was perfect for collection and shipment inasmuch as the parasites were mainly in the pupal stage and if cooled down would remain so for some time before emergence. A large part of the tree was removed and the material was packed in insect-tight boxes, which were placed in the cool-room of the steamer *Tahiti* at a temperature of about 3 °C (38 °F). However, no unparasitized mealybug stock was obtained and this remained a problem. Meanwhile, because Australian potatoes, or citrus fruit, etc., could not be brought into California because of quarantines, Compere obtained American-grown potatoes from an American ship in Sydney Harbor just before departure and used these to continue shipboard propagation of mealybugs. The mealybug supply was alleviated considerably when during a stop-over in Wellington, New Zealand, he found citrophilus mealybug in abundance on grapes and fruit trees and obtained a box of heavily infested grapes to use as mealybug breeding stock.

During the three-week voyage to San Francisco, Compere set up a temporary insectary in a vacant hospital room on the *Tahiti* and tended the cultures daily. New host mealybug stock was available in abundance from the material collected in Wellington. From San Francisco the material (except for the quarantined grapes) was sent on at once (about March 15) to the Riverside quarantine insectary.

Both *Coccophagus gurneyi* and *Tetracnemus pretiosus* were readily propagated at Riverside, their life cycles being only about three weeks. The first field colonies of *C. gurneyi* were liberated in June 1928 and the first field recovery was made on July 24, a very promising indication. Within a year the species was thoroughly established throughout the infested area of southern California as well as in the San Francisco Bay area, and insectary propagation was stopped. *T. pretiosus* cultures were supplied to the insectaries of Los Angeles and Orange Counties on April 23–4 and at the same time colonies were released in the field. The first recovery was made on August 15, although it was doubtless established before this, and it was soon found everywhere.

By the spring of 1929, within one year of release, there was a very appreciable reduction in the number of mealybugs in the districts where the parasites had been well established. Local insectaries which formerly had mass-produced *Cryptolaemus* continued to produce and distribute the parasites during 1929, so that by the spring of 1930, virtually the entire citrus acreage of southern California had been colonized and both parasites thoroughly established.

In the spring of 1930, two years after the first releases, the usual 'peak hatch' of mealybugs failed to occur and complete economic control was achieved. No infestations of any economic importance have occurred since that time. From my own experience I can safely say that today it might take a specialist anywhere from a day to a week to find even his first specimen. At the time of the successful control by parasites it was shown by surveys that savings in Orange County alone amounted to from $500000 to $1000000 annually. This county represented about one-half of the then-infested citrus acreage (the mealybug was still spreading) so that overall savings to the citrus industry alone amounted to from $1000000 to $2000000 annually. The entire cost to the State of California was $1700, exclusive of Compere's salary of $150.00 per month, or all told less than $2600. (See Compere and Smith, 1932.)

Citrus blackfly in Cuba, 1930

This species, *Aleurocanthus woglumi* Ashby, like the spiny blackfly discussed earlier, is not a true fly but a member of the whitefly family Aleurodidae. Its name derives from the shiny black color of the nymphs and pupae. Like the related scales, mealybugs and aphids it sucks the plant sap. Badly infested leaves wither and drop off and complete defoliation may occur in unchecked infestations resulting in almost complete loss of crop. Before biological control was attained in Cuba, eradication was futilely attempted and then expensive and repetitive spraying programs were conducted, but in spite of them the citrus blackfly continued increasing from year to year. This blackfly was first found in Jamaica in 1913, then in Cuba and the Bahamas in 1916, Panama in 1917, Costa Rica in 1919, and in more and more other countries and islands of the area over the years.

Because of its presence in Cuba so close to Florida, there was real danger of its accidental introduction into the great Florida citrus-growing areas. It was reasoned by those concerned in the United States that if effective biological control could be attained in Cuba and other infested Caribbean islands the danger of entry into Florida or other gulf states would be greatly lessened. As a consequence, the United

139

States Department of Agriculture entered into an agreement with the Cuban Department of Agriculture, Commerce and Labor to attack the problem co-operatively.

It was known from published records and museum specimens that the citrus blackfly was of Oriental origin, but even more important, Professor Filipo Silvestri had published in 1926 and 1928 that important parasites of the citrus blackfly occurred in the Orient. It will be recalled that he did this work while on foreign exploration assignment in 1924–5 for the University of California at Riverside, and that information gained on the same trip led to the complete biological control of the related spiny blackfly in Japan. It is of interest that the original stimulus leading to the US–Cuba co-operative project apparently originated with Professor J. F. Tristan of San Jose, Costa Rica (where the blackfly was a pest) who, having read Silvestri's papers, set in motion a chain of correspondence in 1927 that finally culminated in the importation of parasites to Cuba. It was this background information that led Dr C. P. Clausen, then of the US Department of Agriculture, to discover and import natural enemies from the Orient.

Clausen began foreign exploration in May 1929 and finished in August 1931. Two separate trips to tropical Asia were involved. P. A. Berry of the USDA was in charge of the receiving, culture and colonization work in Cuba. Clausen made studies and observations in the Philippines, Thailand, Malaysia, Java, Sumatra, Burma and Ceylon but eventually settled on Singapore as the center for collection and shipment of parasites. Clausen found five species of parasites and nine of predators to attack the citrus blackfly. Of these, he rated three parasites *Eretmocerus serius* Silvestri, *Prospaltella divergens* Silvestri and *P. smithi* Silvestri, to be important and effective in the order named and the predators to be of little consequence.

In addition to the usual problems of maintaining living cultures of hosts and parasites during lengthy sea voyages, this work was complicated by the desire to use non-citrus host plants of the blackfly because of the danger of introducing citrus diseases into Cuba. It was with difficulty that an infestation of citrus blackfly was obtained on mango seedlings adequate to justify their being sent to Cuba. This first shipment was sent in Wardian cages from Singapore in March 1930 and arrived in Havana late in April. From this material forty-two female and nineteen male *Eretmocerus serius* emerged along with thirty-four female *Prospaltella divergens*. The latter was not successfully

Fig. 31. Twelve Wardian cages containing citrus plants infested with citrus blackfly on shipboard en route to Singapore to be inoculated with parasites for return to Cuba. From Clausen and Berry (1932).

cultured but the former ultimately provided the control sought. Two additional shipments emphasizing the *Prospaltella* spp. and one predator were made. Both involved more elaborate planning and preparation than the first. The second shipment was sent on citrus to New York (where citrus could be imported) with the idea of rearing the adult parasites out there and trans-shipping them on to Havana. Forty-three female *Prospaltella divergens* and fifty-one female *P. smithi* were forwarded to Havana but none arrived alive. However, forty-two adults of the predator *Catana clauseni* Chapin were received alive in Havana and successfully cultured. They were colonized beginning December 1, 1930 and although they increased rapidly in some cases and reduced heavy infestations of the blackfly, they were unable to maintain the blackfly at low levels and were eventually supplanted by *Eretmocerus*.

The third shipment, made direct to Cuba on citrus plants originally sent from Cuba to Singapore and kept under quarantine conditions there, arrived in Havana June 3, 1931 (see Fig. 31). It consisted almost entirely of *Prospaltella divergens* and although 750 adults emerged in Havana no reproduction occurred, either in the laboratory or in the field. A few *P. smithi* were also received but also failed to reproduce.

141

Thus the first small shipment was the only one of any consequence. A few of the *E. serius* from this shipment were directly released in the field but most were used for laboratory culture, which occurred readily. Soon large numbers were available for field liberation which began in late June and early June 1930. Shortly thereafter, the parasites became so abundant in the release sites that insectary culture no longer was necessary, it being much simpler to transfer field-reared parasites from grove to grove.

Eretmocerus increased and spread so rapidly from the first small releases that complete control occurred prior to August 1, 1931 in the first groves colonized, or in about one year. Frequently citrus groves in which *Eretmocerus* had been released six months previously would show enormous peak populations of the parasite and three months later the groves were usually completely cleaned of the pest. It was estimated that one initial release of from 100–500 female parasites in the center of a five-acre grove would provide commercial control in from eight to twelve months. Roughly this meant the reduction during this period of the pest population by a mere initial handful of parasites from at least 100 million blackflies per five acres of heavily infested grove to just a few individuals per tree. By 1932–3 biological control in Cuba was essentially complete.

Amazingly, all this resulted from the initial stock of only forty-two female *Eretmocerus* which survived the first shipment in 1930. The total cost of the entire project as far as I can ascertain was about $40000, about half being contributed by Cuba and half by the USA. This included expenses for travel and research in the Orient, collection and shipment of material, establishment and distribution of natural enemies in Cuba and some other countries.

From Cuba, *Eretmocerus* was soon sent to other islands. In April 1932, J. G. Myers introduced one large shipment of *Eretmocerus* into Jamaica from Cuba. Recoveries were made in July and within a year it was nearly impossible to find a specimen of the citrus blackfly on the original release trees. In fact, Mr H. W. Edwards, who had received and colonized the parasites, made a standing offer of one shilling for each blackfly found on these trees. Similar results occurred in other islands. *Eretmocerus* was introduced into the Bahamas in October 1931, recovered two months later, and was doing effective work by May 1932. It was introduced into Haiti by Dr Dozier in August 1931. Subsequently over the years it has been introduced into several other Caribbean islands or Central American countries with generally outstanding results. The major exception has been Mexico, and that story is illustrative of how so-called biological control failures may only be indicative of lack of research emphasis or premature termination of a project.

Eretmocerus serius was a 'failure' in Mexico, at least as compared to its work in most Caribbean islands. The citrus blackfly was found in the State of Sinaloa on the west coast of Mexico in 1935 and, in spite of quarantines, rapidly spread during the next few years throughout the major citrus areas of all Mexico, not only causing enormous damage there but creating consternation in the bordering citrus-growing states of California, Arizona and Texas. Again for the same reasons as with Cuba and after small-scale importations of *Eretmocerus* in 1938 failed to result in establishment, the US Department of Agriculture developed a formal co-operative project with the Mexican Department of Agriculture in 1943 to import *Eretmocerus serius*. Colonies were shipped in from the USDA Panama laboratory and released in the States of Colima, Nayarit and Sinaloa. The parasite became well established at several sites and subsequently was generally distributed as new areas became invaded by the blackfly. Even though the parasite became abundant it did not effect the control previously experienced in other countries, except in a few small areas of high humidity. It was concluded that climate was reducing the effectiveness of this parasite and that additional ones should be sought abroad in areas having climatic conditions more comparable to the Mexican areas.

Therefore in 1948–50 the search was directed to semi-arid areas of India and West Pakistan, where a series of parasites were discovered and successfully imported, that gave complete biological control throughout Mexico. This truly outstanding achievement will be related in the next chapter. (See Clausen and Berry, 1932.)

Sugar-cane borer in the Caribbean area, 1932–3

This is to be but a small part of the sugar-cane borer story. Biological control research has been going on for many years now with this borer, *Diatraea saccharalis* (Fabricius), and related species. It has been quite successful in some islands or districts: less so in others. Much of this variability has been due to the degree of research emphasis, or lack of it, and to differing climates and philosophies of control. Quite a number of parasites are known and many are or were originally restricted to particular islands or areas. Much remains to be done.

143

For example, Dr Myers suggested that the possibility should be investigated of effective parasites occurring in New Guinea, which would be adapted to parasitism in thick canes. To my knowledge this has not been done.

In the Amazon basin, Dr J. G. Myers conducted some of the most rigorous and primitive foreign exploration ever engaged in by any entomologist anywhere; on the other hand he was possibly the first to utilize commercial airlines for the shipment of parasites when in 1932 he took advantage of Pan American's recently inaugurated Caribbean flights to ship parasites from Cuba to Antigua.

Dr Myers had some definite hypotheses regarding biological control ecology that directed his quest, as was the case with Compere and others. He was dealing with native species that had adopted sugar-cane as a host plant. He based his research and explorations on two main ideas: (1) there were many primitive 'ecological islands' in South America and the Caribbean area where unknown parasites of *Diatraea* might exist on wild host plants because they were isolated from sugar-cane areas, and (2) the known parasites of *Diatraea* occurring in sugar-cane areas might not be as well adapted to living in the sugar-cane habitat as was *Diatraea*. According to Myers:

There is surely no valid ecological or practical difference between a pest introduced without its parasites and an indigenous insect which, in a circumscribed biological or geographical island, has learned to live upon a cultivated crop, while its parasites, although perhaps already abundant in the area, even on the edge of the fields, have not yet learned to or are in some way prevented from, attacking it in its new host-plant. The line of control endeavor should here take the course, not of trying hopelessly to establish the parasites in the cultivations, but, in accordance with the older and proven technique, of introducing another and more efficient parasite from outside.

That he was justified in his assumptions is borne out 'by the fact that the most promising parasite so far discovered, the Amazon fly (*Metagonistylum minense*), was first found, not in sugar-cane, but in a wild host plant, in a primitive plant community' deep in the Amazon basin.

Before importing the Amazon fly, Myers had been engaged in the introduction of a tachinid fly parasite of *Diatraea*, *Lixophaga diatraeae*, from Cuba into the Lesser Antilles. The first attempt failed, according to Myers, because it was largely a single-handed effort lacking a full-time experienced worker on the receiving end. Later, during March to May 1932, Myers, along with his assistant L. C. Scaramuzza and

144

some skilfully selected and trained workers consisting of a Spaniard, a Cuban Negro, a white Cuban, a Portuguese and a Haitian, sent nearly 7000 puparia of the parasitic fly to the entomologists, Mr H. E. Box in Antigua and Mr Mestier in St Kitts via the rather new Pan American Airways flights. The spread of the fly and the progress of parasitism were speedy. The next year this tachinid was sent to St Lucia with similar results, and has since been introduced to many other areas.

Dr Myers spent several years in nearly continuous foreign exploration. Five separate major journeys were made in northern South America. This account will be restricted to the one involving discovery and the importation of the Amazon fly, a major parasite of the sugar-cane borer. His itinerary was roughly as follows: Leaving headquarters in Trinidad he proceeded to Para (= Belem), Brazil, from which he crossed one of the mouths of the Amazon to the great island of Marajo and then returned to Para exploring the River Moju. Thence he proceeded up the Amazon to the Trapajoz River and up it to Fordlandia and back, continuing up the Amazon to Manaos. From here he branched on to the Rio Negro and Rio Branco to the Brazilian border of British Guiana. From there by the headwaters of the Ireng and the Mazaruni Rivers he proceeded in a circular route to Mt Roraima in Venezuela, returning by the Venezuelan and Brazilian savannahs to the River Uraricuera which flows into the Rio Branco. There, because of lack of communication with Manaos, he returned to the British Guiana border and walked down the cattle trail to the coast, exploring all host-plant associations for sugar-cane borer parasites en route. Altogether about 800 miles were covered on foot – according to Myers 'a method of progression which offers the best conditions for entomological work, and one which ought to be adopted more generally were the time available'. Except for this long trek on foot the entire trip was by water.

Myers had more than his share of the three main difficulties in such South American travel, namely river rapids, disease and shortage of food. On occasion he was deserted under difficult conditions but of all the varied helpers he had, he considered the Indian aborigines to be especially hardworking, intelligent and efficient as entomological assistants. Myers' wife shared much of his work but she was invalided to England late in 1931 with severe malaria contracted in the unhealthy delta of the Orinoco.

All of the material of the parasitic Amazon fly was collected near Santarem on the Amazon in 1933 and essentially all local transport was by water. Virtually all the parasite puparia were collected by means of boats or canoes from *Diatraea* infesting the floating grass-beds of *Paspalum repens*, which reach their maximum development in the vicinity of Santarem. Other parasites also were present but were already known elsewhere and because in this area of the lower Amazon and lower Rio Branco, *Diatraea* was scarce on sugar-cane, it seemed possible that the Amazon fly might play an important role in this scarcity.

At the height of the campaign a small fleet of boats was engaged. Locally a small motor launch, a small sailing boat and eleven dugout canoes were used, employing as many as forty collectors. A 26-foot launch, which could withstand the very heavy seas of the lower Amazon, was bought to make the round-trip journey, carrying parasites from Santarem to Para every two weeks as no other reliable transport was available on a regular basis. The entire population of the lower Amazon was amazed to see the launch successfully make trip after trip through the fifty miles of treacherous open water before Para.

The arrival of the launch in Para, 470 miles from Santarem, was arranged to coincide with the weekly commercial airline flight from Para to Georgetown, British Guiana, where the parasites were to be colonized. This flight took one day, so with the judicious use of ice, the pupal parasites could be kept for up to a maximum of thirteen days and still be unemerged and healthy by the time of their arrival in Georgetown.

All told, six shipments were sent during August to October 1933, totalling some 3000 parasite puparia. They were received in Georgetown and colonized by Mr L. D. Cleare, who also cultured many more in the insectary. By March 1934, only a little over six months after the first shipment was made from the Amazon, the tachinid parasite was recovered in some numbers from six different release fields in two localities. It has since become widely established. (See Myers, 1935.)

Coconut leaf-mining beetle in Fiji, 1933

This beetle, *Promecotheca reichei* Baly, is a native insect in Fiji that originally apparently was well controlled by native natural enemies. However, beginning about the 1880s as trade developed and coconuts became extensively cultivated, the beetle gradually became a serious pest. Severe outbreaks became commonplace. The larvae bore within the leaflets and the adult beetles feed on the leaves externally. In heavy infestations they together caused a reduction of about 75 percent in the leaf surface of every tree over wide areas.

146

A detailed study of the insect and its natural enemies was not feasible until 1929 when sufficient entomological expertise became available from other duties. This investigation showed that all severe outbreaks had one unusual feature in common; only one stage of the insect was present at any one time, i.e. there was no overlapping of generations. This was remarkable in a salubrious climate like Fiji where reproduction can continue throughout the year. Such a climatic situation invariably leads to all stages being present simultaneously, yet such was not the case here. The discovery of the reason behind this and the appreciation of its significance, led to the solution of the problem.

In a nutshell, the principal cause of the outbreaks of the beetle was considered to be due to the indirect adverse effect of a predatory mite, *Pediculoides ventricosus* (Newport), on two native parasite species which otherwise were capable of satisfactorily controlling the beetle and were considered to have done so originally. The mite was undoubtedly accidentally introduced some years previously inasmuch as it is cosmopolitan and feeds on a wide variety of insects. For complex reasons to be briefly explained, the mite caused an 'even-brooded' condition of the beetle and this resulted in the native parasites being rendered ineffective because they attacked only the larval stages and these were largely lacking for long periods of time because of the even-brood. Thus the native parasite populations were greatly reduced and rendered ineffective.

The mite exerted its effect thus. It attacked all larval stages and the pupae of the beetle but not adults or eggs. In the dry season it increased with such incredible rapidity that it would destroy all of the beetles except eggs and adults in a given locality, the adults laid eggs and died and this resulted later in the single-stage condition consisting principally of beetle larvae, but meanwhile the predatory mite population crashed because of food shortage when only adult beetles and eggs were present. When the wet season came the beetles increased again very rapidly – essentially without any check – both because parasites were scarce due to the single-brood condition and because the mite was ineffective during wet weather. T. H. C. Taylor concluded that the mite would have replaced the indigenous parasites and done a good job of control, had it not been decimated by wet weather every year. In the wetter parts of Fiji the beetle seldom became a serious pest, presumably because the mite was held down and the native parasites operated without hindrance.

The preceding knowledge showed that a new parasite must be

147

discovered and led to the formulation of a set of quite definite characteristics that should be possessed by such a parasite in order for it to control the coconut leaf-mining beetle under the single-brooded condition. These requirements mainly included: (1) the parasite should have a more rapid rate of increase relative to the pest than the native parasites, and one generation must require no longer than a month, (2) adults of the parasite should be able to survive the long periods when no individuals of the pest were in a suitable stage for its attack, and (3) it should parasitize all larval stages as well as pupae of the host so that suitable hosts would be available over a much longer period in each pest generation than for a parasite species which attacked only one stage, and thus the period during which the new parasite would lack suitable hosts would be correspondingly shorter. Also it was desired that the parasite should be internal, very active and capable of rapid dispersal and tolerant of the climatic conditions of Fiji.

No suitable candidate parasite was known at the time this study was completed, but in 1930 R. W. Paine's investigations in Java resulted in the discovery of a large number of parasites of a related species of *Promecotheca* (*P. nuciferae* Maulik). This beetle occurred throughout Java but was never a pest – a good indication that the parasites might be effective. Taylor followed this up with detailed studies of the Javanese parasites in 1932–3 and concluded that only one of the parasites, *Pleurotropis parvulus* Ferriere, met the conditions set down for the new parasite desired for Fiji, even though this species was considered to be one of the least important of the complex controlling the beetle *P. nuciferae*, in Java.

This small parasitic chalcid wasp attacks all stages of larvae as well as the pupae of *Promecotheca*, and many individuals develop in each host individual giving it a high potential rate of increase with respect to the host. The life cycle is only some three weeks long as compared to about three and a half months for the beetle in Fiji and perhaps most important, the adult parasites live for five and a half weeks which enables them to survive periods when suitable stages of the host are rare or absent.

Taylor transported the parasites from Java to Fiji in the usual manner of the day. Six, large, wire-gauze-covered cages each containing four seedling coconut palms heavily infested with *Promecotheca nuciferae* of all stages were used. Parasites were included in the cages and were able to reproduce during the voyage. He left Batavia, Java, April 17,

1933 on the S.S. *Van Rees* which traveled from Singapore to Sidney via Java, New Guinea, New Hebrides and New Caledonia. It was necessary to trans-ship at Noumea, New Caledonia, on May 10 to the S.S. *Kareta* in order to go on to Suva, Fiji, where he arrived May 14.

Before arrival in Noumea (four days from Fiji) all palms, soil, containers, etc. were thrown overboard to eliminate any potential pest hazards, after all adult parasites and parasitized larvae and pupae of the host had been collected into glass tubes.

From Suva it was necessary to proceed at once on a chartered motor launch to the Lau group of islands where outbreaks were raging. They arrived at Nabavatu on Vanua Balavu on May 24 (37 days out of Java), where headquarters and an insectary were set up. Some 1200 adults and pupae of *Pleurotropis parvulus*, the preselected parasite, arrived in excellent condition. To be on the safe side, Taylor also imported the two parasite species considered most important in Java. Only one, *Dimmockia javanica* Ferr., was successfully introduced, cultured and liberated in sufficiently large numbers, but it failed to become established, thus justifying the predictions in this regard.

The first liberations of *Pleurotropis parvulus* were made on May 26, 1933 and were continued to April 30, 1934, when so many parasites were present in the field that insectary rearing was no longer necessary. Within a year it had completely controlled all the severe outbreaks of *Promecotheca* that had raged on Vanua Balavu, Kanacea, Taveuni, Mago, Lakeba and elsewhere. Taylor records that it literally attained 100 percent parasitism on all trees, even though in many outbreaks every tree over hundreds of acres of land bore about 4000 beetle individuals. At the first peak of the parasite explosion, about 5000 adult parasites were emerging per tree daily and this continued for about ten days. (It will be recalled that many parasites develop in each host.) Not a single *Promecotheca* individual escaped in many outbreak areas and the parasite dispersed so well that it controlled the pest even on isolated coconut trees hidden in the forest.

The one minor disadvantage to this parasite was that it was too effective. On small islets or very isolated spots of coconuts it would exterminate the pest and then die out itself. This necessitated re-introduction of the parasite if the beetle happened to reinvade. However, this never happened on larger islands or large coconut estates. Today the coconut leaf-mining beetle remains a rarity of no economic importance.

This is an amazing case in many respects but the development in advance of a set of very definite characteristics that the imported parasite would need to possess in order to be successful and then the deliberate preselection of such a parasite from among a group, at least two of which were much more common and effective in the country of origin, is unique I think in the annals of biological control. Not that the foreign explorer doesn't intuitively employ preselection to a considerable extent, but nearly always the parasites given the most chance to succeed are the ones considered to be most effective in the country of origin. Additionally, this case demonstrates the feasibility of biological control of native insect pests. (See Taylor, 1936, 1937.)

Coffee mealybug in Kenya, 1938

The importance of correct taxonomy to successful biological control is nowhere better illustrated than by this project. The coffee mealybug *Planococcus kenyae* (LePelley) was, during the early years of its occurrence as a pest in Kenya, first thought to be the citrus mealybug *Pseudococcus citri* (Risso) and later to be *Pseudococcus lilacinus* Ckll. Consequently for twelve years the wrong natural enemies were sought after and imported and unsuccessfully colonized. It is a most interesting story and the lesson of the necessity for accurate identification still needs to be kept in mind with other projects.

The coffee mealybug was first noticed when a severe infestation on coffee occurred in the Thika district of Kenya in 1923. At first it was assumed to be a native insect but its rapid spread to other nearby districts and ultimately far afield coupled with its lack of any important parasites in Kenya made it evident that it was an introduced insect. It soon became one of the notable mealybug plagues of the world. Coffee was the principal cash crop attacked but severe damage was done to food plants in native gardens and to ornamentals as well. In fact, the cultivation of yams was stopped due to the mealybug and other cropping practices had to be modified. The prosperity of thousands of small native landowners was severely affected. It was estimated that the financial loss on coffee alone, including cost of control efforts, from 1923 to 1939 (when biological control was achieved) was between £1 000 000 to £1 500 000 sterling or approximately $5 000 000 to $7 500 000 US, quite a sum for that period.

During the early period in 1925 when the pest was thought to be the citrus mealybug, a parasite of that mealybug, *Leptomastidea abnormis* (Girault), was sent from Sicily to Kenya. Although no parasites survived the trip it is doubtful if they would have attacked the coffee mealybug.

Another parasite, *Leptomastix dactylopii*, of the citrus mealybug was received later on in large numbers from the University of California at Riverside, but would not successfully reproduce on the coffee mealybug. Later, when the mealybug was considered to be *Pseudococcus lilacinus*, other natural enemies were sought, not only from other mealybug species but especially from *P. lilacinus*. A major effort was made by Dr R. H. LePelley to obtain parasites of *P. lilacinus* in the Orient, its presumed native home, and to import and colonize these in Kenya. During 1936–7 he explored many countries and, particularly from the Philippine Islands and Java, successfully shipped large numbers of parasites and predators to A. R. Melville in Kenya. However, none of the parasites obtained by so much effort would attack the coffee mealybug when tested in Kenya. Some of the predators were cultured and liberated but apparently none became established. By now, natural enemies had been imported unsuccessfully from four continents.

During about the time of LePelley's trip it became evident that the coffee mealybug was a species distinct from *P. lilacinus* and, since much of the world had been searched, most probably was native to Africa somewhere outside of Kenya. Here again luck creeps in. My colleague Harold Compere was exploring for black scale parasites in Africa for the University of California and in 1937 visited Melville in Nairobi, while LePelley was still absent abroad. Compere recalled that he had seen the coffee mealybug in Uganda and told Melville that it was rare there.

Following LePelley's return from the Orient, staff became available for a search for parasites in Uganda and this time A. R. Melville did the exploring with LePelley in charge of the receiving, quarantine, culture and colonization work. Melville went to Uganda early in 1938 and almost at once found the mealybug and sent parasites to Nairobi. LePelley successfully cultured nine species of primary parasites, destroying several species of hyperparasites that were present. Because of lack of insectary space, the five most promising parasites were concentrated on and the other four dropped, with the idea that they could be reacquired if necessary. However, such never proved to be the case. A species of *Anagyrus* near *kivuensis* was colonized in June 1938 and during September–December 1938, 15000 more parasites were liberated. From 1939 to 1941 about an additional 200000 were

151

liberated each year and the whole of the mealybug-infested area was colonized.

Of the five species colonized, three were established, but one, *Anagyrus* sp. near *kivuensis* Compere, is given credit for the outstanding results that occurred. According to LePelley it possessed all the chief attributes of an outstanding parasite; 'it is vigorous, hardy, adaptable, mates readily, and is an excellent searcher. It appears capable of maintaining itself on a very low and scattered mealybug infestation. This insect alone...has completely controlled infestations in districts where for 10 or 15 years it had been necessary to band large areas at great expense.'

The establishment of the parasites rapidly and remarkably reduced the population of the mealybug. By 1941 losses in coffee plantations were reduced by 92 percent and became less and less over the years. The same remarkable clean-up occurred in native gardens and reserves. In 1938 a motorist could easily notice areas of vegetation along the roadside which were black from sooty-mold fungus growing in the honeydew exuded by masses of mealybugs and which stank with the mealybug odor. Two years after liberation of parasites there were no such areas and a detailed search was necessary in order to find any mealybugs at all. When LePelley wrote of the marvelous results in 1943, they had just occurred and he was not quite sure that they would be so completely maintained in the future. He suggested that if ever required, known additional species of parasites could be introduced. That his doubts proved groundless is shown by Dr W. R. Thompson's report in 1956 that complete biological control was continuing. (See LePelley, 1943.)

Comments and conclusions

As we reflect on the cases just discussed quite a few points become evident that today are accepted as standard principles and practices in biological control. One thing is clear: highly trained professional entomologists enthusiastically devoted to their science furnished the main ingredient for success in case after case. Were it not for men such as Riley, Muir, Silvestri, Taylor, Compere and Myers, to name just a few, how many more years would have elapsed before serious pests were subjugated? The personal equation cannot be given too high a rating in this work, nor can basic research and scientific communication. In several cases the solution to a problem lay in studies previously conducted by scientists having no connection with the problem. The acquisition of their information was essential and it emphasizes today's need for a data bank.

It is clear that perseverance may pay off, as with the sugar-cane leafhopper problem in Hawaii which was completely solved only after fifteen years of continuing effort and interest, and just as clear that some projects were prematurely abandoned or insufficiently pursued, such as the citrus whitefly problem in Florida as well as the gypsy moth and sugar-cane borer problems, even though much has been done on the latter two.

From the successful results obtained, quite a number of conclusions are evident: Generally one, and usually not more than two, natural enemy species are responsible for control and these effective natural enemies become established and disperse easily, bringing about control rapidly (usually within nine months to two years) and spectacularly. It is not necessary to import massive numbers when effective natural enemies are concerned. In the case of the spiny blackfly only twenty parasites comprised the initial stock and only forty-two females furnished the stock for the successful citrus blackfly project in Cuba. The importance of correct taxonomic identification of the pest is clearly shown by the coffee mealybug case in Kenya. The same applies to correct identification of natural enemies. The fact that effective natural enemies may be obtained from hosts other than the target pest was established by the sugar-cane beetle borer case, the *Opuntia* cactus case, the coconut moth case and the coconut leaf-mining beetle case and is very important to keep in mind on any project. By inference this also means that native pests may be controlled by importation of natural enemies from related hosts abroad and of course this was actually demonstrated with the coconut leaf-mining beetle in Fiji.

The various cases discussed showed that either predators or parasites acting alone may produce complete control. It all depends upon the particular pest–natural enemy complex involved and no real purpose is served by arguments *a priori* as to which type of natural enemy is better. However, parasites were the major factor in most cases. It is also evident that control may be accomplished by the attack of a natural enemy on any one host stage (egg, larval or pupal) and does not necessarily require a sequence of stages to be attacked. Cases in point include the eucalyptus snout-beetle and its egg parasite and the sugar-cane leafhopper and its egg predator.

Preselection of particular natural enemies for a given job is practiced up to a certain point by all trained foreign explorers, and was eminently successful in the case of the coconut leaf-mining beetle in Fiji, but as has been emphasized by various explorers, the natural enemy they had considered to be best often turned out to be inconsequential and, in fact, the best one even may be overlooked for years, as was *Cyrtorhinus*, the egg predator of the sugar-cane leafhopper. It seems that the proof of the pudding lies in the eating, i.e. all likely candidates should be imported and tried. By likely candidates we mean ones that attack the target pest or related species and that are more than of incidental occurrence in the native home area. Careful quarantine to exclude other, possibly detrimental, organisms must of course always be carried out.

There is no evidence from any of these cases that purposeful importation of any of the natural enemies did any harm, as far as final control of the pest is concerned, regardless of whether the poorest enemies were imported first and the best ones last or vice versa. Neither is there any evidence that complete biological control once achieved ever became reduced over the years. If anything, as in the eucalyptus snout-beetle case, control continued to improve for a number of years.

From a financial standpoint the results were frequently fabulous. The various cases speak for themselves, but several that cost only a few thousand dollars to solve continue to result in savings to agriculture of millions of dollars a year each.

6
Modern foreign exploration and successes

The development of commercial air transport signalled the modern era of foreign exploration. The changes from the earlier years to today have been largely technological ones related to easier, much more rapid means of travel and safer and simpler techniques of shipping and handling natural enemies. Along with this of course have come improved quarantine laboratories and insectaries for culture of introduced enemies, better colonization techniques and increased biological, ecological and taxonomic knowledge in general.

The changes have not been abrupt and there is no clear line of separation. I have arbitrarily chosen the end of the 1930s as the beginning of the modern era. It will be recalled from Chapter 5 that air shipments of sugar-cane borer parasites were made as early as 1932 in the Caribbean and in 1933 from Para, Brazil, to Georgetown, Guyana. However, as will be discussed shortly, the first long-distance intercontinental air shipment apparently occurred in December 1939. Unfortunately, only a few projects were able to take advantage of the increasing air transport facilities before World War II put a stop to such endeavors until 1945.

The modern foreign explorers can often accomplish in days or weeks what previously would have required months or a year or more. Their conditions of travel and living in foreign countries are usually considerably more pleasant and health risks fewer but off-the-beaten-track conditions are still grim in many places. In my own experience I have had to have armed guards in order to travel and collect in certain localities in Burma; have lived in hovels on stilts where the toilet was a hole in the floor; have had pig-intestine soup for what I later recalled was Thanksgiving Day dinner; have had to have local permission and blessing to enter and collect in bandit-infested parts of the semi-autonomous Tribal Territories of West Pakistan and once en route received many required penicillin shots from nearly anyone

155

Fig. 32. (*a*) The insectary of the University of California at Riverside, (*b*) parasite rearing cages in the insectary at Riverside, (*c*) Dr Richard Doutt in the quarantine room of the insectary of the University of California at Berkeley.

I could find, including airline stewardesses, pharmacists and medical orderlies. On the other hand, I have had some lovely collecting in Rio, Tahiti, Japan and other places.

Today, with a little planning, airmail shipments of live natural enemies can be made from nearly any given country to the home insectary as much as half-way around the world in from four to six days or less. Special arrangements utilizing air freight can even reduce this time. Thus the problem of 'bringing 'em back alive' has been greatly alleviated and the need to grow and maintain host cultures abroad solely for importation purposes virtually eliminated. Heated and pressurized cargo space generally furnishes good conditions for the natural enemies. The proper food and moisture conditions merely have to be provided in the shipment package, which also should be well insulated. Refinements may need to be made to suit particular cases, but there is really no technical obstacle left to prevent our successfully shipping live natural enemies rapidly from any one country to any other country in the world.

Another development that has helped considerably has been the ever-increasing construction of biological control insectaries around the world. These not only may serve as headquarters for visiting foreign explorers but as foci of knowledge concerning local natural enemies. Sometimes they may have the natural enemies desired already under culture so that large shipments can be easily made. Many countries, provinces or states and some agricultural industries maintain insectaries (see Fig. 32). Their lack is the greatest where they are sorely needed – in developing countries. This is partially alleviated by the Commonwealth Institute of Biological Control which maintains insectaries in Trinidad, Switzerland, India, Pakistan, Uganda, Sabah, Argentina and Ghana and will carry out special projects for any given country. Also, of course, insectaries with quarantine facilities are necessary in order to preclude the possibility of accidental importation of hyperparasites or other detrimental organisms. Most such insectaries operate under governmental permit and supervision.

Some outstanding modern biological control projects

The fifteen successful projects that follow have been chosen from among many, either because they are particularly interesting or because they furnish valuable insights into biological control principles and practices. Many of the other cases that might just as well have been

157

used are included in the summary of worldwide results later in this chapter. The dates given with each project generally represent the time of importation or establishment of the major natural enemies.

Citriculus mealybug in Israel, 1939–40

During the 1920s and 1930s the Palestine Farmers Federation financed the construction of several insectaries to carry out biological control projects against such pests as the Mediterranean fruit fly and the common citrus mealybug. In 1938, Israel Cohen was appointed Director of these insectaries and it is to him that most credit must be given for the completely successful biological control of the citriculus mealybug *Pseudococcus citriculus* Green, which was an invading pest first noticed in August 1938 when a severe outbreak occurred in some groves in the coastal plain. In 1938, the infestation (then thought to be *Pseudococcus comstocki* (Kuwana)) was spreading rapidly and by 1939 was becoming catastrophic. At a meeting called by the citrus industry in May 1939, the opinion was expressed that 'The intensity of the damage caused and the apparent rapidity of spread threaten to annihilate the citrus industry.' At this meeting it was agreed that spraying experiments should be carried out but that major stress should be on biological control by importation of parasites from other countries.

Attempts to control the pest with oil sprays and other insecticides failed to yield even remotely encouraging results. Although Cohen was not trained as an entomologist, he had studied agriculture at the University of California during the period when another very serious mealybug pest, *Pseudococcus fragilis*, had been completely controlled there by introduced parasites and he was convinced that their hope in Israel lay in a similar direction (letter to author from I. Cohen April 27, 1960). He sent samples of their new mealybug to various experts who identified it as *P. comstocki*. He then wrote to various entomologists to ascertain where parasites of this Comstock mealybug might be obtained. Japan was suggested as the native home but certain parasites were also known to be present in the eastern United States where *P. comstocki* had become established. About this time Dr I. Carmon, the citriculturist of the Experiment Station at Rehovot was about to journey to the United States, so Cohen suggested that he route his return trip via Japan and search for parasites there. Cohen raised funds to cover the extra expenditures and contacted United States Department of Agriculture and University of California entomologists to help and advise Dr Carmon.

With the assistance of a USDA entomologist stationed in Japan, Carmon collected and sent parasites of *P. comstocki* to Israel (then Palestine) in two airmail shipments in December 1939. This apparently represents the first lengthy intercontinental transport of natural enemies by air. Additionally, Carmon personally returned by boat in 1940 with many pupae of the various Japanese parasites of *P. comstocki*. Meanwhile, Cohen had a special temporary laboratory–insectary constructed and invited Dr E. Rivnay to direct it.

Dr Rivnay sorted out the various primary parasites and hyperparasites received from Japan and determined that *Clausenia purpurea* Ishii was the most effective one. The hyperparasites were eliminated, of course. *Clausenia purpurea* was cultured and one hundred specimens colonized under a tent on one tree in April 1940. It became established immediately and spread rapidly. Mass production was started later in 1940 so as to distribute the parasite widely. Trees which received twenty-five parasites in 1940 showed marked decreases in the mealybug infestation by August 1941. In a very short time control was complete and has remained so ever since.

One of the most interesting parts of this story is that the pest was later found to be *P. citriculus* rather than *P. comstocki*. This came about because a Japanese parasite, *Alloptropa burrelli* Mues., which had been established on *P. comstocki* in the United States, would not develop in the presumed *P. comstocki* in Israel, thereby indicating the Israeli mealybug to be a different species. Thus the pest was controlled, one might say, with a blend of skill and luck by a parasite of another mealybug species. However, this illustrates very strikingly the point that effective natural enemies may sometimes be obtained where least expected. It also shows that personal initiative as well as support by government or industry of the biological control effort is of prime importance. Neither Cohen nor Carmon were entomologists, yet between them they collaborated to import a parasite responsible for one of the world's great successes. (See Rivnay, 1968.)

Comstock mealybug in the eastern United States, 1939–41

The Comstock mealybug *Pseudococcus comstocki* is a native of Japan that accidentally became established in the eastern United States and became highly destructive in apple, pear and peach orchards of at least nine States in the late 1930s and early 1940s. Attempts at chemical control were failures, owing to either ineffectiveness or to the economics involved. Search for parasites of the pest was directed to Japan during 1939–41 because several species of parasites were known to attack the Comstock mealybug there. This resulted in five species of parasites being imported and colonized by the USDA Bureau of Entomology and Plant Quarantine. The three most important ones were *Alloptropa burrelli*, *Pseudaphycus malinus* Gahan and *Clausenia purpurea*, although it had been ascertained previously that *C. purpurea* was already accidentally established and generally distributed before the importations. It also proved to be the least important of the three, possibly because it is commonly attacked by native hyperparasites.

Culture and distribution of the parasites in several eastern states resulted in the general additional establishment of *Alloptropa burrelli* and *Pseudaphycus malinus* in all the main infested areas by 1945. These two species increased and spread rapidly. Peak percentages of parasitization in the upper 90s were commonly attained before the mealybug population crashed. Successful control following releases occurred within one or two years. It is of interest that although *Clausenia purpurea* was considered to be the least important of the three main parasites in the United States, yet it was the major factor in biological control of the citriculus mealybug in Israel. This could well be because its hyperparasites were excluded from entry into Israel. Ironically, Israel could have obtained this parasite from the eastern United States in 1939 more readily and cheaply than they did from Japan. (See Haeussler and Clancy, 1944; Clausen, 1956.)

Klamath weed in California, 1944–6

This weed, *Hypericum perforatum* Linnaeus, of European origin, was first reported in northern California in the vicinity of the Klamath River. It increased and spread rapidly and by 1944 it occupied over two million acres of range land in thirty counties. Not only were good forage plants greatly reduced but cattle and sheep lost weight when eating Klamath weed because of its somewhat toxic effect. This resulted in such a great decrease in land values that it became almost impossible for ranchers to borrow money for improvements. Chemical weedkillers were available but not generally practical because of the cost and the inaccessibility of much of the infested land. Professor H. S. Smith, head of biological control work in California, proposed the importation of insects that fed on the Klamath weed as early as 1922 but the idea of deliberately introducing a plant-feeding insect was not acceptable at that time.

Meanwhile, Australia had been fighting the same problem with *Hypericum*-eating insects introduced from England and Europe beginning in 1929, and Professor Smith, in California, followed the progress there with much interest through correspondence with A. J. Nicholson, Chief Entomologist for the Commonwealth Scientific and Industrial Research Organization (CSIRO). Smith finally obtained authorization in 1944 to import three species of beetles that showed promise against the Klamath weed in Australia. It was impossible then to consider importations from Europe because of World War II, but rather easy to bring material from Australia through the co-operation of the United States Army Transport Command. The Australian CSIRO, through Dr Nicholson, offered to collect and prepare the material for shipment. Importations started in October 1944 but problems were immediately encountered in changing the timing of the life cycle so the beetles would be in phase with the Northern Hemisphere seasons. Two species of *Chrysolina* that were in the summer resting state of aestivation responded rapidly in California to fine mist sprays of water to become active and lay eggs within three weeks. The third species, an *Agrilus*, was lost. After starvation tests in quarantine on a variety of economic plants the beetles were ready to be released in the field.

Chrysolina hyperici (Forster) was released in the spring of 1945 and *C. quadrigemina* (Suffrian) in February 1946. Both became readily established but it soon became evident that *C. quadrigemina* was becoming dominant. Distribution throughout the entire infested areas was rapidly made from the original colonies. From one colony of 5000 beetles released in 1945–6, more than three million beetles were collected for redistribution in California in 1950. They were also sent to Washington, Oregon, Idaho and Montana where they became successfully established.

Within ten years after the first release, the Klamath weed was reduced to the status of an uncommon roadside weed in California. Its abundance was reduced by more than 99 percent. Land values immediately increased by three or four times. Loss in weight of cattle and sheep ceased. I have previously estimated (DeBach, 1964a, p. 13) that at least $20960000 in savings accrued to the agriculture industry in California for the period 1953–9 or about $3500000 per year. These savings continue to accrue each year without even taking inflation into account. (See Holloway, 1964.)

This fruit fly, *Dacus dorsalis* Hendel, is a native of the Orient. It probably gained entrance to Hawaii in 1945 via military materiel returning from the western Pacific theater of war. It increased rapidly to epidemic proportions during 1946, attacking a wide variety of fruits. The larval infestations not only rendered most fruits worthless in Hawaii but additionally posed a serious potential problem to the warmer fruit-growing areas of the mainland United States. Chemical control was difficult, expensive, hazardous to health with certain materials and frequently insufficiently effective. As a consequence one of the most massive biological control projects of modern times came into being.

The Hawaiian Territorial Board of Agriculture and Forestry initiated exploration for natural enemies in 1947–8 in the Philippines and Malaysia. They actually imported and established the parasites responsible for the success subsequently obtained but it was impossible to ascertain this during this early stage of the effort. Consequently, in 1948–9, other interested organizations joined into a co-operative effort, including the US Department of Agriculture, the University of California, the Hawaiian Agricultural Experiment Station, the Hawaiian Sugar Planters Experiment Station and the Pineapple Research Institute. Up to September 1951, fourteen foreign explorers collected parasite material from many fruit fly species in most of the tropical and subtropical areas of the world including especially the Philippine Islands, Malaysia, Taiwan, Thailand, Borneo, India, Ceylon, Australia, New Caledonia, Fiji, South Africa, Kenya, Congo, Brazil and Mexico. Shipments consisted mainly of parasitized puparia sent by airmail or air freight and generally reached Hawaii in seven days or less from any given country. All told, more than 4 246 000 fly puparia of over sixty species were sent to Hawaii. About one-third of these were *Dacus dorsalis*, the pest in question. Some eighty species of parasites were obtained from this material, of which sixteen or more larval parasites of the genus *Opius*, six pupal parasites and one predator were cultured and released in the field. Eleven species were recovered initially in the field but the most effective one soon became nearly exclusively dominant.

The story is somewhat confused because various of the imported species of *Opius* were very similar in appearance and some were misidentified at first. Thus the original material received from the

Philippines in 1947 contained the three most important of all the parasites eventually imported, but only one of these, *Opius longicaudatus* (Ashmead), was correctly identified. The other two, *O. vandenboschi* Fullaway and *O. oophilus* Fullaway, were thought to be one species, *O. persulcatus* (Silv.), which actually was not present. The same applied to the next group of shipments received from Malaysia in 1948. Parasites from these shipments immediately became established. *Opius longicaudatus* increased rapidly in the field after its initial release on Oahu in 1948 but suddenly lost its dominant position during the latter half of 1949 to *O. vandenboschi* which had been released initially about the same time. In turn, *O. vandenboschi* was replaced during 1950 by *O. oophilus* which had first been recognized to be established in 1949. Interestingly, in spite of the competition between these three species, each replacement of one by another was accompanied by a higher total parasitization and a greater reduction in the fruit fly infestation. Both *O. longicaudatus* and *O. vandenboschi* had virtually disappeared by 1951 and this status has since continued.

The final result has been a very substantial reduction in the Oriental fruit fly populations in all of the Islands estimated to be on the order of 95 percent as compared to the 1947–9 peak abundance. At that time practically 100 percent of most kinds of fruits were infested. The threat of movement to the mainland has been greatly reduced. Still, some preferred fruit such as guava and mangoes, which up to 1949 were 100 percent infested, are sometimes infested to the extent of 50 percent, but with many fewer larvae per fruit. Yet on average, less than 10 percent of the mangoes are now infested. Many kinds of fruits that were once heavily infested are now virtually free of attack.

This project illustrates the basic importance of accurate knowledge of both taxonomy and biology to biological control. *Opius oophilus* was mistaken for some time as *O. persulcatus*. Had the latter been imported and established early with some degree of success, it is possible that further work, including the ultimate discovery of the best parasite, *O. oophilus*, might have been dropped. It is of interest that *O. oophilus* has also turned out to be the best parasite of the Mediterranean fruit fly in Hawaii, having displaced *O. tryoni* (Cameron), which previously was well established and fairly effective. Had *O. oophilus* been recognized as a valid species and introduced from Malaysia in 1913–14 when importation of parasites of the Mediterranean fruit fly was being initiated, better biological control would have occurred forty years earlier.

The biology of *O. oophilus* differs from that of *O. longicaudatus* and

O. vandenboschi which deposit their eggs in host larvae. The former lays its egg in an egg of the host, then completes development in the host larva. Had this habit been known in 1935–6 when F. C. Hadden undoubtedly but unknowingly imported *O. oophilus* along with other *Opius* species from Malaysia and India for control of the Mediterranean fruit fly, it probably could have been cultured and established. However insectary propagation did not occur, very likely because its habit of ovipositing only in host eggs was not then known and probably only host larvae were provided in the culture unit. If the biology had been understood so that the parasite had become established on the Mediterranean fruit fly at that time, it not only would have provided better biological control of that fruit fly from 1936 to 1950 (when *O. oophilus* finally became well established) but it would have been present to attack the Oriental fruit fly when it first reached Hawaii in 1945 and could well have made the later massive and expensive project unnecessary. (See Bess and Haramoto, 1958, and Clausen, Clancy and Chock, 1965.)

Red wax scale in Japan, 1948

This case might be likened to 'a gift from the gods'. The omnivorous pest *Ceroplastes rubens* Maskell was first found at Nagasaki, Kyushu, in 1897, probably having originated in China. It became a scourge of many economic plants, including citrus, persimmon and tea among others, and soon spread to the main island of Honshu and to Shikoku. No native parasites of any consequence were found attacking it. The introduction of several species of parasites that attacked it in Hawaii and California was attempted in the 1930s but without success. Thus chemical control remained necessary but was not always sufficiently effective because of the protection afforded by the waxy covering of the scale.

About 1942, the red wax scale began to diminish in severity on the southern island of Kyushu. In 1946, after the population of the red wax scale had been reduced noticeably, Professor K. Yasumatsu discovered a new and effective species of parasite, *Anicetus beneficus* Ishii Yasumatsu, that was apparently responsible for the decline. The parasite was then thought to be a race of a closely related species, *A. ceroplastis* Ishii, that parasitized another wax scale, *Ceroplastes pseudoceriferus* Green. Surveys showed that the parasite was not present on Honshu or Shikoku.

The origin of the new parasite remains a mystery to this day. Dr Yasumatsu suggested the possibility that *A. beneficus* may have evolved by mutation from *A. ceroplastis* in relatively recent years. Although no other case of this nature has been demonstrated in biological control, it is not too unlikely a hypothesis because the only major changes would have to have been in host preference and the development of reproductive isolation between the two. They are quite similar morphologically, although distinguishable under high power magnification. They do not interbreed, hence unquestionably are distinct species. Support for Yasumatsu's hypothesis lies in the fact that *A. beneficus* has never been collected outside of Japan, even in the presumed native home of its host, *C. rubens*, in China.

Beginning in 1948, *A. beneficus* was transferred in large numbers from Kyushu to various orchards on the islands of Honshu and Shikoku. It never failed to become established wherever liberated. Results were spectacular, resulting in complete biological control everywhere. One example of the effectiveness of the parasite will suffice. Twenty mated females were released in a heavily infested citrus orchard of 3000 trees. Judging from my own observations in citrus elsewhere probably at least 100000 scales were present per tree or 300000000 in the orchard. Within three years of the single release of twenty parasites, it was nearly impossible to find a live scale in the orchard.

This instance of biological control emphasizes the point that it is not always necessary to go abroad to discover effective natural enemies. There are other similar cases where efficient enemies have been transferred from one part of a country to another with great success. (See Yasumatsu, 1958.)

Purple scale in California and elsewhere, 1948 on

Although the purple scale *Lepidosaphes beckii* (Newman) was one of the world's most serious pests of citrus, it, like many of today's major pests, was never the object of a formalized biological control project. The discovery of the key parasite cannot be attributed just to luck but it was incidental to the search for parasites of the even more serious California red scale. Had a purple scale project been concentrated on specifically earlier, the parasite could have been discovered years sooner, with consequent prior alleviation of the problem and resultant much greater accumulation of savings to agriculture in many countries.

As a matter of fact, the Italian entomologist Filipo Silvestri recorded observing a parasite of purple scale on lemons in Macao, China, during his exploration of South China and Japan in 1924–5 for the University of California. Unfortunately no one followed through on this because it undoubtedly was the parasite in question, *Aphytis lepidosaphes* Compere, that was later to be obtained for the first time years later from nearby Canton, China. We now know it to be the dominant parasite throughout southeast Asia where it maintains the purple scale at very low population levels.

In November 1948, Dr J. L. Gressitt, who was primarily searching for California red scale parasites, sent live material of *A. lepidosaphes* from Canton to the biological control insectary of the University of California at Riverside by airmail. A total of several thousand live specimens were received from the Canton area and from Taiwan through 1949. It was immediately cultured and several small colonies released in the field in southern California during 1949. Subsequent colonizations were made through 1952 to facilitate the rate of increase and distribution. The extremely cold winter of 1949–50 drastically reduced the first colonies, but by the fall of 1950 establishment was evident in most sites. Over the next few years the parasite became thoroughly established, common, and spread throughout all infested areas. It even moved on its own over 100 miles into Baja California, Mexico, from the nearest point of liberation in California. The purple scale infestations were reduced greatly but not to the point of completely satisfactory control. However, chemical applications could be reduced by about half because of the effect of the parasite. We were able to determine from field and laboratory studies that the reason for the parasite not being completely successful in southern California was due primarily to mortality caused by low winter temperatures.

Subsequently, from 1952 to 1968, we made shipments of *A. lepidosaphes* to thirteen other countries or states having serious infestations of purple scale and ironically the parasite was completely successful in subjugating the scale in most of these from which we either have received reports or have made personal observations. Complete success has been reported for Texas, Mexico, Greece and Brazil; Peru reported a substantial degree of control, Chile and Cyprus partial biological control.

This parasite has an unusually good ability to disperse. We have found it to be established by accident in as many countries as it has been sent to purposely and it is credited with completely effective biological control in most of these. Florida is a good example. The purple scale was a very serious major pest there for years. The parasite was first recorded there in 1958 and indications were that it probably had not been present more than two or three years. How it arrived is a mystery, but by about 1960 the scale had been reduced to insignificant numbers. This case emphasizes again how much loss society suffers from lack of sufficient knowledge and emphasis on the biological control approach. (See DeBach and Landi, 1961; DeBach, 1971*a*.)

Citrus blackfly in Mexico, 1949

This is one of the larger projects and great successes of modern times. It developed as a co-operative effort between the Departments of Agriculture of Mexico and the United States because of the danger of spread into the United States.

The citrus blackfly *Aleurocanthus woglumi* Ashby was first found at El Dorado, Sinaloa, on the west coast of Mexico in 1935. In spite of quarantine barriers it spread like wildfire and by the early 1950s was the most serious pest in most of the commercial citrus areas of the country. Chemical control was difficult, sometimes ineffective and prohibitively expensive. If heavy infestations were not controlled within one year complete crop failure would result. In general, growers reported approximately 80 percent crop reduction in heavily infested areas. The threat to the citrus industry was so great that in 1951 the President of Mexico decreed the establishment of a National Blackfly Committee. The Spanish name 'mosca prieta' became a household term throughout Mexico.

After *Eretmocerus serius*, the parasite that had earlier controlled the citrus blackfly in Cuba and elsewhere, had been imported from the United States Department of Agriculture laboratory in Panama and established in 1943 but found to be ineffective except in restricted areas of continual high humidity, other natural enemies were sought in the native home area in the Orient. Herbert D. Smith, of the US Department of Agriculture, went to Malaysia in 1948 to obtain parasites that C. P. Clausen had previously recorded there. He shipped live material the old fashioned way in Wardian cages and also made one air shipment of infested leaves. Nothing came from the Wardian cages and only a few parasites emerged from the airmail shipment but failed to become established. Smith then moved on to India and Pakistan to search in areas more similar climatically to the Mexican citrus areas. He spent eight months there in 1948–9 conducting a wide-ranging survey; then, from November 1948 to April 1950, made twenty-five air shipments of parasitized material to the special USDA quarantine laboratory in Mexico City. Of eight parasites and two predators received, four parasite species became established and three – *Amitus hesperidum* Silvestri, *Prospaltella clypealis* Silv. and *P. opulenta* Silv. – eventually became dominant in controlling the citrus blackfly. A nationally co-ordinated program of great magnitude rapidly arranged for the re-collection of parasites developing in the field and their distribution to all areas of the country. At the peak period of the campaign about 1600 people were employed and hundreds of millions of parasites redistributed. By the end of 1953 the pest was well controlled by the parasites in nearly all groves of the states of Morelos, Vera Cruz, Puebla, Oaxaca, Guerrero, Mexico, Colima, Jalisco, Guanajuato, Hildalgo and San Luis Potosi. By 1955 commercially satisfactory biological control occurred in virtually all citrus areas of the country. Now the term 'avispas' for the parasites became a household word.

Amitus hesperidum was the most generally effective parasite, especially in reducing heavy infestations, but is susceptible to lengthy periods of hot weather, so *Prospaltella opulenta*, which is quite tolerant of hot weather, became the dominant parasite in states such as Sonora or Nuevo Leon. *P. clypealis* attains optimum performance under humid conditions and throughout Mexico in general is more effective than *P. opulenta*. Thus these parasites complement each other very well. Their ecological relationships in Mexico could hardly have been guessed from their distribution and the ecological evidence obtained in India and Pakistan. This affords strong support for the general biological control practice of importing and testing all likely natural enemies rather than trying to prejudge which one will be the best and thereby excluding some. The idea of preselecting the one 'best' parasite is based on the now discounted hypothesis that competition between parasite species may reduce overall effectiveness in host population regulation. In spite of the intense degree of competition that occurred between these three species it was not detrimental to host population regulation but rather enhanced it. (See Smith and Maltby, 1964.)

Rhodesgrass scale in Texas and elsewhere, 1949 on

This so-called scale, *Antonina graminis* (Mask.), a destructive pest of several valuable range grasses, became extremely serious in Texas following its discovery in 1942 and by the early 1950s had completely destroyed thousands of acres of excellent stands of Rhodesgrass. Control with insecticides was economically unfeasible under range conditions. Actually this pest is a mealybug and technically should be called the Rhodesgrass mealybug; however, it has nearly always been referred to as a scale in the literature so we shall follow common usage.

It was known that one internal parasite, *Anagyrus antoninae* Timb., occurred in Hawaii where the scale was only a minor pest, so this parasite was imported early in 1949. It was cultured and released in large numbers and became established, but proved to be of little value because it could not stand the high temperatures and low humidities of southern Texas. Several parasites were imported from France in 1954–5 but no establishment occurred. Then in 1957 a new parasite species, *Neodusmetia sangwani* (Rao), was discovered attacking Rhodesgrass scale near Delhi and Bangalore, India. It was introduced and established in Texas in 1959. Subsequently colonies were sent from there to Mexico, Brazil, Bermuda, Arizona, California and Florida.

The parasite was soon shown to be effective in reducing Rhodesgrass scale to subeconomic levels. Substantial host reductions always followed within one year of the establishment of adequate colonies. This was effective in eliminating losses in yield due to scale damage. There was one major hitch, however; the parasite was functionally wingless (brachypterous) and therefore distributed itself very slowly from foci of colonization since it had to crawl. Females were very short-lived and only dispersed about six feet in their lifetime. To compensate for this an ingenious program was developed. Parasitized scales were collected from colonies in the field, packaged in suitable containers and mass distributed by dropping from airplanes. This has resulted in a great speed-up in attainment of complete distribution of the parasite throughout the infested area of Texas. (See Schuster, Boling and Marony, 1971.)

Effective biological control of Rhodesgrass scale has also been reported from Florida and Brazil by *Neodusmetia sangwani*.

Olive scale in California, 1951–7

This native of the Middle East, *Parlatoria oleae* (Colvée), became accidentally established near Fresno about 1934 on olive. It rapidly spread throughout the Central Valley and into southern California,

169

becoming a major pest of many deciduous fruit crops and ornamentals in addition to olives. Monetary losses due to damage and the cost of chemical control were well over $1 000 000 per year. It not only caused massive plant damage due to heavy infestations but was additionally serious on olives because even one scale per olive fruit would cause discoloration and subsequent cullage. This made it evident from the beginning that biological control on olives would have to be especially efficient.

An intensive program of biological control was initiated in 1949. First, a 'strain' of *Aphytis maculicornis* (Masi) attacking olive scale was imported from Egypt, but proved to be of no consequence. In 1951, H. S. Smith arranged for Dr A. M. Boyce to search for natural enemies throughout the presumed native home of the olive scale, from India through the Middle East, North Africa and the Mediterranean. Boyce was abroad about a year and made numerous consignments to California by air from India, Pakistan, Afghanistan, Iran, Iraq, Syria, Lebanon, Israel, Cyprus, Egypt, Greece and Spain. Even during this relatively modern period he had plenty of adventures, including collecting in rebel areas under armed escorts. Follow-up shipments were made by collaborators from India and Pakistan in 1952–3.

Several species of parasites were obtained and colonized in California, including four so-called 'biological strains' or sibling species of *Aphytis maculicornis*. These were indistinguishable morphologically but laboratory studies showed that they possessed distinct biological attributes, so they were reared and released separately in the field. It was soon obvious that the 'Persian strain' of *A. maculicornis* released in 1952 was the only natural enemy showing appreciable promise in the field, so insectary production, colonization and field study plots were concentrated on this parasite. Over twenty-seven million were colonized between 1952 and 1960 at several hundred sites in twenty-four counties. This illustrates the importance in foreign exploration work of obtaining parasites from all parts of the range of a pest species and of recognizing that distinct biological races or sibling species may be found with distinctly different potentials in diverse parts of the range of distribution.

Soon dramatic results were evident. The Persian *Aphytis* became readily established everywhere and increased rapidly, commonly attaining parasitization rates of 90 percent or more and generally reducing the average olive scale population densities by about 98 or 99 percent. Plant damage *per se* was eliminated. However, even this drastic reduction proved to be economically unsatisfactory on olive in many cases, because, as mentioned, even one scale on a fruit may result in its being culled, and not more than five percent cullage could be tolerated. Since a heavily infested olive tree might have upwards of 1 000 000 scales, a reduction of '99 percent would leave 10 000 scales, which could mean that quite a few fruit might have one or more scales. The parasite was prevented from being more effective because its populations were greatly reduced each summer by the hot dry weather. Otherwise, it undoubtedly would have produced complete biological control everywhere on its own, as it did in certain favorable locations.

The establishment of additional effective natural enemies obviously was necessary. Although the writer was not assigned to this project he knew of the need through colleagues at Berkeley and as a result of a fortuitous combination of circumstances, was able to obtain and ship to California from West Pakistan, the parasite that ultimately made biological control completely satisfactory.

I was searching for parasites of the California red scale in West Pakistan early in 1957 and had gone with Dr M. A. Ghani to a remote village in the Tribal Territories where citrus had been reported. It was to be a brief three-day trip with one day at the village for collecting because of continuing travel commitments. Upon arrival there we found that the altitude was somewhat too high and the climate too cool for citrus, so I spent the day looking for other scale insect parasites on deciduous fruit trees and ornamentals. Olive scale was found and parasite activity was noticeable, especially emergence holes of internal parasites in the dead scales. I knew that no internal parasites were established in California. Consequently I collected as much of this material as I could and we returned to Rawalpindi the next day, where I packaged it and sent it on to the University of California at Berkeley by airmail.

Two species of parasites emerged from this single shipment and both were successfully cultured. Only one, however, the then new species, *Coccophagoides utilis* Doutt, became established. By early 1961 it showed great promise of improving the degree of biological control of olive scale in the two groves in which it was first released in 1957-8. This led to mass-culture and colonization of over 4 000 000 of the parasites during 1962-4 at over 170 sites in twenty-five counties. Widespread, complete biological control soon resulted. *C. utilis* acted as a complementary mortality factor to *Aphytis maculicornis*. Although it only added about four to eight percent additional host mortality to what *A. maculicornis* would have produced alone, this was sufficient to reduce the equilibrium level of the scale population so considerably that virtually no cullage of olives remained. This case provides an excellent illustration of the fruitlessness of trying to evaluate the potential or actual effectiveness of a parasite on the basis of the percent parasitization of the host, and it emphasizes that we should try all available parasites within reason until completely satisfactory biological control is obtained. (See Huffaker and Kennett, 1966; DeBach, Rosen and Kennett, 1971.)

Winter moth in Canada, 1955–60

This moth, *Operophtera brumata* Linnaeus, was looked upon as just a nuisance of shade trees when the project began in Nova Scotia in 1954. It had been found for the first time in 1949 scattered along the southern coast, but apparently was accidentally introduced in the 1930s. It moved slowly and the only threat seemed to be that it might eventually reach more valuable trees elsewhere. It was not until 1962 that it had invaded New Brunswick and Prince Edward Island. Eventually though, based on its range in Europe, the moth appeared capable of spreading across North America. However, the economics of the situation changed in just a few years. Hardwoods now are a valuable commodity and it has been stated that had they been so important in 1954, chemical control would probably have been utilized and biological control attempts passed by.

In a ten-year span following the invasion of the winter moth into Nova Scotia from its home in Europe, damage to oak forests in just two counties amounted to some 26 000 cords of wood per year. Currently this would be worth about $2 000 000. During this period the moth spread over most of the Province. Other forest and orchard trees also were damaged and it has been estimated that probably all oaks would have been killed and a minimum of $12 000 000 loss suffered in this area alone had its attacks continued. However, parasites from Europe were imported and effectively colonized from 1955 to 1960 and two species, *Cyzenis albicans* (Fall.) a tachinid, and *Agrypon flaveolatum* (Grav.) an ichneumonid, became established, the former first in 1955 and the latter in 1956–7. Eventually they brought about complete biological control for a cost of about $160 000.

Initial increase of the parasites was slower than usual and it took about six years following liberation before host population collapse occurred at a given release site. In addition to the monetary savings in Nova Scotia, the rate of spread into new areas has been greatly reduced in proportion to the reduction in host populations by the parasites. The two parasites have been shown to be compatible and strongly complementary. *C. albicans* is the most efficient in reducing high host densities but *A. flaveolatum* is more effective at low host densities. The original collections in Europe may reflect this indirectly. There, the heaviest infestations possible were sought out in order to obtain the most parasites for shipment. In other words small outbreaks were sought out. In such dense host populations the dominant parasite may not represent the best regulatory agent, or even a satisfactory one, when host densities are low, but rather the dominant one may be dependent upon high densities in order to maintain itself. These European collections yielded about ten *Cyzenis* to one *Agrypon*. When these two parasites were first well established in Nova Scotia (1959) host densities were high and *Cyzenis* was much the dominant parasite. By the time host densities at the original sites had been considerably reduced in 1962, *Agrypon* was slightly dominant. In 1963 host densities were too low to obtain adequate parasitization data. The data in Table 6 from the original release sites show the change in dominance of the two parasite species as the host population decreased.

Table 6. *Dominance of the two parasites on* Operophtera brumata

Year	Average percent parasitization by		Average host population density‡
	*Cyzenis**	*Agrypon†*	
1959	10	0.1	60
1960	34	4	75
1961	58	7	70
1962	38	40	37
1963 ⎱ host too scarce to provide data			6
1964 ⎰ on percent parasitization			0

* Established 1956.
† Established 1957.
‡ As measured by percent defoliation of red oak in the vicinity of liberation areas.

These data illustrate the point that in searching abroad for new natural enemies, one should not concentrate only on collecting where the host is most common and easily found. To do so could mean

173

missing the best parasite which may be found where host populations are the lowest.

It is of interest that intensive quantitative population studies of factors effecting the winter moth near Oxford, England, covering some twenty-odd years, did not indicate parasites to be of major consequence. This again raises the question of the value of such studies in the evaluation of the effectiveness of natural enemies in prey population regulation (see Chapters 3 and 7 *re* experimental methods of evaluation). Mathematical model studies in England by G. C. Varley and G. R. Gradwell of winter moth–parasite interactions also have led to predictions by them that in Canada strong oscillations in interacting populations of the winter moth and its parasites will cause damaging outbreaks of the winter moth at nine- or ten-year intervals. It will be interesting to see if this rather unlikely event occurs solely as a result of such interactions between the parasite–host populations. No such instance has yet been recorded among the many other successful cases of applied biological control. (See Embree, 1971; Mesnil, 1967.)

Another interesting point is that this case, as also was true with the eucalyptus snout-beetle in South Africa, is an exception to Clausen's rule. This generally true precept states that if imported natural enemies are destined to become completely successful in host population regulation they will do so either within three host generations or within three years. In this instance it took six to seven years.

Florida red scale in Israel and elsewhere, 1956 on

The biological control of the Florida red scale *Chrysomphalus aonidum* (Linn.) (= *ficus* Ashmead) in Israel stands out as an illustration of the simplicity, ease and inexpensiveness with which biological control can sometimes be accomplished – given an enthusiast to push it. This outstanding success against Israel's worst citrus pest was achieved principally through correspondence, as was the case earlier with the citriculus mealybug in Israel, and was brought about by the same man, Israel Cohen, head of the Technical Division of the Citrus Marketing Board of Israel. No foreign explorer was directly involved. Cohen, who, it will be recalled, was not a trained entomologist, wrote to specialists in biological control of scale insects at the University of California at Riverside in 1955 seeking advice as to where natural enemies might be obtained. He was informed that at least two species of parasites were known in Hong Kong where the scale was indigenous and scarce and that arrangements might be made with S. K. Cheng, a part-time collector for Riverside, to obtain and make air shipments. Cheng was a biology teacher who had originally been trained 'on the job' by Dr J. L. Gressitt of the Bishop Museum, Honolulu, when Gressitt was doing foreign exploration in the Orient for the University of California at Riverside in the 1940s.

Shipments were begun by Cheng in February 1956, reaching a total of seventy-two during the next two years. All told, they contained relatively few parasites, with approximately equal numbers of *Aphytis holoxanthus* DeBach (then thought to be *A. lingnanensis*) and *Pteroptrix* (= *Casca*) *smithi* (Compere) being present. Less than 150 live females and males of *Aphytis* were received in 1956 but laboratory culture was immediately successful with the first few specimens tested and all the others were then released in infested groves in Rehovot, mostly during the period February–May by E. Rivnay and later by David Nadel. These few gave rise to the later millions that reproduced in the field and subjugated the scale. The *Pteroptrix* was not successfully cultured in the laboratory but about 120 individuals were released directly in one grove from December 1956 to April 1957. *Pteroptrix* was not seen again until a few were found in 1960. It has since remained inconspicuous and largely only in the area of original release.

In September 1957, about one and a half years after the first release of *A. holoxanthus*, a homeowner in Rehovot informed Nadel that for the first time in his memory the citrus trees in his backyard were clean of Florida red scale. *A. holoxanthus* was obviously responsible for this and an immediate follow-up survey by Cohen and Nadel of the citrus groves about Rehovot showed a considerable area completely clean of the scale. Bordering this area scale was still abundant but the parasite was extremely common and furthermore was found to have spread as far as twenty kilometers to the north and ten to the south. Further distribution of the parasite in 1957 was then rapidly accomplished by movement of parasitized scales on twigs and branches to new locations and by release of insectary-reared parasites during 1958–9.

Complete biological control was achieved throughout the main citrus-growing area of Israel, the coastal plain, within two to three years after the first liberation. I visited groves in this area in 1960 and during several days of observation saw only a few isolated scales where previously there would have been millions. It has been conservatively estimated that savings of well over one million dollars per year can be attributed to this successful project that cost only a few thousand dollars. Mr Cohen wrote me in late 1959 that in 1956 before the parasites were exerting any effect, 3000 tons of oil were used to spray for the Florida red scale; in 1957 this was halved to 1500 tons; by 1958 – two years after the first release of parasites – it was reduced to 500 tons and in 1959 only 10–20 tons were used.

Regardless of the closed border between Israel and Lebanon, *Aphytis holoxanthus* soon dispersed into that country and produced similar results. It has been purposefully introduced subsequently into Florida, Mexico, South Africa, Brazil and northern Peru with outstanding results and at a cost of only a few dollars to cover the air shipments in most of these cases. Additional millions of dollars in reduced pest control costs and damage are accruing annually from these successes.

Historically and technically there are several points of interest in this case. They all revolve around the facts that inadequate knowledge of the taxonomy of *Aphytis* species and lack of financial support for biological control work prevented the discovery of *A. holoxanthus* and its successful use in the countries mentioned, as well as in some others where it still remains a pest, for at least eighty years.

William Ashmead of the United States Department of Agriculture, stationed in Florida to work on citrus insects, attempted by correspondence as early as 1879 to ascertain the native home of the Florida red scale in order to obtain its natural enemies for use in that State. He was unsuccessful but had funds been available and knowledge sufficient the biological control of the Florida red scale in Florida could have been the first great successful project rather than that of the cottony-cushion scale in California which occurred ten years later. Thus the Florida red scale remained a serious pest in Florida eighty years longer than it needed to.

Another chance was missed when Alfred Koebele reared an *Aphytis* from Florida red scale in Hong Kong, apparently in the late 1890s, and sent the specimens to the United States National Museum. They were misidentified as *Aphytis mytilaspidis* (LeBaron) and subsequently ignored, probably because *mytilaspidis* was common in the United States, but as far as can be told today (they are poorly prepared) they are *A. holoxanthus*. Then in 1924–5, while Professor F. Silvestri was collecting in China for the University of California at Riverside, he recorded noticing differences between the *Aphytis* parasitizing the California red scale and the Florida red scale. He thought the parasite of the former to be *A. chrysomphali* (Mercet) and designated the one from Florida red scale as *Aphytis* sp. Again, this was probably *A. holoxanthus* and had Silvestri formally described it as a new species, as he did with several other important parasites, the resulting publication would have undoubtedly come to the attention of Florida entomologists or others and the successful importation made in this case some thirty years before it finally occurred in Israel. Yet another chance to 'discover' what apparently was *A. holoxanthus* was overlooked following the clues published by T. H. C. Taylor in 1935 in connection with the coconut scale project in Fiji. He recorded a 'form' of *A. chrysomphali* as a parasite of Florida red scale in Java. The pupal stage he pictured is obviously not *chrysomphali* but is identical in appearance with pupae of *A. holoxanthus*. These missed opportunities emphasize, as we do in Chapter 7 and elsewhere, the great need for taxonomic research and for increased foreign exploration and importation of new natural enemies. With many of today's major pests we have done no more than William Ashmead was able to do against the Florida red scale in 1879. (See Cohen and Kamburov, 1968; DeBach, Rosen and Kennett, 1971; Rivnay, 1968.)

California red scale in California, 1957

This scale, *Aonidiella aurantii* (Maskell), is of Oriental origin. It became established in California by the 1870s and for years was the number one pest of citrus, being responsible for losses of millions of dollars annually from damage to trees, loss in fruit quality and cost of insecticidal treatment. Attempts at biological control began in 1889 when Albert Koebele sent in some predatory beetles from Australia, and work has continued with varying degrees of emphasis up to the present. The campaign against the California red scale is the longest in the history of biological control. A detailed and valuable history of the earlier efforts in California has been given by Compere (1961). His account shows how a combination of confused taxonomy and lack of adequate knowledge of biology and ecology prevented the discovery and importation of the most important parasites of the California red scale for fifty or sixty years. The biological and ecological problems involved in working toward a successful solution have been so complex that a large book would be necessary to cover the entire story which is still continuing. Only the briefest resume can be given here.

Up to 1941, several predatory beetles and one parasite, *Aphytis chrysomphali* Mercet, attacked the scale in California. They were generally of no practical significance, although we were able to demonstrate later that *A. chrysomphali* was potentially capable of controlling red scale populations very effectively in mild coastal locations if not interfered with by chemical treatments or by honeydew-seeking ants. Rarely were both of these factors absent from any given grove in the restricted climatic zones favorable to the parasite, so it had been considered to be of no consequence over the years, after it became accidentally established in California about 1900. Inasmuch as virtually all *Aphytis* reared from the California red scale abroad up to 1948 were considered to be *A. chrysomphali*, no attempt was made to import any of these, which, as we shall see, ultimately included the two best parasites now established. Thus the inadequate state of the taxonomy of the genus *Aphytis* caused a delay of some fifty years in the introduction of the most valuable parasites into California and subsequently elsewhere.

The degree of success in biological control of the California red scale in California can now be considered as substantial. It was considered to be a failure for nearly sixty years, however. Completely satisfactory control occurs in some groves year after year and this is essentially the case in entire districts. In groves under good biological control the scale is so scarce as to be difficult to find, even by an expert. Nonetheless, a large amount of chemical treatment is still practiced. I consider the real need for much of this to be questionable or definitely unnecessary, especially in coastal and intermediate climatic zones, but there are certain climatic areas where the parasites currently established are rendered ineffective by cold winter weather, hot summer weather, or both. In general the degree of unfavorability increases with distance from the coast. Thus in the desert areas of the Imperial Valley, the extent of biological control is reduced to a negligible level. In any event, the California red scale has lost the dubious distinction of being California's major citrus pest. Many thousands of acres now go untreated each year with enormous savings to the citrus industry.

Four species of parasites are responsible for the degree of biological control now achieved. All were established between 1941 and 1957, with the last one being the most important. Two species of *Aphytis* are in general the most effective of the natural enemies. Each of these alone can regulate California red scale populations at extremely low levels if habitat conditions are favorable to them. *Aphytis melinus* DeBach, imported by the author from India and West Pakistan in 1956–7, must be rated number one. It is completely dominant in interior areas and generally in intermediate climatic areas but is complemented in its work by the red scale race of *Comperiella bifasciata* Howard, which was imported from south China in 1941. This was established from an original stock of only five mated females. *Aphytis lingnanensis* Compere, imported from southern China in 1947–8, remains generally dominant in coastal districts but is strongly complemented by the red scale race of *Prospaltella perniciosi* Tower imported from Formosa in 1949.

These four parasite species are the last natural enemies to become established and are by far the most effective of all the many species of predators and parasites imported and liberated since 1890. This illustrates the value of continued research and indicates that there probably never is any certain point in time when a given biological control project can safely be pronounced to be a failure. That 'best' parasite may still remain undiscovered.

The discovery and importation of the last and currently best one, *Aphytis melinus*, was a direct result of increased taxonomic knowledge and of previous ecological field studies with *A. chrysomphali* beginning in 1946 and with *A. lingnanensis* starting in 1948. These studies for the first time proved experimentally in the field that species of *Aphytis* can be highly effective in host population regulation. The investigation also demonstrated that parasites can be precluded from exerting adequate control by adverse climatic factors. As a consequence we deliberately sought another species of *Aphytis* from climatic zones similar to the harsher interior zones of southern California. Areas of northwest India and Pakistan were some of the few that were known to be similar, hence were searched. This led to the discovery of *Aphytis melinus*. We still hope to discover another species that will be fully adapted to the most severe weather conditions where citrus is grown in southern California. It may exist in the interior of south China, which has been unavailable for foreign exploration during most of the modern era. Meanwhile, we have sent *A. melinus* to many other countries for use against the California red scale, including Argentina, Australia, Chile, Cyprus, Greece, Israel, Morocco, South Africa and Turkey. It is reported to have become established in all of these, but for the most part results are not yet final.

An interesting sidelight of this project has helped clarify the basic role of competition between parasite species as it related to host population regulation and the biological control policy of multiple species importations. It has been hypothesized by some that, because multiple importations will necessarily involve competition between parasite species, this will result in poorer regulation of host populations. Therefore they have proposed that only the single best natural enemy should be introduced, although how this could be determined *a priori* has never been ascertained. Virtually all biological control specialists disagree with the latter idea both as being impractical and ecologically unrealistic. Results from the California red scale project support this and further demonstrate strikingly that even the most severe competition between parasite species does not interfere with host population regulation but rather enhances it. The story and reasons are as follows.

Admittedly much trial and error has been involved in the eighty-odd-year campaign against the California red scale. About fifty or more species of natural enemies have been purposely introduced; others became accidentally established and certain native ones adopted the red scale. A highly complex and drastic succession of changes has occurred over the years among the various predators and parasites of this scale. Natural enemy species have become established, increased in abundance, sometimes to become dominant, and then later on, as additional species were imported, decreased drastically or even disappeared completely. Meanwhile, there has never been any observation or suggestion made that all this competition between natural enemies has ever proved favorable to population increase of the California red scale at any time. In fact the opposite is true; California red scale populations have continued to decrease.

The most intense and interesting competition has occurred during the past thirty years, principally between species of *Aphytis*, *Prospaltella*, *Comperiella* and several predatory ladybeetles. The interactions now have nearly run their course and homeostasis between the remaining species is being approached. The current situation is that briefly mentioned previously, with *A. melinus* dominant and *Comperiella bifasciata* complementary in interior areas and with *A. lingnanensis* generally dominant and *Prospaltella perniciosi* strongly complementary in coastal areas.

This competition between natural enemies over the years has caused the virtual disappearance by the newer parasites of the predaceous ladybeetles which up to about twenty years ago used to reduce heavy outbreaks of the scale periodically but were unable to maintain it at low levels. Following the establishment of *Aphytis lingnanensis* in 1948, we have documented its role in causing the virtual, if not complete, extinction of *Aphytis chrysomphali* which was the dominant, generally distributed enemy of California red scale twenty-five years ago and which produced excellent biological control in certain favorable habitats. We subsequently have followed the complete elimination of *A. lingnanensis* from interior citrus areas where it was exclusively dominant in the mid-1950s by competition provided by *A. melinus* which was first established in 1957. Meanwhile, we have seen that the apparently less efficient parasites, *Comperiella* and *Prospaltella*, continue to coexist with one or the other species of *Aphytis* and to complement them, because they attack different host stages and are not strict ecological homologs.

In spite of this intense and continuing competition between natural enemies for a single host species the extent of biological control has concurrently increased until today California red scale populations are much lower in general than they ever have been. From careful study of the large mass of biological and ecological data accumulated on this project we see no possibility that the observed results could have been predicted with any accuracy beforehand. Too many variables are involved even in what might appear to be a simple ecosystem such as citrus. We have to conclude that we can knowledgeably restrict the number of promising natural enemy candidates for importation to a relative few, but we cannot predict in advance which one or which combination will be the best in any given habitat, much less in the variety of habitats usually inhabited by a major pest. (See DeBach, Rosen and Kennett, 1971.)

Dictyospermum scale in Greece, 1962

This co-operative pilot project, designed to add impetus to biological control research in Greece, was initiated in 1962 when the author was invited to spend his sabbatical leave as a Senior Fullbright Fellow at the Benaki Phytopathological Institute in Kiphissia, near Athens. It was chosen because it could be carried out rapidly, at little expense, and with good probability of success because the parasites to be tested were known to be effective in other countries. At that time the dictyospermum scale *Chrysomphalus dictyospermi* (Morgan) was the number one pest of citrus in Greece, the California red scale was second in importance and the purple scale third. We imported parasites for all three, but this discussion will cover only the results obtained against the dictyospermum scale. Favorable results were obtained in each case however. Chemical treatment was generally practiced but damage from scale insects often occurred in spite of it. Heavily infested and damaged citrus trees were commonly seen in the principal citrus areas in the Peloponnesus and Crete as evidenced by leaf-drop, killed twigs and scale-encrusted fruits.

Three established species of parasites were found to attack the dictyospermum scale of which *Aphytis chrysomphali* was the most abundant and potentially the most effective. However, as was the case earlier in California against the California red scale, *A. chrysomphali* was apparently precluded by adverse environmental conditions from exerting any appreciably reliable degree of biological control.

At that time we were mass culturing several species of *Aphytis* in the insectary at the University of California at Riverside, all of which had been reared from the California red scale in different countries and imported for trials against that scale in California. The three that we considered most likely candidates for testing in Greece against both the dictyospermum scale and the California red scale were *A. melinus* (originally from India and W. Pakistan), *A. lingnanensis* (originally from south China) and *A. coheni* DeBach (originally from Israel). The former two were known to be effective parasites of the California red scale in certain locations in the field in California as well as in their native homes. *A. coheni* was new and its status unknown.

None of these parasites were known with certainty to occur on dictyospermum scale anywhere in the field (this scale is not a pest in California), but we had found that *A. lingnanensis* and to a lesser extent *A. melinus* and *A. coheni* did very well on dictyospermum scale in laboratory tests at Riverside.

Inasmuch as no scale cultures for rearing of the parasites were then available at the Benaki Institute, direct field colonizations of imported pure cultures of adult *Aphytis* adults were indicated. The main problem, even with air shipment, is that the adult parasites are quite short-lived and suffer considerable mortality within a few days, especially if subjected to temperature extremes en route. The first air shipments from California in October 1962 evidently were transferred en route to Athens and held to await airplane connections, hence took several days. Many of the parasites were dead on arrival but the survivors were colonized. Therefore, special arrangements were made with Trans World Airlines for the next shipment to receive preferential treatment. As a result the next and final air freight shipments of November 1962 arrived within twenty-four hours after leaving Riverside, California. This is probably a record for such long-distance shipment of natural enemies. Fig. 33 shows this shipment being received

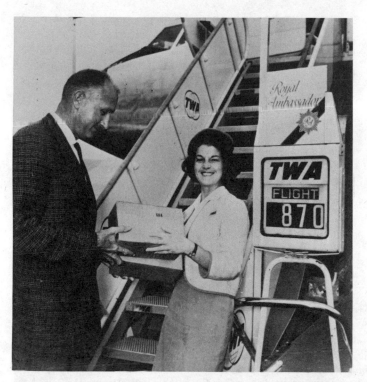

Fig. 33. The author receiving a shipment of several species of adult *Aphytis* parasites in Athens, Greece, only 24 hours after they had been sent air-freight from the University of California insectary at Riverside, California. The parasites were released directly in the field and brought about complete biological control of the two worst scale pests of citrus and substantial control of two others.

by the author at the Athens airport. No mortality occurred among these parasites. They were colonized in the field, even in Crete, within the first or second day after arrival. Substantial numbers ranging between about 8000 to 20000 of each species were liberated.

The following winter of 1962–3 was unusually cold but recoveries were made the following spring in low numbers, with *A. melinus* being the only one of any consequence taken and ultimately the only one to persist. In spite of the fact that about 18000 additional *A. lingnanensis* were liberated in June 1963, a very favorable period, *lingnanensis* failed to become established.

Aphytis melinus increased and spread rapidly during 1963 both on dictyospermum and on California red scale. It was recovered from four of the five sites sampled in October–November 1963, one year

183

Fig. 34. Map of southern Greece and Crete showing the four original localities in which the scale insect parasite *Aphytis melinus* was colonized in October–November 1963. The shaded area shows approximate dispersal of *Aphytis melinus* from these sites by December 1966. It became strongly, if not exclusively, dominant over the originally established *Aphytis chrysomphali* by that time.

after release, and already comprised 79 percent of the total parasite population as compared to 21 percent for *A. chrysomphali*. It had become dominant at the points of liberation within one year; within two years it had completely replaced *chrysomphali* at these sites. After about two and a half years *A. melinus* had successfully dispersed from the original sites some 200 kilometers across country which is cultivated only in scattered areas and is generally quite barren. Other data bearing on this point indicate an effective dispersal rate of about 100 kilometers per year. This far surpasses any of the other species studied which attack *Chrysomphalus dictyospermi* or *Aonidiella aurantii*. This ability to disperse may be related to searching ability and thus may indicate why *A. melinus* is such an effective parasite. By the end of 1966 *A. melinus* was strongly dominant and had virtually replaced *A. chrysomphali* throughout the Peloponnesus and in all areas surveyed in Crete. It had also dispersed to the islands of Lesbos and Chios (see Fig. 34). Soon thereafter it was found for the first time on the mainland of Turkey at Izmir.

Biological control of the dictyospermum scale has been outstandingly complete. At the original release sites in the Peloponnesus near Trejenia it was nearly impossible to find scales on trees that were encrusted three years before. As *A. melinus* spread and became abundant the dictyospermum scale became everywhere reduced to insignificant levels When I revisited Greece in 1968 I was unable to find anything but a rare specimen of this scale on trees which previously I knew to be chronically encrusted. The entire cost of this project as far as the practical results are concerned was only a few hundred dollars, including the cost of importation of the parasites and their field colonization in Greece. There are any number of projects in the world today that could be conducted just as cheaply and easily if the people responsible for decision-making merely had the necessary knowledge that parasites are available. (See DeBach and Argyriou, 1967.)

Green vegetable bug in Australia, Hawaii and elsewhere, 1933–62

This plant-sucking pest, *Nezara viridula* Linnaeus, known as the green vegetable bug, is of cosmopolitan distribution, being found in North and South America, Africa, Australia, New Zealand, various Pacific islands and Japan. Its feeding habits are very broad, including a wide range of fruit and ornamental trees, field crops and vegetables. Such omnivorous feeding characteristics have made it an important pest nearly everywhere it invaded from its native areas in Asia and Africa.

Australia was the first country to start a biological control attack against the green vegetable bug by using the imported egg parasite *Trissolcus basalis* (Wollaston) from Egypt. Large releases of *Trissolcus* were carried out in various States lasting from 1934 to 1943. Results were not always monitored consistently, so most reports circulated abroad that the results were of little consequence, even though *Trissolcus* was well established in all infested States. Consequently this project might justifiably be termed the 'case of the forgotten natural enemies', except in Western Australia which claimed outstanding results early in the game. Otherwise, for some 15–20 years, not much credit was given to the activities of the parasites, especially in areas having relatively cold winters. By 1960 the benefits from the establishment of *Trissolcus* were considered variable – what we would term a partial success. As we have seen the program was rated an outstanding success in Western Australia. Excellent results also were reported from South

Australia and satisfactory control from New South Wales except in inland areas. This was true of other inland areas.

Meanwhile later introductions of other races or strains of *T. basalis* from various countries were made but only the Pakistan race is known to have become established. A more recent review of the situation (Ratcliffe, 1965) shows that the pest is now fully controlled in the inland areas, with most credit for this going to the Pakistan race in these areas. With continuing research efforts Australia finally achieved a complete and outstanding success against this serious pest. This project is an excellent illustration of the value of so-called races, strains or ecotypes in biological control, as well as of the pay-off that may come from continued research.

In Hawaii the green vegetable bug was first discovered in late 1961 and an immediate program of parasite introductions began early in 1962. The success achieved in Australia was already known so parasites were obtained first from there. Other parasites were flown in from Antigua and Monserrat in 1962 and from Florida in 1963. Large-scale mass production of the imported parasites in 1963 yielded 767 525 egg parasites and 15 712 *Trichopoda pennipes* Fabricius, a tachinid, for field release. As a result by 1964, *Trissolcus basalis*, the egg parasite, and two varieties of *Trichopoda pennipes*, especially *T. pennipes pilipes* from Antigua and Monserrat, were thoroughly established.

Trissolcus basalis was first found to be established in August 1962 and thereafter increased and spread with great rapidity. Rearing records from ten sites on Oahu during the last half of 1963, i.e. about one and a half years following first releases, revealed an average egg parasitization of 94.9 percent. This figure continued over the ensuing years during which period egg clusters of the green vegetable bug became difficult to find in the field. The tachinid *T. pennipes pilipes*, which attacks adult bugs, also increased and spread rapidly on Oahu, showing an average parasitization of about 41 percent for the same period. Both of these parasite species later became abundant on the islands of Hawaii, Kauai and Maui. Complete economic control was achieved first on Oahu and Kauai and has been general on all islands since 1965. (See Davis, 1967.)

Results in New Zealand where the bug was discovered in 1944 were achieved by the importation of *Trissolcus basalis* from Australia in 1949. Serious damage was soon nullified and by 1950, 80 percent parasitization was reported. In 1952, 90 percent parasitization was recorded in certain districts. Overwintering bug populations were

186

greatly reduced that year. Apparently some fluctuations still occur but there has been a gradual decline in the severity of plant damage and the current situation is satisfactory (see Cumber, 1964). The opportunity apparently remains for New Zealand to import and establish one or more other species or strains of parasites.

Trissolcus basalis was imported into Fiji from Australia in 1941. Establishment occurred readily. Also *Trichopoda pennipes* was imported from Florida but establishment is uncertain and results are unknown (O'Connor, 1960). Similarly *Trissolcus basalis* was introduced into a number of other Pacific islands including Tonga (1941), New Caledonia (1942–3) and Samoa (1953) with establishments recorded in each case but biological control results are unavailable.

Walnut aphid in California, 1959 and 1968

This aphid, *Chromaphis juglandicola* Kaltenbach, is a native of the Old World that invaded California at about the beginning of this century. It soon covered all the walnut-growing areas of the State. In spite of attacks by several native natural enemies, the aphid frequently literally covered the trees with exuded honeydew and the resultant black sooty-mold fungus that grows in it. Thus for years, routine insecticidal treatments were necessary, beginning with nicotine sulfate in the early days and progressing to a variety of synthetic organophosphates and chlorinated hydrocarbons in more recent years. These posed the usual problems of upsets, resurgences, development of resistance and drift of toxic materials outside the area being treated.

A change in tactics to biological control obviously was desirable but there has been a long-standing idea prevalent among entomologists that aphids may not be particularly amenable to biological control because they can multiply so rapidly in the spring that damage is done before their natural enemies can catch up with them. Dr Robert van den Bosch, who was in charge of this project, suspected that this applied principally to the less effective, high-density, omnivorous-feeding natural enemies but perhaps not to more host-specific forms. He therefore concentrated his search on the latter and in southern France in 1959 he found a parasitic wasp, *Trioxys pallidus* Haliday, having a high degree of host specificity. It was successfully imported into California and became eminently effective against the aphid in the coastal plain of southern California, spreading rapidly and destroying a very high percentage of the host population. However, the problem was not completely solved because this parasite was not well adapted to conditions in northern and especially central California where, in spite of large-scale releases, it apparently never became permanently established. Evidently the French strain of *T. pallidus* lacked genetic characteristics enabling it to reproduce and survive to any extent in areas of extreme summer heat and low humidity.

Recalling that *Trioxys pallidus* had been observed and collected during 1960 on the hot, dry, central plateau of Iran, van den Bosch obtained live specimens from there in 1968. They were cultured and colonized in central California that summer and fall with spectacular results. Small releases made in June and July gave rise to abundant parasite populations which had dispersed significantly by fall. Further releases were made in the Central Valley in 1969 from insectary cultures. Surveys of release plots in October 1969 showed the parasite to be established in all new release plots and to have spread to a distance of at least eight miles.

The biological control impact of the Iranian *T. pallidus* was closely evaluated during the 1969 and 1970 seasons. It was shown that, starting with a low initial population early in the year, the parasite could increase rapidly and markedly reduce aphid populations by summer or fall. The extent of control was such that very few aphids escaped parasitism to reproduce. As a result very few individuals were present to start the next year and of these over 90 percent were parasitized by parasites that had survived the winter. Population indices showed an average reduction of from 2550 aphids per sample in mid-May 1969 to only eight per sample in mid-May 1970. During 1970 the parasite was found to be present and often abundant in most sites sampled, even though some of these were many miles from the nearest known areas of previous establishment.

By 1971–2, biological control of this aphid could be said to be complete throughout California, except where upsets occurred due to the adverse effects of insecticides used against the codling moth or the walnut huskfly and to a lesser extent from the Argentine ant, interfering with the parasites.

Had taxonomy remained in the alpha stage and the existence of ecotypes not been appreciated, the Iranian *Trioxys pallidus* probably never would have been imported because it is indistinguishable morphologically from the French form imported and established in 1959. It would have been considered to be already established in California. Instead of a complete success, only a partial success would have been achieved. How many more of these opportunities remain undiscovered? I am sure there are a great many but only strong support for, and rigorous dedication by, well-trained bio-ecologists thoroughly familiar with biological control will supply the ultimate answers. (See van den Bosch, Frazer, Davis, Messenger and Hom, 1970.)

Lesser successes and their value

Most but not all of the fifteen cases just discussed have been considered complete successes. Obviously there are all degrees of success possible in applied biological control importation projects, but for convenience they can be divided into complete, substantial and partial degrees of success. These categories may be defined as follows: (1) Complete biological control refers to the successful reduction of a major wide-spread pest to a non-pest level and its permanent maintenance below the economic threshold so that insecticidal treatment becomes rarely, if ever, necessary. (2) Substantial biological control includes cases where economic savings are somewhat less pronounced because of the pest or crop being less important or by the crop area being less extensive or by the control being such that occasional insecticidal treatment is indicated. The latter should mean a reduction in chemical treatment of 75 percent or more. Also control can be complete over most of the pest area but only substantial or partial over some smaller portion of it. (3) Partial biological control includes cases where the pest is definitely reduced but not consistently so, or is not maintained regularly below the economic injury level. Thus regular chemical treatment may remain necessary but may be reduced by approximately 50 percent; intervals between treatment may be lengthened and out-breaks occur less commonly. Partial control can easily mean a saving of 50 percent in reduced treatment costs and a concurrent reduction in environmental pollution. When evaluating published records of successes for purposes of tabulation we also include under this category cases where complete or substantial biological control is obtained in only a minor portion of the infested area, or where we are dealing with minor pests or incipiently established pests as well as insufficiently documented cases which infer a greater degree of success. Partial successes tend to be overlooked or discounted by the average ento-mologist because they are not as obvious as complete or substantial successes, but they do represent important pest reductions and often may be the key to being able to reduce insecticidal treatment enough to make integrated control programs feasible. Even though partial successes tend to be overlooked or discounted, nonetheless they often represent a considerable saving as measured by reduction in damage, lessened need for treatment or reduced hazard of spread.

It might be thought that partial successes constitute the majority of results obtained in biological control. This is far from the case. Seventy-five percent of the successes in control of insect pest species have been either complete or substantial (DeBach, 1971b) whereas only twenty-five percent have been partial. This is discussed in more detail in the second section following.

Summary of worldwide results against weeds

Since 1865, well over 100 species of weeds, representing more than sixty plant genera and thirty families, have been studied as possible objects of biological control importation projects. Research has progressed to the stage of natural enemy importation and colonization against about fifty of these weed species to date. This reflects a rapid recent expansion of this field, particularly in North America during the last decade or so. Up until now North America included about half of the weeds studied as possible targets for biological control projects throughout the world.

Most of the weeds considered for biological control until about 1960 were alien, perennial species infesting relatively undisturbed terrestrial habitats, predominantly grazing lands. However, more recently, an increasing number of annual and biennial, aquatic and semiaquatic, native as well as alien weeds have been objects of biological control research.

The successes achieved in biological weed control have utilized insects as natural enemies for the most part. The plant-feeding insects involved have been a diverse lot representing seven orders and thirty-three families, with about half of the families represented belonging to the Lepidoptera. The biology, form and habits of the natural enemies involved in successful results are widely diverse. Between them they variously attack all of the major vegetative or reproductive parts of these plants considered as a whole. Up to now most successes have been registered against perennial alien rangeland weeds. Perhaps this reflects a concentration of effort on this type of weed until recent years.

Judging by the published results available, a rather high degree of success has been achieved relative to projects attempted. As mentioned, importations of weed-feeding natural enemies have been made against about fifty weed species. Published results have been made for a little over half (27) of these weeds, which have involved forty-one projects in eighteen countries, states or territories. Of these forty-one projects, thirty-one or about 75 percent have achieved a measurable degree of success. Eight projects have been rated as complete successes, nine as substantial successes and fourteen as partial successes, with ten successes bridging these relative categories in terms of control results. Some 55 percent of reported successes fall in the complete or substantial categories. This must be considered an impressive achievement warranting increased emphasis on this ecological approach. [Information furnished by Dr R. D. Goeden, see also Holloway (1964); Andres and Goeden (1971).]

Summary of worldwide results against insect pests

Recently I tabulated and analyzed the number and extent of success obtained from biological control importation projects against insect pests on a world basis (DeBach, 1971b).

It was found that the importation method alone had resulted in the permanent control (either complete, substantial or partial) of at least 120 species of pest insects in nine major orders of insects. Forty-two of these pests were completely controlled; forty-eight species were substantially controlled and thirty fell in the partial control category. Additionally, various of these pest species were subsequently controlled in other countries following the first success, so that all together there have been at least 253 successful projects worldwide up to 1970. Perhaps 10 percent more could be added to this total up to the time of publication of this book. However, for the most part the results from these are still not sufficiently complete for inclusion. This is by far the greatest number of successes achieved by any one non-chemical method, with the possible exception of cultural control which to my knowledge has not been tabulated. The use of resistant plant varieties or irradiation-sterilized insects each apply thus far only to control of a few pest species. All other non-chemical methods combined would add only a few more.

The tabulation showed that natural enemies had been imported against some 223 species of insect pests and some measurable degree of success obtained with the 120 pest species mentioned earlier. This represents some degree of success with over half (54 percent) of the species involved and includes completely successful control of forty-two species. Thus these formerly serious and major pests no longer require chemical treatment in the country where the natural enemy was introduced. A total of ninety species are included in the combined categories of complete and substantial control. The latter category means that only very occasional treatment is needed, or perhaps that complete control was not achieved over the entire range of the pest. Only thirty, or 25 percent, of the pest species controlled fell in the category of partial success. The authenticity of these successes (aside from the cases where formal experimental proof was presented) is vouched for by the fact that nearly one-third of the pest species controlled (35) were again successfully controlled in other countries following the first success.

The preceding data show that the chances of obtaining some significant extent of success against any given insect pest species from importation of natural enemies are about 54 in 100. In view of such truly outstanding results, it seems a remarkable indictment against our profession that only about 223 pest species have been subjected to the natural enemy importation method whereas there are approximately 5000 species of insect pests recorded worldwide. In other words over 95 percent of the world's insect pests have had no biological control importation project directed against them.

The analysis of all importation projects reveals that the chances of obtaining a degree of control (i.e. either complete or substantial) that would nearly or completely eliminate the need for further insecticidal treatment included four pest species out of ten, or 40 percent. This is a very impressive success ratio and the economic savings have been correspondingly great. The dollars returned in savings resulting from reduced chemical treatment costs and lessened crop damage for each dollar invested have been carefully estimated as being about 30 to 1. In California alone they have amounted to well over $200 000 000.

These results belie the opinions sometimes expressed in the literature by the casual writer, or by entomologists unacquainted with the field, to the effect that biological control is the best method of all when it works but it is seldom successful. Such statements obviously do not stand up against the information just presented and it appears that they are based on a misconception of what constitutes success in biological control. They mistakenly interpret lack of success as being the proportion of imported natural enemy species that fail to become established. This proportion is in the neighborhood of 70–80 percent but cannot be equated with the ultimate success of a project because only one or two natural enemies out of a large number imported needs to be successful. In fact, as we have seen in Chapter 3, the most effective enemies tend to displace or exclude the less effective ones, so a high establishment ratio is not to be expected. In the long run it is not the proportion established, or the proportion established to successes achieved, but rather the cost–benefit ratio that is really important and we have already shown this to be a very good 30 to 1. With insecticides it is estimated to be only about 5 to 1.

The research and development cost of one new chemical pesticide in the market place is now about $4 000 000 or more. The research and development cost to obtain one new natural enemy will be only a small fraction of this, ranging from less than $100 to several hundred or even occasionally tens of thousands of dollars, but I believe the average would not be more than a few thousand dollars per entomophagous species.

The analysis thus far has been concerned only with the proportion of target pest *species* against which successful results have been obtained. However, successful results have been repeated with quite a few of these species in other countries. The cottony-cushion scale has been controlled in over thirty countries following the first success in California and the woolly apple aphid in twenty-five. These represent the extra, easy dividends in biological control. The original project may cost from a few hundred to many thousands of dollars but the repeat or transfer projects often cost only the amount of an airmail shipment and some correspondence.

The total of all successful *projects* from original importations as well as from subsequent transfers of natural enemies to other countries is over 253. This includes 133 more successes than if the original target species alone were considered, i.e. the number of successes were more than doubled. Over 75 percent of these successful projects fall in the substantial or complete control category. The value of these repeats should not be minimized. They are just as important to the country in which they occur as was the first success in the original country.

There are ten leading countries or states in the world that account for over half of the successful importation projects thus far obtained. It has been shown that it is not latitude, longitude, or climate, the island or continental status, or the type of crop or pest, but rather simply the amount of support and research effort that has been directed toward the importation and colonization of new natural enemies that has accounted for the pre-eminent status of these countries in the biological control field. In some of these leading countries one or a few devoted individual scientists have been largely responsible for the progress made.

It has often been assumed that biological control only works well in tropical or subtropical areas; however, worldwide results show that the majority of successes have occurred in temperate areas. This is interpreted as being related to the greater amount of research effort being expended in temperate areas rather than to a direct correlation with climate. Certainly tropical areas are quite favorable to the activity of natural enemies and there is some indication that the proportion of complete successes has been greater in such areas. The important thing to realize is that there doesn't appear to be any climatic zone where significant biological control of agricultural pests may not be achieved.

There appears to be little doubt that importation of new natural enemies from abroad should generally receive first priority in all biological control efforts (including conservation and augmentation) as well as in all other non-chemical approaches to pest-management ecology. It is obvious that much greater research emphasis and financial support is needed. The probability of success of the method has been shown to be very good; it has general application; results are permanent; the cost–benefit ratio is highly favorable with initial costs being relatively low and recurrent costs essentially nil; problems relative to the adverse effects of chemical insecticides are reduced or eliminated by its successful use and no adverse effects on the ecosystem occur from biological control. No other method approaches this totality of favorable aspects.

As long as we ignore, anywhere in the world, an effective natural enemy capable of controlling one of our major pests, we are postponing cheap, reliable and permanent control until we import such enemies; yet we continue to do just this with 95 percent of the world's insect pests. The cost of other treatments and crop loss in the interim may justly be charged against the entomological profession. This was strikingly illustrated by several of the successes discussed earlier in this chapter and in Chapter 5, where it was shown that, but for lack of effort and adequate research, various serious major pests could have been subjugated years before they finally were. (See DeBach, 1971 b.)

7
Maximizing biological control through research

Applied biological control can be viewed as a discipline or profession like the field of medicine. It concerns problem solving which, nowadays especially, is achieved through research. Such research is immensely diversified in medicine and likewise in biological control. Both include an imposing gamut of more discrete and specialized biological disciplines and the research involved must cover a broad spectrum of biological principles, practices and procedures. In the case of biological control we are concerned with all of the varied disciplines involved in ecology and this does not leave much science out. This chapter emphasizes research on biological control of insect pests, but similar sorts of research are just as important with biological control of weeds or other organisms. Principles of biological control of weeds have been discussed by Huffaker (1964).

As a broad phase of ecology, and depending on the project, biological control is most likely to encompass research on: (1) biology including behavior, developmental cycles, physiology, genetics, reproduction, nutrition and culture; (2) systematics, phylogeny and biogeography; and (3) population biology.

Despite the substantial progress that has been made in the field of biological control there is no doubt that its application could be greatly increased. Applied results largely depend on basic taxonomic, biological and ecological research and the amount of such research remains much too small considering the enormity of today's problems. The paucity of support is evident from the fact that the majority of state universities or their experiment stations in the United States have departments of entomology but only a handful have even one man specializing in biological control research. Aside from their internal budgets, all receive unsolicited donations for research principally from chemical companies. The following figures reported for one of the largest entomological departments (including the largest biological control research group) in the country are quite revealing in this connection. In the two years 1969 and 1970, $8536.91 were donated for biological control research, whereas $494 187.77 were donated for other entomological research, predominantly on chemical pesticides. Of the problems that biological control could help materially in solving, I refer principally to: (1) protection of the food supply from pests, (2) protection of humans, wildlife and general environmental quality from toxic chemicals used in pest control, (3) protection of the public health and well-being by biological control of vectors of disease and of nuisance pests, and (4) economic savings to growers and consumers.

From the analysis of worldwide successes in classical biological control of insect pests discussed in Chapter 6, it is abundantly clear that the single most important characteristic of the ten leading countries or states achieving the most successes have been their amount of research support for dedicated, well-trained scientists assigned to biological control importation projects. In this respect Hawaii, a tiny land area, leads the world. California follows closely. Both have vigorously supported biological control from approximately 1890 on. They, plus the other leading countries or states, are so widely distributed geographically and the projects so varied that it is obvious that neither latitude, climate, island or continental status, nor type of pest or crop, can be assigned a major influence on successful achievement of biological control. Here we have been referring to an analysis of importation projects, but it should go without saying that the two other main phases of applied biological control, conservation and augmentation, require as much and probably more research effort. The complexity of adequate field studies necessary for a really scientific understanding of how to manipulate established natural enemies to increase their effectiveness offers a formidable research challenge.

Systematics and biological control

The broad dependence of classical biological control importation projects on systematics – more accurately nowadays on biosystematics – furnishes an excellent example of the absolute necessity for basic research. True, some projects would be successful on an empirical basis, but the failures would be, and have been, greater because of lack of adequate knowledge of systematics. Perhaps only the need for detailed studies in population ecology in order to solve problems in the conservation and augmentation phases of biological control is quite so critical.

In biosystematics the taxonomist goes much further than is the case with so-called alpha-taxonomy, which relies principally on morphological characteristics to distinguish between species. If two specimens look the same to a given taxonomist he will call them the same species. However, the morphological and coloration criteria used as distinguishing characteristics differ greatly between taxonomists, so that one man might include several valid species under one species name whereas another might name as different species, several races or variants of what was actually one species. The biosystematician uses other aids to help in determining what actually constitutes a valid species. This may include data on biology, physiology, habits, sound-production, type of pheromone produced, etc., but the ultimate test (with bisexual species at least) is whether or not one population interbreeds with another population and produces the normal number of viable and fertile offspring. Failure to do so is, with very few exceptions, proof that distinct species are involved. With parasitic and predatory groups, data on host or prey relationships, host plant, and microhabitat preferences are often useful taxonomic tools and obviously of utmost importance in biological control. The adequate taxonomist also acquires data on strains or races, geographical distribution and phylogenetic relationships with other species or groups.

What we have been leading up to is that, more frequently than not, a natural enemy species cannot be used in biological control importation projects until it is discovered and recognized as a distinct species. This usually means receiving a formal scientific description, but even this is not always enough because as Compere (1969) has pointed out, 'of the named species, few have been adequately described; and of these, fewer still classified with regard to natural relationships. The great majority of described chalcidoids cannot be identified with any degree of certainty on the basis of existing descriptions.' Also, if a species is misidentified, the error might likely be made that it is already established or else that it is a parasite of another host species with the consequence that it would be ignored. Of course, accurate identification of the host or prey (pest) insect also is critical, especially where highly specific natural enemies are concerned; but generally speaking, pest insect taxonomy receives more adequate research support. However, if the host is misidentified, a parasite may be imported that comes from another host species and will not attack the one we are striving to control.

Just how serious is the lack of biosystematic knowledge affecting applied biological control? It is far worse than anyone, even most experts in the field, realize. Good general reviews and discussion of this question will be found in Schlinger and Doutt (1964) and Sabrosky (1955).

The problem can be analyzed from the standpoint of: (1) undiscovered or unnamed species, (2) species misidentified because of poor taxonomy, (3) unrecognized species because they are so morphologically similar to already known species that only careful biosystematic studies will reveal them, and (4) the occurrence, detection and value of races or strains of species. Before going on, however, there is a corollary problem nearly as critical. The applied biological control specialist must be enough of a taxonomist to easily keep up with the literature so as to keep abreast of all new taxonomic advances of importance to him. A perfect parasite for his purposes may be described from Afghanistan, but if he does not learn of this, he is postponing its usefulness for an indefinite period.

The undiscovered (i.e. uncollected) and unnamed (i.e. collected but not recognized as new) species of parasitic Hymenoptera (the order which contains the most effective and most numerous species of natural enemies) constitute by far the vast majority of the species that actually exist. The English specialist on parasitic Hymenoptera, G. J. Kerrich, estimated (1960) that if the parasitic Hymenoptera had been studied to the same extent as have the Coleoptera, there would be about 500000 described species, whereas there are less than 50000. In other words, and because not all Coleoptera are yet known, possibly considerably less than 10 percent of the parasitic Hymenoptera are known to science and 'available' for use in biological control. Another estimate he used supports this overall figure; that is, of the Ichneumonidae of tropical America, tropical Asia, Africa, and Australia, only about 10 percent have been described. In this regard we should note that this group includes many of the larger, more readily seen and collected, parasites. Finally he makes the amazing, but not unjustifiable, 'guesstimate' that as many as 1000000 species of the superfamily Ichneumonidae may exist in the world. This figure is a total commonly used for all insects.

Dr Henry Townes (1971), a world authority on the Ichneumonidae, made the somewhat more conservative estimate that about 70 percent of the parasitic Hymenoptera are still undescribed species and that there is not even a scrap of biological information concerning 97 percent of the species. In other words, not even the hosts are known for

97 percent, so these are of greatly reduced usefulness for employment in biological control projects. In any event, if the unknown species of parasitic Hymenoptera constitute somewhere between 70 and 90 percent of the species actually in existence, it is obvious that we have just begun to scratch the surface in the search for insect natural enemies and are even much further behind in the absolutely essential knowledge of the host or microhabitat preferences. Townes points out that the Ichneumonidae comprise 20 percent of all parasitic insects and that, from the biological control viewpoint, the most important thing to know is their microhabitat preferences. They tend not to be host-specific but specific to certain situations – for example, to borers of various species in certain twigs or to cocoons of several species under the bark of a particular tree. Thus with many ichneumonids we should look for species that occur in a specific microhabitat, not necessarily for a species that attacks the host we wish to control. This knowledge is the product of good biosystematic research.

The problem of misidentified species because of poor taxonomy has several causes, but the results are self-evident. A natural enemy species, perhaps undescribed and new to science, but wrongly given the name of a described species, may be as effectively hidden as if it were never collected (DeBach, 1960). Expert systematists know that this occurs commonly. It stems directly or indirectly from the great shortage of professional systematists. The scientists in our national and other museums are spread thinly and are often called upon to identify specimens in families or genera with which they have only a superficial acquaintance. The problem may be compounded when the field worker, unable to obtain identification of his submitted specimens rapidly, undertakes his own identification with an insufficient background. Publication of mistakenly identified species, or worse, of inadequately or erroneously described new species may result. This is not to discourage the field man from such activity, because his contribution is probably necessary to help close the gap. It is urged, however, that he develop considerable expertise, preferably in groups of restricted size, before publishing descriptions of new species.

A considerable, but unknown proportion of the undescribed natural enemies may be so because they are so-called sibling or cryptic species. Such species are valid ones but are so similar morphologically to one or more others as to be unrecognizable from them. They can only be detected by the biosystematic type of investigation mentioned earlier. Few systematists have the time, facilities or money for such work, inasmuch as it entails culturing the host and parasite or predator and prey and studying living specimens. Probably most of such studies have been done in connection with biological control projects. A glimpse of the potential from such research and of what lies hidden may be obtained from studies of the genus *Aphytis*. The species of this genus include the most important parasites of armored scale insects throughout the world, hence have received more than usual emphasis.

We have found that what only a few years ago was considered to be one species, *A. chrysomphali*, was, in fact, a complex of sibling species. Actually, each of the originally described, more common species in the genus is now known to include a group of sibling species. All told, eighteen out of about seventy-six species (i.e. approximately 25 percent) fall into this sibling category (DeBach, 1969). The importance of recognizing such cryptic species is that each may attack different hosts which is knowledge essential in biological control, and even if they attack the same host species, they will have different inherent capabilities for biological control. Hafez and Doutt (1954) found that the *Aphytis maculicornis* imported for control of the olive scale included four so-called biological strains or sibling species, all indistinguishable from one another but possessing distinct biological attributes. The 'Persian strain' was the only one that proved to be effective in biological control.

Subspecific categories (so-called races, strains, ecotypes, subspecies and semispecies) are of real importance in biological control. Again, biosystematic studies are necessary for their detection. Races with distinct host preferences do exist and, as such, are the practical equivalent of distinct species. Two races of the parasite *Comperiella bifasciata*, imported into California, represent an excellent example. They are morphologically indistinguishable and cross readily in the laboratory with resulting normal progeny production and sex ratios. The Chinese race may prefer the California red scale as a host, but it develops well in the yellow scale; the Japanese race strongly prefers the yellow scale and virtually never completes development in the California red scale. They occur together in the field in the San Joaquin Valley of California where somewhat surprisingly, because they hybridize readily in the laboratory, they maintain their distinctness. The Japanese race is always the one reared from yellow scale there and the Chinese race from the California red scale. Apparently the hybrids are not as well adapted as either parent is to their particular host – hence, natural selection continually operates to eliminate the hybrids and to maintain the integrity of the two races.

SOLID ARROWS   DASHED ARROWS   DOTTED ARROW
= Fertile F₁   = Sterile F₁   = No hybrids

■ 41 – 51%   ☰☰☰ 5–16%   ········· 0%

▨ 31–40%   – – – 1–5%

▨ 15–30%
                    ⟶ Only undirectional cross obtained.
▬ 5–14%   Arrow points to ♀ parent.
── 1–4%   ←→ Bidirectional cross obtained.

Fig. 35. The crossing relationships of some geographical forms of the *Aphytis lingnanensis* complex. These forms are indistinguishable on a morphological basis one from the other, yet all degrees of reproductive isolation are evident. From Rao and DeBach (1969).

Semispecies exhibit considerable reproductive isolation, whereas races by definition do not. In biosystematic studies of imported and cultured *Aphytis* we have found the species *lingnanensis* to contain a complex of semispecies as is shown by Fig. 35. Although none of these can be distinguished morphologically, differences in host preferences and other biological characteristics make certain of them the practical equivalent of different species.

Many examples could be cited wherein lack of adequate systematics has precluded successful biological control for a number of years, as well as a few where good systematics has helped, but space limitation necessitates restricting these to several only. Reflection will tell us that the cases we know of represent only the few that have finally been solved. The ones chosen here are associated with the successful projects treated in Chapters 5 and 6.

The final outstanding biological control of the sugar-cane leafhopper in Hawaii was delayed about fifteen years because its predator, *Cyrtorhinus mundulus*, was so poorly known as to be thought to be a plant-feeding insect. Success with the coffee mealybug in Kenya was delayed a dozen years or so because of misidentification of the mealybug as another species. As a result, an unnecessary wild-goose chase was conducted in the Orient to obtain parasites from the wrong mealybug. It was not until the mealybug was correctly identified that its native home was found and effective parasites imported. On the positive side of the ledger, the successful biological control of the citrus blackfly in Cuba and other Caribbean countries, stemmed directly from the earlier publication by F. Silvestri of a systematic paper describing *Eretmocerus serius* (the parasite that later accomplished the job) as a new species reared from the citrus blackfly in Malaysia.

The successful establishment of the effective 'Persian strain' of *Aphytis maculicornis* on the olive scale in California doubtless was delayed a number of years because of the failure in those days to duly appreciate the existence of sibling species. Failure to determine that the parasite of the Florida red scale in Hong Kong was not *Aphytis lingnanensis* but actually a new species, *A. holoxanthus*, precluded the importation of that parasite into Israel for an indeterminate number of years. Following its importation in 1956, it gave complete control of Israel's then worst citrus pest. Adequate biosystematics could have made it available many years earlier. Although it has since been sent to several other countries, each with similar excellent results, certain ones – apparently because of lack of knowledge of the literature – have not yet taken advantage of what would be a 'free ride' today. Florida did so in 1959 with spectacular results, but it is most apropos of our discussion to note that eighty years previous to this, in 1879, William H. Ashmead, who was an excellent taxonomist, was attempting to learn of the native home of the Florida red scale in order to obtain its natural enemies for Florida. Had systematics been far enough advanced then, Florida would have had biological control eighty years earlier, with a consequent savings of the many millions of dollars that were spent over the years for insecticidal control. Another chance was missed about the end of the last century because Albert Koebele reared an *Aphytis* from the Florida red scale in Hong Kong which was sent to the National Museum in Washington, but mistakenly identified as

A. mytilaspidis and subsequently ignored. These specimens were examined by my colleague, Dr David Rosen, in 1970 and he considers them to be *A. holoxanthus*, the principal parasite of the Florida red scale. Still another opportunity was missed in the 1920s during T. H. C. Taylor's work on the coconut scale in Fiji. An *Aphytis* reared from the Florida red scale in Java was misidentified as a form of *A chrysomphali* – a cosmopolitan species. From Taylor's figures of the pupa it is definitely not *A. chrysomphali* but very likely *A. holoxanthus*.

The California red scale story in California includes a long history of confusion of the scale with related species as well as misidentification of parasites. Inadequate systematics was responsible for the failure for many years to successfully import and establish *Comperiella bifasciata* parasitic on the California red scale as well as of *Aphytis lingnanensis* and *A. melinus*. The latter two are the principal red scale parasites in California but were not imported earlier in the mistaken belief that they were *A. chrysomphali*, a species already present in California and thought to be of little consequence. We now know from biosystematic studies that what was once thought to be the single species, *Aphytis chrysomphali*, parasitic on the California red scale in the Orient and elsewhere, and accidentally established in California, includes at least seven species having different biological adaptations.

The final example, previously discussed in Chapter 6, also comes from California but illustrates an improving trend in appreciation of the use of biosystematics in biological control research. A monophagous parasite *Trioxys pallidus* of the walnut aphid, a major pest of walnuts in California, was discovered and introduced from France about 1959. It was colonized in all principal walnut-growing areas, quickly becoming established and effective in control in coastal San Diego County, but it never became established in the commercially important San Joaquin Valley area despite massive colonizations. Studies indicated that the parasite was not adapted to the hot, arid climate of the San Joaquin Valley. This led to the likely presumption that either ecotypes, sibling or closely related species might occur in climatic zones similar to the San Joaquin Valley. Finally, an Iranian race or ecotype – possibly a sibling species – indistinguishable from the French form, was discovered and imported in 1968. It readily became established and rapidly spread with the result that the walnut aphid is now under complete biological control in the San Joaquin Valley.

Biology and biological control

Basic research on the biology of a natural enemy or of the host or prey insect can be the key to success in any given project. Several examples will suffice to illustrate this.

For years researchers had been importing parasitic species of Aphelinidae in the genera *Casca, Physcus, Coccophagus* and others, for use against scale insects and mealybugs. Some of these parasites appeared very promising in the native home, yet time after time culture attempts following importation were unsuccessful. Finally, it was discovered that their very unusual and complicated developmental biology was the reason for previous failures. The usual type of repro-duction and development in parasitic Hymenoptera, it will be recalled, is for females to mate soon after emergence, store the sperm from the male in the spermatheca and then, depending on external stimuli, either release sperm as eggs are being laid to fertilize the eggs and produce female offspring, or retain the sperm in the spermatheca so that the eggs remain unfertilized and produce male progeny. Both males and females develop as primary parasites.

The unusual type mentioned has been referred to as hyperparasitic male development. There are variations but generally in such cases the unfertilized, and therefore male-producing, eggs develop only on a female larva or pupa of their own species. In some other cases males develop only on immature females of another parasite species. When such a species is imported and culture attempted, the usual procedure would result in starting with all fertilized females (because in shipments both sexes are present and the males are quite efficient) which would lay only fertilized female-producing eggs because the host culture would not contain parasite larvae or pupae to trigger the deposition of male-producing eggs. Hence no males would be available in the next generation and the culture would be lost. Often the same trials were repeated over and over. The key to the discovery of this pheno-menon lay in biological studies done in Fiji with coconut scale parasites. Final clarification was accomplished by Dr S. E. Flanders at the University of California, Riverside, in the 1930s. As a result of these meticulous studies, it has since been possible to successfully culture and establish several species which previously would have been, or actually were, lost. One striking example involves *Coccophagoides utilis* which has been the final 'straw' to effect successful biological control of the olive scale in California. This species has hyperparasitic males which develop on female pupae or prepupae of their own species. Even so it was successfully cultured from a single shipment yielding only a few specimens from an isolated area in the Tribal Territory of West Pakistan. Had it not been known that this species was in a group likely to have hyperparasitic male development, the chances are great that culture would not have been achieved and that the olive scale would remain a much more serious problem today.

Means of breaking obligatory diapause of natural enemies are critical to certain projects when the species are imported from the Southern Hemisphere or vice versa. If one imports them during the best season for colonization in the Northern Hemisphere, spring or early summer, and they are a species in winter diapause from Australia, they will not complete development under usual insectary conditions and the culture will be lost. Studies on the effect of photoperiod on natural enemies have enabled the successful breaking of diapause in certain cases; in others it was more complicated, involving an indirect effect operating through the host plant or host insect.

Knowledge of the biological or nutritional requirements of natural enemies may furnish the key to their successful establishment or effective operation. In connection with ichneumonids, the most numerous parasitic family, Dr Henry Townes has stressed that host species that do not occur in the microhabitat of the exploring female parasite are never attacked, even though in the laboratory they may be suitable hosts. Thus, much effort could be wasted on futile mass rearing and field colonization of an imported species that looked promising in the laboratory on the host desired to be controlled. On the other hand, within its own microhabitat, consisting say of pupae occurring in leaf rolls, it may attack a large variety of host species. Thus, as briefly mentioned previously, rather than trying only to obtain new ichneumonids that attack the particular host we wish to control, success may likely be achieved by importing ones attacking other hosts occurring in similar or identical microhabitats.

Another biological characteristic of adult ichneumonids that is essential to establishment of new species and to effectiveness of native ones is that, like other insects, they have a high ratio of evaporative surface to body water, hence lose water easily. Since they do not feed on plant tissue, they must in general drink free water daily. Thus, the availability of moisture in the form of dew or rain is the dominant feature in the bio-ecology of adult ichneumonids. Such knowledge may better enable us to manipulate them in certain cases and in others not to waste time trying to establish them in areas lacking in frequent dews or rain.

Some cryptic relationships between parasites or predators and host plants are not only biologically interesting but affect the success of certain natural enemies. Several attempts to import the California red scale parasite *Comperiella bifasciata* in the early days failed because, before air transport, infested plants had to be taken to the Orient to have the scales parasitized there and then returned to California. Citrus could not be used because of quarantine restrictions. Therefore, the sago palm *Cycas revoluta*, an excellent and very hardy host of the scale, was used. Although the parasites oviposited freely in the scale on *Cycas*, none completed development and for some time it was thought that the wrong 'strain' of the parasite had been obtained. Actually, it was finally found that the *Cycas* plant confers immunity of the California red scale developing on it to *Comperiella*. A similar effect has been noted with the famous vedalia beetle. It will not develop on cottony-cushion scale growing on the ornamental *Cocculus*, and does poorly on others such as maple and scotch-broom. Host-plant-induced immunity of a host to a parasite or predator could lead to false conclusions as to its effectiveness or even presence in a particular area.

Ecology and biological control

To a large extent biological control is dependent on ecological research. In the discussion of the three major phases of biological control that follow this section, the need for, and value of, ecological research and knowledge will be covered as it applies to each. Here discussion will be limited to only one of the most important illustrations of how to maximize biological control through ecological research. This particular one is necessary for all phases of biological control because it enables us to determine whether we need to emphasize importation of new enemies, conservation, or augmentation of established enemies, or all three.

Precise methods of evaluation of the effectiveness of natural enemies in pest population regulation were lacking for years. Without such methods one cannot determine whether effective natural enemies of a given pest are actually absent from a habitat or whether they are present but rendered ineffective by some sort of adverse environmental condition. If it can be shown that they are lacking, then obviously research should be started on the importation of new ones; if they can be shown to be present, but in some manner rendered ineffective, then other research approaches to alleviate the situation are indicated. Although today the general methods are known, research on refinements, and on application to applied research lags badly and by some ecologists the experimental approach even has been disregarded. This important subject has been discussed in some detail by DeBach and Bartlett (1964), Huffaker and Kennett (1969) and DeBach and Huffaker (1971).

The first experimental technique for the measurement of the effectiveness of a parasite in biological control was developed about twenty-five years ago. Others followed until today there are both alternative and complementary techniques. Experimental methods were developed because quantitative statistical methods, although valuable for other purposes, do not provide the rigorous proof of control (or its lack) by natural enemies that is needed. Periodic census and life-table data furnish useful information, but such quantitative methods, including modeling techniques and regression analysis, are inadequate for the measurement of the regulatory impact of natural enemies on host or prey populations. A major weakness is that they do not distinguish between cause and effect. For example, does the host population drop because of the activity of parasites which then necessarily follow suit or does it drop from climatic effects and the parasite population *then* follow suit?

One absolute essential to any adequate evaluation method is that the study be conducted in test blocks of sufficient size and quality so that natural enemies will have had the opportunity to express their full effectiveness and will not have been repressed by artificial adverse conditions. Experimental evaluation plots are then established within the main study block. This will be discussed further in the section on research on conservation of natural enemies.

Experimental methods of evaluation may be divided into two categories, namely (1) exclusion methods and (2) interference or repression methods. In the former, natural enemies are excluded from a 'plot' (anything from a part of a leaf to an entire tree or a group of plants) usually after being artificially removed and also without otherwise significantly affecting the pest population.

Cages of one sort or another are usually used for exclusion but various kinds of barriers may be employed for certain predators. These tests must always involve a series of paired comparisons, starting with comparable population densities, so that one series of cages completely excludes enemies, whereas another series utilizes the same sort of cages but includes enough means of ingress and egress for enemies for them to operate normally within the 'open' cages. The open cages are designed so as not to change the microhabitat significantly more than the closed cages, so they furnish an evaluation of any effect of the cages *per se*. The time involved depends on the organisms but may run from weeks or months to a year or more. Cages are only suitable for certain types of insects, mainly ones tending to be restricted in their movements. The technique employed in each case, of course, must be designed with the habits of the organisms involved in mind.

If the host or prey population increases after a period of time in the exclusion cages, but not in the non-exclusion cages, it can be concluded that enemies were responsible for the previously observed prey population density. If there is no change the conclusion is that the enemies are lacking or completely ineffective. Once designed properly the tests are simple; only a 'before' and 'after' count actually is necessary.

Interference methods similarly involve paired-plot comparisons but differ in that natural enemies are not completely eliminated or excluded but rather are seriously decimated and rendered inefficient for a lengthy period of time from one series of plots. The check plots are not interfered with in any way. Again, initial prey population densities in each must be comparable.

Long-lasting insecticides, such as DDT, which are highly toxic to the natural enemies involved but relatively non-toxic to the prey population, have usually been used. Comparison of prey population densities between the treated and untreated check plots after a sufficient period of time has elapsed, will reveal whether or not the natural enemies were responsible for the originally observed population density in the untreated study plots. If there has been a striking increase, this is evidence that natural enemies were responsible for the original population density on the untreated trees. This is because the toxic chemical makes a poor natural enemy out of an effective one and causes the prey population to rise to a higher average density (see Chapter 3). If there is no change, some other factor such as climate was responsible for the natural control observed.

In some cases, especially with phytophagous mites, it has been stated by some but denied by others that insecticidal residues may have a stimulatory effect on reproduction in addition to any adverse effect on enemies. This question remains controversial, but in employing an insecticidal interference method, this possibility should be kept in mind and checked out, preferably by using some other type of experimental method simultaneously. Hand removal of natural enemies from certain plots over a period of time but not from others is one such. It seems to be an ideal method, but is time consuming and expensive. The so-called 'biological check method' is another. It utilizes honeydew-seeking ants in certain plots to interfere with natural enemies while having no effect on the prey, and at the same time it excludes ants from the check plots. It has no known disadvantages except that it is of restricted application to plants or crops having honeydew-seeking ants present.

The 'trap method' provides another alternative. It involves the regular treatment with toxic insecticides of a barrier zone surrounding a central untreated block. With care and plots of sufficient size, chemical drift is kept out of the central block. However, natural enemies moving in and out through the barrier zone are killed and so become reduced in efficiency in the central block. An increase in prey population density in the central block shows that natural enemies were responsible for the original density. In general, the 'trap method' tends to work best with rather sessile prey species and with ones not affected by the insecticides used to trap the natural enemies in case some accidental drift of the insecticides should occur into the central untreated block.

By the use of such techniques we were able to show in several cases that what were considered to be serious pests actually represented upsets from one cause or another. It was also possible to prove that *Aphytis chrysomphali*, which was thought to be an ineffective parasite of California red scale in California, actually was highly effective in all coastal citrus areas if not interfered with by ants or chemicals. The tests likewise showed that *A. chrysomphali* was ineffective in interior areas because of adverse effects of climate. This knowledge led to further foreign exploration for related but better adapted species of *Aphytis* and resulted in the discovery and importation of the most effective parasites obtained during seventy years of effort in California.

Importation of new natural enemies

The importation and establishment of new exotic natural enemies encompasses the single greatest opportunity for increasing and maximizing biological control. Foreign exploration, especially with exotic invading pests, is the classical and first approach in applied biological control, but the applicability of this method against native pests bears re-emphasis.

A substantial number of native pests have been controlled by the importation of natural enemies from abroad, including such well-known cases as the coconut moth and the coconut leaf-mining beetle in Fiji, the sweet potato leaf-miner in Hawaii, the coconut hispid in the south Pacific Marianas and Carolines, the sugar-cane beetle in Mauritius and the red coconut scale in the Western Carolines. Most of the successful natural enemies came from closely related host species but not all.

Much indirect evidence also supports such possibilities. A number of introduced pests have been controlled by parasites and predators imported from abroad where they attacked related species. It is a well-known fact that native natural enemies commonly adopt accidentally introduced hosts and may exert satisfactory control. There are also instances where a purposefully imported parasite has achieved control of both the target pest and another pest, as well as cases where the parasite did not provide satisfactory control of the target pest but did of a related pest. This all means that many such parasites exist that would be suitable candidates to introduce against native pests. The possibility of biological control of native pests also seems especially promising with the use of introduced ichneumonids, or other types, that select a particular kind of microhabitat in which to parasitize a host rather than selecting a particular host species.

It will be recalled from Chapter 6 that, up to 1970, importation of new natural enemies alone resulted in the permanent control of 120 pest species. Forty-two were completely controlled, forty-eight substantially controlled and thirty partially controlled. Inasmuch as various of these pest species have been controlled in more than one country, the grand total of successful projects worldwide is 253. No other non-chemical method of pest control can compare with this record, but I consider that the surface has just been scratched. This seems obvious when we remember that somewhere between 70 and 90 percent of all parasitic Hymenoptera remain to be discovered. It seems obvious when we find that most pests, even in the countries leading in biological control, have not had any biological control research directed toward them. It seems even more obvious when we know that certain countries have serious pests, yet fail to import a recorded effective natural enemy of that pest when they could do so merely by a written request to an insectary in a neighboring country. These examples and many more emphasize that there are multitudinous opportunities being neglected, mainly because of a lack of trained personnel, research support and administrators who are unable to assess correct priorities.

A small indication of what new leads adequate foreign exploration can uncover is revealed by recent emphasis on discovery of parasites and predators of houseflies and other fly pests by E. F. Legner. It had been assumed that the geographical distribution of the four major parasitic species was largely complete; however, he found, for example, that one of the best ones, *Muscidifurax raptor*, was either absent or infrequent in East Africa, Mauritius, Australia, New Zealand, Samoa and Hawaii, while it was common in other similar climatic areas. Obviously, it should be imported where absent. It was also demonstrated that this species includes various strains and reproductively isolated forms having differing biological characteristics and hence, could represent valuable introductions into new areas. Another parasite, *Tachineaphageus zealandicus*, was found only in the Southern Hemisphere, where it ranges through diverse climatic conditions. Because it attacks fly larvae, it occupies a niche that is largely unutilized in other parts of the world, hence is a prime candidate for importation into many countries.

How should we determine priorities for research in biological control and each of its three main phases, as compared to other aspects of pest management? The past records, advantages, disadvantages and relative probabilities of success of other non-chemical methods will be covered in Chapter 9. It will be shown that no single one, and probably not all combined, have the breadth of opportunity and application that biological control does.

The priority importance of the three phases of applied biological control research – importation, conservation and augmentation – must be determined by ecological studies of the faunal complex of an agro-ecosystem in chemically untreated study blocks including the utilization of experimental methods of evaluation (see previous section) in order to determine which of the pests present constitute 'real' ones and which are man-made upsets resulting from insecticides or other artificial practices. If certain pests are shown to be real ones, in the sense that they lack effective established natural enemies, then the first priority with respect to them is importation of new exotic natural enemies. If, however, the 'pest' is demonstrated to be a man-made one resulting from an upset of a non-target species or is a magnified one resulting from resurgence of a target pest, then in the first case research on conservation should be stressed and in the latter case, both research on conservation as well as importation of new natural enemies should be emphasized concurrently.

If, after thoroughly adequate foreign exploration has been conducted and the problem of a real pest or of a resurgent one has not been solved, then, and generally only then, research on augmentation of natural enemies should be emphasized. All research on foreign importation should not be dropped, however, because rarely do we know that the search really has been adequate. For example, just recall the number of years before the finally successful natural enemy was found in connection with many of the famous projects.

From the preceding it is clear that foreign exploration and importation should always receive first priority in biological control research, with the one exception that if the 'pest' has resulted from an upset, then research on conservation should be stressed.

The number of successes that have occurred in recent years (see Chapter 6) along with the other reasons presented, clearly show that biological control by importation has not reached a point of diminishing returns but rather needs greatly increased research emphasis. Every example of fortuitous biological control (see Chapter 3) represents a case where man could have achieved the same results earlier if research had been adequate.

Some people have been critical of the probability of achieving success in biological control and have usually based this on the ratio of the number of enemies imported to those established. We have discussed this question (DeBach, 1971b) and shown that the establishment ratio actually is relatively good (about 1 in 4) but in any event, this is not the really important criterion nor is the proportion of natural enemies established to successes achieved. Rather, the cost–benefit ratio is the critical measure and it is very good. We have shown benefits to be at least thirty times as great as costs in California over a period of about forty-five years. This probably represents a good international average. Hawaii would probably be better, but some others might be poorer. The cost–benefit ratio for insecticides is commonly rated at about 5 to 1. It really does not matter if nine natural enemies fail to become established if the tenth one produces complete biological control and saves millions of dollars. It merely means that a certain amount of time and money was wasted on the first nine. It now costs at least $4 000 000 to research, develop and market one new pesticide. Even then it has to prove itself in competition with others. It is in a sense comparable to a newly imported natural enemy. Both remain to be finally tested in the field. However, the research and development costs for one new natural enemy will amount to only an infinitesimal fraction of that of a new insecticide. Just recently I discovered and imported two effective new parasites at a cost of less than $500.00. I have also been involved in the importation of quite a few already known natural enemies into countries which lacked them, where the cost has been considerably less than $100.00 per species. Such transfers have resulted in several outstanding cases of complete biological control. Other projects will cost considerably more, but I estimate at the most, generally less than a few thousand dollars per entomophagous species.

An analysis of all worldwide importation projects to 1970 shows that some significant degree of success has been achieved with about 54 percent of all target pest species. Substantial or complete success was obtained with about 40 percent of all target pest species which means that a degree of control was attained that essentially eliminated any further need for insecticidal treatment. To me this is such an astounding success ratio that it is difficult to understand why every single pest of any consequence does not have a team of biological control specialists assigned to do research on it. However, there is one hitch that would have to be straightened out first. There are currently many more recorded pests than there are adequately trained specialists in biological control.

If, instead of talking about the degree of success obtained against target pest species, we consider it from the standpoint of all successful projects, we then find that the number of worldwide successes more than doubles because certain pest species have been subjugated by enemies – usually but not always the same ones – in more than one country. Of these successful projects more than 75 percent were in the substantial or complete category. Thus success in one country may have reverberations around the world so that many benefit. If all countries were doing as much research in this area as the leading ten, the problems solved would jump enormously.

How can research in discovery, importation and colonization of new natural enemies be maximized aside from what has already been said? Assume that the priority has been determined to be importation. It should go without saying that the work should be handled by one or more trained specialists with good quarantine facilities available. It has just been pointed out that there is a shortage here that needs correction. Preferably, the entire project should be in charge of one

213

man who has overall responsibility for foreign exploration, importation, quarantine, culture, colonization and evaluation of results. The number of personnel necessary might range from two to five or more depending on the importance and urgency of the project.

Certain procedures should be followed in order to best determine: (1) where to go, (2) how to discover the enemies wanted, (3) which species among many to choose (if some choice is required for practical reasons), (4) which are likely to be better – parasites, predators or pathogens, (5) which habits and characteristics are signs of an effective enemy, and various others. This subject has been covered by Bartlett and van den Bosch (1964).

Obviously a first step is to consult the literature to determine where the pest occurs and especially where it is not considered a problem, as well as what natural enemies are recorded and any evaluations of them. Sometimes the latter can be obtained by correspondence, but generally foreign exploration is necessary and desirable in order to achieve a really thorough check of natural enemies occurring abroad.

Based on ecological principles, an analysis of successful and unsuccessful projects, personal experience and the experience of many other biological control specialists, I have developed (DeBach, 1971 b, c) a series of conclusions and recommendations regarding biological control importation principles, policies, and practices, as follows:

(1) Exotic pests are obviously suitable subjects for biological control by importation of natural enemies, but native pests also have been controlled by imported enemies and should receive serious consideration. Effective natural enemies may be obtained abroad from either the target pest or from species related to it or from the same type of microhabitat.

(2) The ultimate success of a given natural enemy candidate for importation *cannot be accurately predicted in advance*, but we can find and select good probabilities. The effectiveness of natural enemies can be evaluated – experimentally or otherwise – in the country where they occur and their potential estimated. An effective natural enemy can be deduced to have the following characteristics: (*a*) high searching ability, (*b*) high degree of host specificity or preference, (*c*) good reproductive capacity relative to the host, and (*d*) good adaptation to a wide range of environmental conditions. The most essential characteristic is high searching ability. It should be borne in mind that a really effective enemy may be scarce in its native home because it regulates the host population at low levels.

(3) A really effective natural enemy becomes established easily and rapidly if correctly handled; usually the first year. Intensive and continued research effort should not be wasted on ones that don't. Rather, additional species or strains of species should be sought. Complicated and expensive programs are not necessarily required to achieve successful results.

(4) Multiple importation, either simultaneously or chronologically, of diverse natural enemy species is the only practical manner of obtaining the best natural enemy for a given habitat, or the best combination of natural enemies for this habitat, or the best combination for the entire host range.

(5) Multiple importation of similar species of enemies is not ecologically unsound because competition between natural enemies normally is not detrimental to *host population* regulation; in fact, the displacement of a fairly effective established enemy species by another imported species means that the second one is even more effective and will produce even better host population regulation. Although competing natural enemy species may affect the individual efficiency of each other, their *combined* effect in host population regulation is greater.

(6) There usually is one best enemy for each pest species in a *given habitat*, and one frequently is sufficient for complete biological control. Often, however, a second or third enemy species may add to host population regulation and may in fact be necessary to achieve satisfactory biological control. The best enemy species may differ for different host habitats; hence there is generally no single best natural enemy extending throughout the range of a pest species. Therefore, all natural enemy species of any promise should be imported and each one colonized in all of the different habitats within the range of the pest species.

(7) The best natural enemy may not be found until all natural enemies are known; hence basic studies in biosystematics are of utmost importance and need increased emphasis and support. Current knowledge is woefully inadequate.

(8) The genetics of natural enemy populations needs to be taken more into consideration. Collections should be made over the range of a species with the view of obtaining either distinct races or ecotypes which would best fit the host and the new environment, or of obtaining sufficient genetic variability among the imported stocks so that natural selection would result in the best fit becoming established.

(9) From a *practical* standpoint, long-term basic ecological research

on a 'real' pest species need not precede importation of new natural enemies. Such studies are not likely to help a *really effective* enemy and obviously the enemy cannot effect control unless it is imported. Any delay in discovery, importation and colonization of a really effective natural enemy merely lengthens the period that the pest species remains a problem.

(10) No geographical area or crop or pest insect should be pre-judged as being unsatisfactory for biological control attempts. The wide variety of successful results now obtained from importation of natural enemies suggests that nearly anything is possible.

(11) Direct pests (i.e. ones that at low population densities directly damage the marketable item, such as fruit) are suitable objects for biological control but the probabilities for success may be somewhat lower than with indirect pests which can exist at higher population densities without causing economic damage.

(12) Basic research on importation policy, and on the population ecology and genetics of colonizing species, should receive more emphasis but should not reduce in any way continued and increasing emphasis on current procedures for importation of new enemies.

I have no doubt that if trained people could be assigned to this research area in insignificant numbers and with adequate support, more problems in applied entomology could be permanently and rather rapidly solved than by any other approach.

Conservation of natural enemies

Effective conservation of established natural enemies is absolutely essential if biological control is to work at all. The process involves manipulation of the environment to favor natural enemies, either by removing or mitigating adverse factors or by providing lacking requisites. A general discussion of this subject may be found in van den Bosch and Telford (1964).

The efficiency of established effective natural enemies can be so greatly affected by adverse factors that they will be rendered incapable of controlling the pest satisfactorily. The same factors can prevent a newly imported enemy from being effective or even becoming established. Although there are a number of such factors, the major overriding ones today, as we have seen, are insecticides. At the risk of repetition it is imperative to restress this. The upsets of non-target insects caused by the effects of insecticides on natural enemies may last for up to three or four years after a given insecticide application has been made. Obviously, if they are used very often the normal balance will never be reattained. The toxicity of an insecticide, its residual life, as well as the frequency and type of application all interact to determine the degree of adversity to natural enemies. There is no question but that the indiscriminate use of pesticides will preclude the general possibility of obtaining satisfactory biological control. The only acceptable approach to preserving effective biological control of non-target organisms is to employ selective pesticides at the least injurious time and in the least disruptive formulation. Even then they should only be used when it is established to be really necessary based on scientifically established economic injury thresholds. A recent successful example of the pay-off of research in this area applies to fly control. It was shown conclusively that the practice of applying insecticides to the larval breeding sites in dung in commercial dairy, poultry, feed-lot and stable environments destroyed almost 100 percent of the natural enemies. These natural enemies were shown to be able to cause more than 95 percent destruction of the fly population. If only the resting sites of the adult flies on walls, etc. were sprayed the parasites were not interfered with. When this practice was combined with staggered removal of manure deposits, again in order to preserve enemies, fly control of maximum effectiveness at minimum cost was attained.

Once the phenomenon of suppression of effectiveness of enemies has occurred and biological control either has been reversed or prevented from occurring, the real ability of the enemies is hidden and generally forgotten, if it was ever known. It can only be brought into the light by ecological studies in chemically untreated plots using experimental check methods in the manner previously discussed. This constitutes the main foundation for research to develop better conservation.

In this regard the key lies in the selection of study sites and the design of appropriate ecological experimentation and observation. There has been a massive neglect of such research. Study areas must be so selected that cryptic interference phenomena do not mask or preclude biological control unbeknownst to the investigator. One cannot learn about the true potential of natural enemies in an inadequate size plot which, even though unsprayed directly, may be subject to heavy drift of insecticides from adjacent plots. By the same token, such a plot may magnify adverse effects of weather or of emigration or immigration of pests or natural enemies. To be adequate, a study plot must be large enough to be completely representative of the much

217

larger surrounding faunal-complex area. It should go without saying that no chemical pesticides or other natural enemy disruptive practices should be permitted unless absolutely necessary.

Various other adverse cultural practices should be eliminated if at all possible. Then the plot must be studied and experimental checks conducted for a sufficiently long period to be certain that balance has been achieved. This can require two, three or four years, depending upon how thoroughly natural enemy–prey interactions were disrupted initially. It all boils down to making the study site as ideal for natural enemies as possible. Only then can their true potential be determined, and this is the only logical starting place to develop future corrective procedures for maximizing natural enemies in any given crop. The fact that what is done in the study site may not be practical in the crop should be disregarded. It is first necessary to find out which natural enemies are inherently effective and which are not, and to isolate the factors responsible for nullifying the effectiveness of the potentially good ones.

The opportunity of solving problems through research is virtually as great with conservation as through foreign importation, because so many pest problems are man-made but so few are recognized as such. However, we have but to recall the great extent of natural biological control known to occur and the increasingly large numbers of upsets and resurgences plaguing us today to realize the need for research on conservation.

Of course, various other factors are adverse to natural enemies and must be determined for each particular case. Cultural practices used in cropping as well as cultural pest control techniques may be detrimental from the overall viewpoint. For example, regular discing which produces much dust may lead to substantial increases in mite and certain insect populations. The reason is that dust kills small predators and parasites while having little effect on these pests. We have demonstrated that by washing the dust from citrus trees at weekly intervals, populations of the California red scale will be reduced by about one-half due to increased efficiency of parasites. Cultural pest control techniques such as burning or plowing under stubble or harvest residues may sometimes do more harm than good. Burning can destroy only parasitized larvae remaining in the stems while the healthy ones escape because they have entered the soil to pupate. Each case needs to be investigated separately, both with respect to the target insect and to other members of the faunal complex.

The adverse effect of honeydew-seeking ants on natural enemies has already been mentioned in connection with experimental check methods. Thorough ant control is an absolute necessity if satisfactory biological control is to be attained on various fruit tree and other crops. However, application of this knowledge lags and with various crops the adverse effect of such ants remains to be investigated.

Weather is another environmental factor known to have strikingly adverse effects on natural enemies and on their ability to produce satisfactory biological control. In general, not much can be done to diminish the ill-effects of weather extremes, but research may indicate some possibilities as well as indicate what is needed in the way of new natural enemies. The weather that the insect experiences in its microhabitat can be modified by manipulation of irrigation, by use of cover crops, by modification of pruning techniques or by changes in mass-harvesting practices. In alfalfa it has been shown that harvesting large acreages all at one time greatly decimated the exposed natural enemies, whereas if the fields were harvested in alternate strips on a chronological basis, predators and parasites would be conserved and natural biological control greatly improved.

Aside from adverse factors, natural enemies may be neutralized by lack of certain necessities. The reliance of most adult ichneumonid parasites on a daily drink of water has been mentioned. Sources of honeydew or nectar are essential to many adult parasites and predators but are often periodically in short supply. The most outstanding development in solving this problem stems from Dr Kenneth Hagen's research with supplementary diets. By spraying applications of yeast hydrolysate and sugar he has demonstrated important increases in predation in alfalfa, cotton and peppers. Experiments in the USSR have emphasized the need of adult parasites for supplementary food. As a consequence nectar-producing plants are planted in orchards to provide food for adult parasites of the codling moth, the San Jose scale and others. Availability of nesting sites for predatory *Polistes* wasps as well as for insect-eating birds limits their efficiency. F. R. Lawson and R. L. Rabb increased mortality of hornworms on tobacco by providing nesting boxes for *Polistes*. There are major projects in Spain and other European countries to control forest pests by providing nesting sites and drinking water for insectivorous birds.

Alternative hosts or prey may be necessary for certain natural enemies. Dr R. L. Doutt found that the principal parasite of the grape leafhopper required an alternate host species in order to overwinter in the vineyards and that this other leafhopper occurred on wild blackberries. By planting small patches of blackberries near vineyards he was able to achieve satisfactory biological control. This example represents a type of habitat diversification and there are many others that have been shown to favor natural enemies and perhaps act as trap crops at the same time. E. J. Hambleton and J. E. Wille in Peru increased the effectiveness of enemies generally by crop diversification and specifically by planting strips of corn in cotton fields to attract the earworm *Heliothis* so as to more rapidly increase the supply of parasites and predators. Raul Castilla Chacon in Mexico has planted corn plots adjacent to cotton for the same purpose. V. M. Stern and his colleagues planted strips of alfalfa in cotton to attract *Lygus* bugs and increase predation. However, careful experimental field studies are necessary in order to determine the most favorable type of diversification. For example, Robinson, Young and Morrison (1972) found that biological control in Oklahoma cotton was improved by adjacent plantings of sorghum but somewhat reduced by adjacent plantings of corn. In very few instances has adequate research been done in this area of conservation. From what little has been done, it appears that the opportunities for natural enemy management may be just as promising as certain programs developed for wildlife management.

Augmentation of natural enemies

Augmentation of parasites or predators to increase their effectiveness involves their direct manipulation either by mass production and periodic colonization or by some type of planned genetic improvement (see DeBach and Hagen, 1964). Although research on means of augmentation seems to strike a popular chord, it should in general be given the lowest priority in biological control research endeavors and not resorted to until it has been determined that the solution does not lie in foreign exploration and importation of new natural enemies or some type of conservation. The latter approaches can solve the problem permanently, and often very cheaply. Augmentation techniques are more expensive to develop as well as to apply. As implied by the name, periodic colonization is a repetitive process which can be just as costly as insecticidal control. This is not to imply that augmentation of certain natural enemies may not be the ultimate key to complete biological control in a given faunal complex; rather it is meant to put research priorities in perspective.

Augmentation attempts should usually be restricted to those natural enemies which have been demonstrated by research to be inherently effective in prey population regulation but are prevented from doing so principally because either they are not adequately adapted to weather extremes, are not synchronized with the necessary stages of the host, or are otherwise rendered ineffective by periodic environmental unfavorability. There is little hope of accomplishing anything practical by trying to change an *inherently* ineffective enemy into a good one. In other words, we should not work with an enemy primarily because it is easy to culture.

Many projects have been developed involving mass production and periodic colonization. The use of insect pathogens in this manner appears especially applicable. The literature in this field is voluminous but a good cross section of it as well as an outline of research needs is contained in an article by Surtees (1971). Active interest in the use of pathogens for controlling vectors of disease is being shown by public health entomologists. Demands are becoming more urgent and frequent to completely curtail the use of DDT and other persistent chemicals for vector control. Additionally, resistance of mosquitoes and flies to various insecticides has become serious in some areas, so that other approaches are indicated. With the backing of the World Health Organization and the co-operation of many insect pathologists, it appears that a strong research program will develop.

In agricultural pest control, *Bacillus thuringiensis* has come to be commercially produced and utilized on a wide scale, mainly against lepidopterous pests, but it is somewhat questionable whether it should be considered as a natural enemy or an 'insecticide', because the killing action comes from toxic crystals included in the bacteria and usually the organisms do not reproduce in the field. In any event, it constitutes an excellent selective mortality measure with no known ecological drawbacks.

The successful use of mass releases by spraying of insect viruses has been demonstrated in large-scale tests with the cotton bollworm, the cabbage looper, the citrus red mite and others and offers a great deal of promise. A breakthrough is needed to achieve cheap commercial production of viruses on artificial media. An interesting example of research leading to promotion of virus epizootics in populations of the Swaine jack pine sawfly in northeastern Canada has been reported by Smirnoff (1972). Periodic outbreaks of this sawfly cause defoliation of jack pine stands and many affected trees die. To prevent these losses, a particularly virulent strain of a nuclear polyhedrosis virus, *Baculovirus swainei*, shows promise through manipulation. The objective is to introduce the infectious disease into healthy sawfly populations. Various techniques of accomplishing this were investigated and the most practical one involves introduction of the virus by the dissemination in the forest of infected cocoons which give rise to infected adults. These fly to the trees and move about spreading the disease by laying diseased eggs. By the time the first larvae from these eggs have died from the disease, indigenous larvae are infected. The third and fourth instar indigenous larvae all succumb but the fifth instars that are simultaneously present proceed to spin cocoons after becoming infected and the adults from these cocoons contribute to the spreading of epizootic centers in the population.

It is expected that the induced viral epizootic will spread naturally into surrounding infested areas at the rate of about one mile per year. Acceleration of spread could be achieved by wide distribution of the infected cocoons.

Virus can also be sprayed to attain similar results but more technical difficulties are involved to achieve practical results. To obtain the infected cocoons for dissemination in the field to initiate epizootic centers, jack pine trees infested with numerous fourth and fifth instar sawfly larvae are sprayed with a virus concentration of two million polyhedra per ml. Branches bearing inoculated larvae are then cut and the larvae allowed to spin cocoons. These cocoons are then put in containers from which later, emerging adults can escape, and distributed in the field to create epizootic centers by dropping them in infested stands from a helicopter, throwing them from a car or transporting them deep into the forest by horse. This method eliminates many difficulties associated with mass production of the virus.

Species of the egg parasite *Trichogramma* have been utilized more than any other entomophagous enemies for mass release. Much of the early field work was empirical and did not include experimental checks. Good results have been claimed in many cases: others were admittedly unsatisfactory. The main reason for controversy stems from the inadequate research basis for many of the projects including the misidentification of species, so that completely unsuitable stocks were cultured and released. It was thought for some years that only one species, *T. minutum*, occurred in the United States. Recently, Lawrence R. Ertle of the USDA Biological Control Insects Research Laboratory at Columbia, Missouri, demonstrated the existence of eight species among twelve populations tested by reciprocal crossing. Today, however, there seems to be little question but that mass releases of *Trichogramma* spp. are achieving good results, especially in cotton in the United States and Mexico and against a variety of pests of several major crops in the USSR.

In Mexico there are government *Trichogramma* insectaries scattered throughout the country. A good example is one at Torreon, Coahuila, that started in 1963 under the direction of Raul Castilla Chacon of the Direccion General de Sanidad Vegetal. They produce hundreds of millions of *Trichogramma* annually for release against the bollworm (*Heliothis* spp.) and the pink bollworm (*Pectinophora gossypiella*), the two worst pests of cotton in this large area. When they started, massive applications of insecticides were being made, yet losses and costs were so high as to be virtually prohibitive; since 1963, losses have declined substantially each year coincidentally with significant reductions in insecticide usage. The results are attributed to *Trichogramma* which parasitizes a high proportion of the eggs of each pest species. It is interesting that the pink bollworm and the *Heliothis* bollworm are still feared major pests in certain areas of the United States and elsewhere where *Trichogramma* mass releases have not been adequately tested, if at all.

The Soviet Union leads the world in research and application of mass releases of species of *Trichogramma*. The Plant Protection Institute of the USSR studied seventeen ecotypes of four species, both in the laboratory and field, to determine their biological characteristics and their relative potentialities with respect to twelve important pest species. As a result, fifteen intraspecific forms of three species were selected and today are in common use in pest management in the USSR. In 1968, about six million acres reportedly received releases of *Trichogramma* produced in numerous insectaries at a cost of a few cents per acre. The Ministry of Agriculture produced thousands of millions of *Trichogramma* egg parasites which were used on a total area of about four million acres against more than ten species of pests. *Trichogramma evanescens* is used in many areas against *Agrotis segetum* and against the cabbage moth, the corn borer and other moths infesting fields of winter grains, sugar-beets, cabbage, corn and potatoes. *T. embryophagum* and *T. pallida* are used to control the codling moth on apples in regions where the pest has only one generation. In general, pest numbers have been reduced by about 80 to 85 percent and substantial increases in yield have resulted with wheat, corn, sugar-beets, cabbage and apples.

Basic research was responsible for this. First, taxonomic studies of

Fig. 36. Six plots of cotton showing increases in yield in the three plots white with cotton that received releases of green lacewings to control bollworms (right foreground, left center, and right background) as compared to the three darker plots that received no natural enemies. From Ridgeway and Jones (1969).

natural populations clarified the various species and ecotypes involved along with their host preferences. Then ecological studies pinpointed the preferred conditions under which the several forms performed best. Various *Trichogramma* species and forms show different specializations according to pest species and to habitats. Some prefer open fields and live near the ground. Those attacking the cabbage moth eggs prefer moist conditions, while those attacking corn borer eggs in corn fields are drought-resistant. *T. cacoeciae pallida* and *T. embryophagum* are forest-dwellers capable of populating the tree tops. In orchards they prefer eggs of the codling moth to those of other moths. *T. c. pallida* populates the whole tree whereas *T. embryophagum* prefers the upper parts of the tree. *T. pini* as a forest-dweller populates the upper parts, even of high trees. Consequently, in the USSR, the use of the several species and forms of *Trichogramma* has been arranged according to zones, regions, crops and pests in relation to the biological and ecological qualities of the parasites. This is an elegant system that has evolved to its present state from the early, more or less isolated, empirical, use of *Trichogramma*. It is now the main basis for integrated control which also stresses use of microbial bioinsecticides and the minimization of chemicals (see Scepetilnikova, 1970).

In the United States, R. L. Ridgeway and S. L. Jones (1969) have recently experimentally demonstrated excellent control of the bollworm

Heliothis on cotton in Texas by the mass release of the green lacewing *Chrysopa carnea*. These releases reduced bollworm larvae by 96 percent and resulted in a three-fold increase in yield of seed cotton. The difference in yield is shown graphically in Fig. 36 by the plots white with cotton as compared to the darker ones that received no green lacewing releases. These general predators appear promising for use in a number of mass release programs. They are currently being produced in a commercial insectary in California for use against a variety of pests (for more detail, see Chapter 8).

F. D. Parker (1971) and colleagues conducted some very impressive experimentation in Missouri that successfully controlled the serious imported cabbageworm and another pest. Although most cabbage growers in Missouri considered three species of aphids and three Lepidoptera to be major pests, the studies by Parker, F. R. Lawson and R. E. Pinnell of the United States Department of Agriculture's Columbia, Missouri Biological Control Laboratory indicated that only one, the imported cabbageworm, is a real pest, except for occasional outbreaks of the others. The principal manipulative methods were based on studies showing primarily that the main established parasite, *Apanteles glomeratus*, of the imported cabbageworm was not well synchronized with early spring populations of the host; the host density of the first two generations was too low for the parasite to increase satisfactorily and overwintered parasite densities were too low because of winter mortality and attacks of hyperparasites. Two new species of parasites, *Trichogramma evanescens* and *Apanteles rubecula*, were imported to partially solve the problem. Then mass releases of *A. rubecula* and *T. evanescens* were devised to synchronize and increase parasite density and additionally, early spring host density was brought to a level satisfactory for early parasite increase and continued synchronization by artificially releasing cabbage butterflies in the field. The combined effect of releasing the two parasite species as well as the host resulted in substantial increases in host mortality of the cabbageworm and the production of nearly all Grade A, No. 1 cabbage heads in a series of test plots. None of the check plots produced marketable cabbage (see Fig. 37). Seven other pests or potential pests were present. The cabbage looper was controlled in the experimental plots by releases of *T. evanescens* and by spraying with a virus. The other species were held under natural biological control. Later studies (Parker and Pinnell, 1972) showed that control could be obtained either by managing the pest population with releases of both the pest and its parasites or by

(a)

(b)

Fig. 37. (*a*) Typical damage caused to cabbage by the cabbageworm in plots not having biological control augmented as compared to (*b*) Grade A, No. 1 cabbage produced in plots receiving mass colonizations of the parasites *Trichogramma evanescens* and *Apanteles rubecula*, as well as purposeful early field releases of the host in order to increase host–parasite synchronization. Courtesy of Frank D. Parker.

releasing only parasites at timely intervals. Releases of *T. evanescens* alone controlled the host population during favorable weather; if extended periods of cold and rainy weather persisted, especially when the plants were beginning to mature, releases of *A. rubecula* at a rate of about 5000 adults per acre controlled the escaping host population. This is an outstanding example of what can be accomplished by appropriate research.

It would appear from preliminary experiments that good possibilities exist for increasing the effectiveness of natural enemies by selective breeding or other genetic manipulation. However, up to now, research has been limited and no practical results have been obtained in the field. Laboratory studies on selective breeding have demonstrated increases in tolerance of parasites to insecticides, and to temperature extremes, have produced changes in host preference of parasites and have led to improvement of sex ratios in mass-reared species. This may be an especially important research area for mass-production methods where inbreeding and genetic drift could lead to deleterious changes. I consider the possibility of changing the host preference of an enemy especially worthy of investigation because one can choose a highly effective enemy to start with, so that the major desirable characteristics are already 'built-in'.

Another interesting approach has been suggested by Legner (1972). He made reciprocal crosses between imported strains of widely geographical separated populations of synanthropic fly parasites. Expressions of hybrid vigor were found in F_1 through F_3 generations of crosses from climatically similar but geographically isolated areas. This indicates the possibility of producing superior synthetic strains through directed heterosis for use in mass-release programs and widens our view for biological control manipulations.

8
Utilization by
the public

Anyone who grows plants, and to a lesser extent those who raise animals, are automatic recipients of a great deal of natural biological control. Additionally, they can take certain measures to increase the degree of biological control they enjoy if it is not sufficient to start with. Satisfactory natural biological control of ornamentals and shade trees is the rule: exceptions are rare, as inspection of home yards and parks will reveal. The exceptions, of course, are the things we hear about – the occasional serious pest species which can cause great damage if not controlled.

The dooryard horticulturist, home gardener or the small-scale grower who utilizes local markets often has certain advantages over the large commercial farmer as far as the utilization of biological control and the minimization of pesticides is concerned. The former do not have to be concerned with 'cosmetic' appearance of their produce nor of its shipability, so they can overlook minor insect damage and thus suffer no industry-imposed cullage, while being able to harvest at the peak of flavor. The absence of non-essential cullage means a few fruit or vegetables can actually be lost entirely to insects without necessarily suffering any appreciably greater losses per plant than the large-scale farmer who sprays regularly and so has large pest-control bills. In addition to vast monocultural acreages that tend to be faunistically impoverished, the large-scale commercial farmer often has more constraints imposed upon him by outside sources such as government and industry which may make it more difficult to utilize biological control to its maximum. He also has more at stake economically and this may tend to keep him on the insecticide treadmill. These are differences in degree only, however. One should not infer he cannot utilize or increase biological control, but only that more expertise and sophisticated methodology may be required, as is discussed in Chapter 10.

On the other hand the commercial farmer may do very well without resorting at all to insecticides as the following excerpts from *Natural History* (Hall, 1972) indicate.*

On...January 17,...I...read an Associated Press dispatch...crediting our new Secretary of Agriculture with stating that if pesticides were banned from farming, we could not feed all Americans. That dispatch followed the departmental line, as expressed by the administrator of the Research Service of the US Department of Agriculture: 'As we cope with...a more populous world...one of the greatest needs is production of food for billions of people. At present such production requires the use of pesticides' (*Science*, June 19, 1970).

The statement that pesticides are required to grow food crops is repeated so often by employees of the Department of Agriculture that many citizens believe it is true. Actually, it isn't. Individuals and local organizations of agriculturists in many parts of the United States have been, and are, demonstrating that the use of pesticides (herbicides and insecticides) is not necessary in food production.

One example is a 107-acre farm that I manage in Marysville Township, Miami County, Kansas. Five acres are pasture, 22 are woodland along a creek, and 80 are cultivated. No pesticides have ever been used on growing crops on this farm. Corn, milo, soybeans, and wheat are the crops raised now. For any given year in the period from 1886 through 1964 there was little or no difference in the yields from farms with comparable ground throughout the township. However, in the seven years since then, herbicides were introduced on neighboring farms and the yield per acre on my 80 acres has been greater than on comparable land, especially when soybeans were planted where corn had been grown the year before. On the comparable land, residues of herbicides applied to inhibit the growth of broad-leaved weeds in corn fields accumulate in the soil, causing the soybeans, themselves broad-leaved plants, to be puny. Other kinds of herbicides applied in order to inhibit the growth of grasses in soybean fields accumulate in the soil and cause the corn plants, themselves grasses, to be puny, especially when corn is planted where soybeans had been grown the year before...Considering the common interest, it would seem that, in Miami County, for each 2500 acres of cultivated land there should be at least five instead of four farmers and that they should control weeds by cultivation and should not use pesticides. This system produces more bushels per acre and more total bushels.

Furthermore, under this system the fish in the creek grow big and do not die prematurely because of pesticide residues, which have already stilled the

* From 'Down on the Farm' by E. Raymond Hall, *Natural History Magazine*, March 1972. Copyright © The American Museum of Natural History, 1972.

spring voices of five bird species in the woodland on and around the land that I manage.

The example outlined above is only one strand of the web that regulates the lives of man, other animals, and plants in the current green (agricultural) revolution, but illustrates why I am very tired of being informed that pesticides are required to grow enough food crops.

If the reader is inclined to discount the observations and opinions of author Hall as coming from just an unscientific farmer, it should be mentioned that he received a Ph.D. from the University of California at Berkeley in Zoology, he was Chairman of the Department of Zoology of the University of Kansas and was a Vice-President of the American Association for the Advancement of Science. This is only one instance of hundreds or thousands of growers in the United States and other countries who are producing crops of superior quantity and quality while using pesticides rarely, if ever.

The idea that the private individual can utilize and even increase biological control is not new. Some eighty years ago C. V. Riley (1893) wrote:

There are...two methods by which these insect friends of the farmer can be effectually utilized or encouraged, as, for the most part, they perform their work unseen and unheeded by him...These methods consist in the intelligent protection of those species which already exist in a given locality, and in the introduction of desirable species which do not already exist there.

Regarding the former, i.e. conservation of natural enemies, Riley considered that the 'husbandman' would be restricted in what he could accomplish. Also Riley did not yet recognize the potential possibility of mass production and periodic colonization of natural enemies. (Importation work with new natural enemies was then, as today, restricted to official agencies and so is outside the scope of private endeavors, aside from the individual utilizing the results.) However, he went on to say:

That a knowledge of the characteristics of these natural enemies may, in some instances, be easily given to him [the public] and will, in such instances, prove of material value, will hardly be denied. The oft-quoted experience which Dr Asa Fitch recorded, of the man who complained that his rose-bushes were more seriously affected with aphides than those of his neighbors, notwithstanding he conscientiously cleaned off all the old parent bugs (he having mistaken the beneficial ladybirds for the parent aphides) may be mentioned in this connection...But for the most part the nicer discriminations as to the beneficial species must be left to the trained entomologist.

Riley was certainly correct for his time and to a considerable extent remains so today. There are limitations on what the individual can do to utilize or augment biological control of certain pests, because many pest problems require considerable time, money and professional research for their solution. However, there is no question but that the interested home-owner, gardener, farmer, forester, poultry producer, etc., often can take advantage of today's increased knowledge and commercial availability of natural enemies to foster biological control of pests in the area of his concern.

Conservation

The greatest possibility for utilization of biological control by the public lies in the conservation of established natural enemies along lines discussed in Chapter 7. We have already emphasized the great extent of biological control that occurs naturally and the importance of not disrupting it. In many cases in the home garden, dooryard or commercial farm this will be all that is necessary for adequate pest control. Some good references for the layman on practical biological and ecological control include *Common Sense Pest Control* (Olkowski, 1971), *Gardening Without Poisons* (Hunter, 1971) and *Organic Farming Methods and Organic Markets* (Steffen, 1971).

The activities of natural enemies can be conserved and fostered by individuals in various ways. The most important is by restricting the use of pesticides to the minimum that is absolutely necessary to prevent pest damage. Chemicals should never be used on a so-called 'insurance' or 'calendar' basis without regard to whether the pest actually constitutes a hazard at the time or whether natural enemies are in the process of reducing or regulating the pest. When it appears on the basis of careful counts or observations that a pesticide may be necessary, only short-lived, non-persistent materials highly selective for the target pest should be used. Microbial insect pathogens such as preparations of *Bacillus thuringiensis* are especially suitable in this regard but there are also relatively safe selective chemical pesticides. Among them, plant-derived materials such as rotenone, derris, ryania and nicotine are generally safe when properly used.

Bacillus thuringiensis first became available commercially in the United States in 1958. It has since been produced by at least six companies in the United States and six in other countries, as shown in Table 7.

Table 7. *Insect pathogens developed by industry and various agencies in recent years**

Group	Pathogen	Product name	Source
Bacteria	*Bacillus lentimorbus* Dutky	Japidemic	Ditman Corp., USA
	B. popilliae Dutky	Doom	Fairfax Biological Labs., USA
	B. sphaericus Neide	—	International Minerals Chemical Corp. (IMC), USA
	B. thuringiensis Berliner	Agritrol	Merk and Co., USA
		Bakthane L69	Rohm and Haas Co., USA
		Bactospeine	Pechiney Progil Lab. Roger Bellon, France
		Bathurin	Chemapol, Biokrma, Czechoslovakia
		Biospor 2802	Farbwerke Hoechst, Germany
		Biotrol BTB	Nutrilite Products, Inc., USA
		Dendrobacillin	Moskovs, zavod. bakt. preparatov. atov., USSR
		Entobakterin 3	All-Union Institute Plant Protection, USSR
		HD-1 (Experimental)	Abbott Lab., USA
		Parasporin	Grain Processing Corp., USA
		Sporeine	Laboratoire LIBEC, France
		Thuricide	IMC, USA
Fungi	*Beauveria bassiana* (Balsamo) Vuillemin	—	IMC, USA
		Biotrol FBB	Nutrilite Products, Inc., USA
	Metarrhizium anisopliae (Metch.)	—	IMC, USA

* From Falcon (1971). Copyright © 1971, Plenum Publishing Corporation, New York. Reprinted by permission.

Group	Pathogen	Product name	Source
Nematodes	DD-136	Biotrol NCS	Nutrilite Products, Inc., USA
Polyhedrosis viruses	*Heliothis* virus	Biotrol VHZ	Nutrilite Products, Inc., USA
		Viron/H	IMC, USA
	Neodiprion virus	Polyvirocide	Indiana Farm Bureau Co-op Assoc., USA
	Prodenia virus	Biotrol VPO	Nutrilite Products, Inc., USA
	Spodoptera virus	—	IMC, USA
		Biotrol VSE	Nutrilite Products, Inc., USA
	Trichoplusia virus	—	Biological Control Supplies, USA
		—	IMC, USA
		Biotrol VTN	Nutrilite Products, Inc., USA

Of all the insect pathogens listed, *B. thuringiensis* is the only one registered for use on food crops in the United States. It can be used on more than twenty crops, in addition to use in forests and on shade trees and ornamentals for the control of more than twenty-two insect pests, all, or virtually all, of them lepidopterous caterpillars or larvae. The other species of *Bacillus*, comprising the 'milky diseases', are used in the soil to control Japanese beetle larvae. The other pathogens listed largely remain experimental. Their future potential is discussed by Cameron (1971), and a book edited by H. D. Burges and N. W. Hussey (1971) covers the basics, application and potential of insect pathogens rather thoroughly.

Good lists, sources and discussions of selective materials as well as of other alternative non-chemical measures may be found in Briggs (1970), Hunter (1971) and Olkowski (1971). It should be recognized that any pesticide – no matter how non-toxic to humans or other vertebrates; no matter how short-lived or how selective – has the *potential* of causing upsets or resurgences in any given ecosystem or habitat. Each decision to use a chemical should reflect this possibility, but this is not to say that in any given instance a decision to spray or dust is not the best one under the circumstances. Shirley A. Briggs,

Executive Director, Rachel Carson Trust for the Living Environment Inc., 8940 Jones Mill Road, Washington DC 20015, maintains a revised list of pesticides classified according to their use, persistence, human or mammalian effects and adverse effects on non-target organisms.

Pests are often mistakenly sprayed at a time when their natural enemies would have controlled them completely within a few days and before damage resulted. Such a procedure invariably has a greater adverse effect on the parasites and predators than on the pest, with the consequence that the pest rapidly increases again and requires another treatment. The mere fact that 90 or 95 percent of the pest are killed – by whatever means – has a seriously upsetting effect on the attainment or maintenance of natural balance. Various so-called non-poisonous materials such as oil sprays, talc (used as a carrier for insecticides), nutritive zinc formulations and even road dust, have been shown to decimate natural enemies and cause upsets. Some highly-toxic organophosphates and others which have quite a short residual life may be looked upon by wildlife conservationists as relatively safe chemicals to use because they do not accumulate and build up in the food chain; nevertheless, various of these can cause catastrophic upsets of non-target insects because of their intense effect against insect parasites and predators and such effects are compounded when these materials come to be applied frequently. How much have we gained when we eliminate DDT or a like material because of its long residual life, if we apply one or more highly toxic substitutes so frequently that they are, in effect, present constantly?

In home gardens and yards simple water-spraying with the garden hose, hand-picking of larger insects and various other methods can often be used in place of insecticides in cases where natural enemies do not do a satisfactory job. Water-sprays have the added advantage of removing airborne dust which is deleterious to many small natural enemies and may be the reason why biological control is not satisfactory. When hand-picking is used to remove pest eggs, larvae or pupae, these can be placed in suitable containers having a mesh screen cover which will permit parasites to emerge, escape and continue to propagate but prevent the pest from escaping. Another protective control device is the use of wide burlap or corrugated cardboard bands around the trunks of ornamental or fruit trees to trap caterpillars, pupae or adults of certain species that seek such concealing shelter. In 1971, an entomologist in Connecticut completely eliminated an infestation of caterpillars of the notorious gypsy moth from his yard trees by applying a wide strip of burlap around the trunks, overlapping the top, then later removing the strips and knocking the accumulated larvae into a container of kerosene to kill them. Nearby neighbor's trees were defoliated.

Aside from the use of upsetting chemicals, the presence of honeydew-seeking ants, where they occur at all commonly, possibly has the next greatest adverse effect on natural enemies. Ants of this type attend many homopterous pests such as aphids, soft-scales and mealybugs for their syrupy secretions and at the same time kill or drive away natural enemies. Since they do not discriminate between species of natural enemies, ants can also cause increases in non-honeydew-producing associated pests. For satisfactory biological control, ant control is a must if they are at all abundant and are tending colonies of honeydew-producing insects. Often they can be excluded from trees or large shrubs by mechanical or sticky barriers, otherwise commercially available ant poisons can be used. However, it should be recognized that many ant species prey on pest insects and are beneficial. Only ants definitely running on plants and primarily obtaining honeydew secretions from aphids, mealybugs and the like, should be controlled.

One thing that is very important to natural enemies is that they have a favorable habitat. This can vary greatly with different species but the greater the floral and faunal diversity that is present in a backyard or garden, the greater is the chance that a given natural enemy species will find a suitable source of alternative hosts or prey when the primary one becomes scarce; will find the necessary free water, nectar, pollen or honeydew essential for adult nutrition and reproduction; and will find suitable nesting sites or protective shelter. A diversity of pest species, even though in low numbers, helps to maintain a diversity of general predators or parasites which assist greatly to maintain balance if a more specific natural enemy becomes temporarily decimated for one reason or another. A chronological sequence of plants is highly important to the maintenance of natural balance. If a vegetable garden is abandoned during part of the growing season, serious upsets between predator–prey interactions will result. The natural disappearance of certain or all annual plants during the winter is not of so much consequence because both pest insects and natural enemies have evolved and adapted to such natural changes.

Augmentation

Individuals can foster biological control by personally collecting and introducing natural enemies from other nearby places where they are abundant or by purchase from commercial insectaries and dealers. However, the public should clearly realize that not every species of natural enemy, in fact usually not many different species, will do the particular job they want. Parasites and predators tend to be specialists to a greater or lesser degree, especially the best ones which are invariably limited to a restricted prey or host list. Not just any natural enemy will do and the problem of the non-specialist is to learn which will be suitable for a particular pest problem. Once this is determined the enemies should be colonized in close proximity to the pests under favorable weather conditions.

There are many popular and professional misconceptions stemming from lack of knowledge concerning this type of manipulation of natural enemies. As in the case of medicine, there are bona fide, scientifically-based cures and there are quack cures. The size or ferocity of a natural enemy is no indication of its effectiveness. The spectacular praying mantis, which is commonly offered for sale, is a very general predator which is not likely to materially reduce the population of any particular target species, but rather will feed indiscriminately. The ladybeetle *Hippodamia convergens* has been collected by the million for years in the western United States from overwintering aggregations of adults and sold by the gallon from California to Texas or even farther afield. The hitch is that these beetles are in a state of ovarian diapause and are not in a physiological condition to feed and reproduce until they have left their aggregation sites naturally in response to changes in weather conditions. Hence, when they are collected and released in the fields artificially they fly away seeking to aggregate again, rather than remaining to feed and reproduce. Later, often the same or other species will increase naturally in the field and the farmer, failing to recognize the difference, will assume he has been responsible for the results, whereas actually he has wasted his money. Today certain insectaries feed the adult *Hippodamia* beetles with a special diet after they are collected, so that their reproductive ability is awakened and they are ready to feed and lay eggs when they are released in the field. Only such preconditioned ladybeetles should be purchased.

The mass colonization of egg parasites of the genus *Trichogramma* is carried on worldwide against a variety of pests, often with spectacular success but many times with utter failure. One main reason for the failures has been that species of *Trichogramma* can be very specific to a particular pest or habitat but in the past entomologists have failed to recognize the minute differences between certain species, so that sometimes the wrong ones have been produced and colonized. Thus, when purchasing such parasites, it should be known that the species in question prefers the pest one wishes to control.

There are also excellent completely successful examples of how natural enemies can be conserved and augmented in rather small restricted habitats. In England and the Netherlands experimental pest management in glasshouses has been demonstrated after a great deal of basic biological research (Hussey and Bravenboer, 1971). It relies principally upon the mass production and periodic colonization of various natural enemies, the initial seeding of certain others as well as the pest itself at appropriate times in order to establish the necessary balance early, and the judicious use of selective chemicals, especially fungicides, when necessary.

Red spider mites are controlled on glasshouse cucumbers by deliberately introducing about 10–20 female mites onto every cucumber plant within a few days of planting. Subsequently, two predatory *Phytoseiulus* mites are introduced onto every second plant and a continuing natural balance is established below the economic injury level. This program can be modified to fit particular circumstances. In Holland in 1969 about fifty private nurseries adopted this technique and achieved successful biological control of mites. A single grower reared the predatory mite and sold it to the others. The greenhouse whitefly on cucumbers is commonly controlled by rearing its parasite *Encarsia* in an insectary, introducing whiteflies early at the rate of four per plant, then two weeks later releasing *Encarsia* at the rate of eight per plant. The temperature must average over 18 °C. The cotton aphid on cucumber was successfully controlled by releasing one third-instar larva of the ladybeetle *Cycloneda sanguinea* for every twenty aphids, followed by the introduction of small cotton plant seedlings bearing about fifty aphids, half of which were parasitized by *Aphidius flavipes*.

With glasshouse chrysanthemums the young cuttings are usually artificially inoculated with low populations of both aphids and their parasites within a few days of planting. A good natural balance then follows. For red spider mite control, the cuttings are infested at separate foci with the prey mites, followed three weeks later by the introduction of ten predatory mites at each of the same foci. Often aphids are present on the new cuttings, hence in such cases need not be introduced. Subsequently aphid parasites are introduced after about 17, 24 and 31 days in order to achieve overlapping of generations and synchrony of balance.

Yield increases of glasshouse cucumbers of at least 20 percent, amounting to $7200 per acre, have been reported where biological control was used. These yield increases are attributed partly to superior red spider mite control by the predatory mites as compared to chemical control and partly to the lack of phytotoxicity under a biological control program, whereas with the alternative chemical method, frequent applications of petroleum oils and acaracides cause plant damage. Integrated control of glasshouse cucumber pests is now practiced commercially with material supplied by two commercial firms.

It will not always be easy for the public to obtain positive answers as to the best natural enemy for a particular problem or where to obtain them. Some likely sources of such information include eco-logically-oriented entomologists of State University Agricultural Ex-periment Stations, of other universities, of the United States or other national Departments of Agriculture, the state or provincial Depart-ments of Agriculture, county agents or extension specialists. Once an individual knows the correct natural enemy or enemies for a particular pest problem he may either purchase it, if available, or personally obtain it from naturally occurring infestations of the same pest. Obviously a certain amount of expertise is needed but this is not beyond the scope of the interested, intelligent layman. One of the best sources of information now available will be found in the recently reorganized (1971) Inter-national Organization for Biological Control. One of the main objectives of this global organization is the dissemination of information and the promotion of biological control in all its aspects. Any individual interested in biological control can join the IOBC for a nominal annual fee and receive the journal *Entomophaga* and a newsletter, which are devoted to articles and information on biological control. Currently there are three regional sections with two in the formative stage, namely: the West Palearctic Regional Section, the Western Hemisphere Regional Section, the South and East Asian Regional Section, the Tropical Africa Regional Section and the Pacific Regional Section. Information regarding the organization may be obtained from Professor Carl Huffaker, President, IOBC, Division of Biological Control, University of California, Berkeley, or from Professor V. Delucchi, Secretary

General, IOBC, Entomologisches Institut der ETH, Universitatstrasse 2, Zurich 8006, Switzerland.

Lists including some important sources of natural enemies that are available commercially in the United States have been presented in Hunter (1971) and also are available on request from the Utah State University Extension Services, Logan, Utah 84321, and the California State Department of Agriculture, Bureau of Entomology, Sacramento, California. The Association of Applied Insect Ecologists, 100 No. Winchester Blvd, Executive Suite 260, Santa Clara, California 95050, can furnish commercial sources of natural enemies and lists of consultants on biological and integrated control. One of the largest and most reliable private insectaries producing a variety of insect natural enemies for sale to the public is Rincon-Vitova Insectaries, Inc.,* PO Box 475, Rialto, California 92376. All of the natural enemies they produce have been demonstrated to be effective when used under the proper conditions. To aid the public in utilizing these beneficial insects to their greatest advantage this firm issues informative leaflets regarding each. The following statements distributed by them are ones concerning green lacewings, which are proving to be one of the better kinds of natural enemies for periodic mass release in the garden, orchard and farm; and concerning parasites for biological-integrated control of pest flies.†

GREEN LACEWINGS (*Chrysopa carnea*)

The green lacewing is a delicate, rather broad-winged insect of a beautiful pale green color, with eyes of a bright metallic gold (they are also known as Golden Eyes). The membrane of the wings is transparent, and also pale green. Adults are from $\frac{1}{2}$ to $\frac{3}{4}$ inch in length. They have a characteristic fluttering flight, and sometimes rise from the plants when disturbed especially at twilight. Adult lacewings themselves are not predaceous, but feed on honeydew, nectar, and pollen.

Lacewings deposit their eggs at random over the plants. The adult lacewing first makes a stalk, which looks like a tiny hair to the naked eye. It lays its eggs on top of the stalk. The eggs themselves are pale green and oval-shaped.

In several days, lacewing larvae hatch from the eggs. The larva, also known as the aphid lion, is an indiscriminate feeder on almost any pest in the garden. It is probably the best but least appreciated predator in

---

* No intent to endorse products of the firms mentioned over certain others is intended.

† Reprinted by permission of J. Everett Dietrick, Rincon-Vitova Insectaries, Inc., PO Box 95, Oakview, California 93022.

agricultural and garden crops. The tiny larvae (no longer than $\frac{3}{8}$ inch) are alligator-shaped, and either gray or brownish gray in color. They are active searchers, moving continually over the plant in search of food. The larva seizes its prey, punctures it with long, sickle-shaped jaws, and sucks out its body fluids. They destroy aphids, spider mites, leafhoppers, thrips, all sorts of moth eggs, and caterpillars; and they are particularly well-known as predators of red mites.

After 2 or 3 weeks in the larval stage, the immature lacewing pupates, spinning a globular cocoon with silken thread. After about 5 days in the cocoon, the adult lacewing emerges, cutting a round hole in the top of the cocoon. The cycle then repeats itself.

The life cycle of lacewings is directly influenced by climatic conditions. Under summer conditions a complete life cycle can occur within a month, and thus many generations can occur each year. Lacewings over-winter as adults, but with difficulty; they should be recolonized each spring.

Although lacewing eggs can be 'seeded' into the garden, they must have a beneficial habitat there, or they will leave once they have matured. If the habitat in the garden is suitable, they will remain in the garden and lay their eggs, providing many generations of lacewings for your garden. For general suggestions on habitat maintenance, see our brochure entitled Biological Control: An Ecological Approach to Pest Management for Farms, Ranches, and Gardens. In addition, there are several gardening practices which are especially beneficial to lacewings. These predators are nocturnal insects; that is, they are active at night, and during the day they huddle together in a sheltered spot. Lacewings, since they are so tiny, lose their water content easily. To prevent dehydration, they need a high humidity habitat during the daytime. For this reason, the plants should be close enough together to sustain a high level of humidity all day long.

There are 4 main sources of nutrition (food and water) that should be made available to lacewings. The first is pollen, which can be obtained from flowers; so have some flowering plants in the garden area. The second is nectar, which is obtained from the plants themselves; many plants have glands called 'nectaries', which 'bleed' a sweet sap that lacewings can feed on. The third is the honeydew given off by certain insects; therefore, the plants should be strong enough to harbor tolerable levels of aphids, whiteflies, and other honeydew-producing minor pests. The fourth source of nutrition is free water, given off by grasses, plant leaves, etc. Tiny 'cover crop' patches of unmowed grasses and flowers will contribute to a habitat that will attract and retain lacewings. In fact, all these recommendations will contribute to the vigor of the garden itself.

240

Rincon-Vitova, Inc. markets lacewings as freshly laid eggs that will hatch in a few days. It is impossible to determine a set amount to be purchased; this depends completely on the natural complex already present in the garden, and on the severity of the problem. We recommend at least the minimum order for a small garden. The minimum order consists of approximately 3000 to 5000 lacewings eggs. Since the eggs are so tiny, it is extremely difficult to package a precise amount; however, we do guarantee at least 3000 to 5000 eggs per package. They should be ordered as needed, beginning early in the spring, so as to 'seed' these predators into the garden. Additional releases made in all pest situations as they develop will help give maximum biological control. Lacewings may be used on orchard pests, too; eggs and larvae can be placed where the branches of the tree touch the ground or on the crotch of the tree, or they can be 'salted' onto the leaves.

The lacewings you receive are deposited on the brown paper with enough food on it to sustain the hatching immature larvae (aphid lions) for 2 to 3 days after hatching. After receiving the eggs, keep them at temperatures above 70 degrees. Best results are obtained when the eggs are kept at around 80 degrees. The eggs may be refrigerated to delay hatching, but this is not recommended, for the quality of the larvae and adults will be reduced proportionately to the length of refrigeration time. Therefore, you should order lacewings as you are ready to use them. The eggs should be kept in the bag in which they are shipped, and released as soon as possible after hatching. At 80 degrees, the eggs will hatch soon after the date marked on the package.

When laid, the eggs are pale green and perched on the ends of tiny stalks produced by the adult lacewings as they lay their eggs. On approximately the second day, they turn gray. On the third day, they hatch and turn white. After hatching, some of the eggs may still appear gray, but close inspection will reveal them to be empty. After emerging from the eggs, the tiny larvae can be seen crawling about the paper. To inspect the larvae, you may carefully pull the paper from the bag – the larvae will not 'run away'. Soon after hatching, however, the larvae crawl to the bottom of the bag in search of food. If the eggs are empty and the larvae cannot be seen, they are probably at the bottom of the bag. The larvae must be released as soon as possible after hatching, unless they are released within 1 to 2 days after hatching, the lack of food will cause them to begin killing each other.

Make the release by placing the paper throughout the area to be 'seeded'. Make sure to tear the bag open completely so that all the larvae will crawl away. They will feed on pest insects as they continue their life cycle to become adult lacewings. The larvae have no wings, so they are not as easily dispersed as some beneficial insects, but they are hardy, and have been measured to travel as far as 80 feet for their first larval meal. Moving over the plants, they will walk a total of up to seven or eight linear miles in their larval lifetime.

CULTURAL, BIOLOGICAL, AND CHEMICAL CONTROL OF FLIES. INTEGRATED FLY CONTROL

Rincon-Vitova's program of integrated fly management takes advantage of the natural control factors that kill flies, by establishing and aiding this biological control complex on poultry ranches, feed lots, dairies, other animal pens, and backyard fly breeding sites. When established effectively each season, the complex of predators and parasites can yield up to 95% destruction of immature flies. Today it is necessary to biologically control flies. Overdependence on pesticides has brought on a genetic resistance to chemicals in flies, and so-called 'superflies' have developed. Due to the very short life cycle of the fly, resistance develops far more quickly in flies than in their natural enemies. If flies are exposed to pesticides during each of their life stages, resistance develops 60 times faster than if the adult stage alone is exposed (this negates the principles of using larvacides for fly control).

Rincon-Vitova entomologists offer a supervised control program that advises the farmer of the best control techniques, the proper application times, and the most economical methods. This service includes colonizations of insectary-grown fly parasites, concentrating on spots where fly breeding occurs, throughout the year. The entomologist makes periodic visits to the ranch to assess the biological control and fly density.

The parasites themselves are tiny, wasp-like insects that attack all the common species of flies found in animal dung. They can accelerate their kill rate and their own development in response to increases in fly populations. We grow 3 species of fly parasites: Spalangia endius, Tachinaephagus zelandicus, *and* Muscidifurax raptor. *The parasites puncture the pupal case to feed on the blood of the fly, and they lay their eggs in the larvae and pupae of flies in the manure pile. The parasite eggs hatch in the immature flies, and the larvae develop by eating the flies. They grow into adult parasites, and the cycle repeats itself. A release program augments the natural biological control complex by adding more parasites to destroy more flies, and thus grow even more parasites. The effectiveness of parasites extends beyond the number of parasitized pupae. The stronger, more active*

242

flies attract the parasites, and are killed in greater numbers. Those weaker, inactive flies who may escape parasitization lay less eggs than the strong flies, and transmit more weak inherited characteristics to their offspring. Thus biological control becomes a genetic force to interact with the flies and suppress their population growth.

The predators and parasites work under a variety of ecological conditions. Some predators work in wet situations, and others work in dry conditions. All the composting organisms of bacteria, fungi, mites, insects, and even small animals, aid in the decomposition of animal dung. Many of these attack the immature flies in the manure. Some aid in drying the manure; there is more to biological drying of manure than just dehydration due to climatological effects. This can be seen in the shrinking of the manure as it dries, rather than a glazing or crusting over as in the drying of mud. Some organisms aid in drying by encapsulating much of the water in manure in their bodies. This activity is important to fly control, as well as to odor control. Aerobic (oxygen-loving), non-smelling bacteria live in composted aerated manure, as opposed to the ammonia-producing, odorous, anaerobic bacteria that live in wet manure. Mechanical stirring of manure is rarely necessary where the biological fly control complex is working.

The predators and parasites live entirely within the manure, never becoming pests themselves; one must look closely in order to see them at all. Most predation and parasitization occurs at night. The tiniest predators eat mostly fly eggs and small maggots, while the larger ones devour the larger maggots. The parasites eat the larger maggots and fly pupae that are too tough for the predators. This interaction of biological control organisms yields a very high degree of fly population suppression.

Pesticides, however, need not be abandoned completely; indeed, they should be used to reduce peaks in adult fly density, for no fly control program can be 100% effective at all times. Peaks in fly density may be caused by disruption from necessary farming procedures; this should not trigger an all-out pesticide attack in an attempt to eradicate all flies. Adult fly populations must be controlled to abide by public health standards, but peak densities of flies must be suppressed by intelligent, selective use of pesticides (only when needed, and in the way that is least disruptive to the biological controls). Sprays should always be directed at adult fly populations; the manure should never be sprayed, for the natural enemies will die in greater numbers than the flies. Sprays can be in the form of peripheral surface sprays or baits (with sugar or molasses added as attractants). Sprays are most valuable in situations where flies have migrated onto the ranch and immediate kill of a large number of adult flies is desired. Selective use of pesticides slows the development of resistance in flies, leaving the pesticides effective for future control when needed.

In order to derive maximum benefits from biological fly control, existing predatory and parasite fly enemies must be preserved in the animal dung. Once the biological control complex is established in the piled manure, it is important to culturally manage this dung in order to avoid driving away the beneficial insects during cleanout. Certain management techniques are suggested that are not too disruptive to the predators and parasites.

One such technique is alternate row cleanout leaving a dry pad. The best time for cleanout is early summer, after the spring increase in flies. When all the manure is cleaned out at one time, almost all the beneficial insects are either removed with the manure or driven away. Cleaning out only alternate rows of manure preserves half the habitat of natural enemies. They are concentrated and ready to move into the new piles of manure that are beginning to form in the cleaned out rows. After a month or so, fresh droppings will have built back a control complex, so that the remaining rows may be cleaned out with minimum disruption. Leaving a 6 to 8 inch pad of droppings under cages at cleanout time further aids in providing a base to start immediate drying of the fresh droppings, and preserves the habitat of the biological control organisms. Other management techniques include control of water leaks, good aeration of barns, and good animal nutrition to insure firm dung deposits. In dairies and feed lots, gathering of manure into piles reduces the surface exposed to fly breeding, and attracts the biological control complex. Concrete floors beneath the poultry cages are an advantage; the fly larvae, seeking a dry place to pupate, are forced to the edge of the concrete, where the parasites are better able to reach them.

We have had up to 5 years of successful fly control on ranches. The program is not an immediate success, due to its very nature; it is a long-term suppression of the fly problem, rather than spectacular short-term quick kills (which are disruptive and inefficient). Often the beneficial species are nearly eradicated by excessive use of pesticides, along with disruptive cleanout practices that prevent establishment of any effective biological controls. Under our program, it takes about 3 to 6 months to grow back the complex of beneficial organisms. Greater success is apparent by the second year, when numbers of complaints drop and cleanout costs are visibly reduced. The insects develop little or no resistance to chemicals, rendering selective pesticide use even more effective, and there is little or no chance that pesticide residues will form in the animal products.

The cost of colonizing a ranch depends on the size of the ranch and the extent of the problem. For poultry farms, an average cost of 2 to 3 cents per chicken per season will pay for a one year program of weekly or bi-weekly releases during the fly season. Dairy, feedlot, and backyard stable costs would be figured on the basis of manure weight per animal; the cost for horses and cows works out to about 50 to 80 cents per animal per year for a one season fly program. We prefer to spread the cost and program over the period of time that flies are a problem; this makes our program as effective as possible. In addition, we sell a single colony, and a 4-colony program in 4 releases, for small ranches and backyard fly problem areas.

In connection with green lacewings it should be noted that Dr Kenneth Hagen and colleagues of the Division of Biological Control, University of California, Berkeley, have found an effective supplementary food for these predators and others, Wheast®, which is available commercially. Dr Hagen is a pioneer in the development of supplementary foods for entomophagous species. He has stressed the absolute necessity of such species either having natural food available in their habitat or of man supplying it artificially. Experiments carried out with natural populations in the field using a spray of Wheast plus sugar plus water (4.8:5.8:20) induced premature and increased oviposition of green lacewing adults and three- to five-times the number of ladybeetle adults being present in the food-sprayed plots as compared to unsprayed plots. In cotton about three green lacewing eggs were found per plant one week after spraying with the Wheast food mixture as compared to one per plant in the unsprayed plot. Certain other natural enemies appeared to have been favored by the food spray (Hagen, Sawall and Tassan, 1970).

A source of natural enemies primarily for importation and establishment purposes is the Commonwealth Institute of Biological Control which maintains highly professional insectaries in various parts of the world. They furnish a wide variety of natural enemies on a contract basis to various governments, organizations or even individuals. For example, in Europe the CIBC maintains colonies of the predatory ant *Formica polyctena* for colonization of needed areas. Field observations have shown that a single colony of *F. polyctena* is able to save more than ten oak trees from defoliation by *Tortrix viridana*. Information may be obtained by writing to Dr F. J. Simmonds, Commonwealth Institute of Biological Control, West Indian Station, Gordon Street, Curepe, Trinidad, West Indies.

There are quite a few commercial sources of insect pathogens as indicated previously. Two prominent ones are Nutrilite Products, Inc.,

5600 Beach Blvd, Buena Park, California 90620, and International Minerals and Chemical Co., Crop Aid Products Department, 5401 Old Orchard Road, Skokie, Illinois 60076. Biocontacts, Inc., of 11221 SW. 24th Avenue, Gainesville, Florida 32601, is a relatively new firm started in 1971 with F. R. Lawson as Technical Director. He was formerly in charge of the USDA Biological Control Laboratory at Columbia, Missouri. Biocontacts' primary activity has been research on the development of more economical production methods for nuclear polyhedral viruses of Lepidoptera. They are also developing integrated fly control in poultry houses by adapting the methods worked out in California.

Political action

Individuals, organizations, farming industries and other commercial enterprises interested in fostering biological control for their own use or as a means of reducing chemical pollution of the environment are greatly hampered by the general lack of information and emphasis on biological control furnished by federal, state, university and commercial agencies dealing with pest control. Political action is a potentially powerful means of increasing support for and the use of biological control. Various conservation, environmental protection and consumer organizations are already capable of influencing legal decisions, legislation and financing in the right direction. Interesting and informative accounts of such possibilities are given in the books *Since Silent Spring* (Graham, 1970, especially Chapter 21) and *Unfit for Human Consumption* (Harmer, 1971, especially Chapters 16 and 17). The environmentally oriented public can and should effectively press the issues of clean food *vs* poisoned food, the right of a farmer not to have his crops receive drift of toxic chemicals applied by another nearby farmer, the adverse effects of the use of non-selective and environment-polluting pesticides [as the Environmental Defense Fund (EDF) and other organizations have done successfully with DDT and are continuing to do with other dangerous pesticides], and the setting by the agricultural industry and government of ridiculously high standards for 'cosmetic' appearance of foodstuffs even though no actual damage or loss of crop occurs, so that the farmer is forced to apply un-needed insecticides or fungicides in order to produce a product without a single blemish. Taste and nutritional quality should be the goals but they are often sacrificed in today's market.

It is generally estimated by ecologists that at least half of the insecticides now used are unnecessary. With proper emphasis on biological control there is no telling to what minimum the use of insecticides could be reduced. Such emphasis can be greatly increased by group pressure for expansion of research on and support of biological control by federal, state and local governments and universities.

9
Other
biological methods

Other non-chemical approaches to pest management include three methods of proven practical usage in the field as well as several still in the idea or pilot-testing stage. The three main methods now in practical use include: (1) the development of plants resistant to insects, plant diseases and nematodes, (2) cultural techniques or habitat modification designed to control pests, and (3) the genetic technique of sterile-male releases in the field in order to mate with wild females and prevent progeny production. Other genetic techniques such as habit modification, use of lethal genes, etc. mainly await the first pilot tests. The use of insect pheromones to attract and trap or otherwise neutralize pests is still largely in the pilot-testing stage although lure-traps have been successfully used in some instances. The competitive displacement of pests by non-pests remains in the idea stage.

There are other potentially useful control techniques which may be borderline between being a biological method or a chemical method (which indeed pheromones may be). These include the use of the so-called 'third-generation' pesticides, juvenile hormones or their analogues, and ecdysones, the growth and molting hormone of insects, or their analogues, to prevent successful completion of the life cycle or otherwise disrupt physiological processes. These much publicized techniques, however, are still in the research or preliminary pilot-testing stage after some fifteen to twenty years of research. As an example of potentialities, H. A. Röller has reported that 20 mg of synthesized cecropia moth juvenile hormone were effective in controlling codling moth infestations of individual apple trees. In another case, Zoecon of Palo Alto, California, reported that a large-scale 1972 field trial against three species of mosquitoes in Panama with an ecdysone analog killed 100 percent of mosquito larvae within twenty-four hours at a concentration of two ounces per acre. Marketing of these materials in the United States is not anticipated before 1974. However, Robert L.

Benson has discussed how insects could develop resistance to hormones, pheromones and chemosterilants and Bernard J. R. Philogène has suggested that insect hormones and pheromones are not as good prospects as formerly expected.

Still other approaches that are non-biological but may be ecologically non-disruptive include use of electromagnetic energy, especially in light traps, which have shown promising results in some large-scale experiments with the tomato and tobacco hornworms and other pests. Other methods, none of which have more than limited application, include mechanical exclusion, heat, and light and sound to disrupt biological patterns; use of chemosterilants, which prevents reproduction but is not yet developed as a practical commercial method, and there remains a serious problem of safety in field applications; use of repellents, which as yet has no application in agriculture but does against certain pests of public health or veterinary importance and antifeedants which also have not as yet been developed to the stage of commercial usefulness with one or two exceptions. Of course, another chemical technique that can be ecologically non-disruptive involves the use of selective insecticides. This actually is of much greater immediate practical importance than any of the other chemical or physical methods mentioned above and will be discussed further in Chapter 10. The remainder of this chapter will be devoted to the other biological methods mentioned in the first paragraph and an evaluation of their relative potential as compared to each other and to biological control. Two useful general references covering the subjects just mentioned are by Kilgore and Doutt (1967) and by the National Academy of Sciences (1969).

Plants resistant to pests

This method offhand appears to offer such an excellent means of controlling insect pests that it seems surprising that its application has been relatively limited in the overall scheme of pest management. The principle involved consists of artificially altering the plant species genetically, or selecting naturally available plant varieties, so that the plant is not as satisfactory a host to the pest as it was originally. The changes can be classed as physical or biochemical. The former include such characteristics as hardness or hairyness, the latter involve chemicals in the plant that might repel the insect, mask the plant as a host or affect development of the insect. The resistance of wheat to the cereal leaf beetle in Michigan, for example, is due to the presence of pubescence on the leaves. Resistance to the wheat stem sawfly is largely due to solid stems as contrasted to hollow stems, which permit greater egg and larval survival. The resistance to the Hessian fly is principally antibiotic in nature since most larvae die when feeding on resistant plants. Resistance to the greenbug is mainly due to tolerance, i.e. the ability of the plant to tolerate aphid attacks. The principle applies as well to resistance of animals to various parasites. Levels of resistance of practical value to internal parasites have been shown in cattle, sheep, goats and chickens but even less work has been done here than with plant resistance.

According to Pathak (1970) the development of plant varieties resistant to the Hessian fly, wheat stem sawfly and grape phylloxera represent the main examples of this method. Newsom (1965) lists the wheat stem sawfly, the Hessian fly, the European corn borer, the spotted alfalfa aphid, greenbug, and chinch bug as being more or less satisfactorily controlled on some crops in the United States. In Hawaii the development of a sugar-cane variety resistant to the beetle borer was credited, along with introduced parasites, with successful control. There are various other examples around the world, including ones that have been empirically adopted from naturally occurring resistant varieties. Success in breeding resistance to *Empoasca* leafhoppers into cotton has been achieved in Africa, Australia and India. Some other plant varieties more or less resistant include: corn to the corn leaf-aphid, corn earworm and corn rootworms; alfalfa to the pea aphid; rice to the striped borer, the green leafhopper and the rice delphacid; beans to the Mexican bean beetle; and cabbage to the potato leafhopper and the striped flea beetle.

The economic savings from certain projects have been enormous. About ten million acres of wheat are now being planted with Hessian fly-resistant varieties in the United States. Painter (1968) concluded that fifteen million dollars a year in increased yield was being attained in Kansas alone from the use of Hessian-fly-resistant varieties and Luginbill (1969) calculated the savings for the entire nation for the year 1964 to be 238 million dollars. Reduction in damage by the wheat stem sawfly has resulted in similar great savings. No chemical control of this pest has been economically possible, but the use of the resistant varieties Rescue and Chinook permits the profitable growing of wheat on 1 800 000 acres in Canada and over 600 000 acres in the United States. Sawfly populations were reduced to a minimum over a period of several years. Previously losses in the Great Plains area of Canada and the United States ranged up to 75–85 percent. A $6000000 loss was estimated for North Dakota alone in 1944. It has also been estimated that the use of resistant corn varieties, particularly for the European corn borer, has saved about $100000000 per year in the United States alone.

It is impossible in such a short review to include details of the principles or the research involved in plant resistance to pests, nor can all sources be cited. The following will be found useful to the interested reader: Beck (1965), EPPO Report (1970a), Luginbill (1969), National Academy of Sciences (1969), Painter (1951, 1958, 1966), and Pathak (1970).

The Kansas Agricultural Experiment Station has been the leader in the United States with a formal project since 1926. They have approved for distribution to farmers eleven crop varieties resistant to various insects, including varieties of sorghums, alfalfa, corn, barley and wheat (Painter, 1960). According to Painter the following are the important characteristics of insect resistance as a pest control measure:

1. In contrast to chemical control, which is sudden and often rapidly decreasing in effect and often presents a toxic residue problem, resistance is cumulative and continuing and is without residue problems. The combined use of plant resistance and insecticides may therefore give greater than additive control and perhaps be longer lasting.
2. The breeding of insect-resistant varieties requires the continued cooperation of plant breeder and entomologist.
3. The production of a resistant crop plant variety requires ordinarily ten to fifteen years, although sometimes there are means of shortening this time.
4. The effect of a resistant variety has been to increase the yield or quality of the crop and often to decrease the insect population even in neighboring susceptible varieties.
5. The use of resistant varieties involves no direct cost to the user and perhaps adds to the value of an otherwise improved variety. Where the margin of profit per acre is small the use of resistant varieties reduces the cost of production and increases stabilization.

A distinct advantage of using resistant plants is its compatability with other methods of control. Insects feeding on resistant plants may be less vigorous and more easily killed by weather or more easily handled, if necessary, with reduced amounts of insecticides. Predation has been shown to be greater on some resistant varieties, and natural enemies are always given a relative advantage if the rate of increase

251

of their prey is diminished as it is even on moderately resistant plants. Thus even a slight increment in resistance could lead to an increase from partial to complete biological control.

Currently, plant resistance to over 100 species of pest insects is known and it is being studied for over sixty insect pest species at the present time. A few varieties have been developed that are resistant to more than one insect pest species and even to some pathogens. Needless to say, these will have greater practical utility and more ready acceptability to the grower. Additionally, and actually on a much grander scale, plant resistance has been developed to many plant pathogens and nematodes. This also is advantageous to biological control because the chemicals otherwise used against those organisms can cause upsets.

If the method is so potentially effective, valuable, compatible with other pest control techniques and ecologically non-disruptive, as I concur it is, why hasn't it been utilized to a much greater extent? There are a complex of reasons.

The research involved requires a multidisciplinary approach which, although often relatively simple, is expensive. A large team effort may be required including entomologists, plant breeders, agronomists, geneticists, plant pathologists and economists. This means that such work is not as likely to be done by a small institution, state or even a single country. In fact it appears that large-scale governmental support is necessary and that this should be co-ordinated into co-operative international programs (see EPPO Report, 1970a). This, for instance, would be the only logical means of obtaining an adequate source of the enormous genetic variability available within a given crop. A correlative objective of such teams would be to check new plant varieties developed for other purposes for possible loss in resistance to pests. In cotton considerable effort has been devoted to developing commercial varieties having low gossypol content because this chemical is toxic to non-ruminant animals and has disadvantages in processing cottonseed. However, low-gossypol cotton has proved to be very attractive and susceptible to several cotton insects and in fact such cotton is attacked by insects not previously known as cotton pests.

Painter states that the production of a resistant crop plant variety requires ordinarily ten to fifteen years, although it may be shortened in certain cases. However, with tree crops the time required may be even longer. Obviously, with a team effort involved, this means a large outlay of money before results are obtained. This time factor also may not be attractive to scientists who are often under pressure to 'produce'.

There are also continuing biological and ecological screening problems to be certain that the development of plant varieties resistant to the target pest does not lead to reduced resistance to some other pest or potential pest or otherwise change the variety, or the ecosystem, in some undesirable way. The new strawberry varieties that were grown in California because of their resistance to pathogens, lost much of this advantage because they were severely damaged by the cyclamen mite which had been only a minor pest on the earlier varieties. There are also cases, such as the pea weevil in Finland, where rather careful programs of selection carried out for at least five years with a large number (94) of plant strains resulted in no increase whatsoever in resistance, so results are not guaranteed. In fact, resistance to oligophagous insects is often unknown in either the plant species or genus. For instance, this is the case with *Haplodiplosis equestris*.

Technical problems such as the fact that screening methods are insufficiently developed for large numbers of plants and that the genetic basis of resistance to insects is often complex pose additional difficulties. For example, in some aphid species, resistance even differs between the alate and the apterous generations.

Finally, once a resistant variety has been developed there remains the formidable problem of grower and consumer acceptance. If, for example, the pest can easily be controlled by insecticides, there may be considerable reluctance to plant a new variety. Habits are not easy to change. It is probably not coincidence that the most outstanding results have been obtained against pests for which no satisfactory chemical control existed – the Hessian fly, the wheat stem sawfly and the grape phylloxera.

Even after a resistant variety has met with commercial acceptance, the development of new biotypes, or physiological races, of the pest may occur. The artificial development of resistant plants is a genetic and evolutionary procedure and similar events can just as well occur naturally in the pest to overcome the plant resistance. Selective breeding for plant resistance may therefore become a continuing process. Thus far, biotype development has not occurred nearly as rapidly or as generally with insect pests as it has with fungus diseases, such as wheat rust, which has several hundred biotypes. In the United States, Painter (1966) recorded only six pests which had developed biotypes to overcome plant resistance. This included the Hessian fly and five aphids but was not general over the range where the resistant varieties were grown. The Hessian-fly-resistant wheat varieties in California and Kansas remained so. The biotype that overcame resistance in Indiana was controlled by additional sources of resistance. In fact resistant varieties are available for all six biotypes of Hessian fly. No evidence of the development of biotypes in the wheat stem sawfly with respect to the famous resistant variety Rescue has been observed. This is true also with corn resistant to the European corn borer, although some of the varieties have been grown continuously since 1949. The apple variety Winter Majetin, which was recorded as resistant to the woolly apple aphid as early as 1831, still retains its resistance. Thus biotypes represent a potential problem in any given case, but do not appear to be serious enough with insect pests to restrict increased research and development.

It can be concluded that this is an elegant method having potentially broad application for pest population regulation in spite of some drawbacks. It is under-researched and undersupported. Large-scale co-operation and financing on a national and international basis is indicated. It has such obvious advantages it certainly should be exploited more thoroughly.

Cultural methods

This is one of the oldest methods of pest control and was probably in successful empirical use before the underlying biological reasons were known. It is reported that, for centuries, Chinese farmers have used particular grain-planting dates to prevent damage by the rice borer, the wheat stem maggot and a pest of millet. The disposal of crop residues was recommended in Europe as early as 1897 in order to reduce overwintering populations of the European corn borer.

Cultural control involves altering the habitat in any of many diverse ways to make it less favorable for pest reproduction and survival. Effects can be direct on the pest or indirect, such as by favoring natural enemies or increasing plant tolerance, or they can include a combination. Habitat modification can involve manipulation of such parameters as planting or harvesting times, cultivation, plant spacing, irrigation, crop rotation, trap crops, habitat diversity, fertilizers, pruning, thinning, soil preparation, and sanitation. Manipulation of water levels is an example in aquatic ecosystems.

The research and application of cultural methods must be based on a biological and ecological foundation just as much as any other technique. A thorough knowledge of the pest's life history and habits is particularly essential, including precise information on its natural enemies. Similar knowledge of its plant or animal host may be just as necessary. The discovery of the most vulnerable developmental stage or stages of the pest's life cycle is a prime requisite. Then the habitat, farming practices or others must be modified so as to strike at the pest in its most susceptible stage. At the same time an understanding of the ecosystem is necessary because habitat modification deleterious to one pest could well favor one or more others.

Cultural control techniques were more commonly used before the advent of organic insecticides made such methods sometimes seem cumbersome and complicated. Now that very serious side-problems have arisen from the use of insecticides there is a strong resurgence of interest in cultural methods. Many have been and still are quite effective. Today, as a rough estimate, there may be 100–200 instances of cultural control being used more or less effectively against a diversity of pests in various countries. However, there does not appear to be any general review of the number, type and effectiveness of cultural methods on a world basis, so it is difficult to compare the potentialities, costs and returns with other methods. There is no doubt that such methods may furnish the key to the achievement of overall satisfactory pest management in any given crop or area. In fact, studies of tobacco insects by Baumhover and colleagues in North Carolina clearly suggest that since the suppression of the hornworm by cultural methods, there are probably no real pests on that crop except occasional ones. Rabb's (1969) data on the tobacco hornworm distinctly show the importance of planting dates, early stalk destruction and sucker control in reducing pest populations. The pink bollworm, a key cotton pest, is successfully controlled in Central Texas almost entirely by cultural controls. Various component techniques including area-wide stalk destruction, legally set plowing-under times for the shredded crop residues, suicidal emergence of the adult moths, preharvest defoliation, modern cotton-ginning operations, and sanitation around the gins, add up to provide satisfactory control.

A rather thorough discussion of this subject will be found in National Academy of Sciences (1969), Chapter 10. Some examples derived from many sources follow. They are listed under various of the general headings given in paragraph one of this section.

Planting time

The crop can be grown when the pest is inactive or when the susceptible stage of the crop occurs when the pest is least abundant. The Hessian fly in the United States furnishes an outstanding example in use for many years. However, it only applies to the fall brood, not to the spring generation. The adults of the fall brood emerge and live for only 3–4 days. When the winter wheat crop is planted after this generation is over, few eggs will be deposited on the plants. Dates for delayed sowing of winter wheat have been established by entomologists in Hessian-fly-infested states. The method is strongly complementary to the use of resistant varieties but also can be used alone. It has been estimated (Pimentel *et al.* 1965) to have a potential saving, if rigorously followed, on the entire wheat acreage of $114 000 000 a year against a total research cost of about $2 000 000 and a yearly maintenance cost of about $20 000. This represents an exceptionally high return on the research investment and costs the growers nothing. On the other hand, if the entire acreage were treated with chemicals, the cost would be about $80 000 000 per year. This result alone should offer sufficient incentive for society and the responsible institutions to finance research on cultural methods on a much grander scale.

Growing pickling cucumbers in the spring before the pickleworm invades from the Gulf Coast states where it overwinters, provides control. The notorious pink bollworm and boll weevil of cotton can be held down by planting all cotton in an area within a short period of time so as to prevent extension of the fruiting period which favors increases of these pests. Also planting during the earliest favorable period for an area makes early stalk destruction possible and reduces overwintering populations. The early planting of corn in the northern United States may enable it to mature before the corn earworm and the fall armyworm can migrate north from the southern states where they overwinter. The corn seed maggot can be controlled by timing planting so that the corn seed is not present when the females emerge and are capable of laying eggs. The sorghum midge is effectively controlled in the high plains of Texas if the crop is planted soon enough to bloom before the first week in August. In certain areas the beet leafhopper is likely to cause damage unless planting is delayed until after the spring leafhopper migration. In the Sudan, timing of planting and size of acreage of alternate hosts influence the extent of infestation by the *Heliothis* bollworm. In the USSR, late planting of summer wheat caused reduced infestations by a flea beetle and a thrips. Early sowing of wheat during May in India freed the crop from attacks of a gall moth, whereas sowings made in late June or early July were heavily infested.

Cultivation

Methods of tilling the soil which coincide with susceptible life-history stages of pests have long been used. Not only is a thorough knowledge of the biology of the pest in question necessary, but the effects must be compatible with other faunal interactions and with good agronomic practice. As mentioned earlier, the whole ecosystem must be studied in relation to any given proposed habitat change. High mortality of overwintering pupae of the corn earworm is accomplished by fall plowing. Deep spring plowing that buries all plant fragments destroys many larvae of the European corn borer and the survivors crawl to the surface where they are exposed to weather and natural enemies and are further decimated. The wheat stem sawfly has been reduced as much as 75 percent by turning under of stubble. The grape berry moth can be greatly reduced by plowing so as to bury the overwintering cocoons under a layer of soil through which they are unable to emerge.

The best control for the pale western cutworm and some others in Canada is to summer-fallow fields and then *not* till them in August and September. The soil becomes crusted and the moths will not lay eggs on it. On the other hand in Canada, clean summer fallowing every second or third year to eliminate plants on which wireworms feed, will reduce their populations to non-economic levels.

Harvesting

Both time and manner of harvesting can be manipulated to reduce pest populations. Harvesting the crop just as soon as it is mature reduces damage to sweet-potatoes by the sweet-potato weevil, to Irish potatoes by the potato tuberworm, to peas by the pea weevil and to cabbage by thei mported cabbageworm and related species as well as by the cabbage looper. Losses from the sugar-cane borer in heavily infested sugar-cane can be reduced if the cane is cut as early as possible. A selective cutting system works well in control of the western pine beetle in ponderosa pines in some areas. It involves the early detection, cutting and removal of those trees most likely to be attacked by the beetle.

In alfalfa, strip-harvesting on a chronological basis not only gives strikingly better pest management in that crop but lygus bug infestations in adjacent crops may be reduced (van den Bosch and Stern, 1969). The alfalfa field is cut in alternate strips so that two different ages of plants occur simultaneously in the same field and it becomes a much more stable environment than if an entire field were cut at one time and laid bare. One series of strips are cut when the others are about half-grown. The lygus bugs move into the younger strip when the older one is cut, instead of flying into adjacent crops as they would if the entire field were cut at once. The natural enemies also move with them and are conserved. Although the bugs lay eggs in the half-grown hay, the hay is harvested about fifteen days later, hence many of the eggs and newly hatched nymphs are removed or destroyed. In Wisconsin, damage to alfalfa by the potato leafhopper could be reduced in most years by making the second cutting at the late-bud or very-early-bloom stage. The alfalfa weevil may be controlled by early cutting of the first and second crops.

Irrigation and water management

Reservoirs, irrigation developments and natural aquatic habitats provide breeding sites for pest mosquitoes, biting midges, horseflies and others. Populations of these pests often can be minimized or eliminated by proper manipulation. Many techniques adapted to particular circumstances are well developed, including use of water-impervious canals to prevent seepage, use of drains to prevent ponding and to provide self-draining, the regulation of amount of irrigation water use in fields so that none remains standing, management of reservoirs, etc., by completely removing vegetation from the summer fluctuation zone of the permanent pool, by artificially varying water levels to minimize conditions favorable to mosquito reproduction and diverse others. Artificial impoundment is a practical means of minimizing reproduction of salt marsh mosquitoes and biting midges in some marshes. The marsh is continually flooded by pumping or stream diversion, for example. The mosquitoes and midges then breed only at the water edge inside the impoundment, instead of throughout the marsh, and wave action and predation by fish at the edges may virtually eliminate mosquito breeding.

Irrigation or flooding can be manipulated to control various soil-inhabiting insects. Sugar-cane borers in the seed cane are subjected to flooding in some countries in order to control them. Flooding of rice paddies for a minimum of five days after harvest substantially reduces larval and pupal populations of the rice stem borer. Manipulation of irrigation regimes has been shown to have a great impact on pest populations in cotton in California. However, irrigation may be a two-edged sword. Increases in various pests have been recorded following irrigation or flooding This again emphasizes the fact that no cultural technique should be considered only from the viewpoint of controlling a given pest. The whole agro-ecosystem must be taken into account.

Sanitation

This general technique has been successful against a number of pests. Destroying harvest residues or plant refuse may prevent damage to future crops. The method may cause direct mortality to vulnerable stages or remove breeding or hibernating sites. As in other cultural techniques a thorough knowledge of the ecology, biology, life cycle and habits of the pest must be obtained before the most scientifically sound method can be developed.

The housefly is a good example of the need for sanitation. Satisfactory control by insecticides or any other means is virtually impossible if proper disposal or manipulation of animal dung, etc., is not carried out. Substantial reduction of cotton boll weevil populations have been obtained in Texas by early-fall destruction of cotton plants as soon as possible after harvesting but before the first killing frost. Such a procedure resulted in only 27 percent punctured squares by late July of the next season as compared to 63 percent punctured squares where the plants were not destroyed. The former figure is economically acceptable. If the stubble of the harvested corn crop is plowed out of the soil in the fall, low winter temperatures will kill the overwintering larvae of the southwestern corn borer and effect control. In areas of warmer winters, control can be obtained by plowing stubble under several inches of soil so that the adults can not emerge. The practice of cutting and burning cotton plants soon after harvest, as well as fall plowing, has been carried on for many years in order to destroy hibernating larvae of the pink bollworm. However today, area-wide stalk-shredding following harvest, along with plowing under of the refuse, is looked upon as the best pink bollworm control technique. These combined operations can reduce late-fall populations by at least 95 percent.

Control of the sweet-potato weevil is aided by destruction of sweet-potato crop residues by plowing during the winter to expose the roots and vines to freezing temperatures, good sanitation of storage facilities and elimination of infested potatoes prior to storage. Overwintering sugar-cane borers may be killed in large numbers by plowing-under the millable sugar-cane and high stubs left in fields after harvest. Similarly, destruction of tobacco stalks after harvest decimates tobacco hornworm larvae, tobacco budworm and corn earworms, thus resulting in lower initial populations the following season. Removal and destruction of slash residues following logging operations is especially important in reducing the amount of breeding by several species of bark beetles and preventing outbreaks from developing.

There are other applications too numerous to mention. Sanitation appears to offer wide potential in insect control and justifies more research emphasis, even though it does not always provide completely satisfactory control alone. It would appear to be particularly useful against most stalk-boring insects and rootworms of annual crops where harvesting and plowing techniques may be manipulated to reduce pest populations.

Crop rotation

The principle involved here is to follow one crop by another one botanically unrelated so that the pests of the first crop are unable to feed on the subsequent one. However, such techniques may or may not coincide with good agronomic practice and each case must be decided on its own merits. Crop rotation tends to be most successful with pests having both a limited host range and powers of dispersal.

Grass crops following legumes generally greatly reduce damage from white grubs. For example, the white-fringed beetles reproduce freely on such legumes as peanuts, soybeans and velvetbeans, but adults feeding on grasses, including corn and small grains, lay few eggs and additionally the grasses are not damaged as much by a given number of larvae. Proper rotation gives adequate control; legumes followed by legumes results in rapid increase in this pest.

Space limitation precludes discussion of other proven techniques such as use of trap crops, habitat diversity, manipulation of fertilizer regimes, pruning, thinning and soil preparation. However, it is obvious that there are a great number of actual and potential pest control techniques available by manipulation of cultural practices. This is the

260

only non-chemical method of pest control that approaches biological control in the number of successful applications.

There are some difficulties and disadvantages to the method. The practical application of scientifically sound cultural techniques may remain difficult to put into practice because nearly complete adoption over a wide area may be necessary, especially where free-flying or migratory pests are involved. Also the measures are largely preventative and must be put into practice a considerable time previous to insect damage. This is a psychological disadvantage in getting users to adopt the method because they prefer to see immediate results. There also is likely to be a reluctance to adopt a method that may not provide complete economic control. Then there is a formidable extension task in seeing to it that proper timing and application of the particular technique is carried out. From the entomologist's viewpoint, he must realize that any cultural control technique may have widespread inter-actions in the agro-ecosystem; so broad, yet basic, interdisciplinary long-term research is required. As in the case of insecticides, it must be determined that the treatment to reduce the target pest does not have other effects which are adverse. Also, as crop production techniques change or new varieties are introduced, new cultural controls may be necessary, so research must be considered a continuing proposition.

The advantages are that many cultural control techniques can be integrated into normal practices with little or no additional expense to the grower. Some methods in use are so simple and cheap that growers do not even realize they are practicing pest control. Additionally they do not result in pollution problems, nor are they subject to the development of resistance as are insecticides. It seems obvious that cultural methods must play an increasing role in so-called integrated control or pest management.

Genetic methods

Genetic pest control connotes the manipulation and use of genetic material in a manner deleterious to pest insects. Except for the 'sterile-male' technique, the method is still in the idea, laboratory or pilot-test stage. The potential applications are based on principles and techniques discovered and proven by geneticists working principally in laboratories.

Genetic methods can be divided into two categories: (1) autocidal methods, and (2) habit modification. In the former, lethal and sterility factors are incorporated into the field population in order to reduce

261

its density. In the latter, the pest population is not necessarily reduced but its habits changed, so that for example a mosquito species might be modified from a human-biter to an animal-biter. The principal obstacle to the realization of most possibilities lies, not in the creation of suitable genetic traits in the laboratory, but rather in their incorporation into a field population in such a way that they will not be rejected and eliminated. This is theoretically feasible and an interesting field experiment was conducted in Burma, where a population of the common house mosquito was apparently eradicated by the release of cytoplasmically incompatible males. This is about all that can be claimed at present except as discussed below. The reader is referred to articles by Foster, Whitten, Prout and Gill (1972), Smith and von Borstel (1972), Whitten (1970, 1971) and National Academy of Sciences (1969, Chapters 9 and 15) which, along with the references cited therein, cover this complex field very adequately.

The control of insect populations by the release of sterile males has been demonstrated with at least five insect species (LaChance, Schmidt and Bushland, 1967). This spectacular technique has been termed autocidal control and involves using an insect species to bring about its own self-destruction. Very briefly it is accomplished by irradiating laboratory-reared males of the species to an extent sufficient to disrupt the genetic function of the sperm nucleus but not appreciably interfere with the normal ability of the male to mate or of the sperm to penetrate the eggs of the female. However, such 'fertilized' eggs fail to develop, so a wild female mated with a sterilized male produces no progeny. If sterile males are released in large enough numbers in relation to the wild population they will fertilize more females than will the wild males. The advantage is cumulative in each generation, hence eradication may be achieved within a few generations under ideal conditions. Unfortunately ideal conditions, either biologically, ecologically or economically do not occur very often. Thus the only really major success thus far has been with the screw-worm which was eradicated from the island of Curaçao in 1954, from Florida in 1958–9, and which currently is being controlled in the southwest (Texas to California) by massive annual releases of sterile males. Migration of wild flies from sources throughout Mexico, however, prevents eradication. Eradication or control of this major economic pest has paid handsome dividends and it illustrates the value that such unique approaches can have on occasion. The benefits have been estimated to average $20 000 000 per year in the southeastern states and about $100 000 000 per year in the southwest, where about 99 percent reduction in infested livestock has been achieved.

The other most promising results have been obtained against tropical fruit flies. A low infestation of the Oriental fruit fly was eradicated from Guam in 1963, but tests on three other islands were not completely successful. The melon fly was eradicated from Rota Island in 1963 using a combination of a bait spray and sterile-insect releases, and the field cockchafer eradicated from a seventy-four acre plot in Switzerland in 1962. The boll weevil is reported to have been eradicated from a small isolated field by the release of chemically sterilized males. Chemosterilants have been under intensive investigation but are not as yet practical. They offer the advantage of treating the wild population directly and thus avoiding the mass-rearing necessary with gamma radiation.

In addition, tests with the Mediterranean fruit fly in Spain and Hawaii, with the Mexican fruit fly in Mexico, the Queensland fruit fly in Australia and the codling moth in the United States and Canada showed sufficiently effective results to indicate this to be a promising method, either for control or perhaps for eradication under ideal circumstances. However, practical application of the technique in these cases has not been achieved even, for instance, after fifteen years of research in Canada and the United States on the codling moth. Various other pilot tests have failed to produce appreciable results.

From these results, representing about two decades of intensive and quite expensive research, it is apparent that the sterility principle will not be practical for controlling or eradicating many insect species but it may be spectacularly successful against some major insect pests. In fact E. F. Knipling, the guiding force behind the method, has stated that the sterile-insect technique will not be practical for controlling or eliminating established populations of most of our destructive insect species. The method will not be feasible for those that have a wide host range, are sporadic in appearance, or which do not cause high economic losses. Additionally the released insects must be distributed evenly throughout the range of the wild population and such field populations must be low enough to achieve an effective ratio between released and natural populations. Laboratory and other aspects also have to be favorable; mass-rearing must be cheap, sterility must be produced without other adverse effects so that sterilized males are competitive with wild males and the females preferably should mate only once during their lifetime.

The advantages of the method are that if eradication can be achieved the problem is solved permanently, barring reintroductions, and the method is highly selective for the target pest and ecologically non-disruptive, at least where radiation sterilized insects are concerned. Great savings can be obtained against serious major pests of expensive commodities, as illustrated by the screw-worm.

Use of pheromones

The ability of an insect to locate a mate and to copulate once it has been found, is often directed by natural specific chemicals produced by the insect called pheromones. Natural chemical attractants and mating stimulants have been shown to occur in many pest insects. They are often effective in incredibly small concentrations; one caged virgin female of the introduced pine sawfly attracted over 11000 males. Some have been chemically identified and even synthesized. Also, chemical lures have been synthesized, so that it becomes a moot question whether we are dealing with a chemical or a biological method. Its high specificity for particular target insects, however, makes this approach highly desirable.

Such phenomena gave rise to the intriguing idea of using these natural (including living insects) or artificial pheromones to attract and trap insects, to lure them to contact poisons, chemosterilants or pathogens or to mask the location of females by saturating the environment with synthetic sex pheromones. Such techniques could offer highly specific control methods with little or no ecological side-effects.

An example of possibilities is furnished by the eradication of the Oriental fruit fly on Rota Island where the artificial 'pheromone' or attractant, methyl eugenol, lured the male flies to a poison-coated surface. A similar but more important achievement was the eradication of the Mediterranean fruit fly from about one million acres in Florida in 1956–7. The cost was about $11000000. A different approach has been illustrated experimentally recently by my colleagues, H. H. Shorey and L. K. Gaston, who volatilized synthetic cabbage looper sex pheromone in the field and, when evaporative sources were as much as 300 meters apart, obtained 99 percent male inhibition, i.e. reduction in presence of males, so that most of the females in the area would remain unmated. It was considered that, if the treated area were sufficiently large to prevent immigration of mated females from the outside, a reduction of the pest in the next generation could be expected.

A similar possibility has been suggested by Beroza (1971) in connection with the gypsy moth and its synthetic attractant, Disparlure. The same article not only is of general interest but provides a good list of additional references.

Thus far, effective means of control of insect populations utilizing insect pheromones and artificial chemical attractants have been quite limited. The research involved is difficult and costly, hence target pests should be chosen carefully based on preliminary promising findings and with due regard to the probability of success being achieved more easily, cheaply or completely with other approaches. It appears that adequate control from pheromones or attractants probably can only result if they are so highly effective as to be able to reduce the pest population to low levels in the treated area and are used over a large area, so that immigration of the pest from the outside would not negate the effort.

They may find much more general use, however, in sex-pheromone traps or 'lure-traps' designed to assess the population density of a pest and thereby economically and accurately determine economic thresholds. Integrated control may thereby be made feasible. A good illustration involves the use of such traps in apples in El Dorado County, California, to determine the number of codling moths present, hence the need for treatment (Bethell *et al.* 1972). Five live virgin adult females were used per trap to catch male moths. This gave an index to total numbers. In orchards where moths were indicated to be low the insecticide program using Guthion for codling moth control was reduced and this led to a subsequent decrease in the need for mite control. At the beginning of the test program in 1968, a total of twenty-three codling moth applications were made and eighteen contained an acaracide as well, whereas in 1971, a total of sixteen applications were made and only three contained an acaracide. By 1971 costs were $15 to $50 per acre less than with the traditional insurance type of spray program, and pest control was just as good. Sacramento County growers adopted the program in 1971 and saved $58 per acre on 1100 acres of commercial pears, with just as good pest control as before.

Competitive displacement of pests by non-pests

Competitive displacement between ecological homologs is now generally accepted as an ecological principle. Briefly stated it says that different species having identical ecological niches (i.e. ecological homologs) cannot coexist for long in the same habitat. Ecological niche in this context means the role played by an animal in the habitat based on its *precise* food, spatial and habitudinal requirements. In other words, and even more briefly, two species of insects having *exactly* the same food or other essential requirements cannot coexist in the same habitat for any extended period of time. They do not have to actively fight for the food or be aggressive towards one another, but the food must be exactly, not superficially, the same. Feeding on the same plant or even on the same leaf, is not necessarily enough. One example of ecological homologs would be where two species need to feed on the upper midrib of the same leaves in the same area of the same plant species. However, they could coexist if one fed and lived on the upper leaf surface whereas the other was restricted to the lower leaf surface. In this latter case they would not be homologs. In cases of true homologs one will always eliminate the other, barring immigration, alternative hosts and other possible modifying factors. There are now many recorded cases of competitive displacement in the field and a large number have been demonstrated experimentally in the laboratory (see DeBach, 1966).

The fact that such displacement (i.e. eradication or extinction) of one organism by another has occurred naturally, eventually led to conjectures that the phenomenon might be manipulated to man's advantage in pest control or eradication (see DeBach, 1964b). However, from the precise nature of the interactions it is evident that the principle will not be of broad application to all or even most pest species. It should, however, have as broad, or even broader, a potential as the sterile-male technique. In an ideal case, competitive displacement should be attained with a minimum of cost and effort, and eradication or permanent high-level control could result. The technique merely involves the discovery of a harmless ecological homolog of a pest and its introduction and colonization. If the introduced homolog has a competitive advantage, as ultimately expressed by the greatest F_1 progeny production, it will eventually eliminate the other. The principle operates very much like natural selection and survival of the fittest.

In applying the principle of competitive displacement for control or eradication of a pest, obviously one cannot risk trading one pest for another, which might be as bad or possibly even worse. Especially suitable cases need to be chosen and extremely careful selection of the candidate species would have to be based upon sound biological and ecological studies. The most likely applications involve use of non-pests to control or eradicate pests, and this would seem to generally rule out trials with phytophagous insects. However, it must be borne in mind that the critical competition can occur between any active stage of the life cycle, i.e. any larval or nymphal stage, or the adult stage. Thus it is conceivable that the adults of a phytophagous pest which required a specific nectar from a wild host plant, might be displaced by an introduced phytophagous species with the same requirements as an adult but whose immature stages fed only on weeds. Other potentially suitable targets among phytophagous insects include insect vectors of plant pathogens. Often such vectors occur in low numbers and are only damaging because they transmit a plant disease, which, however, is very serious. Such vectors could be replaced by an ecological homolog that was a non-vector and it could exist on the plant even in considerably higher numbers without doing the same amount of damage, perhaps even none. An even better possibility exists where vectors overwinter on an obligate alternative wild host plant as the beet leafhopper largely does in California on Russian thistle. The introduction of another leafhopper restricted to Russian thistle which could out-compete the beet leafhopper on that plant, might well solve this major problem. Some other possibilities are mentioned in the previous citation.

The likelihood remains that most potential applications involve public health, livestock, or nuisance pests such as mosquitoes, biting flies and midges, and others, where the larval food is of no economic importance or actually is unwanted. Thus competition in water between mosquito larvae of different species could lead to displacement of one species by another with no detrimental effects to man or the environment. There is no reason why a species whose adults are non-human biters, or non-vectors of disease, could not be introduced, and displace a serious pest mosquito through the medium of larval competition. The same idea applies to biting flies, gnats, houseflies and others. E. F. Legner and E. C. Bay have suggested to me that the *Hippaletes* eye-flies that are such a nuisance in many parts of North America, include species in the Caribbean area that are not attracted to man. Should their larvae, which develop in the soil or in decaying organic material, be ecological homologs, this problem could possibly be solved.

Some preliminary tests have indicated good possibilities. The house fly has various competitors for dung or other types of larval media. There is no problem here with introducing any coprophagous competitor, which has neither nuisance nor disease transmission potential. In fact, in Australia the CSIRO has an active project involving the introduction of insects to compete with fly larvae for cattle dung. Pilot tests in California have shown that a stratiomyiid fly, which has little nuisance value, can eliminate the housefly under certain conditions, apparently by larval competition for food. After World War II, attempts with chemicals to eradicate a serious mosquito vector of malaria, *Anopheles labranchiae*, in Sardinia, led after two or three years to another, previously rare species, *A. hispaniola*, becoming dominant, while *A. labranchiae* became scarce. *A. hispaniola* is not a vector of malaria. This apparently occurred because of differences in habits of both adults and larvae of the two species which favored relative survival of *A. hispaniola* under the chemical treatment imposed. Had such treatment been continued longer, extermination of *A. labranchiae* could have occurred, not from the chemical treatments alone but from the competitive advantage conferred on *A. hispaniola* by these measures. Thus, the process of competitive displacement can be swung in favor of the species we wish to be the winner by using treatments selectively adverse to the other. High-level ecological research was behind the work described and will be essential to any project of this nature. Currently, competitive displacement tests are in progress on one island of the Marquesas involving the introduction of *Aedes albopictus*, a non-vector of the dreaded filariasis disease, to compete against *Aedes polynesiensis*, the local established vector of the disease. Results are pending. Tests are also being considered in the Marquesas involving the inter-island transfer of a simuliid blackfly that bites only birds, for competitive displacement of a simuliid that is a serious biting pest of humans. Competition occurs between the larvae and certain historical and observational evidence indicates that the bird-biting species may be dominant.

This method definitely has good possibilities that are largely being overlooked, especially when one considers that it probably applies most readily to insects of public health, nuisance and veterinary importance and that such insects have not as yet yielded as readily to traditional biological control methods. These insects, such as malaria mosquitoes, also continue to constitute one of the great sources of environmental pollution with 'hard' insecticides. Competitive displacement offers one of the few techniques where eradication can be expected or achieved. In most cases its application could be extremely cheap because the natural reproduction of the introduced competitor would do the job. However, only highly competent and careful eco-logically oriented scientists should carry out such projects.

Comments and conclusions

In this chapter I have tried to objectively discuss and evaluate the potential of biological methods of pest control other than biological control, especially in agriculture. Aside from biological control, there are really only four methods of proven practical importance in the field: cultural control, use of resistant plants, use of the sterile-male technique and chemical attractants including pheromones. The practical use of the sterile-male technique remains so limited after two decades of intensive research and trials, as far as the number of pest species involved is concerned, that it cannot be expected to play other than an occasional very specialized role in pest management. Other genetic methods remain in the idea or pilot-test stage. Another 'biological' method mentioned, insect pheromones and their synthetic doubles, artificial chemical attractants, show good practical results in several cases and additional practical indications of promise but again their use will probably be limited at best. The use of competitive displacement of a pest by a non-pest, or some similar phenomenon, appears to have promising practical applications, especially in public health and veterinary entomology, but it remains largely in the idea or pilot-test phase. Various other techniques – biological, chemical and physical – have received considerable publicity but they remain largely unproven for practical pest management in agro-ecosystems. They include juvenile hormones and ecdysones, chemosterilants, repellants, anti-feedants and others.

Thus, if we are to avoid the unilateral use of insecticides in crop ecosystems and rely instead on ecologically sound insect pest manage-ment programs, we are currently predominantly dependent upon three principal biological techniques or methods and one chemical technique, namely: biological control, cultural control, the use of insect-resistant host plants and the use of selective chemical insecticides (or the selective use of insecticides).

From the historical record as well as projected promise and from comparisons of advantages, disadvantages, costs *vs* returns, ease of application and other considerations it is clear that the first priority on a general basis should go to research on biological control and especially on importation of new natural enemies. Cultural control methods are indicated to deserve a strong second in emphasis. The development of pest-resistant host plants should also receive strong support. In spite of the relatively few pest species that have been controlled by this method, it appears to have much greater potential than has been realized. The sterile-male technique should be pilot-tested wherever there seems to be a reasonable chance of success against an otherwise refractory major economic pest. Pioneering research should, of course, continue along the lines mentioned previously, as well as others, but not at the expense of more proven or more likely methods. These, of course, are general priorities and with some certain specific pest could well be reversed, but adequate preliminary ecological studies would have to determine this. However, unless biological control research had been *thoroughly* carried out previously, there would seem to be no reason to change priorities. The word thoroughly is emphasized because, for instance, it will be recalled that we consider that the possibilities for biological control of the gypsy moth have not been thoroughly followed through in spite of an enormous amount of work expended on it years ago. Various other previous biological control projects also fit in this same category. A very good case in point involves the codling moth, the most destructive pest of apples and other pome fruits. As mentioned earlier, research and pilot-testing directed toward the sterile-male technique has been going on in the northwest and in Canada for some fifteen years. A large-scale pilot-test including twenty-five square miles and involving chemical and cultural control as well as the release of sterilized male moths was initiated in 1970–1. This will cost a very large amount of money. There were no plans to import new natural enemies of the codling moth, even though there are over one hundred recorded enemy species and only two species have thus far been imported into North America from the native home in the Old World. A bona fide biological control importation project emphasizing this pest has never existed, yet it could be done for a small fraction of the cost of the above-mentioned project. This is a classic example of mis-direction of research priorities.

10
Escape from the pesticide dilemma

A very substantial reduction in the application of insecticides going as far even as their complete withdrawal in some agro-ecosystems can best be attained by the application of basic ecological principles to pest insect problems. Pest problems are bio-ecological problems, not chemical ones. The empirical and unilateral use of chemicals to attempt to hammer pests into submission by repeated costly blows is, as we have seen in Chapter 1, increasingly failing to provide a solution. Pest resurgence and upsets in natural balance combined with the ever increasing development of resistance by pests to the poisons used against them – all problems brought on by the pesticides themselves – clearly show that a rapid and drastic change is necessary in order to achieve control of pests in an ecologically and economically satisfactory manner.

Even with the continual development of new and presumably better pesticides combined with their greatly expanded usage, chemicals are not controlling pests in general as well as previously. Percentage losses due to insect and plant diseases increased since the 1942–51 period according to USDA records (Pimentel, personal communication). For example, a 3.5 percent loss of corn from insects was reported for the period 1942–51 as compared to a 12.0 percent loss for the period 1951–60.

In the United States, pesticide production increased from about 100 million pounds in 1947 to nearly a billion pounds in 1971. It continues to increase. In California agriculture alone, the number of acre-treatments rose from about 7.3 million in 1960 to over 15.0 million in 1971. Better pest control is not resulting from these massive increases. The need for change becomes even more urgent when the serious side-problems generated by the use of pesticides are considered, such as hazards to human health, killing of fish and wildlife, adverse soil effects, hidden social costs and others. These so-called external costs, as well as many of the other economic considerations to be analyzed in a pest

271

management program, are multi-faceted and too involved to consider here. A good overview of them has been presented by Smith (1971 *a*).

An excellent summary of the pesticide problem as illustrated in cotton, the importance of natural enemies, and the need for an alternative ecological approach has been presented by Professors Ray F. Smith and Harold T. Reynolds (1968), two of the world's leading exponents of integrated control, as follows:*

The actions of parasites, predators and pathogens are important causes of pest mortality in many cotton agro-ecosystems. In other areas, especially where heavy use of pesticides has eliminated the natural controls, such biotic mortality may be minimal. The importance of parasites and predators in cotton agro-ecosystems has been most clearly demonstrated by the unleashing of secondary pests through the use of broad-spectrum organic insecticides. Also, in many instances, there have been tremendous resurgences of 'primary target' pest species following the use of pesticides. These pest resurgences and secondary outbreaks are largely the result of the elimination of parasites and predators. There are many examples of such pesticide-induced outbreaks including those of bollworm, tobacco budworm, cotton aphids, and spider mites in the Cotton South of the United States. Jassid control with DDT, Sevin or Zectran results in increased incidence of whitefly in the Sudan. It should be emphasized that it would not be long possible to produce most crops, including cotton, economically or at all without the regulatory impact of beneficial species upon the pest complex...

The use of chemical pesticides without regard to the complexities of cotton agro-ecosystems, especially the fundamental aspects of the population dynamics of pest species, has been the basic cause of the exacerbation of cotton pest problems over the past 10 to 15 years. A review of these problems in many cotton-growing regions of the world shows a common pattern. Typically, at first the introduction of the widespread use of modern pesticides to cotton agro-ecosystems results in significantly increased yields of seed and lint. But then more frequent applications are needed, the dosages must be increased to achieve control and the treatment season is extended. It is noted that the pest populations now resurge to new higher levels rapidly after treatment. The pest populations gradually become so tolerant of the pesticide that it is useless. Another insecticide is substituted and the pest populations become tolerant to it too, but this happens more rapidly than with the first chemicals. At the same time, pests that never caused

* From *The Careless Technology: Ecology and International Development*, edited by M. Taghi Farver and John P. Milton, copyright © 1969, 1972 by The Conservation Foundation and the Center for the Biology of Natural Systems, Washington University. Reprinted by permission of Doubleday and Company, Inc. and Tom Stacey, Ltd.

damage in the area previously or only occasionally become serious and regular ravagers of the cotton fields. This combination of pesticide resistance, pest resurgence, and unleashed secondary pests causes greatly increased production costs and often brings on an economic disaster...

The integrated control approach attempts to avoid the pitfalls of pest control...There is now ample evidence that the integrated control approach with its strong ecological inputs has proved to be a better approach to solve a wide variety of pest problems than has a total reliance on pesticides... Integrated control attempts to use a combination of suitable control techniques in as compatible a manner as possible to maintain the pest populations below defined economic injury levels. Integrated control derives its uniqueness of approach from its emphasis on the fullest practical utilization of the existing mortality and suppressive factors in the environment.

The cotton pest control situation...is not unique. Similar crises are upon us or are soon to be faced in the control of mosquitoes, deciduous fruit pests, spider mites on many crops, house flies, cabbage loopers on vegetables, ticks on cattle and many other situations where pesticides have been used intensively. In many of these situations, time is running out. The world population is facing a most serious food crisis. This is the crisis that faces crop protection specialists all over the world. We believe that with an imaginative approach to the management of agro-ecosystems this challenge can be met, that pests can be controlled without continued exacerbation of the magnitude of the problem...

The change to sound ecological and biological principles in pest control has come to be referred to variously as integrated control or pest management. There are somewhat different ideas as to what these terms mean as well as different definitions. One thing is certain, however; integrated control does not merely refer to some more or less random mixture of different control methods. It must be based primarily upon careful biological and ecological studies of the pest complex and the natural control factors involved in a particular crop habitat. In a broad sense integrated control means the integration of chemical control *with* biological control and other non-chemical approaches, not the opposite. My colleague Professor Ray F. Smith has characterized integrated control thus:

It is clear that not all the important crop pests have adequate biotic controls as they are now handled in modern agro-ecosystems. However, even with these pests we may have biotic agents which give partial controls. The task of the plant protection specialists is to conserve and protect these hidden natural controls and partial control agents and mold them with other controls (resistant plant varieties, chemical controls, cultural controls) into a sound economic protection system. This is another way of describing the integrated control approach.

There is now a huge amount of literature dealing with the subject of integrated control but much of it is either general or theoretical. Some good articles of broad interest include Doutt (1964a), Doutt and Smith (1971), FAO (1966), Smith (1971a), Smith and van den Bosch (1967), van den Bosch *et al.* (1971) and Wood (1971b). A wealth of important articles too numerous to list pertaining to pest management and biological control will be found in the *Annual Proceedings of the Tall Timbers Conference on Ecological Animal Control by Habitat Management, Tallahassee, Florida*. Outstanding specialists from various countries are invited to present papers at this Conference each year. Four volumes were issued through 1973 by the Tall Timbers Research Station, Tallahassee, Florida.

The objectives of pest management in a crop ecosystem are to optimize yield and quality while minimizing pesticidal pollution, other adverse environmental effects and cost. The opinion is held by many ecologically oriented entomologists that a good portion of these objectives could be met nearly immediately because probably at least 50 percent of pesticide chemicals are now used unnecessarily. A good example of what can be done in this regard is illustrated by the management of sugar-cane borer populations, the key sugar-cane pest, in Louisiana (see Hensley, 1971). The maximum number of annual insecticide applications was reduced from twelve to three – a 75 percent decrease – in one decade from 1960 to 1970. This somewhat primitive system of pest population management (in the author's own words) takes full advantage of the suppressive effects of a large complex of arthropod predators, varietal resistance and adverse weather conditions. These are supplemented by the judicious use of insecticides only when necessary. The reduced chemical application system was developed by research which led to the adoption of the following principal practices: (1) discontinuance of insecticidal control of the first generation after research had shown that larvae of this generation did not destroy enough young tillers to reduce yield and that insecticidal control of the first generation did not provide sufficient suppressive effect on the second generation to justify cost; (2) discontinuance of fixed weekly application schedules after a reliable economic injury threshold had been established which recommends treatment or retreatment of second and third generation infestations only when 5 percent of the stalks are infested with small larvae; (3) improvement in field survey methods for detecting potentially damaging infestations by replacing a system of observing plants for superficial feeding signs of larvae that may have later been eliminated by predators or other ecological mortality agents with a system based on the presence of live larvae in leaf sheaths; (4) use in control programs of highly effective synthetic organic insecticides that permit long intervals between applications and that cause minimum damage to natural enemy populations; and (5) more emphasis on host plant resistance as a means of controlling the sugarcane borer and reducing insecticide use.

Two other examples involving potential rapid drastic reduction in pesticide use are furnished by Dr Perry L. Adkisson (1971) from Texas. In the Pecos Valley insecticides are applied from ten to twelve times annually to cotton. However, entomologists of the Texas Agricultural Experiment Station at Pecos produced a crop for each of the three years 1968–70 with almost no insecticide. They accomplished this principally because cotton in the area actually had no key pest such as the boll weevil that apparently lacks effective natural enemies hence requires major insecticidal treatments. Insect outbreaks in the Pecos crop generally are induced by the unwise use of insecticides that kill natural enemies and thereby cause secondary pests, mainly the bollworm, to develop to damaging numbers. Unfortunately, at the time of writing, the producers in the area had not yet followed the practices that have been shown to work.

The results produced at Pecos strongly indicate that supervised control of insect pests by trained specialists could drastically reduce the amount of insecticides used in cotton, even without the development of new technology, according to Dr Adkisson. He considers that insecticide use on cotton in most areas of the United States might be reduced by perhaps 50 percent without reduction of yields. Since nearly half of the total agricultural insecticides applied in the United States is used on cotton, this means that it appears possible in the immediate future on just this one crop to eliminate 25 percent of the total national use of insecticides. Dr Adkisson also presents data showing that the amounts of insecticide used on grain sorghum for control of the greenbug are two to five times greater than that actually needed to control the pest. When the greenbug appeared as a pest about 1967 only $100000 per year was spent on sorghum pest control; three years later in 1970, $14000000 was spent on insecticides to control the greenbug and related pests. Based on the figures presented, from about $7000000 to $11000000 of this amount was unnecessary

275

and was wasted. In other words, insecticide use could be immediately reduced by from 50 to 80 percent in this case and still obtain the same degree of control.

Other striking possibilities for immediate drastic reduction in pesticide usage have been cited by Smith (1971b) concerning a recent investigation carried out by Richard D. Strong, Commodity Specialist of the California Farm Bureau Federation. Strong studied the economics of pest control for up to five years in from 1000 to 4000 acres in Valencia citrus orchards, Thompson seedless grape vineyards and in cotton, to evaluate the economic effect of switching from traditional to integrated control in the San Joaquin Valley. The traditional pest control in each case represented that typically used on most of the acreage in the Valley. The integrated control program which was recommended by research entomologists and applied insect ecologists was a modified one based on utilization of current technological knowledge regarding natural enemies, selective pesticides and economic thresholds. The yield and quality under the integrated control program was essentially the same as under the traditional program. The cost of pest control on citrus was $101 per acre with the traditional program, $45 per acre for the integrated program, for a net saving of $56 per acre and a reduction in pesticide costs of over 50 percent.

The cost of pest control on grapes was $48 per acre for the traditional program, only $16 per acre for the integrated program for a saving of $32 per acre and a reduction in pesticide cost of about 67 percent. The pest control costs per acre on cotton were $25 for the traditional program, $12.50 for the integrated program, giving a reduction in cost of 50 percent. It is emphasized that these were not perfected integrated control programs, the research workers associated with them have already established substantial improvements and have prospects for additional improvements in the future.

The role of biological control in integrated control

We have already stressed (Chapters 3 and 7) the great extent of biological control that occurs naturally in all agro-ecosystems. This natural control furnishes by far the greatest part of the foundation upon which ecological pest management must be built. Without it, we would be unable to produce crops of any magnitude or quality; with it, we can concentrate on the few problem species that for one reason or another are not held under natural biological control.

As pointed out in Chapters 7 and 8, biological control can be fostered and increased in several ways. The optimization of *established* natural enemies through conservation practices offers the most immediate and direct means of decreasing insecticidal chemical pollution and reducing pest control costs. It constitutes the main aspect of integrated control since about 99 percent of all potential pests are already under biological control. The remaining one or so percent of the species that constitute actual pests may need to be controlled chemically at the moment, but with proper research emphasis may still be subjected to biological control through importation of new natural enemies or augmentation of established ones by means of mass production and periodic colonization or other techniques of biological control (see Chapter 7). When biological control cannot be achieved by these techniques the alternative non-chemical methods discussed in Chapter 9 should be rigorously investigated. When serious major pests are involved, probably several of the most promising approaches can and should be investigated simultaneously, because a rapid solution to the costly annual losses is necessary. Systems analysis is being developed as a potent tool in the optimization of pest management. A good discussion of the possibilities involved is given by Stark and Smith (1971).

Selective chemicals and selective means of application can furnish an immediate first step toward integrated control by substituting them for the hard chemicals that kill a broad spectrum of natural enemies (see also Chapter 8), or by timing applications or reducing dosages so that more natural enemies are spared. Another selective technique is to treat only a portion of the crop (strip, spot or skip-treatments) at a particular time, so as to leave reservoirs of natural enemies. An elegant example of this is detailed by Stern (1969). He and colleagues found that early season chemical treatment for lygus bugs in cotton eliminates many natural enemies and often triggers outbreaks of other pests such as bollworm, cabbage looper and spider mites. These in turn require special treatment. However, early season lygus bug treatments can largely be avoided. First, movement of the lygus bug adults into cotton from alfalfa (where they are a minor problem) can be restricted by strip-cutting of alfalfa or by growing trap-strips of alfalfa in the cotton fields. Second, much higher populations of lygus bugs can be tolerated in cotton without economic loss than was previously considered to be possible. The application of this knowledge will greatly reduce the use of insecticides in the first half of the growing season and therefore minimize the occurrence of upsets and resurgences.

General adoption of these techniques by farmers can mean a reduction in pest control costs of millions of dollars.

It should be realized that to seek the highest possible percentage kill of a given pest with a chemical generally is ecologically disruptive. The degree of mortality produced should be designed primarily only to prevent the peak populations that will cause economic loss. Thus 80 percent mortality, rather than 98 percent, may be sufficient for the immediate chemical control needed and it will cause fewer upsets or resurgences and additionally will reduce the rate of development of resistance to pesticides.

What is the real need for chemical control?

We have just estimated and shown examples that strongly indicate that approximately 50 or more percent of insecticides currently used in agriculture are unnecessary. Generally speaking however, the people who use them consider that insecticides are basically required for crop protection, hence they must be shown that their belief is incorrect if they are to change. Thus the real, as opposed to the apparent, need for chemical control must be objectively investigated in all crop ecosystems by means of bio-ecological study and experimentation as well as by economic analysis and questions such as the following answered.

Have chemicals used previously decimated natural enemies causing upsets and resurgences resulting in new or worsened man-made pests? Has resistance to the pesticides developed so that the chemicals used no longer kill the target pest, only other organisms? Is chemical over-kill practiced, i.e. are greater dosages and more frequent applications used than are necessary? Are erroneous or misleading crop-loss claims used to justify need for chemicals? Are asserted gains in production from chemical use accurate or could other factors such as fertilizers, etc., be responsible? Are artificial crop quality standards of a cosmetic or other nature imposed on the farmer which force him to use costly chemical treatments and thereby trade inconsequential blemishes or minor damage for toxic residues in the produce? Are the economic injury thresholds and economic injury levels (which are indications of the need for treatment or the level at which economic loss starts) scientifically accurate, merely rough estimates or only educated guesses? For example, sprays for the bud moth larvae in Canada used to be applied arbitrarily. It is now known that five bud moth larvae or less per 100 apple leaf clusters do not constitute an economically important population. Hence, sprays are now omitted at these densities because resulting damage is below the 5 percent level generally tolerated by the industry. Very few economic thresholds have been determined by economic entomologists using appropriate experimental field study, and even fewer have been adequately determined in chemically untreated check plots as compared to chemically treated ones. The fact that the economic injury threshold is not a constant for a given pest species is often overlooked. It will be completely different in a crop that has been frequently sprayed as compared to the same crop which has been unsprayed or very little sprayed for a period of time. The decimation of natural enemies causes this. In frequently sprayed crops economic injury thresholds are reached at much lower pest population levels because when natural enemies are eliminated the pest population resurges much more rapidly. An international conference on prediction, forecasts and assessments of economic thresholds was held in Vienna, Austria, in 1969. Many of the papers presented relate to means of determining ahead of time whether or not a given insect will become a problem in a particular season. This obviously is basic to our ability to reduce the use of pesticides (EPPO Report, 1970b).

When the preceding questions, and doubtless others, have been appropriately answered, it will become apparent how much chemical treatment is being carried out unnecessarily. It will also indicate the the directions in which further research is needed to solve the remaining problems. In my experience and from numerous literature reports it seems definite that in any major crop the answers to the preceding questions will be affirmative for from several to many pests, as well as non-target organisms. I personally know from many years of field experimentation that in California alone, many thousands of acres of citrus annually receive from one to several unnecessary pesticide applications.

We cannot emphasize too strongly that the answers to most of the questions posed can only be obtained by conducting simultaneous experimental comparisons between adequately designed test plots receiving minimal or no chemical pesticides as compared to similar plots receiving the usual commercial quota of pesticide treatments. (See Chapters 3 and 7.)

Supervised control

Even after the answers are known regarding the degree of unnecessary use of pesticides and their adverse effects, and after research has shown to what extent effective natural enemies of the various pests are present, it is not necessarily an automatic or easy matter to switch to integrated control from a heavy chemical program. First, recall the habit-forming, narcotic-like effect of insecticides (see Chapter 1) and the concomitant, very real and often difficult problem of withdrawal from chemicals. The change to ecological pest management is a practical matter to the farmer and he is not prepared to suffer any interim financial losses during the changeover. Even his imagined possibility of loss may make him quite reluctant to change his traditional program. The integrated control pioneers, A. D. Pickett and N. A. Patterson, wrote in 1953:

There are great difficulties involved in combining biological and chemical control under field conditions. It is similar in many ways to the relationship between preventive and curative medicine. As Wigglesworth has stated 'The public loves the hospital, the doctor and the bottle of physic; while the advances in preventive medicine which have transformed our lives are scarcely noticed. So too it creates a greater impression on the mind to destroy an infestation of insects that can be seen, than by some simple change in practice to prevent any infestation from developing.' Had the staff of our laboratory developed an insecticide that would control the oystershell scale as effectively as the mere changes in program that allowed nature to take its course, they would have been assured of a place in entomological history.

In many, possibly most, crop ecosystems where chemical pest control has been relied on heavily, spraying and dusting cannot merely be stopped with the assurance that biological control will take over. Natural enemies may have to be reintroduced or otherwise manipulated or other non-chemical measures taken, based on what research has shown to be feasible. The grower generally cannot be expected to have the detailed knowledge of pest and natural enemy biology and ecology essential to implement such a program. He needs a specialist trained in ecological pest management, i.e. an applied ecologist who can constantly check and evaluate population developments and inter- actions in the field. Today's large-scale agriculture nearly makes it mandatory that pest management should be under the direction of a trained and licensed supervising applied ecologist who is responsible for all decisions relating to this matter. Such a specialist can be compared to a general medical practitioner, veterinarian or pharmacist in his use of complicated materials and techniques. There is a shortage of such trained personnel now but more and more are entering the field. Various universities in the United States are now emphasizing graduate training in pest management and the National Science Foundation and the Ford Foundation have supported certain programs with financial grants. The Association of Applied Insect Ecologists is an organization of pest management specialists. Information concerning their objectives and programs may be obtained from Maclay Burt, Executive Secretary, AAIE, 100 No. Winchester Blvd, Executive Suite 260, Santa Clara, California 95050.

The current shortage of applied insect ecologists must be rapidly overcome if ecological pest management is to be expanded at a rate commensurate with the need. California probably has more practicing applied insect ecologists than any area of comparable size in the world, yet their number is pitifully meager compared to those employed in the unilateral use of pesticides. The income of this infant industry for consulting pest management services amounts to only about one percent of the total product value of agricultural pest control-related industries, whereas pesticide salesmen (some 6000 in the State alone) and commercial pesticide applicators take in about 99 percent of the total spent on agricultural pest control.

The extension entomologist is a necessary link between the researcher, who finds out what it is possible to do, and the supervising entomologist or applied ecologist who carries out the program. The role of the extension entomologist in pest management is well summarized by Strayer (1971).

Examples of integrated control

Emphasis on the need for integrated control is so great today that some think it is a new idea; however, strong general *support* for integrated control is really what is new. Actually, it began developing more or less empirically many years ago when combinations of biological control, cultural control, chemical control and sometimes plant resistance were used to control pests on a single crop. Practical applications in California employing both insectary-reared natural enemies and chemicals were carried out in citrus groves at least as early as the 1920s. C. V. Riley even envisioned integrated control in 1893 when he wrote:

our artificial insecticide methods have little or no effect upon the multiplication of an injurious species, except for the particular occasion which calls them forth, and occasions often arise when it were wiser to refrain from the use of such insectides and to leave the field to the parasitic and predaceous forms.

It is generally when a particular injurious insect has reached the zenith of its increase and has accomplished its greatest harm that the farmer is led to bestir himself to suppress it, and yet it is equally true that it is just at this time that nature is about to relieve him in striking the balance by checks which are violent and effective in proportion to the exceptional increase of and consequent exceptional injury done by the injurious species. Now the insecticide method of routing the last, under such circumstances, too often involves, also, the destruction of the parasitic and predaceous species, and does more harm than good...it not only emphasizes the importance of preventive measures [cultural control], which we are all agreed to urge for other cogent reasons, and which do not to the same extent destroy the parasites, but it affords another explanation of the reason why the fight with insecticides must be kept up year after year, and has little cumulative value.

Actually the term integrated control is somewhat inappropriate because it implies that two or more distinct methods of pest control must be combined in an optimal manner to achieve the desired results, whereas in some instances at least, biological control alone will suffice. In Hawaii, for example, complete biological control of all sugar-cane pests was obtained, and in California avocados enjoy essentially complete natural biological control. Nearly all major pests of coconut in Fiji were controlled biologically by the late 1930s. There are other examples (one was cited in Chapter 8) and larger portions of more crops will be brought under complete or virtually complete biological control in the future. Perhaps ecological pest management would be a better term than integrated control because it is less restrictive and the term itself has broader implications. Be this as it may, pesticides are now being used more or less heavily in most commercially grown crops around the world so the term integrated control will certainly continue into the foreseeable future to apply to the switch to ecological pest management in these crops. The two terms are used more or less interchangeably in this Chapter.

All of the examples of integrated control that follow represent sequels to cases of non-target insect upsets, pest resurgences and/or resistance to insecticides which were so serious that an alternative to the unilateral use of pesticides was urgently mandatory. The upset phase of most of the following examples has been discussed in Chapter 1.

Apples in Nova Scotia and Quebec

In many areas apple growers are burdened by fifteen or more pesticide applications each year. Most need relief from this increasingly intensive program. A good example of what can be done and one of the pioneering and best known cases of integrated control was developed in Nova Scotia by A. D. Pickett and colleagues beginning just after World War II. A review of this work is given by MacPhee and MacLellan (1971 b). Apple production has been a well-established agricultural industry there for about a century. The pest control program developed in Nova Scotia as it did in the United States with nearly total dependence upon the unilateral use of chemical pesticides. As time went on new pest problems developed and some old ones became more serious. The European red mite and the gray-banded leafroller, not important enough to be mentioned in earlier literature, were major pests by the early 1940s. The oyster-shell scale became an extremely destructive pest for the first time in the 1930s. The codling moth and the eye-spotted bud moth became noticeably more serious.

These upsets and resurgences combined with a loss of traditional overseas markets after the war and the consequent need to reduce costs emphasized the need for a new approach. Ecological studies of the impact of the pesticides used showed that the traditionally used sulfur fungicides killed the parasite and a predaceous mite of the oyster-shell scale but were harmless to the scale. The substitution of copper-based fungicides and Ferbam for sulfur proved to be harmless to the natural enemies and natural biological control again resulted. Other selective fungicides have since been incorporated into the program. Native predators were found to be capable of controlling the European red mite if not interfered with by chemicals. Use of selective chemicals for other pests resulted in no further need for miticides.

The program as it stood by 1955 (all integrated control programs are dynamic and may be changed) had narrowed the Nova Scotian growers' list of spray chemicals to glyodin, captan, bordeaux and mercury eradicants as fungicides for plant disease control; and nicotine, lead arsenate and ryania as insecticides. All of these as used are relatively selective in sparing natural enemies. The virtual elimination of sulfur, dormant oils, dinitrocresol, the chlorinated hydrocarbons, carbamates and the organophosphates from the program greatly reduced some of the more important apple pests.

Plant-feeding mites and scale insects, as mentioned previously, became conspicuous by their absence. The eye-spotted bud moth, a serious pest for many years, was reduced to its lowest level in thirty years by 1955. At that time by adopting modified spray programs many Nova Scotian growers were averaging only two sprays per year. About 90 percent of them had adopted the program by the late 1950s and have continued ever since. No acaricides were used but adequate spraying for the apple scab disease was always followed. The conservation of the natural enemy fauna by this program substantially reduced production costs, increased production of good fruit, improved the growth of the trees, reduced hazards to growers and consumers and of course to the environment.

It should be noted that this program, like several others, was developed because the growers had their backs to the wall. Had traditional pesticides continued to provide control without serious side-problems and increasing costs, very likely no change would have been sought. The integrated control program developed, involved principally conservation of natural enemies through substitution of more selective pesticides. Stress on importation and augmentation of natural enemies might further appreciably enhance the program.

In Quebec work on 'modified' and 'commercial' spray programs in apple orchards, designed to reveal gross effects of each program on predator–pest relationships, was initiated in 1951. The results have been reported by LeRoux (1960). A survey was made of the various spray programs in use in the major apple-growing regions of the province, and their effects on the beneficial predator fauna were determined from predator counts made in orchards receiving each program. Orchards were categorized on the basis of the predominant spray materials in use as: (a) fungicide–DDT–parathion, (b) fungicide–lead arsenate, (c) fungicide alone, and (d) unsprayed or neglected. Results showed that such highly toxic pesticides as DDT and parathion, irrespective of the fungicide with which they were combined, markedly reduced the predator populations as compared to treatments with fungicides and arsenicals or with fungicides alone. There were still greater differences between insecticide-sprayed orchards and those that received no sprays. In the latter, however, much of the foliage was destroyed by apple scab. In orchards where DDT had been used for three or more consecutive years, pests of economic importance such as the European red mite *Panonychus ulmi* and the red-banded leafroller *Argyrotaenia velutinana* were on the ascendency. Of all the programs surveyed, the fungicide–arsenical program destroyed the least number of predators while giving sufficient pest control to keep crop damages at a minimum.

The 'modified' program tested was of the fungicide–arsenical type and its basic ingredients were the fungicide glyodin and the insecticide lead arsenate. Glyodin was applied each season; the insecticide was applied only as needed. Additional pesticides were used only when special control measures were required. The 'commercial' program with which it was compared was of the fungicide–DDT–parathion type and the main materials used were the fungicides Magnetic 70 and glyodin, and the insecticides DDT, parathion, malathion and lead arsenate. The number of fungicide and insecticide applications made was the same as that made by the average grower based on his own assessment of apple scab and arthropod pest situation in his orchard. Each program is defined as follows: *modified spray program* – program using corrective sprays (insecticides, acaricides) only to control insects and mite pests, and preventative sprays (e.g. fungicides) mostly to control apple scab. Only spray chemicals known to be relatively innocuous to natural enemies of apple pests were selected; *commercial spray program* – program using preventative sprays only (fungicides, insecticides, acaricides to control scab, insects and mites). Little or no emphasis placed on the selection of spray chemicals innocuous to natural enemies of apple pests. The program was in effect the one used by Quebec orchardists, guided by the annual spray calendar.

Results reveal that for a five-year period the 'modified' spray program gave as clean a crop as that obtained with the 'commercial' program and for approximately half the cost. To carry out the 'modified' spray program, an average of 9.2 fungicidal and 2.2 insecticidal sprays were applied at a cost of $0.65 per tree. The average in apple yield per tree was 6.4 bushels. The program resulted in a build-up from low to high densities of beneficial forms and the maintenance of medium to low densities of destructive forms. The overall control of apple pests for the five years was good considering that on the average 90 percent of the crop was saleable. It would appear that much of the effectiveness of the 'modified' program was due to increased activity of arthropod predator and parasite complexes, and bird predation, which contributed an added degree of control of insect pests. To carry out the 'commercial' spray program for the same period an average of 12.4 fungicidal and 6.0 insecticidal sprays were applied at an average cost of $1.14 per tree. The average yield in apples per tree was 5.2 bushels. The program resulted in the practical elimination of all natural control agents with the maintenance of medium to high densities of destructive forms. The overall control of apple pests for the five years was good with 90 to 95 percent of the crop being saleable. The dollar returns for the crop were substantially greater for the 'modified' or integrated control plots than for the 'commercial' plots. The total returns per 1000 trees for the five-year period were $10500 more for the 'modified' plots than for the 'commercial' plots.

According to LeRoux, the results indicate that a more thorough and intensive approach is needed if the mechanisms of orchard epidemiology are to be more clearly understood and methods of manipulating the orchard environment towards more efficient pest control are to be devised. Favoring effective populations of natural enemies of orchard pests is an ecological problem and to elucidate the problem more adequately, an attempt should be made first to study the natural limitations of orchard pests populations and their interrelationships in the apple orchard habitat.

Citrus in California, South Africa and Israel

The Fillmore Citrus Protective District in Ventura County, California, comprising some 8800 acres, is a unique co-operative pest control association that has been under the supervision of a trained entomologist, Howard Lorbeer, for over forty years. The author has co-operated closely with Mr Lorbeer for many years. The district maintains its own insectaries to produce natural enemies as needed, and uses only a minimum of selective insecticides. They have nearly perfected integrated control and as a result their pest control costs are the lowest of any district in California and their fruit quality and quantity among the highest.

This has not always been the case. Prior to about 1940 most of the citrus orchards in the district were fumigated annually with hydrogen cyanide gas or sprayed with oil to control the black scale which was the major pest of citrus in southern California at that time. Other treatments were applied for a variety of less critical pests. The black scale problem was largely solved following the successful importation of a new parasite, *Metaphycus helvolus*, from South Africa in 1937 by the

University of California at Riverside. This parasite generally produced satisfactory biological control and has been supplemented by periodic release of insectary-reared parasites in some Fillmore district groves. For the ten-year period 1960–70 an average of less than five percent of the groves were sprayed each year to control black scale. This alone amounts to an annual savings of $40 per acre or more than $300 000 per year for the district.

The Fillmore Citrus Protective District originally was organized in 1922 to assist in the chemical eradication of the California red scale which had just been found for the first time in several orchards in the district. That was its sole purpose for the first four years but gradually a program of pest control based primarily upon biological control has been evolved and insecticides now are used mainly to quickly bring an infestation which threatens economic loss back to the level where effective biological control can be re-established. During the period of this development up to about 1960, the California red scale, a serious pest present elsewhere in southern California was successfully prevented from establishing a foothold. However, by 1960, more and more small foci of infestation were found, so that it became economically unrealistic to continue red scale eradication efforts. Fortunately a promising new red scale parasite had been imported from India and Pakistan by the University of California at Riverside and established elsewhere in southern California in 1957. It was colonized widely in the Fillmore district immediately upon cessation of eradication efforts in 1961 and has given excellent biological control of the red scale ever since. Supplementary releases of insectary-reared parasites have been made as needed. Otherwise, the integrated control program might have been largely nullified at that time by the necessity to use major insecticidal applications against this key pest. As it turned out only a very few acres – about one percent – in the district have had to be sprayed each year for the California red scale.

All told in the district, ten insects that are serious major pests in other districts or other countries are being completely controlled by their natural enemies. These include the black scale, California red scale, yellow scale, brown soft scale, dictyospermum scale, cottony-cushion scale, and four species of mealybugs. Four of these were major pests at one time or another in the Fillmore district but now are either minor or innocuous ones due to importation of new natural enemies. Three other pests partially controlled by native natural enemies are the citrus red mite, citrus aphid and orangeworm. More acreage is treated for these latter than for anything else in the district but these are generally selective minor treatments and the average for everything remains less than one spray per acre per year.

In addition to their emphasis on biological control (including control of ants which interfere with natural enemies), much of the success of the Fillmore district in achieving such outstanding integrated control must be ascribed to their long-standing policy of discouraging the use of highly toxic, broad-spectrum insecticides, particularly DDT, parathion, malathion and sevin.

A successful integrated control program for citrus pests in South Africa is developing rapidly. The following is derived from an article by Bedford (1969). The major task which now faces South Africa is the selection of insecticides to replace undesirably toxic ones and to formulate a balanced integrated control program for every group of pests, according to host plant and area involved, while also introducing additional natural enemies whenever possible. The integrated approach to South African pest control problems was suggested by Ullyett as long ago as 1948.

Chemical control programs for citrus

Following the introduction of parathion in 1948 for the control of California red scale *Aonidiella aurantii* on citrus in South Africa, more and more emphasis was placed on the chemical control of citrus pests until the cost of insecticide applications began spiralling and outbreaks of various pests tended to become more frequent, especially from about 1950 to 1964.

They have on citrus a complex of over thirty insect pests which are attacked by about 200 or more species of parasites and predators. As nearly all citrus growers were using parathion and often mercaptothion and Gusathion as well, they destroyed most of the natural enemies in their orchards, as well as greatly reducing the chances of establishing newly introduced parasites and predators.

At least eight species, or about one-third of the most important citrus pests, have at one time or another built up excessively as a result of the use of modern insecticides. Some pests which were originally of minor importance, and even insects which were quite unknown as pests, suddenly reached the status of severe major pests. It is now known that the increase of these pests is simply due to the wholesale destruction of their natural enemies by insecticides. This destruction was then increased in Rustenburg orchards by additional applications of organophosphates, which in turn led to an increasing number of applications of acaricides such as Systox, Tedion, light–medium petroleum oil, Ovex, Kelthane WP, and finally Kelthane MO and Orchex N 695 (narrow distillation range emulsive spray oil). To climax everything, parathion, which often causes outbreaks of the citrus red mite *Panonychus citri*, was still registered and used to 'control' this pest. Some orchards required up to five sprays in one season to control *P. citri*, following one parathion spray.

When the originally used HCN fumigation, cryolite and sulfur dust were replaced by parathion, this material controlled California red scale, as well as *Chrysomphalus aonidum*, *Scirtothrips aurantii* and the American bollworm *Helicoverpa armigera* simultaneously. The annual spray program was initially one application of parathion every September at petal fall. Repercussions of various pests gradually became more and more serious. Even California red scale was suspected to have become resistant several years ago and from three to six parathion sprays were sometimes applied in one season in the Transvaal lowveld.

By about 1964, the control of citrus pests in the Rustenburg area was often a complicated and costly procedure requiring constant orchard inspection, so that growers were most distressed.

An example of a spray program which was applied in a Rustenburg Navel orchard, from June 1963 to May 1964, was as follows:

1963: June		Parathion and Ovex for California red scale and citrus red mite.
	August	Mercaptothion and Ovex for soft scale (*Coccus* spp.) and red mite.
	September	Parathion and Kelthane for California red scale and citrus thrips. (Kelthane to suppress red mite.)
1964: January		Kelthane for red mite.
	May	Mercaptothion, Ovex and oil, for California red scale and red mite (latter causing fruit drop).

(Note 5 sprays for citrus red mite in one season.)

The transition period and corrective control

Ullyett and Simmonds warned that citrus pests could temporarily reach damaging proportions when in transition from chemical control to biocontrol. California red scale and *C. aonidum* both tend to do this, and the problem is solved by applying a corrective spray of parathion plus Rogor or preferably Rogor and a narrow-range light summer oil for the former, or Rogor only for the latter. Packhouse culls have been as high as 27.3 percent for California red scale and 49.5 percent for *C. aonidum* (Florida red or Circular purple scale) when this precaution was not taken in two Navel orchards which became heavily infested. Another step towards integrated control is therefore the selection of insecticides for corrective sprays for temporary or occasional use, again avoiding insecticides like parathion if at all possible. If losses during the transition to integrated control are not likely to be excessive, it may be wiser to accept them rather than to apply potent sprays. For instance, the mealybug *Nipaecoccus vastator* increased in a Valencia orchard when the normal parathion spray was omitted and culls reached 6.5 percent in one load of fruit. Natural enemies finally controlled this infestation.

Integrated control programs for citrus

It has now been proved that California red scale, Florida red scale and citrus red mite can be brought under commercially satisfactory biological control in practically any Rustenburg orchard, and an integrated spray program is now recommended for those citrus pests still requiring chemical control. The routine spray program for integrated control in 1968 is given below.

June   Lime sulfur or chlorobenzilate for citrus bud mite *Aceria sheldoni*.
Early September   Dieldrin application to tree trunks for ant control.
Mid-September   Thiodan for bollworm (only if necessary).
Late September–October   Tartox plus sugar (1st appl.) for citrus thrips.
October   Tartox plus sugar (2nd appl.).

It will be noticed that the major pests requiring control measures vary in the HCN, the parathion and the integrated control programs. In other words, the citrus grower has unknowingly selected some of his major pests according to the spray program which he has followed.
In South Africa a slightly different combination of introduced natural enemies and insecticides is required in each climatic area

according to the major citrus pests involved. When an integrated control project is commenced, one should obviously attempt to bring as many pests as possible under complete biocontrol, especially if suitable enemies are available in other countries. For this purpose the Department of Agricultural Technical Services introduced parasites and predators of *A. aurantii*, *C. aonidum* and *Lepidosaphes beckii*. As a result *C. aonidum* has been reduced to an incredibly low level of subeconomic infestation by *Aphytis holoxanthus*, while DeVilliers has also had very promising results with *Aphytis lepidosaphes* on *L. beckii* (purple scale or citrus mussel scale) in the Eastern Cape.

When initiating an integrated control program such as the one just referred to, published lists of the relative toxicity of different pesticides are consulted. Chemicals which have a high median lethal concentration to beneficial insects and which also show a relatively long persistence, such as parathion, mercaptothion, Gusathion and DDT are to be avoided completely. Those at the bottom of the scale, such as Kelthane, lime sulfur, chlorobenzilate, tartar emetic, etc., are usually safe to use. Those in an intermediate position, such as Thiodan and Rogor, must at first be used with caution and only included in the program if they prove to be safe. Thiodan incidentally has presented no problems in the integrated control orchards, while Rogor has been used as a corrective treatment for *C. aonidum*. Relative toxicity tests can be misleading however, as lime sulfur and Thiodan (endosulfan) have been shown to be toxic to certain natural enemies. The final answers must be sought in the orchard.

Entirely new compounds should rather not be used at all in established integrated control orchards until adequately tested in both field and laboratory.

Insecticide trials with large blocks of trees

Statistically valid proof that an insecticide gives better control of a pest than on the untreated control trees may be quite misleading if a few scattered control trees are surrounded by trees sprayed with an insecticide with a long residual effect against entomophagous insects. Treated trees serve as trap trees for natural enemies. The natural enemies of California red scale are never given a chance to prove their worth in insecticide trials consisting of single-tree or two-tree replicates, conducted in plots in which the natural balance has already been destroyed by parathion.

One approach to the problems at Rustenburg is to leave experimental blocks of at least 48 to 52 trees (4 rows of 12 or 13 trees each) for each treatment and control, and also to conduct long-term experiments to determine any erratic results or repercussions to be expected from treated and untreated blocks. Such experiments are more difficult, present problems of compensation for losses and often extend over at least two seasons, but they are imperative for an unbiased evaluation of biocontrol and for the final selection of insecticides for integrated control.

Another approach is to treat the two halves of an orchard separately (total about 300 to 1000 trees) and to replicate the treatment in three or more orchards, preferably on different farms.

New insecticides for citrus

In view of the fact that Delnav and Abate are promising new insecticides for use against the citrus thrips in South Africa, it was considered essential to test out the effect, if any, on the natural enemies of California red scale by means of field experiments. Only insecticides which have proved to be compatible with an integrated control program can be safely recommended in orchards in which California red scale is under biological control.

A pilot experiment was commenced in young Navel and Valencia orchards at Rustenburg in October 1968, in order to find out whether Delnav (15 fl oz per 100 gal water) and Abate (8 fl oz per 100 gal water) showed any tendency to increase California red scale when sprayed twice at a fourteen-day interval for thrips control in three biocontrol orchards. A few trees also received three additional sprays of these insecticides in January and February 1969, as the citrus thrips is sometimes controlled in late summer to protect flushes of young growth. A portion of one orchard continued to receive an annual spray of parathion for comparison.

By January 1969, unexpected differences in the California red scale population had already showed up in the Delnav and Abate experiments as compared with the blocks receiving the recommended integrated spray program (including lime sulfur and tartar emetic). The final average preharvest scale numbers per fruit obtained in May–June 1969 were: 0.13 for parathion, 2.57 for biocontrol, 10.58 for Delnav (two sprays) and 17.19 for Abate (two sprays). Five sprays of Delnav and of Abate increased the number of scales to 41.71 and 155.50 respectively.

292

It is quite obvious that both Abate and Delnav can be detrimental to the natural enemies of California red scale. Abate also caused a severe infestation of *Coccus hesperidum* which resulted in a heavy growth of sooty-mold on the leaves and fruit.

The importance of selecting insecticides for the integrated control of insect pests is obvious. The initial problem is to develop a commercially satisfactory integrated spray program. Once this is achieved, no new insecticides, miticides or fungicides should be included in the program until adequately tested in the field. The entire program could be jeopardized if the biological control of any pest were severely disrupted. In South Africa, if California red scale flared up, the grower might resort to spraying with parathion which would be detrimental to the integrated program and place him in the same situation as before.

Israel is the only country in which satisfactory integrated control for a crop has been developed for the entire nation. The story has been thoroughly told by Harpaz and Rosen (1971) and is well worth looking up. Aside from developing the necessary foundation of bio-ecological research to make the program technologically feasible, a major reason for this unique achievement lies in the organization of the citrus industry under the Citrus Board of Israel. The Board not only constitutes the sole marketing authority, but finances pest control research and extension work and maintains a large insectary for natural enemy production. Perhaps most importantly, it is authorized to regulate and carry out pest control operations on a country-wide scale. Thus the Board can obtain a meeting of the minds of the ecologically-oriented research entomologists of the country as to the best program to follow and it can then implement this program. This keeps individual growers and private pest control operators from proceeding on a haphazard, perhaps deleterious, pest control progam.

A key development in this program concerned modification of a chemical method of repeated cover sprays of chlorinated hydrocarbons used against the serious Mediterranean fruit fly and adoption of selective treatments against the rust mite. The new fruit fly treatment entailed use of strip sprays of a poison bait containing protein hydrolysates as a powerful attractant for the fly females and malathion as a poison. The bait is sprayed from the air at a very low rate down to less than one pint per acre. The highly mobile flies find the scattered spots of bait but natural enemies of non-target species are largely spared. The bait spray is applied only as needed, based on an effective

293

lure-trap technique of sampling fruit fly populations. This method enables the natural enemies of several previously serious scale and mealybug pests to control their hosts without interference. The switch to selective acaricides for rust mite control not only aided in better biological control of scales and mealybugs being obtained, but also enabled natural enemies of the mite to increase to the extent that the mite has recently ceased to be a pest of major economic importance.

Tropical perennial crops in Malaysia

Following application of broad-spectrum, long-lasting insecticides, especially DDT, dieldrin and aldrin, serious pest upsets occurred on oil palms (Wood, 1971 b) and cocoa (Conway, 1971). On oil palms in west Malaysia the occasional use of the insecticides mentioned for minor outbreaks of bagworms, nettle caterpillars and other insects led to the ever-increasing need for additional treatments for several years until the bagworms and nettle caterpillars were no longer occasional pests but constant ones. The more insecticide was used, the worse the problem became. Furthermore, even with these very strong but non-selective insecticides, sometimes a 40 percent crop loss occurred and it took several years for the trees to recover from defoliations. It was initially hypothesized, and later on detailed field studies showed, that natural enemies of these pests no longer existed in effective numbers in the treated groves and that the worst outbreaks occurred after the initial use of DDT, endrin and dieldrin. The recognition of these facts made the need for selective insecticides obvious. Experiments then showed that trichlorphon or lead arsenate gave sufficient control of the pest populations but were selective and allowed the natural enemies to survive. Further field studies showed the ideal time to spray; this was when young bagworms were emerging and before maximum parasite activity developed. This resulted in an integrated control program where the pests are normally under biological control but occasional outbreaks of the bagworms are successfully controlled with a selective insecticide.

Similar spectacular results occurred with cocoa in Sabah. The new cocoa plantations planted in primary forest clearings with some trees left for shade were attacked by native borers which sometimes caused dieback or even death of cocoa trees. This led the growers to adopt dieldrin sprays which initially gave control. However, subsequent to the use of dieldrin, leaf-eating caterpillars became a problem and this led to more spraying with a wide variety of non-selective insecticides. As a result several more pests in various taxonomic groups appeared in outbreaks of increasing intensity until finally very severe defoliation by several species of bagworms occurred. Conway, realizing that these outbreaks were probably upsets resulting from decimation of natural enemies, recommended that spraying be stopped. When this was done, some of the pests began to disappear more or less rapidly, and this was associated with increased parasite activity. However, bagworms still constituted a pest so were controlled with selective sprays of trichlorphon. Concurrently, studies revealed that a particular common native shade tree species was host to the original bark borer pest but was relatively uninjured by it. Removal of this tree solved the bark borer problem which had led to the whole chain of events.

Cotton in Peru

Doutt and Smith (1971) describe how the chemical cart ran away with the biological horse. They were speaking of the closed, circular self-perpetuating system employing a completely unilateral method of chemical pest control that did not even bother to ask the question of whether a treatment was really necessary or could be justified economically. This they termed the *pesticide syndrome*.

In cotton they discuss how the pattern of crop protection has tended to pass through a series of five phases as follows: (1) *Subsistence phase* – primitive, non-irrigated local agriculture, low yields, and no organized program of crop protection. The crop protection that occurs results from natural control, inherent plant resistance, hand picking, cultural practices and rare chemical treatments. (2) *Exploitation phase* – irrigated agriculture on new land, crop protection measures introduced to protect the large and more valuable crops. These are often necessitated by the changed ecology. Such measures are nearly always solely dependent on chemical pesticides. They are used intensively and often on fixed arbitrary schedules. At first these techniques are successful, resulting in high yields of seed and lint. (3) *Crisis phase* – develops after a variable number of years of heavy use of pesticides. Frequency of application of pesticides increases to maintain control; pest populations become so resistant to particular pesticides that they are useless. Another pesticide is substituted but the same events occur, only more rapidly. New pests arise and old ones resurge rapidly following pesticide treatment due to upsets of natural enemies. All this occasions a greatly increased application of pesticides and causes greatly increased production costs. (4) *Disaster phase* – because of high pesticide costs and failing control, cotton can no longer be grown profitably. First, marginal farmers cease production. Eventually cotton production becomes unprofitable in the entire area. This has occurred or is occurring in several countries. (5) *Integrated control* or *Recovery phase* – a crop protection system is devised comprising an ecological approach to pest management with strong reliance on natural enemies in combination with other appropriate techniques including cultural control, resistant host plants and selective pesticides.

The pattern outlined above is well illustrated by the famous case history of cotton in the Cañete Valley of Peru. The initial phases will be omitted here. The later phases can be covered only briefly. Beginning in the early 1950s, the new organic insecticides (especially DDT, BHC and toxaphene) began to be used and some culture methods (new cotton strains and irrigation) changed. Yields increased by over fifty percent in four to five years. The idea developed that the more pesticides used the better. They came to be applied like a blanket over the entire Valley. Beneficial parasites and predators were decimated. The number of treatments increased year after year and started earlier each year. By late 1952 resistance had developed to BHC by aphids. By mid-1954, toxaphene failed to control the leafworm. In 1955–6, boll weevil reached high levels early in the season, then a new moth pest, *Argyrotaenia*, appeared. Next, the bollworm *Heliothis* exploded and showed a high resistance to DDT. Organophosphorus compounds were substituted for the chlorinated hydrocarbons. The period between treatments was progressively shortened from 8–15 days down to three days. In the interim a whole complex of previously innocuous insects rose to serious pest status. Not surprisingly the 1955–6 season was an economic disaster for the cotton growers of the Cañete Valley. Millions of bales were lost. In spite of the tremendous amounts of insecticides used in futile pest control attempts, yields dropped to less than half of what they were only 2–3 years before.

This catastrophe forced on the Cañete growers the realization that they could not rely on pesticides alone. They appealed to their Experiment Station for help and this led to the development of a successful integrated control method. Changes in pesticide practices were made, cultural control methods improved, perennial cotton (which enabled carryover of certain pests) prohibited, natural enemies were reintroduced from other areas and fostered in various ways. Use of synthetic organic insecticides was generally prohibited and there was a return to the more selective arsenicals and nicotine sulfate. These changes and others were made legal regulations of the Ministry of Agriculture with the approval of the growers. As a result there was a rapid and striking reduction in the severity of cotton pests. The entire group of formerly harmless species, which cropped up in the organic insecticide period, reverted to their innocuous status. The intensity of key pest problems also decreased so that there was an overall reduction in direct pest control costs along with better control. By the next year the yield increased markedly and since has averaged out at the highest yields in the history of the Valley.

Similar stories could be told for other cotton areas in other countries. Large areas in Mexico around Torreon, Durango; Culiacan, Sinaloa and Hermosillo, Sonora, where treatments had become excessive yet were still failing have developed programs leading to greatly reduced use of pesticides. Each of these areas has its own large insectary that produces millions of *Trichogramma* egg parasites for field release against bollworms. Both experimental and some commercial programs in Texas and California are achieving similar results. Various problems remain to be solved in many places, but the prognosis for ultimate development of a high degree of sophisticated pest management in cotton on a worldwide basis appears good.

Conclusions

It is clear from the examples discussed and from many others in the literature that we are in either the crisis or disaster phases connected with unilateral pest control with chemicals on nearly all major agricultural crops in one place or another. These failures of the chemical method are mainly due to adverse effects on natural enemies compounded by increasing development of resistance by pests to pesticides. The achievement of complete control by natural enemies is the ideal goal and generally the most practical single approach to pest management. However, even though its use can be very greatly expanded, this must be based on increased bio-ecological research that will take time. Also there will be refractory pests not amenable to control by natural enemies and these will require other control strategies. Meanwhile, the immediate application of current ecological knowledge and technology to the pesticide dilemma can rapidly lead to general reductions of about fifty percent in the use of pesticides, with consequent greatly reduced environmental pollution and production costs and often with increases in yield and quality. An immediate change to more selective chemicals and to selective means of application and timing will go a long way towards this initial achievement but concurrent manipulation of certain natural enemies may be necessary or desirable. Adequately trained supervising entomologists will generally be necessary to implement such a program.

Further scientific sophistication in pest management stressing conservation, importation and augmentation of natural enemies will solve additional key pest problems and will further significantly reduce the need for chemical pesticides. In some cases the need will be eliminated completely. Refinement of cultural controls (including mechanical controls) and development of resistant host plants furnish additional potent general tools for use in integrated control. The other non-chemical methods of pest control discussed in Chapter 9 may furnish the key to optimal pest management in certain instances but are not yet of very general applicability. Each ecosystem is different and objective decisions for the ultimate in *optimal* pest management in a given instance must be based on thorough bio-ecological research on the organisms involved and the integration of this knowledge with economic, social and other realities. Systems analysis and modelling should prove to be a potent tool in this regard.

Bibliography

Adkisson, P. L. (1971). Objective uses of insecticides in agriculture. In: *Agricultural Chemicals – Harmony or Discord*, ed. J. E. Swift, pp. 43–51. Univ. Calif. Div. Agric. Sci. 1–151.

Andres, L. A. and R. D. Goeden. (1971). The biological control of weeds by introduced natural enemies. In: *Biological Control*, ed. C. B. Huffaker, pp. 143–64. Plenum Press, New York. 511 pp.

Askew, R. R. (1971). *Parasitic insects*. American Elsevier Publ. Co. Inc. New York, 316 pp.

Baltazar, Clare R. (1966). *A catalogue of Philippine Hymenoptera*. Pacific Insects Monograph 8. Bishop Museum, Honolulu, 488 pp.

Bartlett, B. R. and R. van den Bosch. (1964). Foreign exploration for beneficial organisms. Chapter 9 in: *Biological Control of Insect Pests and Weeds*, ed. Paul DeBach. Reinhold Publ. Corp. New York, 844 pp.

Beck, S. D. (1965). Resistance of plants to insects. *Ann. Rev. Entomol.* **10**: 207–32.

Bedford, E. C. G. (1969). The selection of insecticides for the integration of biological and chemical control of citrus pests. *S. Afr. Citrus J.* **431**: 3, 5, 7, 9, 10.

Beroza, M. (1971). Insect sex attractants. *American Scientist*, **59**(3): 320–5.

Bess, H. A. and F. H. Haramoto. (1958). Biological control of the oriental fruit fly in Hawaii. *Proc. 10th Int. Cong. Entomol.* (1956) **4**: 835–40.

Bethell, R. S., L. A. Falcon, W. C. Batiste, G. W. Moorehead and E. P. Delfino. (1972). Sex pheromone traps determine need for codling moth control in apple and pear orchards. *Calif. Agric.* **26**(5): 10–12.

Briejér, C. J. (1967). Zilveren Sluiers en Verborgen Gevaren. *Silvery Veils and Hidden Dangers*. Leiden.

Briggs, Shirley A. (1970). Safer pesticides for home and garden. Appendix I, pp. 275–97, in: *Since Silent Spring*, Frank Graham, Jr. Houghton Mifflin Co. Boston, 333 pp.

Burges, H. D. and N. W. Hussey. (1971). *Microbial control of insects and mites*. Academic Press, New York and London, 861 pp.

Cameron, J. W. MacB. (1971). Insect pathogens and their potential for regulation of insect populations. *Proc. Tall Timbers Conf. Ecol. Anim. Contr. Habit. Mgmt*, **3**: 267–77.

Carson, Rachel. (1962). *Silent Spring*. Houghton Mifflin Co. Boston. 368 pp.

Clausen, C. P. (1956). Biological control of insect pests in the continental United States. *US Dept. Agric. Tech. Bull.* 1139, 151 pp.

(1962). *Entomophagous Insects*. Hafner Publ. Co. New York, 688 pp.

Clausen, C. P. and P. A. Berry. (1932). The citrus blackfly in Asia, and the importation of its natural enemies into Tropical America. *US Dept. Agric. Tech. Bull.* 320, 59 pp.

Clausen, C. P., D. W. Clancy and Q. C. Chock. (1965). Biological control of the oriental fly (*Dacus dorsalis* Hendel) and other fruit flies in Hawaii. *US Dept. Agric. Tech. Bull.* 1322, 102 pp.

Cohen, I. and S. Kamburov. (1968). *Biological Control Institute.* Citrus Board Israel, Rehovot, 43 pp.

Compere, H. (1961). The red scale and its insect enemies. *Hilgardia*, **31**(7): 173–278.
(1969). The role of systematics in biological control: a backward look. *Israel J. Entomol.* **4**: 5–10.

Compere, H. and H. S. Smith. (1932). The control of the citrophilus mealybug, *Pseudococcus gahani*, by Australian parasites. *Hilgardia*, **6**: 585–618.

Conway, G. R. (1969). A consequence of insecticides – pests follow the chemicals in the cocoa of Malaysia. *Nat. Hist.* **78**(2): 46–51.

Conway, G. R. (1971). Ecological aspects of pest control in Malaysia in: *The Careless Technology – Ecology and International Development*, ed. M. T. Farvar and J. P. Milton. Natural History Press, New York, 1030 pp.

Cumber, R. H. (1964). The egg-parasite complex (Scelionidae: Hymenoptera) of shield bugs (Pentatomidae, Acanthosomidae: Heteroptera) in New Zealand. *New Zealand J. Sci.* **7**: 536–54.

Davis, C. J. (1967). Progress in the biological control of the southern green stink bug *Nezara viridula* variety *smaragdula* (Fabricius) in Hawaii (Heteroptera: Pentatomidae). *Mushi*, **39** (Suppl.): 9–16.

DeBach, P. (1958). The role of weather and entomophagous species in the natural control of insect populations. *J. Econ. Entomol.* **51**(4): 474–84.
(1960). The importance of taxonomy to biological control as illustrated by the cryptic history of *Aphytis holoxanthus* n. sp. (Hymenoptera, Aphelinidae), a parasite of *Chrysomphalus aonidum* and *Aphytis coheni* n. sp., a parasite of *Aonidiella aurantii*. *Ann. Entomol. Soc. Amer.* **53**(6): 701–5.
(1964a). *Biological Control of Insect Pests and Weeds.* Reinhold Publ. Corp. New York, 844 pp.
(1964b). Some ecological aspects of insect eradication. *Bull. Entomol. Soc. Amer.* **10**(4): 221–4.
(1966). The competitive displacement and coexistence principles. *Ann. Rev. Entomol.* **11**: 183–212.
(1969). Uniparental, sibling and semi-species in relation to taxonomy and biological control. *Israel J. Entomol.* **4**: 11–28.
(1971a). Fortuitous biological control from ecesis of natural enemies. In: *Entomol. Essays to Commemorate Prof. K. Yasumatsu*, pp. 293–307. Hokuryukan Publ. Co. Ltd. Tokyo, 389 pp.
(1971b). The use of imported natural enemies in insect pest management ecology. *Proc. Tall Timbers Conf. Ecol. Anim. Contr. Habit. Mgmt*, **3**: 211–33.
(1971c). Principios y possibilidades del control biologico de las plagas. *Boletin Soc. Entomol. Peru*, **6**(2): 39–47.

DeBach, P. and Loukia C. Argyriou. (1967). The colonization and success in Greece of some important *Aphytis* spp. [Hymn. Aphelinidae] parasitic on citrus scale insects [Hom. Diaspididae]. *Entomophaga*, **12**(4): 325–42.

DeBach, P. and B. R. Bartlett. (1964). Methods of colonization, recovery and evaluation. Chapter 14 in: *Biological Control of Insect Pests and Weeds*, ed. Paul DeBach. Reinhold Publ. Corp. New York, 844 pp.

DeBach, P. and K. S. Hagen. (1964). Manipulation of entomophagous species. Chapter 15 in: *Biological Control of Insect Pests and Weeds*, ed. Paul DeBach. Reinhold Publ. Corp. New York, 844 pp.

DeBach, P. and C. B. Huffaker. (1971). Experimental techniques for evaluation of the effectiveness of natural enemies. In: *Biological Control*, ed. C. B. Huffaker, pp. 113–40. Plenum Press, New York, 511 pp.

DeBach, P. and J. Landi. (1961). The introduced purple scale parasite, *Aphytis lepidosaphes* Compere, and a method of integrating chemical with biological control. *Hilgardia*, 31(14): 459–97.

DeBach, P., D. Rosen and C. E. Kennett. (1971). Biological control of coccids by introduced natural enemies. Chapter 7 in: *Biological Control*, ed. C. B. Huffaker. Plenum Press, New York, 511 pp.

DeBach, P. and R. A. Sundby. (1963). Competitive displacement between ecological homologues. *Hilgardia*, 34(5): 105–66.

Dodd, A. P. (1940). *The biological campaign against prickly pear*. Commonwealth Prickly Pear Board, Brisbane, Australia, 177 pp.

Doutt, R. L. (1964a). Ecological considerations in chemical control. Implications to nontarget invertebrates. *Bull. Entomol. Soc. Amer.* 10(2): 83–8.

(1964b). The historical development of biological control. Chapter 2 in: *Biological Control of Insect Pests and Weeds*, ed. Paul DeBach. Reinhold Publ. Co. New York, 844 pp.

Doutt, R. L. and R. F. Smith. (1971). The pesticide syndrome – diagnosis and suggested prophylaxis. In: *Biological Control*, ed. C. B. Huffaker, pp. 3–15. Plenum Press, New York, 511 pp.

Embree, D. G. (1971). The biological control of the winter moth in eastern Canada by introduced parasites. Chapter 9 in: *Biological Control*, ed. C. B. Huffaker. Plenum Press, New York, 511 pp.

EPPO Report. (1970a). Report of the international EPPO/EUCARPIA conference on plant breeding for resistance to animal pests. *European and Medit. Pl. Prot. Org.*, Paris, Publ. Series A, no. 54, 94 pp.

(1970b). Report of the international conference on methods for forecasting, warning, pest assessment and detection of infection. *European and Medit. Pl. Prot. Org.*, Paris, 206 pp.

Essig, E. O. (1931). *A History of Entomology*. Macmillan Co. New York, 1029 pp.

Falcon, L. A. (1971). Microbial control as a tool in integrated control programs. In: *Biological Control*, ed. C. B. Huffaker, pp. 346–64. Plenum Press, New York, 511 pp.

FAO. (1966). *Proc. FAO Symposium on Integrated Pest Control*, 3 vols. Rome.

Flaherty, D. L. and C. B. Huffaker. (1970). Biological control of Pacific mites and Willamette mites in San Joaquin Valley vineyards. I. Role of *Metaseiulus occidentalis*. *Hilgardia*, 40(10): 267–308.

Foster, G. G., M. J. Whitten, T. Prout and R. Gill. (1972). Chromosome rearrangements for the control of insect pests. *Science*, 176(4037): 875–80.

Georghiou, G. P. (1971). Resistance of insects and mites to insecticides and acaricides and the future of pesticide chemicals. In: *Agricultural Chemicals – Harmony or Discord*, ed. J. E. Swift, pp. 112–24. *Univ. Calif. Div. Agric. Sci.* 1–151.

Goedaert, J. (1662). *Metamorphosis et historia naturales insectorum I*, pp. 175–8. Jacobum Fierensium, Medisburg.

Graham, F., Jr. (1970). *Since Silent Spring*. Houghton Mifflin Co. Boston, 333 pp.

Haeussler, G. J. and D. W. Clancy. (1964). Natural enemies of Comstock mealybug in the eastern United States. *J. Econ. Entomol.* 37: 503–9.

Hafez, M. and R. L. Doutt. (1954). Biological evidence of sibling species in *Aphytis maculicornis* (Masi) (Hymenoptera, Aphelinidae). *Canadian Entomol.* 86: 90–6.

Hagen, K. S., E. F. Sawall, Jr. and R. H. Tassan. (1970). The use of food sprays to increase effectiveness of entomophagous insects. *Proc. Tall Timbers Conf. Ecol. Anim. Contr. Habit. Mgmt*, **2**: 59–81.

Hagen, K. S., R. van den Bosch and D. L. Dahlsten. (1971). The importance of naturally-occurring biological control in the western United States. Chapter 11 in: *Biological Control*, ed. C. B. Huffaker. Plenum Press, New York, 511 pp.

Hall, E. R. (1972). Down on the Farm. *Nat. Hist.* **81**(3): 8, 12.

Harmer, Ruth Mulvey. (1971). *Unfit for Human Consumption*. Prentice-Hall, Inc. Englewood Cliffs, New Jersey, 374 pp.

Harpaz, I. and D. Rosen. (1971). Development of integrated control programs for crop pests in Israel. In: *Biological Control*, ed. C. B. Huffaker, pp. 458–68. Plenum Press, New York, 511 pp.

Hensley, S. D. (1971). Management of sugarcane borer populations in Louisiana, a decade of change. *Entomophaga*, **16**(1): 133–46.

Holloway, J. K. (1964). Projects in biological control of weeds. In: *Biological Control of Insect Pests and Weeds*, ed. Paul DeBach, pp. 650–70. Reinhold Publ. Corp. New York, 844 pp.

Howard, L. O. and W. F. Fiske. (1911). The importation into the United States of the parasites of the gypsy moth and the brown-tail moth. *US Dept. Agr. Bur. Entomol. Bull.* 91, 312 pp.

Huffaker, C. B. (1964). Fundamentals of biological weed control. In: *Biological Control of Insect Pests and Weeds*, ed. Paul DeBach, pp. 631–49. Reinhold Publ. Corp. New York, 844 pp.

(1971). The ecology of pesticide interference with insect populations. (Upsets and resurgences in insect populations.) In: *Agricultural Chemicals – Harmony or Discord*, ed. J. E. Swift, pp. 92–104. *Univ. Calif. Div. Agric. Sci.* 1–151.

Huffaker, C. B. and C. E. Kennett. (1956). Experimental studies on predation: predation and cyclamen mite populations on strawberries in California. *Hilgardia*, **26**(4): 191–222.

Huffaker, C. B. and C. E. Kennett. (1966). Biological control of *Parlatoria oleae* (Colvee) through the compensatory action of two introduced parasites. *Hilgardia*, **37**(9): 283–335.

Huffaker, C. B. and C. E. Kennett. (1969). Some aspects of assessing efficiency of natural enemies. *Canadian Entomol.* **101**: 425–47.

Huffaker, C. B., C. E. Kennett and G. L. Finney. (1962). Biological control of the olive scale *Parlatoria oleae* (Colvee) in California by imported *Aphytis maculicornis* (Masi) (Hymenoptera: Aphelinidae). *Hilgardia*, **32**: 541–636.

Huffaker, C. B. and P. S. Messenger. (1964). Chapters 3 and 4 in: *Biological Control of Insect Pests and Weeds*, ed. Paul DeBach. Reinhold Publ. Co. New York, 844 pp.

Huffaker, C. B., P. S. Messenger and P. DeBach. (1971). The natural enemy component in natural control and the theory of biological control. In: *Biological Control*, ed. C. B. Huffaker, pp. 16–67. Plenum Press, New York, 511 pp.

Huffaker, C. B. and C. H. Spitzer, Jr. (1951). Data on the natural control of the cyclamen mite on strawberries. *J. Econ. Entomol.* **44**(4): 519–22.

Huffaker, C. B., M. van den Vrie and J. A. McMurtry. (1969). The ecology of tetranychid mites and their natural control. *Ann. Rev. Entomol.* **14**: 125–74.

Huffaker, C. B., M. van den Vrie and J. A. McMurtry. (1970). Ecology of Tetranychid mites and their natural enemies: a review. II. Tetranychid populations and their possible control by predators: an evaluation. *Hilgardia*, **40**(11): 391–458.

Hunter, Beatrice Trum. (1971). *Gardening Without Poisons*. Berkeley Publ. Corp. New York, 352 pp.

Hussey, N. W. and L. Bravenboer. (1971). Control of pests in glasshouse culture by the introduction of natural enemies. In: *Biological Control*, ed. C. B. Huffaker, pp. 195–216. Plenum Press, New York, 511 pp.

Kerrich, G. J. (1960). The state of our knowledge of the systematics of the Hymenoptera Parasitica, with particular reference to the British fauna. *Trans. Soc. Brit. Entomol.* **14**: 1–18.

Kilgore, W. W. and R. L. Doutt. (1967). *Pest Control – Biological, Physical and Selected Chemical Methods*, ed. Wendell W. Kilgore and Richard L. Doutt. Academic Press, New York and London, 477 pp.

Kirby, W. and W. Spence. (1815). *An Introduction to Entomology*. Longman, Brown, Green and Longmans, London, 285 pp.

Kirby, W. and W. Spence. (1826). Diseases of insects. In: *An Introduction to Entomology: or Elements of the Natural History of Insects*, vol. 4, Longman *et al.* London, 634 pp.

Koebele, A. (1890). Report of a trip to Australia to investigate the natural enemies of the fluted scale. *US Dept. Agric. Bur. Entomol. Bull.* **21**, 1–32.

Kuwana, I. (1934). Notes on a newly imported parasite of the spiny whitefly attacking citrus in Japan. *Proc. 5th Pac. Sci. Congr.* (5): 3521–3 (1933).

LaChance, L. E., C. H. Schmidt and R. C. Bushland. (1967). Radiation-induced sterilization. Chapter 4 in: *Pest Control–Biological, Physical and Selected Chemical Methods*, ed. Wendell W. Kilgore and Richard L. Doutt. Academic Press, New York and London, 477 pp.

LeBaron, W. (1870). The chalcideous parasite of the apple-tree bark-louse (Chalcis [Aphelinus] mytilaspidis, n. sp.). *Amer. Entomol. Bot.* **2**: 360–2.

Legner, E. F. (1972). Observations on hybridization and heterosis in parasitoids of synanthropic flies. *Ann. Entomol. Soc. Amer.* **65**(1): 254–263.

LePelley, R. H. (1943). The biological control of a mealybug on coffee and other crops in Kenya. *Emp. J. Exp. Agric.* **11**(42): 78–88.

LeRoux, E. J. (1960). Effects of 'modified' and 'commercial' spray programs on the fauna of apple orchards in Quebec. *Ann. Soc. Entomol. Quebec*, **6**: 87–119.

Luginbill, P. (1969). Developing resistant plants – the ideal method of controlling insects. *USDA, ARS Production Res. Rept.* **111**, 14 pp.

McMurtry, J. A., C. B. Huffaker and M. van den Vrie. (1970). Ecology of tetranychid mites and their natural enemies: a review. I. Tetranychid enemies: their biological characters and the impact of spray practices. *Hilgardia*, **40**(11): 331–90.

MacPhee, A. W. and C. R. MacLellan. (1971 *a*). Cases of naturally-occurring biological control in Canada. In: *Biological Control*, ed. C. B. Huffaker, pp. 312–27. Plenum Press, New York, 511 pp.

MacPhee, A. W. and C. R. MacLellan. (1971 *b*). Ecology of apple orchard fauna and development of integrated pest control in Nova Scotia. In: *Proc. Tall Timbers Conf. Ecol. Anim. Contr. Habit. Mgmt*, **3**: 286 pp.

Massee, A. M. (1954). Problems arising from the use of insecticides: effect on the balance of animal populations. *Rep. 6th Commonwealth Entomol. Conf. London*, pp. 53–7.

Mellanby, K. (1967). *Pesticides and Pollution*. London.

Mesnil, L. P. (1967). History of a success in biological control: the winter moth project for Canada. *Tech. Bull. no. 8, Commonw. Inst. Biol. Contr.* 6 pp.

Muir, F. (1931). Introduction in: *The Insects and Other Invertebrates of Hawaiian Sugar Cane Fields*, Francis X. Williams. Expt. Sta. Hawaiian Sugar Planters Assoc. 400 pp.

Myers, J. G. (1935). Second report on an investigation into the biological control of West Indian pests. *Bull. Entomol. Res.* **26**: 181–252.

National Academy of Sciences. (1969). Insect-pest management and control. Chapters 6, 9, 10 and 15, in: *Principles of Plant and Animal Pest Control*, vol. 3. Natl. Acad. Sci. Wash. DC, Publn. 1695, 508 pp.

Newsom, L. D. (1965). Controlling insect pests and diseases for efficient production for United States agriculture. *Proc. 14th Ann. Meet., Agr. Res. Inst., Natl. Acad. Sci., Wash. DC.*

    (1967). Consequences of insecticide use on nontarget organisms. *Ann. Rev. Entomol.* **12**: 257–386.

O'Connor, B. A. (1960). A decade of biological control work in Fiji. *Agric. J. Fiji,* **30**(2): 44–54.

Olkowski, Helga. (1971). *Common Sense Pest Control.* Consumers Coop. of Berkeley, Inc. Richmond, California, 52 pp.

Painter, R. H. (1951). *Insect resistance in crop plants.* Macmillan Co. New York, 520 pp.

    (1958). Resistance of plants to insects. *Ann. Rev. Entomol.* **3**: 267–90.

    (1960). Breeding plants for resistance to insect pests. In: *Biological and Chemical Control of Plant and Animal Pests*, pp. 245–66. Amer. Assn. Adv. Sci., Wash. DC, Publn. 61, ed. L. P. Reitz, 273 pp.

    (1966). Lessons to be learned from past experience in breeding plants for insect resistance. In: *Breeding Pest Resistant Trees*, pp. 349–66. Proc. NATO and NSF Symposium. Pergamon Press, New York.

    (1968). Crops that resist insects provide a way to increase world food supply. *Kansas State Agric. Expt. Sta. Bull.* 520.

Parker, F. D. (1971). Management of pest populations by manipulating densities of both hosts and parasite through periodic releases. Chapter 16 in: *Biological Control*, ed. C. F. Huffaker. Plenum Press, New York, 511 pp.

Parker, F. D. and R. E. Pinnell. (1972). Further studies of the biological control of *Pieris rapae* using supplemental host and parasite releases. *Environ. Entomol.* **1**(2): 150–7.

Pathak, M. D. (1970). Genetics of plants in past management. In: *Concepts of Pest Management*, ed. R. L. Rabb and F. E. Guthrie, pp. 138–57. North Carolina State University, Raleigh. 242 pp.

Pemberton, C. E. (1948). History of the Entomology Department Experiment Station. HSPA 1904–45. *Hawaiian Planters Record,* **52**(1): 53–90.

Peterson, A. (1936). Biological control of insects at the University. In: *Conference on biological methods of controlling Insect Pests.* Dept. Agric. Entomol. Branch, Ottawa at Belleville, Ontario June 25–6, 1936, 1–86, mimeo.

Pickett, A. D. and N. A. Patterson. (1953). The influence of spray programs on the fauna of apple orchards in Nova Scotia. IV. A review. *Canadian Entomol.* **85**: 472–8.

Pimentel, D. et al. (1965). In: *Restoring the Quality of our Environment*, pp. 227–91. The White House, Washington, DC, 317 pp.

Pimentel, D. (1971). *Ecological effects of pesticides on non-target species.* Executive Office of the President, Office of Science and Technology, Washington, DC, 1–220.

Rabb, R. L. (1969). Environmental manipulations as influencing populations of tobacco hornworms. *Proc. Tall Timbers Conf. Ecol. Anim. Contr. Habit. Mgmt,* **1**: 175–91.

    (1971). Naturally-occurring biological control in the eastern United States, with particular reference to tobacco insects. In: *Biological Control*, ed. C. B. Huffaker, pp. 294–311. Plenum Press, New York, 511 pp.

Rao, S. V. and P. DeBach. (1969). Experimental studies on hybridization and sexual isolation between some *Aphytis* species (Hymenoptera: Aphelinidae) I. Experimental hybridization and an interpretation of evolutionary relationships among the species. *Hilgardia*, **39**(19): 515–53.

Ratcliffe, F. N. (1965). Biological Control. *Austr. J. Sci.* **28**, 237–40.

Report of the Environmental Pollution Panel, President's Science Advisory Committee. (1965). *Restoring the Quality of our Environment.* The White House, Washington, DC, 317 pp.

Report of the Secretary's Commission on Pesticides and their Relationship to Environmental Health, parts I and II. (1969). US Dept. Health, Educ. and Welfare, Washington, DC, 677 pp.

Reynolds, H. T. (1971). A world review of the problem of insect population upsets and resurgences caused by pesticide chemicals. In: *Agricultural Chemicals – Harmony or Discord*, ed. J. E. Swift, pp. 108–12. Univ. Calif. Div. Agric. Sci. 1–151.

Ridgeway, R. L. and S. L. Jones. (1969). Inundative releases of *Chrysopa carnea* for control of *Heliothis* on cotton. *J. Econ. Entomol.* **62**(1): 177–80.

Riley, C. V. (1893). Parasitic and predaceous insects in applied entomology. *Insect Life*, **6**: 130–41.

Ripper, W. E. (1956). Effect of pesticides on balance of arthropod populations. *Ann. Rev. Entomol.* **1**: 403–38.

Rivnay, E. (1968). Biological control of pests in Israel. *Israel J. Entomol.* **3**(1): 1–156.

Robinson, R. R., J. H. Young and R. D. Morrison. (1972). Strip-cropping effects on abundance of predatory and harmful cotton insects in Oklahoma. *Environ. Entomol.* **1**(2): 145–9.

Rudd, R. L. (1964). *Pesticides and the Living Landscape.* The University of Wisconsin Press, Madison, 320 pp.

(1971). Pesticides. In: *Environment – Resources, Pollution and Society*, ed. W. W. Murdock, pp. 279–301. Sinauer Assoc. Inc. Stamford, Conn. 448 pp.

Sabrosky, C. W. (1955). The interrelations of biological control and taxonomy. *J. Econ. Entomol.* **48**: 710–14.

Scepetilnikova, V. A. (1970). Perspektiven der Kenntnis und Anwending von Eiparasiten der Gattung *Trichogramma* zur Bekampfung land-und forstevirt-schaftlicher Schadlinge. (The prospects of the study and use of egg parasites of the genus *Trichogramma* to control agricultural and forest pests.) pp. 117–36. Summary in English. Tagungsbericht der Deutschen Akademic der Landwirt-schaftwissenschaften zer Berlin. Biologische Bekampfungsmethoden von Forstschadlingen.

Schlinger, E. I. and R. L. Doutt. (1964). Systematics in relation to biological control. Chapter 8 in: *Biological Control of Insect Pests and Weeds*, ed. Paul DeBach. Reinhold Publ. Corp. New York, 844 pp.

Schuster, M. F., J. C. Boling and J. J. Marony, Jr. (1971). Biological control of rhodesgrass scale by airplane releases of an introduced parasite of limited dispersing ability. Chapter 10 in: *Biological Control*, ed. C. B. Huffaker. Plenum Press, New York, 511 pp.

Silvestri, F. (1909). Consideration of the existing condition of agricultural ento-mology in the United States of North America, and suggestions which can be gained from it for the benefit of Italian agriculture. *Bull. Soc. Ital. Agric.* **14**(8): 305–67. (Transl. and reprinted in: *Hawaiian Forester and Agric.* **6**: 287–336, 1909.)

305

Smirnoff, W. A. (1972). Promoting virus epizootics in populations of the Swaine jack pine sawfly by infected adults. *Bio-Science*, **22**(11): 662–3.

Smith, H. D. and H. L. Maltby. (1964). Biological control of the citrus blackfly in Mexico. *US Dept. Agric. Tech. Bull.* 1311, 30 pp.

Smith, R. F. (1971*a*). Economics aspects of pest control. *Tall Timbers Conf. Ecol. Anim. Contr. Habit. Mgmt*, **3**: 53–83.

(1971*b*). What is being done by the universities? In: *Agricultural Chemicals – Harmony or Discord*, ed. J. E. Swift, pp. 138–45. Univ. Calif. Div. Agric. Sci., 151 pp.

Smith, R. F. and H. T. Reynolds. (1968). Effects of manipulation of cotton agro-ecosystems on insect pest populations. 36 pp. mimeo. presented at Conf. on Ecological Aspects of International Development, Warrenton, Virginia.

Smith, R. F. and H. T. Reynolds. (1972). Effects of manipulation of cotton agro-ecosystems on insect pest populations. In: *The Careless Technology: Ecology and International Development*, ed. M. Taghi Farvar and John P. Milton, pp. 373–406. The Natural History Press, New York; Tom Stacey Ltd., London, 1030 pp.

Smith, R. F. and R. van den Bosch. (1967). Integrated control. In: *Pest Control – Biological, Physical and Selected Chemical Methods*, ed. Wendell W. Kilgore and Richard L. Doutt, pp. 295–340. Academic Press, New York, 477 pp.

Smith, R. H. and R. C. von Borstel. (1972). Genetic control of insect populations. *Science*, **178** (4066): 1164–74.

Stark, R. W. and R. F. Smith. (1971). Systems analysis and pest management. In: *Biological Control*, ed. C. B. Huffaker, pp. 331–45. Plenum Press, New York, 511 pp.

Steffan, R. (1971). *Introduction to Organic Farming Methods and Organic Markets*. Rodale Press, Inc. Emmaus, Pa. 140 pp.

Steinhaus, E. A. (1946). *Insect Microbiology*. Comstock Publishing Co. Inc. Ithaca, New York, 763 pp.

(1949). *Principles of Insect Pathology*. McGraw-Hill Book Co. Inc. New York, 757 pp.

(1956). Microbial control – the emergence of an idea. A brief history of insect pathology through the nineteenth century. *Hilgardia*, **26**(2): 107–60.

(1963). *Insect Pathology, an Advanced Treatise*, 2 vols. Academic Press, New York, 661 + 689 pp.

Stern, V. M. (1969). Interplanting alfalfa in cotton to control lygus bugs and other insect pests. *Proc. Tall Timbers Conf. Ecol. Anim. Contr. Habit. Mgmt*, **1**: 55–69.

Strayer, J. (1971). The pest management concept: The extension entomologists' review. *Proc. Tall Timbers Conf. Ecol. Anim. Contr. Habit. Mgmt*, **3**: 21–8.

Surtees, G. (1971). Epidemiology of microbial control of insect pest populations. *Int. J. Environm. Studies*, **2**(3): 195–201.

Swan, L. A. (1964). *Beneficial Insects*. Harper and Row Publ. New York, 429 pp.

Taylor, T. H. C. (1935). The campaign against *Aspidiotus destructor* Sign. in Fiji. *Bull. Entomol. Res.* **26**: 1–102.

(1936). The biological control of the coconut leaf miner (*Promecotheca reichei, Baly*) in Fiji. *Agric. J. Fiji*, **8**: 17–21.

(1937). *The biological control of an insect in Fiji. An account of the coconut leaf-mining beetle and its parasite complex*. Imp. Inst. Entomol. (now the Common-wealth Institute of Entomology), London, 239 pp.

Tooke, F. G. C. (1953). The eucalyptus snout-beetle *Gonipterus scutellatus* Gyll. A study of its ecology and control by biological means. *Union S. Africa, Dept. Agric. Entomol. Mem.* **3**: 282 pp.

Tothill, J. D., T. H. C. Taylor and R. W. Paine. (1930). *The coconut moth in Fiji. A history of its control by means of parasites.* Publ. Imp. Bur. Entomol. (now the Commonwealth Institute of Entomology), London, 269 pp.

Townes, H. (1971). Ichneumonidae as biological control agents. *Tall Timbers Conf. Ecol. Anim. Contr. Habit. Mgmt,* **3**: 235–48.

van den Bosch, R. (1971 a). Experimental field studies on upsets and resurgences of pest populations associated with agricultural chemicals. In: *Agricultural Chemicals – Harmony or Discord,* ed. J. E. Swift, pp. 104–7. Univ. Calif. Div. Agric. Sci. 1–151.

(1971 b). The Melancholy Addiction of Ol' King Cotton. *Nat. Hist.* **80**(10): 86–90.

van den Bosch, R., B. D. Frazer, C. S. Davis, P. S. Messenger and R. Hom. (1970). *Trioxys pallidus* – An effective new walnut aphid parasite from Iran. *Calif. Agric.* **24**(11): 8–10.

van den Bosch, R. and K. S. Hagen. (1966). Predaceous and parasitic arthropods in California cotton fields. *Calif. Agric. Exp. Sta. Bull.* 820, pp. 1–32.

van den Bosch, R., T. F. Leigh, L. H. Falcon, V. M. Stern, D. Gonzalez and K. S. Hagen. (1971). The developing program of integrated control of cotton pests in California. In: *Biological Control,* ed. C. B. Huffaker, pp. 377–94. Plenum Press, New York, 511 pp.

van den Bosch, R. and V. M. Stern. (1969). The effect of harvesting practices on insect populations in alfalfa. *Proc. Tall Timbers Conf. Ecol. Anim. Contr. Habit. Mgmt,* **1**: 47–54.

van den Bosch, R. and A. D. Telford. (1964). Environmental modification and biological control. Chapter 16 in: *Biological Control of Insect Pests and Weeds,* ed. Paul DeBach. Reinhold Publ. Corp. New York, 844 pp.

Whitten, M. J. (1970). Genetics of pests in their management. In: *Concepts of Pest Management,* ed. R. L. Rabb and F. E. Guthrie, pp. 119–35. North Carolina State University, Raleigh. 242 pp.

Whitten, M. J. (1971). Insect control by manipulation of natural populations. *Science,* **171**(3972): 682–4.

Woglum, R. S. (1913). Report of a trip to India and the Orient in search of the natural enemies of the citrus white fly. *US Dept. Agric. Bur. Entomol. Bull.* 120, 58 pp.

Wood, B. J. (1971 a). The importance of ecological studies to pest control in Malaysian plantations. In: *Crop Protection in Malaysia,* ed. R. L. Wastie and B. J. Wood, pp. 187–96. Incorp. Soc. Planters, Kuala Lumpur.

(1971 b). Development of integrated control programs for pests of tropical perennial crops in Malaysia. In: *Biological Control,* ed. C. B. Huffaker, pp. 422–57. Plenum Press, New York, 511 pp.

Yasumatsu, K. (1958). An interesting case of biological control of *Ceroplastes rubens* Maskell in Japan. *Proc. 10th Int. Congr. Entomol.* (1956) **4**: 771–5.

Index

310

311

importation policy, 56–7, 168, 172, 181, 194, 206–7, 213–16, 269
  see also foreign exploration; research, importance of
imported cabbageworm, 225, 226, 257
India, 72, 157, 168, 182, 250, 257, 287
  biological control of prickly pear, 78
  foreign exploration in, 114–16, 162, 164, 167, 168, 169–70, 179
Indiana, 254
Indian Museum, Calcutta, 114
Indonesia, 125, 126
insectaries, 119, 134–5, 157, 168, 225, 236, 237
  of CIBC, 157, 245
  commercial, 239, 286
  in Israel, 293
  of Mexico, 223, 297
  of University of California, Berkeley, 156
  of University of California, Riverside, 138, 156
  of USDA, 222, 225, 246
insecticides, *see* pesticides
insect pathology, 76, 77, 78
  see also diseases; pathogens
insect vectors, *see* vectors, of disease
insurance treatments, 21
integrated control, 265, 269, 281
  conservation, importance of, in, 277
  definitions and objectives of, 273–4, 277–8
  examples of: in apples, 283–6; in citrus, 276, 286–94; in cocoa, 294–5; in cotton, 275–6, 277; with flies, 242–5, 246, 273; in glasshouses, 237–8; in grain sorghum, 275–6; in oil palms, 294; in sugar-cane, 274–5; with *Trichogramma*, 225, 227
  natural enemy importation, importance in, 194, 291, 297
  partial biological control, importance in, 189–90
  priorities for research in, 211–12, 269–70
  problems in application of, 280–1, 287, 289–90, 293
  review of, 274
  savings from, 273, 274–6, 277–8, 284, 285–6, 287, 297
  see also augmentation; biological control; conservation; pesticides, reduction of; selective control techniques; selective insecticides; supervised control
International Minerals and Chemical Co., 246

International Organization for Biological Control (IOBC), 238
Iran, 170, 188
Iraq, 170
Ishii, T., 117, 118
Israel, 65, 89, 160, 170, 179, 182
  biological control of: citriculus mealybug, 158–9; Florida red scale, 174–7, 202
  Citrus Marketing Board, 174, 293
  integrated control, in citrus, 293–4
Italy, 75, 76, 82, 104, 114, 117

Jamaica, 65, 139
  biological control of citrus blackfly, 142
Japan, 74, 89, 114, 136, 157
  biological control of: red wax scale, 164–5; spiny blackfly, 117–18, 140
  foreign exploration in, 102, 103, 104, 105, 106, 107, 159–60
Japanese beetle, 45
Java, 106, 108, 115, 134, 140, 177, 203
  foreign exploration in, 110, 111, 125, 126, 133, 148, 149, 151
Joppinae, 32

Kansas, 229, 250, 254
Kansas Agricultural Experiment Station, 251
kelthane, 289, 291
Kenya, 202
  biological control of coffee mealybug, 150–2, 153
  foreign exploration in, 162
Kershaw, J. C., 111, 112
Kincaid, Trevor, 101, 103, 105
Kirby, William, 76, 79, 80
Kirkaldy, G. W., 106
Klamath weed, 160–1
Klee, W. G., 93, 97
Koebele, Albert, 92–9, 106, 107, 108, 110, 136, 176, 177, 202
Kollär, Vincent, 81, 82
Krassilstschik, Isaak, 77
Kuwana, I., 117, 136
Kuwana, S. I., 105

ladybeetles, 245
  see also Hippodamia convergens; Coccinellidae
Lampyridae, 39
Lantana camara, 78
latania scale, 63
Lawson, F. R., 219, 225, 246
Lea, A. M., 129
lead arsenate, 283, 284, 285, 294
leafhoppers, see *Empoasca*

Lebanon, 170, 176
LeBaron, William, 87
LeConte, J. L., 77
Leeuwenhoek, Anton Van, 73
Legner, E. F., 211, 267
legumes, 260
lemons, 63, 166
  see also citrus
LePelley, R. H., 150–2
Lepidosaphes beckii, 291
  see also purple scale
Leptomastidea abnormis, 151
Leptomastix dactylopii, 151
Lestophonus, see Cryptochaetum
Levuana irridescens, see coconut moth
light traps, 249
lime sulfur, 12, 290, 291, 292
Lixophaga diatraeae, 144
Lixophaga sphenophori, 111, 113
London Entomological Society, 83
long-tailed mealybug, 63
Lorbeer, Howard, 286
Louisiana, 274
Lounsbury, C. P., 129, 132
Lygus, 220, 258, 277

malaria, 268
malathion, 285, 288, 293
Malaysia, 125, 140, 202
  foreign exploration in, 107, 110, 126,
    162, 163, 164, 167
  integrated control in, 294–5
  upsets: on oil palms, 17; on cocoa,
    17
mango, 163
manipulation of natural enemies, see
  natural enemies, management of;
  augmentation; conservation
Marchal, Paul, 60, 104
Marianas Islands, 210
Marquesas, 268
Martinez, Juan, 83
Maskell, W. M., 93
Massachusetts, the gypsy moth and
  brown-tail moth in, 100, 103, 104,
  105
Mauritius, 72, 93, 210, 211
mealybugs, 33, 287, 290, 294
Mediterranean area, 66, 136
Mediterranean fruit fly, 158, 163, 164,
  264, 293
Melanesia, 125
Meloidae, 39
Melville, A. R., 151
mercaptothion, 288, 289, 291
mercury fungicides, 283
Metagonistylum minense, see Amazon fly

Metaphycus helvolus, 28, 29, 286
Metarrhizium anisopliae, see green muscardine fungus
Metchnikoff, Elie, 77
methyl eugenol, 264
Mexico, 66, 67, 166, 169, 220, 223
  biological control of: citrus blackfly,
    143, 167–8; Florida red scale, 176;
    purple scale, 166
  Department of Agriculture, 143, 167
  foreign exploration in, 119, 162
  integrated control, in cotton, 297
  National blackfly committee, 167
  upsets in cotton, 14
Michigan, 249
Microgasterinae, 30
micro-organisms, see diseases
midges, 258
milky disease, see Bacillus popillae
Miridae, 44
Missouri, 84, 85, 86, 225
Monserrat, 186
Montana, 161
Morocco, 179
mosca prieta, 167
mosquitoes, 248, 258, 262, 267–8, 273
Muir, Frederick, 50, 107, 108, 109, 110,
  111, 112, 152
multiple parasitism, 26, 56
  see also competitive displacement
multivoltine, 25
Muscidifurax raptor, 211, 242
Myers, J. G., 109, 144–6, 152
mymarids, 28, 130
mynah bird, 72

Nadel, David, 175
National Agricultural Chemicals Association, 21
National Science Foundation, 281
natural balance, see natural control
natural control
  biological, cases of, 63
  definition of, 47
  factors in, 47–9
  proof of, 48
natural enemies
  adverse factors, effect of on, 52, 54, 68,
    69, 147, 178, 179, 182, 188, 208, 209,
    218–19, 233, 234, 235, 243, 244; see
    also pesticides, adverse effects of;
    upsets, of natural balance
  characteristics, of effective, 50, 51, 52,
    148, 149–50, 214, 236; as com-
    plementary mortality factors, 171–2
  of insects, 24–44
  of mammals, 23, 24

317

natural enemies—*cont.*
  management of, 68–70, 230, 235, 236, 237; *see also* augmentation; conservation
  species diversity of, and control, 56–7
  of weeds, 46, 190–1
  see also biological control; importation; parasitic insects; predatory insects
Nemestrinidae, 36
Neodusmetia sangwani, 169
nesting boxes, 219
Netherlands, 237
nettle caterpillars, 17, 294
Neuroptera, predatory
  characteristics of, 40
  families of, 40
  importance of, 40
  prey of, 40
New Caledonia, 65, 149, 162, 187
New England, 100, 101, 106
New Guinea, 110, 125, 144
  foreign exploration in, 107, 112
New Hebrides, 125
New York, 78, 83, 84, 86
New Zealand, 66, 87, 93, 96, 138, 185, 186, 187, 211
Nezara viridula, *see* green vegetable bug
Nicaragua, 14
Nicholson, A. J., 50, 161
nicotine, 283
nicotine sulfate, 297
Nipaecoccus vastator, 290
Nomadacris septemfasciata, *see* red locust
North America, 61, 66, 77, 83, 86, 120, 190, 267, 270
North Carolina, 255
North Dakota, 251
Nutrilite Products, Inc., 245
nutrition, 240, 245
Nygmia phaeorrhoea, *see* brown-tail moth

oak forests, 172, 245
Odonata, predatory, 44
Oecophylla smaragdina, 71, 125
Ohio State University, 62
oil palms, 10, 17, 294
oil, petroleum spray, 289, 290
oleander scale, 63, 66
olive scale, 8, 63, 169–72, 200, 202, 204, 205
olive trees, 8, 63, 169–72
omnivorous leaf roller, 15
Ootetrastichus beatus, 107
Ootetrastichus formosanus, 107
Operophtera brumata, *see* winter moth
Ophioninae, 32
Opiinae, 30

Opius, 30
Opius longicaudatus, 163
Opius oophilus, 163, 164
Opius persulcatus, 163
Opius spp., 162
Opius tryoni, 163
Opius vandenboschi, 163, 164
Opuntia inermis, *see* prickly pear cactus
Opuntia spp., *see* prickly pear cactus
Opuntia stricta, *see* prickly pear cactus
Opuntia vulgaris, *see* prickly pear cactus
orange trees, 5
  see also citrus
Orchex, 289
Oregon, 161
organophosphorus pesticides, 11, 12, 14, 17, 284, 289, 296
Oriental fruit fly, 162–4, 264
Orius insidiosus, 44
ovex, 289
ovipositor, 27, 32, 35, 81
oyster-shell scale, 87, 283

Pacific mite, 6
Paine, R. W., 124, 125, 148
Painter, R. H., 252
Pakistan, 117, 157, 168, 182, 205, 287
  foreign exploration in, 143, 155, 167, 170, 171, 179
Palestine Farmers Federation, 158
pale western cutworm, 257
Panama, 66, 139, 143, 167
Pan American Airlines, 144, 145
Panonychus citri, *see* citrus red mite
Panonychus ulmi, *see* European red mite
Paranagrus optabilis, 107
parasitic insects, *see* Diptera, parasitic; Hymenoptera, parasitic; natural enemies
parasitoids, 25
parathion, 6, 7, 13, 14, 284, 285, 288, 289, 290, 291, 292
Parker, F. D., 225
Parlatoria oleae, *see* olive scale
Pasteur, Louis, 76, 77
pathogenic micro-organisms, *see* pathogens
pathogens
  commercially available, 231–3, 245–6
  general biology of, 26
  general references to, 45
  common groups of, 45
  importance of, 45
  numbers and characteristics of, 45
  use in periodic colonization, 221–2, 225
Patterson, N. A., 280
pea aphid, 250
peach, 159

319

320

shipments, natural enemy—*cont.*
    162, 166, 167, 168, 170, 171, 176, 182, 183, 186, 193, 206
    by sea, 89, 95, 96, 97, 105, 107, 109, 111, 112, 114, 116, 120, 125, 126, 131–2, 133–4, 137–8, 140–1, 148–9, 159
Shorey, H. H., 264
sibling species, 170, 200, 202, 203
Sicily, 150
Silphidae, 39
Silvestri, F., 104, 117, 118, 136, 140, 152, 166, 176, 202
Simmonds, F. J., 245, 289
Simmonds, H. W., 124, 126, 133
simuliid blackfly, 268
Singapore, 126, 140, 141
Sitodiplosis mosellana, see wheat midge
Smith, Harry S., 50, 100, 136, 137, 160, 161, 170
Smith, Herbert D., 167
Smith, Ray S., 273
solitary parasitism, 26
Solomon Islands, 125
sorghum midge, 256
South Africa, 66, 136, 137, 176, 179
    biological control of eucalyptus snout-beetle, 129–32, 174
    Department of Agriculture Technical Services, 291
    foreign exploration in, 162, 286
    integrated control, in citrus, 288–94
    upsets in citrus, 13, 288–90
South America, 66, 145
soybeans, 260
Spain, 114, 170, 219
Spalangia endius, 242
specoid wasps, 43
spider mites, 15, 265, 272, 273, 277
Spinola, M. M., 78
spiny blackfly, 117–18, 140, 153
spotted alfalfa aphid, 250
Sri Lanka, *see* Ceylon
Staphylinidae, 39
sterile-male technique, 262–4, 269, 270
Stern, V. M., 220
strawberries, 6, 7, 253
striped mealybug, 63
Strong, Richard D., 276
successes and projects, 282, 286, 287, 291
    against native pests, 124, 125, 128, 146–50, 153, 210
    conclusions basic to, 152–4, 192–4, 196, 211–16
    famous early, 89–152
    with insect pests, worldwide summary, 191–4, 210, 213

recent, 157–89
savings *vs* costs, 109, 112, 139, 142, 150, 152, 154, 161, 172, 175–6, 178, 185, 192, 193, 194, 202, 212–13, 238
lesser successes, value of, 189–90
with weeds, worldwide summary, 190–1
Sudan, 256, 272
sugar-cane, 106–13, 143–6, 250, 257, 260, 274, 282
sugar-cane beetle, 210
sugar-cane beetle borer, 110–13, 153, 250
sugar-cane borer, 143–6, 153, 257, 258, 260
    first air shipments, 155
    integrated control of, 274–5
sugar-cane leafhopper, 106–9, 153, 154, 202
sulfur, 12, 289
sulfur fungicides, 283
Sumatra, 140
superparasitism, 26
supervised control, 242, 275, 280–1, 298
Surinam toad, 87
Swaine jack pine sawfly, 221
sweet potatoes, 257, 260
sweet potato leaf-miner, 210
sweet potato weevil, 247, 260
Swezey, O. H., 106
Switzerland, 157, 263
Syria, 170
Syrphidae, 42, 43
syrphid fly, *see* Syrphidae
systematics and biological control, 196–203
    subspecific categories: races, strains, ecotypes, subspecies, semi-species, importance of, 201, 203
    see also research, importance of
systems analysis, 277, 298
systox, 289

Tachineaphageus zealandicus, 211, 242
tachinid parasites
    general biology of, 36
    hosts of, 36, 38
    subfamilies of, 38
Tachininae, 36
Tahiti, 133, 157
Taiwan, 65, 66, 136, 179
    foreign exploration in, 107, 162, 166
talc, 12
Tall Timbers Conference, 274
tartar emetic, 291, 292
Tartox, 290
taxonomy, *see* systematics
Taylor, T. H. C., 124, 125, 126, 133, 134, 135, 147, 148, 149, 152, 177, 203

tea, 18
tea tortrix, 18
tedion, 289
TEPP, 10
Terry, F. W., 106, 107, 111
Tetracnemus pretiosus, 138
Texas, 23, 65, 66, 143, 166, 225, 256, 259
   biological control of Rhodesgrass scale,
     168–9
   cultural control of pink bollworm, 255
   integrated control, 275, 297
   upsets: in citrus, 13; in cotton, 13, 14
Texas Agricultural Experiment Station,
   275
Thailand, 140, 162
thelytoky, 27
Thiodan, 290, 291
thiuram, 12
Thompson, W. R., 100, 152
ticks, cattle, 273
Timberlake, P. H., 100
Titus, E. S. G., 101
toad-flax, 78
tobacco, 255, 260
tobacco budworm, 14, 260, 272
tobacco hornworm, *see* hornworms
Tonga, 187
Tooke, F. G. C., 129, 130, 131, 132
Tortrix viridana, 245
Tothill, J. D., 60, 100, 124, 125, 134
Townes, Henry, 205
toxaphene, 14, 15, 16, 296
Toxoptera aurantii, *see* black citrus aphid
Trans World Airlines, 182
trichlorophon, 294, 295
Trichogramma, 88, 237, 297
Trichogramma embryophagum, 223, 224
Trichogramma evanescens, 223, 225, 226,
   227
Trichogramma minutum, 222
Trichogramma pallida, 223, 224
Trichogramma pini, 224
Trichogramma spp., 222, 223
trichogrammatids, 28
Trichopoda pennipes, 186, 187
Trinidad, 145, 157, 245
   foreign exploration in, 134
Trioxys pallidus, 187
   French strain, 188, 203
   Iranian strain, 188, 203
Trissolcus basalis, 35, 185, 186, 187
   Pakistan race, 186
Tristan, J. F., 140
Trouvelot, Leopold, 100
Tryphoninae, 32
Turkey, 65, 179, 184
tussock moth, 102

Tyroglyphus phylloxerae, 87
Tyron, Henry, 118

Uganda, 157
   foreign exploration in, 151
Ullyett, G. C., 288, 289
Union of Soviet Socialist Republics
   (USSR), 77, 219, 223, 224, 256
   foreign exploration in, 101, 102, 103,
     104, 105
   Ministry of Agriculture, 223
   Plant Protection Institute, 223
United States, 46, 60, 86, 88, 118, 222,
   223, 224, 250, 251, 253, 256, 272, 275,
   281
   amount of pesticides used in, 13, 20,
     271, 275
   biological control of Comstock mealy-
     bug, 159–60
   ladybeetles, use of in, 236
   pathogens, use of in, 45
United States Army Transport Command,
   161
United States Congress, 114
United States Department of Agriculture
   (USDA), 60, 86, 92, 93, 94, 100, 114,
   136, 140, 143, 158, 159, 160, 162,
   167, 168, 176, 222, 229, 271
United States Department of State, 94
United States National Museum, 176, 202
University of California, 117, 151, 158,
   162, 166
   at Berkeley, 171, 245
   at Riverside, 89, 136, 140, 151, 166,
    174, 175, 176, 182, 204, 287
University of California Citrus Experiment Station, 136
University of Washington, 101, 105
univoltine, 25
upsets of natural balance, 2, 11–13, 22,
   216–17, 234–5, 278, 283, 288–9,
   292–3, 294, 296–7
   of brown-soft scale, 13
   of citrus red mite, 12
   on cocoa, 17
   in cotton, 13–17, 272–3, 295–6
   of cottony-cushion scale, 13
   on oil palms, 17
   in tea, 18
   see also pesticides, adverse effects of
Utah State University Extension Service,
   239

Vallisnieri, Antonio, 73, 75
van den Bosch, Robert, 187, 188
Varley, G. C., 174
vectors, of disease, 221, 267, 268

vedalia beetle, 13, 37, 39, 94–100, 135, 206
Vedalia cardinalis (= *Rodolia cardinalis*), see vedalia beetle
velvetbeans, 260
Venezuela, 145
Vesey, Nathaniel, 87
vespid wasps, 40
Villa, Antonio, 82
Vipioninae, 30
viruses, insect, 221–2, 246

Walker, Francis, 79
walnut, 187, 203
walnut aphid, 187–9, 203
Walsh, Benjamin D., 83, 84, 86
Wardian cages, 115, 116, 120, 126, 134, 140, 141, 148, 167
Washington, 161
weather, 194
    effects on natural enemies, 52, 55, 69–70, 132, 147, 166, 219, 225, 290–1
    manipulation of, 219
    role of, in natural control, 47–9, 58
weeds, 195
    biological control: first success, 118; history of, 78; worldwide summary, 190–1

biological control of: Klamath weed, 160–1; prickly pear cactus, 78, 118–23
    natural enemies of, see natural enemies
Westwood, J. O., 79
Wheast, 245
wheat, 249, 250, 256, 257
wheat cockchafer, 77
wheat midge, 83, 84
wheat stem sawfly, 250, 253, 254, 257
white-fringed beetles, 260
white muscardine, 76, 77
Wille, J. E., 220
winter moth, 172–4
Wisconsin, 258
Woglum, Russell S., 114–17
woolly apple aphid, 193, 254
woolly whitefly, 34, 35, 63
World Health Organization, 221

Yasumatsu, K., 164, 165
yeast hydrolysate, 219
yellow scale, 5, 63, 200, 287

Zectran, 272
zinc sulfate, 12
Zoecon Corporation, 248